On the Frontlines

ON THE FRONTLINES

Gender, War, and the Post-Conflict Process

Fionnuala Ní Aoláin

Dina Francesca Haynes

Naomi Cahn

OXFORD
UNIVERSITY PRESS

OXFORD
UNIVERSITY PRESS

Oxford University Press, Inc., publishes works that further
Oxford University's objective of excellence
in research, scholarship, and education.

Oxford   New York
Auckland   Cape Town   Dar es Salaam   Hong Kong   Karachi
Kuala Lumpur   Madrid   Melbourne   Mexico City   Nairobi
New Delhi   Shanghai   Taipei   Toronto

With offices in
Argentina   Austria   Brazil   Chile   Czech Republic   France   Greece
Guatemala   Hungary   Italy   Japan   Poland   Portugal   Singapore
South Korea   Switzerland   Thailand   Turkey   Ukraine   Vietnam

Published by Oxford University Press, Inc.
198 Madison Avenue, New York, NY 10016

www.oup.com

Oxford is a registered trademark of Oxford University Press

Library of Congress Cataloging-in-Publication Data
Ní Aoláin, Fionnuala, 1967-
On the frontlines : gender, war, and the post-conflict process / Fionnuala Ní Aoláin,
Dina Francesca Haynes, Naomi Cahn.
     p.   cm.
Includes bibliographical references and index.
ISBN 978-0-19-539664-5 (hardcover : alk. paper) — ISBN 978-0-19-539665-2 (pbk. : alk. paper)
1. Women and war. 2. Women and peace. 3. Women—Violence against.
4. Sex discrimination against women. 5. Women's rights.
6. Postwar reconstruction. I. Haynes, Dina Francesca. II. Cahn, Naomi R. III. Title.
JZ6405.W66N5   2012
305.42—dc22   2011016419

9 8 7 6 5 4 3 2

Printed in the United States of America

CONTENTS

ACKNOWLEDGMENTS

While the formal collaboration between the three of us did not start until the fall of 2008, we feel as though we have been working toward this project for much of our professional careers. Our experiences in different parts of the world, and our work with people in various countries—Fionnuala in Northern Ireland, the former Yugoslavia, and Israel/Palestine; Naomi in Canada, the United States, and the Congo; Dina in Croatia, Bosnia and Herzegovina, Serbia and Montenegro, South Africa, Chad, and Botswana—have all contributed to our understandings of these issues. Books of this scope and this breadth—which involve the balancing of multiple jurisdictional locations added to teaching, other research commitments, activism, and families— do not reach completion without significant assistance and support. Our list of "thank yous" is extensive because we have received so much encouragement and assistance from so many different individuals and institutions. We would like to thank the following people who gave of their time, experience, opinions, and wisdom during the course of writing this book. Foremost, we thank Martha Fineman and Janie Chuang for bringing us together. Martha's *Feminist Conversations* has brought many projects and feminists together over the years, and we are collectively in her debt for the conference on transition and feminism that brought us to share intellectual space for the first time. We also heartily thank our many readers: Diane Marie Amann, Christine Bell, Christine Chinkin, Janie Chuang, Tony Gambino, Jennifer Green, Oren Gross, Ruth Rubio Marin, Siobhan Mullalley, Sean Murphy, Jaya Ramji-Nogales, Gabriele Russo, and Susan Williams for so graciously reading early drafts and offering such helpful comments and suggestions. All are experts in many of the fields this book traverses, and all were generous with their time.

The administrative support of Nicole Gruhot and Jessica Kubis at the University of Minnesota made manuscript production possible. We thank our research assistants: Sabrina Andrews, Morgan Laurie, Nicole Dapcic, Mary Chichorelli, Jose Recio, Michael Sinclair, Elizabeth Super, KT Farley, Moira Heinges, Sara Wilkinson, Jennifer Cornell, Sean Burke, and Maya Zahn for their invaluable assistance with research, editing, and footnotes. We thank the Robina Foundation through the University of Minnesota Law School for supporting the research throughout. This book has benefited enormously from the feedback we have received at numerous conferences: the University of Baltimore Third Annual Feminist Legal Theory Conference, the William & Mary Women and the Law Journal Symposium, the New Perspectives on Gender and Human Security at the University of Wisconsin, the Sexual Violence and Conflict in Africa Conference at Carlton University (Ottawa), the Hirsch Lecture at the New England Law School, and the Comparative Constitutional Design Conference at the University of Chicago Law School. We thank our deans for their continual support and encouragement: David Wippman at Minnesota, John O'Brien at New England, Frederick Lawrence at George Washington Law School, and Paul Carmichael at the University of Ulster have ably facilitated our work on this book. Dave McBride at Oxford University Press has been a wonderful editor.

On the Frontlines

Introduction

Afghanistan. Liberia. The Democratic Republic of Congo. Rwanda. East Timor. Northern Ireland. The former Yugoslavia.

Over the past quarter-century, each of these countries has experienced deeply divisive and highly destructive conflicts. Each is at a different point on the spectrum of emerging from such conflicts and addressing the causes of conflict and rebuilding. Each of these countries has responded in different ways, with varying degrees of intervention and assistance from the international community, to the challenges of creating a new society with new institutions to allow movement forward. Countries in the post-conflict transition process provide multiple opportunities for transformation on many different levels, including; accountability for human rights violations committed during hostilities; reforming local and national laws; reintegration of soldiers; rehabilitation and redress for victims; the establishment or reestablishment of the rule of law, human rights institutions, and governance structures; changing cultural attitudes; and improving socioeconomic conditions. These opportunities are rare in stable and nontransitional societies and explain in part why societies in conflict garner such significant international and institutional attention. The opportunities for massive transformation are, in theory, open-ended.

In this book, we seek to explore the role that gender plays in the construction and implementation of the post-conflict transitional process. For our purposes, gender refers to the social construction of what is defined to be masculine or feminine within any particular culture, and includes our reflections on symbols, theories, practices, institutions, and individuals.[1] Our specific intention is to probe how women fare and to articulate our views on how various legal and political processes might work better for women.

In undertaking this work, our approach is feminist in form and in methodology. Multiple strands of feminist theorization provide the foundations for our analysis, and some offer contradictory advice on how to proceed. Indeed, there is no simple "one-size" feminist position on many of the issues that we examine in this book. As feminist scholars influenced by varying theoretical outlooks, we draw on a wide range of feminist approaches and theories to inform our thinking on the numerous issues addressed in this book. Nonetheless, our focus remains "on the ways that gender—the social construction of masculinity and femininity—organizes political, personal and intellectual life."[2] Viewing processes of transition in conflicted societies through the lens of the multifaceted social movement that constitutes feminist theory and action provides a unique means to assess political, social, and economic change as it works or does not work for women. This methodological choice affirms the importance of a gender lens by firmly unmasking the ways in which situations and constructs appear neutral, but are in practice gendered masculine. We situate women's concerns to the forefront of our inquiries and ultimately seek a recalibration that requires rethinking both the masculine and the feminine in conflicted and post-conflict settings.

Our methodology draws on the working and familial experiences of all three authors, who have each lived and worked for extensive periods in conflicted and post-conflict societies.[3] We also seek to give adequate space to the lived experiences of women in multiple conflicted societies while acknowledging that secondary academic and policy sources have significantly influenced our thinking. Our approach is politically engaged and has as its goal the transformation of social and domestic arrangements that penalize women because of their sex. The processes of representation, analysis, and interpretation focused on women in conflicted societies "risk[s] silencing, mutilating or denigrating the voices of the subjects of our research,"[4] and we acknowledge the difficulties of retaining their voices while privileging our own. There is a clear hazard when engaging in post-conflict reconstruction and transitional work of imposing a Western conceptual frame, thereby reifying race and gender inequalities. There is no easy answer here, but we hope our consciousness of and sensitivity to these complexities will allow us to engage in ways that are meaningful to the societies whose conflicts we address.[5]

There are many different kinds of transitional processes—transitions from authoritarian states as a prime example. This book, however, while drawing on some key lessons from those change processes, is firmly focused on examining the gendered dimensions of societies emerging from extreme, systematic, and institutional violence. We recognize that transitions from conflict take place in multiple ways and through varied mechanisms: locally generated political "deal" making; formal peace negotiations between various armed groupings; and peace agreements endorsed, supported, and underpinned by the international community and regional organizations. In all these contexts we ask "the woman questions." How are women and girls visible—or invisible—within the processes that define and shape the cessation of communal violence? How are men and boys represented, and what does their visibility or their absence within the process to end or contain violence signify? What does the absence of reference to gender signify in such contexts, and how does such absence affect the substance of any particular agreement (whether local or international) to end violence? How does the failure to properly ask and answer these questions undermine the short-, medium-, and long-term construction of post-conflict societies?

Assessing the conflict and post-conflict landscape with a gender lens is complicated. Despite this, many policymakers and scholars understand that in order to achieve substantive gender equality, a gender-sensitive lens is required so that we see how gender hierarchies "shape our ways of thinking, knowing and doing and therefore have patterned consequences."[6] The independent value of a gendered assessment of post-conflict processes remains contested. In this legal and political space of ending or transmuting conflict, women still struggle to influence policies that affect them directly and indirectly. They remain subordinated by dominant discourses that minimize or ignore the value of placing the needs and views of women at the center of the conversation about ending violent communal behaviors,[7] even though such placement is absolutely central to ending societal violence. Women are the group most historically marginalized and excluded from the peacemaking and peacebuilding process across all jurisdictions and conflicts.[8] A gender-centered lens of analysis, followed by practice, enforcement, and oversight, has the possibility for transformative effect on women's lives in post-conflict societies. Gender centrality is a means to make more effective the policy and practice of ending conflicts and ensuring that they do not recur. Without this attention, traditional gender dichotomies may be further entrenched and exacerbated during times of extreme violence and may extend into the post-conflict phase.

Conflicts affect both men and women, but women face additional issues during and after wars that men do not, including, of course, pervasive sexual violence, forced impregnation, reproductive violence, sexually transmitted diseases, and forced abortion. Women and their children experience internal displacement and dominate the refugee populations across conflicts. Women are also differentially affected because of their role as the primary caretakers of the household and family. In this regard, traditional gender dichotomies may be further entrenched and exacerbated during times of extreme violence.

By contrast, during some conflicts in which aspects of a functioning state and economy continue to exist, women can take on roles as workers and laborers outside of the home, opportunities which would never transpire were the society not in conflict. In this way, as other feminist scholars have noted, conflict opens up intended and unintended spaces for empowerment, "effecting structural and social transformations and producing new social, economic and political realities that redefine gender and caste hierarchies."[9] Frequently, however, women are the least often employed or employable because of their legally enforced second-class status in many conflict zones. Across most post-conflict transitions, women are the first to be fired and the last to be hired with the large exception of the false economy built up around the presence of the international community, in which women are paid to fill the "camp follower" positions as housekeepers, cooks, administrative employees, and, of course, for sex. Peacemaking agreements and transitional structures, however, rarely account for these paradoxical roles.[10]

While women are missing from key positions in peace negotiations and government, they often dominate in civil society movements that create "safe" and neutral spaces in conflicted societies. In this latter role, women often provide the grassroots networking and social support structures that are relied upon by local and international elites to embed peace processes. The consequence, however, may be that international actors and others are essentializing the women on whom they so rely, relegating them to "soft" civil society roles, rather than establishing them in the political infrastructure. Women also get the "soft" end of legal norms and legal enforcement. This makes them potentially more vulnerable in the post-conflict terrain in ways that are complex and difficult to address.

Women's roles also include being violent actors in aggressive and conflicted societies, both in undertaking primary acts of violence and in lending substantial support to men who carry out such actions. Even where women are not engaged as combatants, they often create the social and economic networks that support and enable violence to continue. Research examining the overlap between women's roles and war economies has started to explore the subterranean relationships that intertwine women's agricultural and industrial labor, as well as their functioning within the shadow economy accompanying war, as relevant to enabling the conditions conducive to the maintenance of cycles of violent interaction.[11] Acknowledging those belligerent roles is an important step in avoiding the essentialization of women's positions in conflicted societies. Moreover, it has practical consequences. For example, it provides the means to recognize that women who have been combatants face an array of social and cultural challenges that simply never arise for men during and after war. It also requires us to be sensitive to the vulnerabilities created for men and boys by communal violence, and to understand how the exposure of male defenselessness can act as a precursor to further and cyclical patterns of intergenerational violence. We remain consistently wary of essentializing women as peacemakers and facilitators when we are deeply aware of the complex set of roles women as individuals and as members of broader communities play in enabling and encouraging violence.

The primary focus of this book is surveying the interplay of gender with conflict and post-conflict processes, allied with the recognition that women must be central to the powerful and transformative potential of the post-conflict terrain.[12] Conflict-ending and transitional processes are already deeply gendered, drawing on existing cultural, legal, and political practices that are strongly embedded across societies and cultures. The entrenched gender coding of such processes is predominantly masculine and operates to include or make women visible in highly selective ways. A core concern here is the assumption by states and international institutions that conflict endings are the same for women as for men. We consistently challenge that assumption. We also contest the idea that the end of conflict constitutes the end of violence, confrontation, vulnerability, or related manifestations of war for women. As the motif of this book's title suggests, women are invariably at the frontline of conflict, in the physical and metaphysical sense. Their bodies are in the frontline of military strategy and targeting, and the social networks and spaces women maintain are also frontline targets for destruction and undoing. As examples from multiple jurisdictions indicate, the formal end of hostilities between generally male combatants often have little effect on the quality of life for women as they remain vulnerable and at the vanguard of hazards and threats despite paper agreements between elite actors.

This introduction continues by setting out some key ideas that frame our overall analysis. Section one sets out the framework we utilize to address the legal and political processes that are typically harnessed to subdue conflict. Section two provides a critique of gender mainstreaming and articulates our concept of gender centrality—the application of which we suggest might be a means to recalibrate post-conflict processes to better accommodate women's needs and interests. Section three concludes with an overview of the relevant and developing international legal norms that directly address the roles and rights of women in post-conflict political processes.

KEY THREADS AND THEMES

Several key themes provide a conceptual anchor throughout this book. These include: (1) the notion of gender centrality as a more effective and compelling alternative to gender mainstreaming; (2) the extent to which the relevant international norms have been successful in addressing the gendered aspects of post-conflict processes; (3) the importance of consulting with local populations, and with women in particular, before advancing any post-conflict agenda; and (4) the inadequacy of focusing disproportionately on civil and political rights, whether through accountability mechanisms, rule of law initiatives, or other avenues, to the exclusion of socioeconomic rights and needs. To explore these themes in the post-conflict phases, we adapt Christine Bell's three-stage classification of peace treaty forms to women's experience of post-conflict processes.[13] Bell defines three key stages by which parties to a conflict (whether state, nonstate, or both) typically manage political agreements to end or transition from communal conflict. They are particularly useful to framing women's interface with post-conflict processes because the realities of on-the-ground peace negotiations and their implementation frequently operate to exclude women's meaningful participation. Moreover, the three-stage process frames the issues for negotiation in ways that minimize concerns that we contend are of particular and underappreciated importance to the quality of women's lives.

First, pre-negotiation agreements: Pre-negotiation agreements are concluded prior to any formal peace settlement and invariably revolve around ensuring the presence of those perceived as key political actors at the negotiation table. This phase can be both formal and informal, sometimes evolving organically within a state, but more typically advanced by external cajoling from other states or international institutions. This phase can include broad context-setting initiatives as well as statements of principle. The pre-negotiation stage is likely to exclude women for a number of structural reasons. It is rarely a civil society–dominated phase, but typically includes only state and nonstate military actors at the highest echelons.[14] It is often secret in its operation and, given the high value placed on the ending of public violence, the pre-negotiation phase tends to place disproportionate emphasis on the military outcomes perceived as essential to facilitate broader political engagement. This emphasis on military imperatives tends to displace a focus on other institutional, social, economic, and political issues that operate to stymie the transformative potential of the peacemaking process overall. At various points in this book, we address the impact of pre-negotiation phase exclusions and outcomes for women.

The second phase that Bell identifies involves the "Substantive/Framework" agreements that "aim to sustain ceasefires and provide a framework for governance that will address the root causes of the conflict."[15] These are, in some sense, the classic peace agreements. Examples of these model framework agreements include the Burundi Peace Agreements, the Belfast Agreement, and the Lomé Accords in Sierra Leone. These documents are generally ambitious and far-reaching, not only tackling matters such as demilitarization, prisoner release, amnesty, and the military's status, but also addressing legal and political reform, social and economic reparation and reform, and institutional reform. They set out a framework for the exercise of power, as well as laying the groundwork for mandated government policies across a range of social, economic, and political dimensions. Framework agreement phases are more likely to include women at least in some minimal, and public, form. This is often the most high-profile phase of conflict negotiations and frequently involves international actors and agencies as they support a peace process. This means that local actors are typically under significant pressure to include women in order to legitimize the negotiation process, even if women are not in practice given the space to voice issues that affect them. While there is a greater tendency for women to be represented in this phase of negotiation, their presence may be ethereal and have less impact than is commonly presumed on substantive outcomes that advance women's legal and political interests.

The third phase of agreements identified by Bell's paradigm is "implementation agreements" which "take forward and develop aspects of the framework, fleshing out their detail."[16] Because framework agreements are broadly worded treaty agreements, they frequently avoid detailed outlining of specific implementation measures necessary to transform principle to practice. Some commentators have noted that the inherent and "constructive ambiguity" of peace agreements is often the means to ensure that vastly opposing political entities agree to sign them.[17] This means that much of the difficult work of real compromise can be left to the implementation phase, where both genuine opportunity and pitfalls exist for women.

The purpose of implementation agreements is often technical—they can be seen as simply moving forward the work (with greater detail and clarity) to which the parties have previously committed. In practice, their negotiation and content are far more contested. Often the opportunity to renegotiate offered by this kind of agreement means that parties view them as sites to revisit and regain losses (perceived or actual) in other parts of the negotiation process. At other times, the implementation phase actually does little to move the work forward, not because the implementation procedures are verbally or outwardly contested, but because there is no actual political will to see the agreements through; these are agreements without any intention to perform.[18] Women face significant barriers to involvement in the implementation phase. The first is a barrier of time. Specifically, women often do not have the ability or support to divert their attention from the burden of caregiving and other home-based responsibilities to be free to engage in the politics of the moment. Second is the barrier of capacity; women are often not provided with the security and support necessary to become political actors. Both elements are organically linked. After all, the end of violent public conflict does not usually mean an end to violence for women, and thus the post-conflict environment is not inevitably a secure space for them. This lack of security has a profound practical effect on women's capacity to continue to engage in ongoing political negotiations when hostilities have formally ended: they may not have the physical security necessary to participate or the political status to be included. While representation alone is not a panacea to secure advantageous outcomes for women, the absence of women affects both the substance of agreements made and their effects on multiple dimensions of women's lives.

The presence of women at the negotiating table in any one of the three phases of negotiation or implementation does not translate directly into provision for women's rights in the multiplicity of sites that open up in the post-conflict context. This may be attributable to the political structure in which women were operating (or co-opted), whereby any individual or gendered interest was subordinated to that of the organization or to the good of the greater national project.[19] We endorse the fundamental principle of female representation in peacemaking fora contained in UN Security Council Resolution 1325, accepting both the value and limitations of such presence. Representation raises the further problem of whether quotas are an appropriate and useful tool to ensure a tipping point on presence matching impact, when women are mandated for inclusion in peace negotiation processes. We take a generally positive view of quotas, discussed more fully in Chapter 8, and view them as a necessary but not solely sufficient condition of effective participatory strategies for women. Ultimately, however, mere representation may be insufficient to address the challenges faced by women, and close attention should be paid to the modalities and forms of representation including the requirement of sufficient inclusion. This raises broader questions that are society-specific on the extent to which women experience equality of opportunity and have autonomy guaranteed in any particular state. Intersectionality analysis is also relevant and nicely illustrates the broader psychological point that women "do not bear essential qualities such as kindness and compassion,"[20] and that they should not be assumed to apply when women participate in the broader political domain. And, of course, one woman cannot be presumed to represent the interests of all others: women's interests vary depending on ethnicity, class, experiences, and other factors.

Societies rarely have the opportunity to revisit and remake their basic social, political, and legal compact. Such potentially transformative moments are so rare that their occurrence may in part explain our preoccupation with and interest in societies emerging from conflict. It also explains why feminists and other critical thinkers view such opportunities as particularly important to groups that have been marginalized, underrepresented, and discriminated against. This book provides a full-length consideration of the significant opportunities that allow for the reframing and re-creation of new institutions and processes. Such opportunities are real, but a significant question is—are they real for women?

GENDER CENTRALITY

In this context of addressing the opportunity for massive political and social change, "gender mainstreaming" is a phrase commonly employed by the international institutions and organizations engaged in post-conflict reconstruction. Addressing the success, limitations, or alternatives to gender mainstreaming is essential to our project of evaluating what works and what is missing for women from the post-conflict context. Since the mid-1990s, "gender mainstreaming" has gradually come into vogue in international economic development, peacekeeping, and policy circles as a radical and innovative means of achieving equality for women.[21] Across national and international legal and political discourses that concern women, gender mainstreaming is a highly visible conceptual and practical tool. It has gained, at least rhetorically, significant political traction in international organizations as the stated mechanism to address structural and institutional inequalities associated with gender status.[22] With gender mainstreaming, the primary mode of action is not necessarily to dismantle discrimination, but rather to introduce a conversation about "gender" into policymaking practices and institutions. "Mainstreaming a gender perspective is the process of assessing the implications for women and men of any planned action, including legislation, policies or programmes, in all areas and at all levels."[23] In its attempt to encompass the diversity of different women's interests and to diffuse the oppositional stance that the positive action agenda established (against men), gender mainstreaming marks "neutral" ground by claiming to benefit both women and men. In the peacemaking and peacekeeping context, gender mainstreaming has perhaps been most aptly symbolized by the adoption of Security Resolution 1325, which we discuss more fully below. This resolution aims to centralize or "mainstream" gender by encouraging member states and UN bodies to: fund gender-sensitive technical development and training; consider the different ways that conflict impacts women and girls; and strive to involve women in peace negotiations, policing, peacekeeping, and humanitarian operations.[24]

Gender mainstreaming has become a popular term in international policy and development parlance. Despite its popularity, comprehensive evaluations of its success are limited. Empirical studies are lacking. Further concrete research on the successes and shortcomings of gender mainstreaming in development and post-conflict settings are needed before a more thorough evaluation can emerge. Nonetheless, several preliminary observations can be made based on existing critical assessments. We remain wary of the promises offered by the concept and terminology of gender mainstreaming as a means to capitalize fully on the opportunity offered by the society in negotiation with itself about its future. Most scholars have defined gender mainstreaming in relationship with, and in contrast to, the earlier articulations of "equal treatment" and "positive action" approaches to achieving gender equity.[25] The equal treatment approach highlights individual rights and is grounded in the negative idea that women should not be discriminated against in the public sphere on account of their sex. It is perhaps best characterized by legislation and administrative policies that require equal pay or equal access for women in education and employment. In recent years, the scope of equal treatment policies has expanded to encompass public services and facilities beyond the classroom and workplace.[26] In contrast, the "positive action" approach is rooted in the recognition of biological and social differences between men and women and aims to proactively correct deep-seated social, economic, and political disadvantages that women have suffered as a result.[27]

Both equal treatment and positive action approaches leverage the political system to reorganize gender-based rights in specific ways. Gender mainstreaming, on the other hand, seeks to transform the political system itself (institutions, processes, and norms) and the ways in which it creates and perpetuates gender-based inequalities.[28] According to the United Nations, gender mainstreaming "is a strategy for making women's as well as men's concerns and experiences an integral dimension of the design, implementation, monitoring and evaluation of policies and programmes."[29] The fundamental assertion that increasing gender awareness in policy circles will automatically translate into tangible benefits for both women (and men) in every sector and at every level of decision-making.

To this end, gender mainstreaming endeavors to integrate gender-sensitive practices and perspectives into public decision-making institutions and procedures. On a practical level, gender mainstreaming has been implemented at a variety of different levels. Common gender mainstreaming strategies include: evaluative tools for measuring the differential impact of various policies on women and men, the use of gender-sensitive budgeting,[30] the introduction of gender mainstreaming structures or "units" in an increasing number of government sectors, the creation of gender-sensitive policy analyses, and gender-sensitive research and data production projects. The final dimension addresses the appearance of gender-sensitive legislation and policy across a wide variety of policy sectors and departments.[31] All these activities suggest much action, but how much of it is transferable and how much actually positively affects women's lives in conflict and post-conflict settings? Indeed, gender mainstreaming is both more and less ambitious than its predecessor approaches of "equal rights" and "positive action." Those who laud its ambition do so on the basis of the range of actors and institutions it can influence. From our point of view, however, it does not embrace a particular critique of gender relations (it argues for "gender sensitivity" rather than women's rights) or articulate a particular prescriptive for gender equality reform, so gender mainstreaming is less ambitious, or at least less radical. This lack of ambition is particularly pronounced in post-conflict settings.

One troubling conceptual and practical dimension of gender mainstreaming is its "grafted" aspect. Mainstreaming too often takes the form of being "added on" to a preexisting structure, institution, or policy—it comes from the outside in (the proverbial "add women and stir" approach). As a result, the transformative capacity of mainstreaming and its ability to deeply entrench gender roles and perceptions is highly questionable. Despite some undoubted success, mainstreaming essentially functions as a policy tool to meld in a gender dimension but may not attack the roots of systemic discrimination against women. In post-conflict societies, as the necessity to incorporate gender into law and policymaking has emerged for international institutions and donor states, mainstreaming has become the primary stated vehicle for taking care of women's issues. A positive take on gender mainstreaming might suggest that there may be "much for feminists to celebrate."[32] This assessment would include the achievement of gender-inclusive language recognizing women as full subjects of international law, institutional change that has created more prominent international spaces for feminist ideas, and, finally, the "formal institutional affiliation of women's equality and rights [as] a powerful organizing tool for informal local and international women's networks and movements."[33]

Gender mainstreaming requires careful consideration and critique with an eye to evaluating what gains *have actually* been made by women, under the mantle of the policy and what compromises or limitations the doctrine brings. Diane Otto's hard-hitting critique of the limitations of gender mainstreaming at the United Nations highlights the uneven and precarious gains for women, compounded by some foundational compromises that accompany the gender mainstreaming agenda.[34] Others have noted that those claiming feminist advances in the international arena should avoid being dazzled by language and that it is necessary to "look below the surface" to ascertain what actual differences are being imprinted on the ground.[35] For example, close scrutiny of gender mainstreaming into development programs reveals a marked difference between the rhetoric and reality.[36] A comprehensive review of gender mainstreaming in three key international institutions, the International Labour Organization (ILO), UN Development Programme (UNDP), and the World Bank found that "they all suffered from a lack of commitment of senior managers, poor resourcing, lack of expertise, marginalization within the institution, and failure to translate into concrete action."[37] A similar script emerges when we assess the impact of gender mainstreaming within UN peacemaking and peacekeeping roles. The most biting critique identifies a problem of institutional capture suggesting that UN (and other institutions') engagement with gender mainstreaming is highly selective. In this telling, gender mainstreaming serves to cloak a more problematic approach of avoiding a systematic engagement with the causes and structures of women's inequality. Instead it perpetuates unnecessary gender stereotypes by intense concentration on women as victims (and international institutions as protectors) rather than on asking uncomfortable questions about the root causes of discrimination and exclusion.[38] In this view, the price of admission to international institutional acceptance may be too high for women, as it requires a fundamental set of compromises that endanger genuine engagement with the root causes of inequality and violence.

In spite of this diffusion of "gender" language and gender-sensitive policy analysis, gender mainstreaming is no magic bullet, and its limits are increasingly obvious in post-conflict settings. In post-conflict contexts, gender mainstreaming lacks a feminist social critique and reform agenda, and it has often devolved into a toothless "technical project."[39] Drawing on critiques of gender mainstreaming in the European Union, we suggest that, by displacing or eclipsing equal rights and positive action frameworks, gender mainstreaming may actually weaken feminist advocacy in post-conflict settings.[40] In the post-conflict site, a commitment to equality is a core dimension of advancing women's rights and centralizing their needs. The measure of advancement in this regard lies with substantive equality and autonomy outcomes, not merely equality of opportunity, representation, or "taking women into account." Other studies have noted the limitations inherent in the myopic focus that gender mainstreaming places on policy- and decision-making processes. This book, with others, assent that it is simply "unrealistic to expect social transformation to be attained through public policy processes alone."[41] There is strong evidence adduced throughout our analysis that gender mainstreaming has become a tool of convenience for policymakers, rather than a radical means of achieving gender equality. Thus, in the eyes of policymakers, gender mainstreaming represents a way of improving governance rather than a way of dismantling inequality.[42]

Unlike what we conceptualize as a *gender-central* approach in which the equal rights and social and economic advancement of women are paramount, gender mainstreaming lacks both a clear critique of the gender status quo and a clear articulation of the substance and modalities of gender reform. Gender centrality requires a commitment to a substantive account of gender equality embracing not only equality of opportunity for women but also equality of outcomes, and is axiomatic to advancing the quality and capacity of women's lives in conflicted and post-conflict societies.

The approach necessitates the centralization of women's needs, equality, and autonomy from the inception of any response to a problem to the development and implementation of actions and solutions in the post-conflict environment. By gender centrality, we seek to capture a conceptual and practical approach that starts with gender at the center of any given problem or issue in a post-conflict setting and integrates women specifically from the point of recognition. This point of entry locus is critical to the long-term success of making the post-conflict environment transformative for women. Such transformation goes beyond reform of particular institutions or power arrangements to the heart of women's status and value in society and their capacity to be treated as equals with men.

To be sure, most definitions of gender mainstreaming still include the recitation of "gender equality" as a fundamental goal. According to UN Guidelines, for example, gender mainstreaming assessments should be implemented so that "women and men benefit equally and inequality is not perpetuated."[43] The UN Agreed Conclusions further state that "*the ultimate goal* [of mainstreaming] *is to achieve gender equality*."[44] Problematically, however, "gender equality" is defined too vaguely to set clear benchmarks for future progress or to resolve multicultural differences regarding gender roles and rights. For these reasons, throughout this book, we critically probe the reliance upon the gender mainstreaming framework as the appropriate mechanism by which women's interests and rights are realized in post-conflict settings.

We are convinced that rights and equality-based gender centrality are the keys to transformative outcomes for women. Broadly, two sets of interrelated strategies can be used to centralize women's interests and rights in meaningful ways in conflict and post-conflict settings: (1) relying on external actors who may promulgate mandatory or voluntary standards; and (2) relying on internal actors, such as nongovernmental organizations (ranging from churches to public-interest and other local civic groups) or voters or pressure through the legal system. Both strategies depend on external support from multilateral institutions (such as the World Bank), bilateral aid agencies (such as the U.S. Agency for International Development), and international nongovernmental organizations (such as Amnesty International), to exert pressure on governments and other institutions within countries. They also depend on indigenous nongovernmental organizations, individuals, and responsible governmental officials who can pressure institutions from within the country (often with external support). The external and internal strategies must be integrated, particularly given the difficulties of enforcing both international law and voluntary guidelines from outside the country. A central premise is that gender must be incorporated not only into the so-called hard (civil and political) rights and programs, but into the perceived soft (social, cultural, and economic) as well. As the traction and legally binding effect of social and economic rights have been expanded at the international level,[45] it becomes critically important that such understandings affect the implementation and status of these rights in the transitional context.

RELEVANT INTERNATIONAL NORMS

A third strand of this book includes recommendations for the reform of existing standards and practices that have emerged to regulate and frame post-conflict transitions. Despite a flurry of international policy activity, gender issues remain peripheral to all post-conflict transitions, existing norms capture only a portion of women's needs, and there are numerous gaps in the implementation of existing post-conflict transition standards.[46] Key to this thematic strand is the utility and development of international legal norms and practices applicable to post-conflict settings. Part of the thinking that prompted this book was our recognition that language affirming gender as a relevant category is slowly becoming more central to the discussion of conflict and post-conflict reconstruction, and a flurry of notable international reports and soft law norms have been promulgated. Despite this activity, uncomfortable questions remain as to what practical effects such efforts have had for women in conflicted societies, and moreover whether we can genuinely discern systematic social, legal, and economic changes for women in deeply violent settings.

The contemporary cornerstone of conflict-related norm promulgation incorporating women and girls is UN Security Council Resolution 1325, adopted in 2000, which emphasized the importance of involving women and girls in post-conflict peace processes and "the urgent need to mainstream a gender perspective into peacekeeping operations." The implementation of Resolution 1325 has also involved UN member states (to varying uptake and degree) developing National Action plans as a means to advance implementation of the resolution.[47] In 2002, UNICEF published an evaluation of gender and conflict that was co-authored by Ellen Johnson Sirleaf, now the president of Liberia, which assessed the implementation of Resolution 1325. Two years later, in 2004, the U.S. Department of Defense, the United Nations, and NATO each adopted policies addressing the trafficking of humans in and around military deployments. In 2000, the United Nations proclaimed its Millennium Development Goals, which include gender equality as one of eight goals.[48] The Human Rights Council Resolution 5/1 recognizes the importance of gender integration and specifically mandates as a principle that the Universal Periodic Review "fully integrate a gender perspective" into all aspects of the review.[49]

In June 2008, through Resolution 1820, the UN Security Council affirmed that rape should be treated as a war crime—but only after several countries questioned whether rape really was an appropriate topic for Security Council review.[50] Security Council Resolution 1820 can be read in many ways, but one interpretation is that it stands as an acknowledgment to the failings of Resolution 1325, not least by giving it a preeminent legal status by placing the needs and issues that affect women as a matter affecting international peace and security. The Security Council further expanded its preoccupation with sexual violence in 2009 by the passage of Resolution 1888, requiring that peacekeeping missions protect women and girls from the harms of sexual violence. In that same year, Resolution 1889 addressed the obstacles to women's participation in peace processes and peacebuilding, calling for the UN Secretary-General to submit to the Security Council a set of indicators for use at the global level to track the implementation of Resolution 1325. As we probe ten years on, many feminist critics are both cynical and underwhelmed by the scope of the Security Council resolutions, noting the lack of any vision of gender equality premised on principles of equality of outcomes and autonomy for women.

On September 15, 2009, the General Assembly announced a fundamental consolidation of all agencies and bodies tasked with women's issues broadly defined at the United Nations. It adopted a resolution on systemwide coherence, where it recommended that there ought to be strengthening,[51] consistency, and impact of the UN institutional gender equality architecture by streamlining and combining existing gender institutions. The new unit is envisaged to bring together the Office of the Special Advisor on Gender Issues and the Advancement of Women (OSAGI), the Division for the Advancement of Women (DAW), the UN Development Fund for Women (UNIFEM), and the International Institute for Research and Training for the Advancement of Women (INSTRAW). It is evident that an enhanced (or weakened) body will substantially impact on broader institutional initiatives to advance women's equality and to concentrate institutional international efforts to transform women's lives in post-conflict societies.

In sum, there has been, on one view, an extraordinary amount of political and legal energy devoted to women in the preeminent international institutional settings. This flurry of "soft" and "hard" law at the international level can be interpreted in multiple ways. First, it is a promising advance, signaling the increased importance that key international organizations and states have given to realities experienced by women in war. In this regard, it is to be welcomed, and throughout this book we emphasize those positive legal and political developments that have the capacity to aggregate the benefits of international presence and view for women. Second, and on the other hand, such international declarations and positions can be viewed critically. They represent part of a broader phenomenon that we identify in this book, namely the way in which the term "woman" or "women" can be brought into play (as a legal or political matter) without actually doing any substantive work for the subjects thus conjectured. Merely tacking on gender mainstreaming to preconceived post-conflict priorities, plans, and programs will have little benefit for women and for the societies in which they live if the underlying post-conflict processes are flawed. We remain wary of the traction such new norms bring to peace treaty negotiations on the ground, and new empirical work analyzing the use of Resolution 1325 in peacemaking and peacebuilding processes suggests that it remains unproven whether its deployment actually means that women do better under the "deals" negotiated.[52]

To understand better what various post-conflict reform, rebuilding, replacing, and supporting mechanisms have done for women, we explore a number of key arenas analyzing the range of programs and policies most commonly employed in transitions, including inter alia constitutional reform, legal and institutional reforms, electoral reforms, remedies and reparation, security, and economic development. We point out salient transformative opportunities for women in order to harness the critically important elements of international engagement with conflicted societies to utilitarian and gendered ends. As we pay attention to the places where women are present, we are also aware that those who control and shape these processes—including states, nonstate, international institutions, and actors—often systematically erase women from the post-conflict picture. In particular, local "native" women are invariably marginal to post-conflict processes even when they have undertaken extraordinary efforts to be visible to the decision-makers in such contexts. This narrative of absence is not limited to reporting and oversight, but is itself "mainstreamed" into how states and international institutions undertake transition from conflict across a range of key areas.

In the dominant discourses that accompany intervention and engagement by Western states in sites of conflict, there is an undercarriage of neocolonial attitudes, particularly when the site of struggle involves women. Here, the perceived difference in cultures between Western and non-Western values "diverts attention away from sex inequality closer to home and exoticizes third world women in ways that put the spotlight on cultural restrictions while obscuring other restrictions and obstacles these women face."[53] The dangers of othering non-Western societies and women in those places is particularly evident, and our gaze to conflicted societies can remove us from the cogent realities that Western cultures still practice many forms of sex discrimination and struggle with realizing equality and autonomy for women in multiple spheres.

This book is practically grounded in data, narratives, and field experience, showing how practices and standards leave women out of the post-conflict process. The genealogy of institutional gaps for women traces to omissions from peacemaking and transitional "deal-making," compounding the normative legal gaps that facilitate further exclusions down the line. In setting out how exclusions from such "deals" happen, we link to a broader analysis concerning the status and legal capacities of women in such societies prior to the occurrence of armed conflict. We assert a linkage between these broader social status issues and the realities women confront when seeking to impact upon negotiations concerned with the terms upon which hostilities will end (generally between armed male combatants) and what trade-offs such groups will make with one another to desist from further violence. We explore how the conversations that bring about the end of public hostilities between combatants occur in inaccessible and highly masculine spaces that, of their nature and construct, exclude women. In this analysis, the influence of such international measures as Resolutions 1325, 1820, 1888, and 1889 may be limited as they assume a public open context for the negotiations of conflict endings. They rarely engage with the realities of closed private masculine spaces that pervade the endings of violence across multiple jurisdictions and cultures. International mandates fail to distinguish sufficiently between the particular stages of peacemaking that we outline above and thus fail to grasp the nuances and barriers to transformation that women encounter in each phase. Further, the processes and policies undertaken to engage in post-conflict reconstruction have remained largely the same before and after passage of Resolutions 1325, 1820, 1888, and 1889. The mere tacking on of gender mainstreaming, whereby the same programs are constructed (disarmament, demobilization, and reintegration [DDR], governance, rule of law), but are given a gloss of gender mainstreaming, will never serve to fully allow women to capitalize on transformative post-conflict opportunities.

An overarching goal of this book—after arguing that gender must be central and showing how it is not—is a focus on how to actually make gender central to conflict resolution, peacekeeping, reconstruction, and reconciliation efforts. Integrating gender in the post-conflict process specifically includes: (1) proceeding upon the recognition that sustainable development requires substantive gender equality measured in tangible outcomes; (2) recognizing women's rights to participate in all aspects of the transition; (3) developing and actually implementing laws that respect and foster gender equity; (4) fully implementing a justice component that ends impunity and ensures accountability for crimes committed against women and girls during the conflict; and (5) integrating social and economic rights into the core of the "deals" that are struck between factions and states and endorsed by the international community.

As this book argues, integrating gender into the post-conflict process is insufficient unless gender is integrated into all aspects and levels of the newly developing or rehabilitating state. Doing so involves close attention to what happens to women throughout the transition process. For gender to be absolutely involved, it must be addressed in every issue and at every level, and the invocation of gender should be tested for the benefits it brings to women directly. For example, gender discourses have often focused almost exclusively on holding war crimes perpetrators accountable for sexual violence. We cannot, however, evaluate the credibility and value of such accountability mechanisms without an eye to the broader transitional dynamic of the society in question. While international courts and tribunals have unquestionably made significant inroads on giving greater visibility to the violence experienced by women in certain conflicts, it is not entirely clear that the outcomes for women from narrow accountability processes are entirely positive. Prosecutions for gender-based violence have been few, and despite the best efforts of prosecutorial staff in many cases, women victims have often found the experience of giving evidence highly traumatic and difficult as a practical matter. Moreover, there is a danger that a focus on the "extraordinary" violence of conflict smoothes over the "ordinary" sex-based violence experienced by women in such societies as an ongoing reality. For the individual woman victim, the difference between sex-based conflict violence and ongoing vulnerability to routine sexual violence may be indistinguishable—but for the purposes of transitional legal accountability lines are clearly drawn. Furthermore, the current focus of gender crime prosecutions assumes that both "extraordinary" and sex-based violence are a priority even though other types of violence may be more keenly felt by the women in situ. If asked and consulted, they might ascribe different priorities in the substance, timing, and structure of accountability. In short, these kinds of legal distinctions may do little to engage with the broader realities and context of violence for women in conflicted societies, and may do little to address the fundamental broad-based vulnerabilities of women to violence, whether the state is officially in conflict or not. Addressing gender-based violence is only one of the multiple steps in making gender integral to the post-conflict setting.

In its expansive context, our approach challenges conventional notions concerning the role and rule of law in post-conflict situations. For those of us trained to think in terms of legal solutions, of justice via international, regional, or local tribunals, of prosecutions and investigations and evidence and trials, these concepts must be tested in countries with a minimally functioning justice system, with no means of protecting victim-witnesses, and with only minimal assurance that genocide and gender-based violence will not recur. In these countries, we must be particularly sensitive to what role the law can and should play in ending impunity and restoring confidence that the war wounds can be healed. Finding justice for victims and punishing perpetrators are critical, but there are important contextual issues on how best to proceed as countries struggle to establish new governments. In our focus on legal approaches, we must remember the practical realities that confront victims of gender-based violence as they continue with their lives (often living in the same communities as the perpetrators) and craft remedies that account for these differing, potentially conflicting, realities which themselves may reflect divergent constituencies: a need for punishment, rehabilitation for both victims and perpetrators, and moving on in a politically divided society.

While issues in transitional countries challenge the rule and role of law, they also raise critical issues concerning victimization. Victimization is a complex issue in conflicted and post-conflict societies, and has particular pitfalls for women. In societies where violence is pervasive and endemic, victim status may be difficult to differentiate. Struggles abound in determining who is and who is not a victim. Hierarchies of victimhood proliferate, and women struggle to gain a foothold in that dimension. Women who have been subjected to sexual violence by armed groups are certainly victims,[54] yet they are often scorned and treated by their families and communities not as victims but as outcasts, while the soldiers who committed the crimes are welcomed home. This conduct toward women stems from multiple causes: first, women's legal and social status in many conflicted countries is low, thereby operating against full enforcement of criminal norms; second, and intertwined with the first, while sexual violence is slowly being accepted by the international community as a crime, the translation of that status to cultural norms and legal enforcement remains embryonic internationally and domestically.

This book's theorization involves consideration of the overwhelming emphasis on civil and political rights, illustrated by the calls for war crimes tribunals, in many transition deals. While civil and political rights are foundational, their significance at the expense of other types of rights is open to critique as a masculine construct of the priorities of government and law. Moreover, this skew has a negative impact on women's social, political, and economic status during the transition process. Equally, many men's interests are not well served in devastated social and economic settings when the protection of basic needs is not considered an essential part of any conflict-ending process. Without a broader lens on gendered reconstruction issues, minimal transformative possibilities open up to women, thus squandering the momentum and possibility for offered by the massive transformative potential of the post-conflict process for all. Once again, we stress that only with a broad framework will the measurement of what constitutes success for transitional justice actually encompass the experiences of women.

Reconstruction, then, is a core topic: it is a process that includes security and development, but that does not simply re-create patterns that existed prior to conflict.[55] In this framework, the law is only one of many possible tools (including truth commissions and reparations) to help with the healing and dealing with the past. Likewise, while many of these mechanisms are potentially innovative, they are equally susceptible to the same kinds of gender bias and require the same kind of monitoring and critical analysis as more traditional fora and processes.

This book serves as a primer on the role of gender—focusing on women—in the post-conflict process, beginning with what happens to women during war before examining the issues involved in post-conflict reconstruction. Of course, the post-conflict process does not provide a monolithic opportunity in conflicted states. Not every conflict yields transformation or even obvious potential for transformation. For many societies there is no "post" conflict, merely a pause in the ongoing cycles of violence. For women, there may be no end to violence even when there is an end to violence between combatants in public spaces. In many post-conflict societies, the absence of processes and institutions as a result of the awful effects of war means that the concept of gender centrality is often misplaced, as there is literally "nothing" to graft onto. When the peacekeeping phase lasts for years, and the post-conflict reconstruction process never gets under way, for instance, there are few opportunities to reconceive of gender-positive post-conflict processes because there are simply no processes.

This book draws on a variety of country experiences to illustrate how to include a gender analysis in these processes and map the forms of transition onto the experiences of women. Disaggregating the commonalities and differences that arise for women in varying transitional contexts is a motif throughout. Accordingly, it is critical to integrate fundamental conceptual insights from feminist legal and political theory to the transitional justice context, and to identify how these axiomatic ways of understanding the role, experiences, and violations that women experience are translated (or not) into the post-conflict and transitional justice context. The way forward requires at least the following four steps to make gender central: (1) critically understand the traction of gender-based exclusion, discrimination, and violence as central to the perceived normality of all societies; (2) ensuring gender consciousness in institutional and program development; (3) requiring genuine gender centrality in multiple kinds of institutional settings and programs based on a commitment to women's autonomy and equality of outcomes; and (4) implementing gender equity and monitoring throughout. Where available or appropriate, this book includes relevant and primary commentary from women within the country or region in question, as well as a review of the postcolonialist critiques and admonishments of heavy-handed human rights–based or interventionist approaches. Transformative change for women in deeply chaotic and economically devastated societies may be a slow and uneven process. We accept that reformist but not transformative agendas may also be useful to women in the short and medium term to advance their immediate material and social needs.

The examination undertaken in this book proceeds somewhat chronologically, with the understanding that different conflicts have different ebbs and flows, some moving into peacebuilding phases, but then backtracking to peacekeeping, with some never making it past peacekeeping, and some tilting back and forth between settlement and conflict indefinitely. Part I of this book concentrates on pre-conflict and conflict settings and how women fare within them. Chapter 1 is an empirically drawn chapter seeking to situate the status of women across multiple variables in the context of their subsequent experience of conflict. This examination includes a preliminary assessment of health indicators, educational opportunity, legal status, gender discrimination, and familial roles, as well as literacy. Chapter 2 expands on the introduction and explores a range of theoretical issues that set out our general approach to the topics and the contexts in play. We concentrate particularly on drawing out an analysis of masculinities, victimhood, and combatancy.

Part II provides a background and overview of what happens during the immediate aftermath of conflict, including the disarmament, demobilization, and repatriation processes, and how gender affects the political and economic transition processes. We start in Chapter 3 by probing security issues in post-conflict societies. The necessity of security is an omnipresent point of negotiation and challenge in conflicted societies, and has distinct and important dimensions for women often ignored in the three-stage peacemaking process we outline above. Chapter 4 examines intervention processes and actors, laying the context that brings about a broader range and depth of intervention up to and including peacekeeping. Chapter 5 assesses peacekeeping methods and means, with attention to both the positive and negative dimensions of external military presence for women and men in post-conflict societies. Chapter 6 focuses on the disarmament, demobilization, and reintegration programs [DDR] that are pervasive in post-conflict settings. Here, we pay attention to the forms of DDR that promote certain kinds of masculine assumptions and value, and the impact of such encoding for the transformative potential of military disarmament. Chapter 7 sets out the state of play on international and hybrid criminal accountability for gender-based crimes experienced by women in conflict. It surveys a range of prosecution, sanction, and accountability options at both the international and domestic levels. Chapter 8 scrutinizes broader post-conflict remedies, including truth processes, lustration, and forms of reparation. Finally, Chapter 9 pays close attention to legal reform and its influence on women's lives and opportunities.

Part III emphasizes the dynamics and opportunities available to women as a result of reconstruction and development opportunities. Chapter 10 examines gender and governance issues, and Chapter 11 explores the importance of development infrastructure in the arenas of economics, health, and education.

This book draws in all of the post-conflict actors, ranging from soldiers and civilians to international organizations, local feminists, and members of civil society. This book follows the pattern of programs most often considered by the international actors to be central to post-conflict processes, but acknowledges the points at which the assumptions of centrality might be mistaken. It further follows the programmatic structures selected by international actors (rule of law, governance, human rights institutional building), even while deconstructing the extent to which the international actors have failed to make those structural decisions based on any coherent doctrine accepted across various professional ordering mechanisms. Inherent in this analysis is our attentiveness to the culture of masculinity and patriarchy in international institutional settings, and its influence on how these institutions and their agents operate in post-conflict societies.

Throughout this book, we emphasize that gender analysis requires attention to men and women. Too often, gender analysis involves a focus only on including women rather than recognizing the overlapping, but sometimes different, needs of men and women. Moreover, notwithstanding the cultural, legal, and social variations between countries facing post-conflict issues, the core issues around the centrality of gender remain universal. In undertaking this analysis, we are convinced that addressing the needs of women is not only good policy and practice on its own merits, but that it meets the first principle of conflicted and post-conflict societies—namely, ensuring that violence ends for all and is not reignited.

This book itself takes its place during a time of transition. Conflicts over the centrality of gender during war are ongoing, even as the United Nations and other institutions have taken some steps to recognize women's role in the conflict and post-conflict time periods and gender consciousness is becoming more pervasive. Nonetheless, as this book documents, the process of centralizing gender remains fraught with difficulties and setbacks, and our goal is to ensure that the process continues.

PART ONE

Conflict and Its Dynamics

CHAPTER 1

Before, During, and After Conflict

The Connections for Women

As our Introduction has noted, increased attention is being focused on the experiences of women during armed conflict and war, and gradually more consideration is being given to what happens for women in the aftermath of formal hostilities. Political entities, both domestic and international, have increasingly invoked the experiences and status of women as a means to justify or declare an interest in the resolution of conflict and/or their active intervention in domestic situations.[1] When the U.S.-led coalition invaded Afghanistan in October 2001, one of the stated justifications for the war (in addition to the de facto activation of the self-defense provisions of the UN Charter) was that it would liberate women from "the misogynistic rule of the Taliban."[2] Rhetorical reference to the situations of women before armed conflict abound, but there has been little detailed analysis of how women's prewar status and experiences relate to their conflict experiences or affect the manner in which they are treated in the transitional phase. This chapter seeks to explore that terrain with some rather robust caveats rooted in overarching methodological and empirical constraints that we expand upon below. Section one of this chapter commences with a focus on the importance and availability of multidimensional statistical information available to effectively map women's status across numerous social and economic contexts. The premise of this analysis is that baseline comparative data concerning women's lives helps us better understand how women fare in conflict and post-conflict contexts. We set out the dearth of available information, explain the reasons for its paucity, and explore why the absence of good data creates particularly acute problems of remedy and recognition for women in post-conflict societies. Section two explores the methods available to extrapolate women's economic, social, and legal status from the limited quantitative and qualitative data sources presently available. The analysis probes some relevant measurements with a particular focus on health statistics as a means to show the compounded vulnerabilities that women experience in conflict settings. Section three turns to explore the gender of social capital, with some specific extrapolation from data in the health and education contexts. This section also pays attention to whether there is a correlation between rule of law reform and an increase in social capital for women. The chapter closes by examining various data sources setting out state-by-state ranking on women's status and well-being across multiple factors. We probe how these measurements may affect how we assess the range and depth of harms experienced by women during conflict.

In all of these contexts, it is virtually impossible to draw a direct and causal link between legal status and/or economic capacity to the specifics of violence in any particular conflict. Nonetheless, in addition to identifying a need for sustained empirical research, we suggest that at the very least there is reason to believe that poor economic and social indicators supply some of the conditions conducive to the extremity of violence and social catastrophe that women experience during armed conflict. When women have limited access to law, when women are poor, and when women are culturally and socially viewed as lesser than their male counterparts, it stands to reason that the barriers to adverse treatment may be less than in contexts where women's legal and political standing provides some protection from and redress to violations of their human dignity and equality. We acknowledge that many men are poor and lack access to law in fragile and conflicted states, but we suggest that the additional layer of preexisting exclusions and discrimination that typify women's status in many societies has an additional and compounding effect on the waging of and experiences that follow from war in conflicted societies.

MAPPING THE STATUS OF WOMEN PRIOR TO CONFLICT

The endeavor of mapping the "before and after" of conflict is a complex task. That complexity also reflects the difficulties of women's lives, and in particular how little attention is generally paid in many societies to grasping and articulating the lived experiences of women on their own terms. One way to measure women's lives is with the verifiable manner of statistical analysis. This involves using current reporting by international organizations and institutions to garner a complete overview of women's social, economic, and political standing across multiple jurisdictions. This seems both an attractive and uncomplicated solution to charting the territory of women's status and experiences across common markers in societies that have experienced conflict, and to draw conclusions on a basis of solid foundations.

However, such statistical information only provides a partial glimpse of women's social and legal status. In addition to individually orientated measures that calculate the quality or standard of life (for example, maternal mortality, land ownership, fertility, levels of violence, employment, and occupation levels), broader institutional and structural measurements are necessary. This should include an assessment of the systems that function in any given society to protect women's rights and advance their interests. Such structural measurements might include, for example, the number of domestic violence shelters; the procedures and documentation that operate in the criminal law to address violence against women; the laws and regulations pertaining to voter registration and elections; and the legal procedures in place to address employment discrimination. Only synthesis between the effectiveness of broader social systems allied with individual assessment will likely give a fulsome assessment of how women fare in any particular country setting. Importantly, we stress that it is exceedingly difficult to measure equality of opportunity for women, specifically the ability to make choices in the family, market, and society.[3]

Assessing the status, well-being, and equality that women experience in any country is a more fraught enterprise than one might imagine. As a recent comprehensive report on women's health issued by the World Health Organization confirms, "major gaps in knowledge . . . seriously limit what we can say with real authority about the health of women in different parts of the world."[4] At a basic level, these gaps are illustrated by the complete lack of data collection about the most basic facets of women's lives (epidemiological health data, demographic data, mortality rates, diseases experienced by women, reproductive data across age bands, disability, mental health, and health care services) in many countries. This highlights a broader problem, that basic knowledge disparities are prevalent in our understanding of the challenges faced by women across societies and cultures. The foundations for addressing women's needs and being able to measure progress lie with consistently generating better information about women's lives. At a minimum, vital statistics are needed across a range of arenas including women's health (diseases experienced; maternal, perinatal, and nutritional condition; life expectancy; health care systems and how they respond to women; specific information about women amid disasters, emergencies, and conflict); women's education (access to primary, secondary, and university; literacy rates; and qualitative information about the barriers to access including legal and security impediments); violence against women (prevalence; source of the violence; legal regulation; and enforcement of domestic laws); quantifiable data on water and fuel access; and finally, economic access and opportunities for women (including access to finance; access to the marketplace and economic actors; discrimination in remuneration and conditions of employment). Investment in knowledge and understanding are critical to address the experiences of women in conflict, to assess the roots of the violations that women experience, and the barriers that emerge (or reemerge) in post-conflict reconstruction even as internationally supported policies and programs rhetorically commit to the inclusion and advancement of women's rights and interests. Both quantitative and qualitative information are vital dimensions of any assessment.

As a starting point, many UN reports assessing country situations include a section on women's human rights and relay information relating to gender discrimination or the underenforcement of international norms related to women's rights in that country.[5] But such reporting is often very generalized, and frequently lacks precise factual information on the specifics of women's experiences and the patterns of exclusion, discrimination, or violence they may routinely face. In many such reporting contexts, there is a tendency not to aggregate data by sex and age, a process which would be more likely to reveal the extent of the challenges faced by women.

As outlined above, a lack of available or collected data is the rule rather than the exception in many countries on the issues and problems that most affect women. Lack of oversight may, at most basic, be related to the perceived unimportance of women and women's status. From this baseline there may be no apparent incentive for the state in data collection. In many developing countries there may be insufficient structural and informational capacity to record, assess, and distribute data. This problem is doubly manifest in conflict zones, where the capacity to access data is made triply hard by violence (limiting access), the transience of populations (as a direct result of fleeing violence), and the unwillingness of women in fraught political contexts where ethnicity and identity may be relevant to the causes of conflict to identify themselves in ways that make them increasingly vulnerable. It is also compounded by the unwillingness or inability of those (mainly external intervenors) who collect data.

When data is collected, two key questions arise. First, what data? What baseline information do we need in order to gain a nuanced understanding of women's lives? Second, how do we collect and then analyze data in a way that makes it possible to compare women's standing and vulnerabilities both within societies (relevant to social and economic position), temporally (before and after conflict), and between societies so that some cross-jurisdictional analysis can emerge? For example, some baseline information such as fertility statistics may be a useful indicator across countries and cultures to make valid comparisons about a comparable aspect of many women's lived lives. But even then, in societies where cultural norms dictate earlier marriage and a greater value to multiple childbearing, raw numbers alone may not tell the full story of what it means comparatively to carry children in one society over another, and under what conditions without potentially preferring one cultural set of values related to women and children over others. How to calibrate and disaggregate information about fertility in the context of conflict would also require us to take into account the geographical extent of hostilities, and to probe spikes in reported fertility against reported gender-based violence, child abandonment, or greater prevalence of ostracized women and children in situations that suggest nonconsensual sexual harms. None of this may be apparent from a statistical comparison of births between specific countries or regions per se.

What is clear is that we have very little relevant empirical data to assess the quality and limitations of women's lives across multiple societies. Furthermore, little of this data is consistently gathered on a year-by-year basis, allowing longitudinal study of women's lives over extended periods of time. Data needs to be collected in ways that allow for specific disaggregation by sex and age, thereby allowing for information relevant to gender roles and discrimination to be ascertained.[6] Collecting sex- and age-disaggregated data, as well as other types of information, is just the beginning of a process of empirical study. For the analysis to be useful, specific numbers detailing the extent of the problems and then improvements or deterioration of the situation over time could be tracked. Equally, it is important that parallel empirical information is gathered about men and boys.[7] Only by understanding the correlation between the economic and social disenfranchisement of women and the economic and social vulnerabilities experienced by men and boys can we undertake the kind of integrated, cohesive approach to social and economic protection and equality provision that will have broad social, economic, and political traction. To make sense of inequality, state-specific information is needed to outline the process by which inequality-creating structures are delineated, as well as ascertaining how the state is spending its money to achieve gender parity, and to overcome gender discrimination.[8]

SOME RELEVANT MEASURES

International and national data already gathered can provide useful information about women's lives.[9] In this section we focus on discussing some basic and widely available data sources that allow us to set out some baseline information concerning women's status globally, and in particular in those regions and countries that experience conflict most frequently. From here we draw some tentative conclusions about the social and economic contexts that may prove most challenging to women when conflict is added into the mix. Moreover, we suggest, as other strategic observers have done, that economic and social status may well be linked to conflict outcomes and experiences for women.[10]

Most women live in low-income or middle-income countries, with only 15 percent of the world's 3.3 billion females living in high-income countries.[11] More than one woman in three lives in a low-income country. While in general women live longer than men,[12] there are a number of countries in which women's life expectancy is equal to or shorter than men as a result of the social disadvantages that women face.[13] Life expectancy alone, however, only tells us a very minor part of a woman's story. The extra years of life may be spent precariously, as the social context of women's lives may place exceptional burdens on the quality of life lived. This is particularly true in countries that experience long-term, cyclical, or protracted conflict.

A striking feature of understanding women's life experience is to account for the underlying causes of death and disease. It is generally accepted that there has been an underlying shift in the causes of death and disease over time across multiple countries and encompassing the North/South divide. One conceptual means to capture this difference is entitled "health transition" and is constituted of three interrelated and mutually reinforcing elements: demographic structures, patterns of disease, and risk factors.[14] In the early stages of health transition, women and children face high levels of mortality linked to nutritional deficiencies; unsafe water and sanitation; smoke from solid fuels used for cooking and heating; as well as a lack of care during childhood, pregnancy, childbearing, and postnatal settings. These risks have a high overlap with developing countries and are exacerbated in the contexts of poverty combined with conflict. A related literature on gender inequality and poverty outcomes backed by a growing body of microstudies is establishing connections between variables, and flags the overlap between the perpetuation of poverty and inequality of opportunity for women and girls.[15] In low-income countries, maternal and perinatal conditions and communicable diseases are highly prevalent and account for 38 percent of female deaths.[16] The effects of these risks not only apply to women but have marked intergenerational influence, as women with poor nutrition, infectious diseases, and inadequate care have low-birth-weight infants whose health and chances of survival are compromised.[17] Conflicts compound and extend these risks in societies with poor preexisting health indicators for women, and we underscore the damaging effects that communal violence will have on women's health vulnerabilities.

Educational opportunities and the effects of hostilities on access to schooling illustrate the barriers to education generally for women and girls, and the augmentation of those obstacles in conflict and post-conflict settings. Equal accessibility to schooling in transitional is by HIV/AIDS and the reality of ongoing violence for girls. Again, data tracking the fall-off of girls from formal education processes is limited or of little value given a lack of preexisting conflict data on access to schooling in conflicted societies. More recent policy interventions in post-conflict settings focus on accelerated learning programs and targeted programs to improve school-to-work transition and skill deficits in poor adolescent girls, an important entry point to prevent the intergenerational transmission of poverty.[18] The challenge remains rolling out successful training and education programs in high-fertility, high-HIV/AIDS, and post-conflict settings where there is significantly less or highly compromised institutional capacity.

Socioeconomic adversity and inequality are clearly an essential component of understanding women's lived lives in multiple contexts. Less well understood is that gender inequalities exacerbate demographic stresses and limit potential gains even when demographic conditions improve post-conflict. Adversity has multiple gendered dimensions working to the disadvantage of women's health, education opportunity, and economic security. The most prominent of these factors includes high fertility. At the household level, increases in birth rates puts pressure on household budgets and is associated with poorer human capital to the detriment of children, women, and the household economy upon which most women remain reliant. High fertility linked to HIV/AIDS prevalence (often spread by conflicts with high rates of sexual violence) creates an extraordinary price for women in terms of their maternal mortality, labor force participation, and educational access.[19] There is also increased awareness that women are more vulnerable than men to poverty in old age, based on their lower lifetime earnings, their lack of participation in the formal labor force, and the effects of childbearing on their health and market participation.[20] These vulnerabilities and the nexus between poverty caused or exacerbated by conflict bear particular scrutiny as we think about how the post-conflict terrain should account for preexisting stigmas and detriments that are deeply gendered. Comparative longitudinal data is limited, but studies also indicate that in both high- and low-income countries, levels of maternal mortality may be up to three times higher among disadvantaged ethnic groups than among other women.[21] This point bears particular reflection and scrutiny when we intersect it with violent conflicts that have ethno-national fault lines. One might predict that women from minority or politically marginalized ethnic groups will experience a multiplier effect of disadvantage and harm in such contexts.

Little reliable data is available for the proportion of women living in poverty; however, some extrapolation is possible based on women's more limited access to formal employment in most countries and the cross-jurisdictional reality that much of their labor (in the home and family) is unpaid.[22] Even in formal employment, women earn less than men.[23] The World Health Organization (WHO) notes that "[t]he ratio of female to male earned income is well below parity in all countries for which data are available."[24] The lack of equal access to the formal employment market means that women have less job security and are generally denied the benefits of social protection.[25] In such contexts, when violent hostilities draw male heads of household into conflict-related activities, and/or economic disintegration follows the outbreak of hostilities, the marginality of women's economic status may be further compromised. In addition, the barriers that women ordinarily face in entering the labor market may be considerable. In conflicted societies, where women may seek out the market for survival but are limited by deeply entrenched role assumptions tied up with head of household responsibility and access to public space, the collation of such barriers underscore the economic vulnerabilities women and their dependent children face.

All of these background features are compounded in the context of conflicts and crisis. The WHO has confirmed "that there is a pattern of gender differentiation at all stages of a disaster: exposure to risk, risk perception, preparedness, response, physical impact, psychological impact, recovery and reconstruction."[26]

GENDER, LAW, AND SOCIAL CAPITAL

In thinking about the ways in which we should address the relationship between the status of women prior to conflict and its correlation to conflict experiences and post-conflict outcomes for women, it is useful to look at the relationship between social norms, rule of law (specifically the protections that the legal system provides to women both formally and informally), and gender realities.[27] While it is generally agreed that "rule of law is positively associated with desirable outcomes including GDP levels, financial market development, the rate of investment as well as the volume of trade," a puzzle emerges when we put women in the picture.[28] In parallel, using similar country-level data, Pistor et al. have cogently demonstrated that "the status of women in society is weakly associated with Rule of Law indices and that in poor countries this association disappears altogether."[29] For women, then, it seems that rule of law is not a significant determinant of their status. This finding, if sustained, has a potentially significant effect applied to the experiences of women during and after conflict. Some detailed studies of the gender dynamics of social transformation signify "that the status of women in society is determined primarily by social norms and gender equality and that these norms are only weakly affected by legal institutions."[30] As lawyers, unwilling to entirely cede a lack of consequence to law's application, we would at least assert that formal legal rules have a dampening effect on social norms.[31] Such effects may well be augmented over time. Moreover, legal norms have the capacity to create some contested space as an institutional matter, at least providing fora in which social norms must assert and defend their hold. Nonetheless, such research is profoundly disturbing to any analysis of the extent to which gender inequality can be fundamentally challenged in conflicted societies by rule making alone.

In many countries, women and girls are treated as socially inferior.[32] Unequal power relations promulgated by social and behavioral norms translate into differential access to health resources, to education, to income, and to political voice and are correlated with reduced well-being.[33] The Millennium Development Goals Reports affirm that while women's political participation is expanding in many countries, men still wield political and, by extension, social and economic control in most societies.[34] We suggest that such power and participation differentials have the capacity to have a marked effect on the methods and means of warfare pursued. Equally, it shapes the way in which conflict is ended and whose political voices shape and dictate endings and outcomes.

In assessing the experiences of conflict for women and what kinds of outcomes women gain in conflict resolution processes, some research suggests that we should pay less attention to the formal legal protections and status in the pre-conflict phase and more to informal legal systems and social norms that may exclusively or significantly determine experience and outcomes for women.[35] Social norms here refer "not only to intra-family or kinship relations, but more broadly to the social norms that determine a woman's status in society and constrain her ability to step outside stereotyped roles by pursuing economic, social, or political opportunities."[36] This approach might mean that transformative outcomes are more likely to be delivered for women by the delivery of services, capacity, and remedy at the local and communal level. This grassroots tactic based on a gender-central approach would then ideally operate in ways that are attentive to gender stratification and gender discrimination. It would work with women and men to deliver services, remedies, and opportunities and provide both genders with the tools to socially rebuild, but in ways that would provide alternative baselines of status and equality for women.

The interface of war economics and gender dynamics is a relatively new arena of scholarly exploration but relevant here as we make sense of what economic baselines we use to assess women's capacity and challenges in the post-conflict phase. It poses some challenging realities for feminist analysis.[37] There is an emerging consensus in a small but influential body of literature that there is a natural overlap between entrenched economies of criminality and entrenched conflict—particularly in resource-rich states. Described as "durable disorder," this analysis stresses that global liberalization has deepened the necessity that war economies function on asset realization.[38] In this examination, poverty and dislocation are war's intended outcomes, not its by-product. The shadow economy is entrenched,[39] and criminality is one of the few avenues open to men and women for survival and entrepreneurship in post-conflict settings. In this telling, criminality and informal economies are interlocked and constitute much of the functional economy in the global South. The hollowing out of the state for multiple reasons means that women and men are invariably operating between formal and informal economic settings as a means to provide for their basic needs and advancement. This makes it hard to disentangle the functional from the dysfunctional, but also poses uncomfortable questions about the ways in which women's labor operates to sustain and support ongoing hostilities within and between states.

It follows that as we think about the economic rationality of violence, we also consider pricing the economic costs of conflict in gendered terms. Doing so would facilitate restructuring of how we should think about repair and reparation. As Duggan et al. note in their assessment of the costs of sexual and reproductive violence for women in Guatemala and Peru, "a weak economy coupled with the social and communal fallout of SRC [Sexual and Reproductive Violence] can be so acute that it extinguishes traditional avenues of social and economic survival."[40] Such astute assessments indicate the pressing need to factor preexisting gender inequities into cost and damages assessment. We suggest that understanding the interplay between pre-conflict and conflict vulnerabilities would greatly assist in fully recognizing the causality, degree, and depth of harms experienced by women in conflict contexts.

The link between pre-conflict sexual and reproductive violence for women,[41] coupled with elevated violence in situations of conflict, and violence continuation into the post-conflict phase demonstrates a broad preoccupation of this book, namely that sexual violence in conflict is intricately linked to deep-seated structural violence that is multifaceted in form. There is "a continuum of violence whereby political violence interrelates with economic and social violence in gendered ways."[42] In the context of Guatemala, the Commission for Historical Clarification (CEH) report analyzed the economic costs of the conflict and concluded that the costs of the war "including the loss of production due to death, equalled 121 percent of the 1990 Gross Domestic Product."[43] Political violence erodes the human capital of communities, and women are deeply affected by violent disorder in complex and multifaceted ways. But positively, women are key actors in the reconstruction of social capacity in the aftermath of political violence. Thus, post-conflict reconstruction has an inbuilt incentive to determine the extent to which the lasting impact of gender-based violence and other gendered harms may undermine women's abilities to become productive agents for development and reconstruction.

A PRACTICAL ASSESSMENT OF THE BEFORE AND AFTER

We are wary of drawing direct and conclusive lines between the status of women pre-conflict, their experiences during conflict, and the outcomes women achieve in peacemaking and peace-enforcement contexts. At the very least, we must acknowledge some outlier conflicts wherein women's theoretically strong legal and social protections did not result in fewer or less visible gendered harms during the conflict, for example in the former Yugoslavia.[44] But, we are prepared to point some tentative arrows. Drawing on the Organisation for Economic Co-operation and Development (OECD)'s Social Institutions and Gender Index of 2009, which is based on a detailed assessment of 124 country reports, a ranking system has been developed to determine how a country fares in terms of gender (SIGI ranking), and from this we would make various observations.[45] The ranking includes the following aspects:

Family Code (early marriage of women, polygamy, women's parental authority, and inheritance rights); Physical Integrity (violence against women and female genital mutilation [FGM]); Son Preference (missing women); Civil Liberties (freedom of movement, freedom of dress); and Ownership Rights (women's access to land, access to other property, and access to credit). Examining countries that have either received a UN Peacekeeping Mission since 1990 or received International Monetary Fund (IMF) post-conflict emergency assistance since 1995 or were then undergoing a significant humanitarian conflict, we see a moderate correlation between conflict countries and low SIGI outcomes for women.[46] What the database also reveals is that the worst countries for women (and men, though in relative degree) both by region, and in the world generally, tend to be post- or current-conflict countries.

Another useful comparative data set is the World Bank's "Genderstats" database.[47] Utilizing this database, we sought to compare women's health and economic indicators in post- (and continuing) conflict countries with other (non-conflict) countries by region.[48] Using only the measures of adolescent fertility, birth attended by a skilled nurse, maternal mortality ratio, female/male secondary enrollment, and women in the nonagricultural sector, it is evident that women in conflict countries fare worse than the regional average.[49] At the very least, it points to an obvious contention, that widespread poverty and gendered economic disadvantage will create evident vulnerabilities to multiple kinds of harms (physical, social, and economic) for women in situations of conflict. These harms include the greater likelihood for women of being a refugee or displaced person, and in this realm at least it is entirely clear that women bear a disproportionate cost of conflict as compared to men.[50]

We maintain that there is a correlation between a state's security situation (its fragility) and its gender equity. The World Bank's Global Monitoring Report 2007,[51] which discusses the relationship between gender equality, poverty, and economic growth, notes that poverty rates tend to be lower in countries with more gender equality, that economic growth is positively correlated with gender equality, and that female education has a larger impact on growth than male education.[52] Gender-based violence is "an important development constraint that retards economic growth and poverty reduction."[53] In reflecting on some of the most violent conflicts of recent years, it is worth recalling that as of 2009, Somalia's GDP per capita was $600; Rwanda's GDP per capita was $1,000; Burundi's GDP per capita was $300; and Colombia's GDP per capita was $9,300.[54] That raw economic scorecard also indicates that the correlation between violence, insecurity, and income are not irrelevant to our understanding of the causality of conflict generally, as well as the specificity of gendered violence during hostilities.

Moreover, there is a relationship between a country's ranking on the UN Gender Development Index and the level of violence involved in the country's resolution of disputes.[55] In one study, which compared information from the Heidelberg Institute for International Conflict Research[56] with the UN Gender Development Index,[57] the researchers found that increasing amounts of gender inequality were correlated with a country's likelihood of resolving conflicts by using violence.[58] Although the authors note that correlation is not causation, they hold out the possibility that enhancing gender equity through gender development "may relate to a reduction in violence."[59] Researchers have suggested that states with higher percentages of women in leadership positions are less likely to act aggressively.[60] While we are wary of essentializing the changes that might result from including more women in leadership, we suggest that aside from the equality benefits of representational parity, a fringe plus might also include violence and conflict reduction.

Similarly, where there is a high level of intrafamilial violence, there is also a higher level of violence during processes of dispute resolution, and an increasing likelihood of involvement in conflict.[61] When a country has an abnormally high proportion of men to women (such as in some Asian countries, where sex-selection for boys occurs through abortion, infanticide, and other means), this has historically correlated with increased levels of social instability.[62] A demographic concentration of young men in post-conflict societies has been identified as creating a social contest that involves heightened criminal activity attacking individuals and/or the state.[63] The less likely states are to have laws and practices in conformity with Convention on the Elimination of All Forms of Discrimination Against Women (CEDAW), the more likely they are to be of concern to the international community based on their noncompliance with economic, political, and antiviolence international norms.[64] While treaty signing and compliance have been subject to contested empirical assessments,[65] and it is difficult to draw definitive lines, this additional piece of evidence supports the cumulative picture of the synergetic relationship between gender equality and state security.

In the most cogent recent example of textual invocation of women's rights as a basis for intervention, the situation of women in Afghanistan makes for gripping analysis. The plight of women before international intervention was utilized to significant rhetorical effect galvanizing international support for the conflict. It remains highly contested whether this text for intervention has shaped the gendered nature and priorities of military action within that state. A 2008 synopsis of a report on the status of women in Afghanistan summarizes that:

> The gender development index (GDI) adjusts human development indicators to reflect disparities between men and women along three dimensions: life expectancy and health, knowledge, and standard of living. The GDI for Afghanistan— at .310, one of the lowest in the world—reflects the lack of social and economic opportunity available to Afghan women.[66]

Afghan women postintervention have the second highest incidence of maternal mortality, estimated to be 1,700 per 100,000 live births, which equates to one maternal death every thirty minutes.[67] Almost half the deaths among Afghan women in the reproductive age group are from complications related to pregnancy and childbirth, 87 percent of which are reportedly preventable. Health services remain inadequate, substandard, or inaccessible to women.[68] Afghan culture forbids treatment of women by male doctors, yet nearly 40 percent of the basic health facilitates have no female workers, and basic reproductive health services are available only in 17 percent of health facilities in the country.[69] The literacy rate of Afghans fifteen years of age and older is only 23.5 percent, with 32.4 percent for men and only 12.6 percent for women.[70] Because most of the data here comes years after the international community was entrenched in Afghanistan, it raises significant questions, too, about the extent to which conditions for women can change premised on the presence of the international community and its nascent reconstruction programs alone. At minimum, these figures tend to affirm our earlier contention that substantially advancing women's social capital and making substantive equality gains for women has yet to really be seen in that jurisdiction, and is not advanced by current post-conflict reconstruction mechanisms.

The correlation of gender inequality and state fragility might rest on a variety of bases; reflecting on the movement toward gender equality in more developed countries, gender inequality in fragile states may simply evidence gaps in development in most of these states. Or, it may be that gender stereotypes, rather than biological essentialism, result in men pursuing more aggressive and inegalitarian policies. Dissolving or at least modifying gender stereotypes would allow the integration of peace-based values into domestic and international policymaking.[71] Whatever the source, the result is that "the violent masculinities that dominate in times of conflict" affect "the forms of accountability sought in the post-conflict/post-regime environment [because they] reflect the gender biases that manifest in the prior context."[72] We contend that unless women are involved in policymaking, and unless policymakers explicitly focus on gender, then the inequities will continue as a country moves toward stability. Inclusion of women alone is clearly insufficient without challenging the paradigms that have maintained their inequality and exclusion.[73] To undercut the structural and complex instigating factors that spark violent and gendered conflict, we underscore the need to pay consistent and thoughtful attention to the broader causalities identified in this chapter. Subsequent chapters set out how one might do so across a range of post-conflict arenas and issues.

CHAPTER 2

Gender and the Forms and Experiences of Conflict

We now turn to assess the phenomena of conflict in greater depth, to explore the waging of war and its gendered dimensions, and to reflect on how women and men experience violence in different and similar ways. War comes in multiple forms, and we use multiple terms to describe its occurrence. These include armed conflict, internal armed conflict, civil war, total war, cold war, and war on terror, to name but some of the phrases of capture. A multitude of legal and political mechanisms, ranging from international treaties to regional charters, exist to regulate, control, and contain conflict. The physical, psychological, and structural outcomes of conflict are invariably devastating and do not merely abstractly epitomize communal and state disputes writ large. Despite generally agreed applicable legal norms such as the Geneva Conventions and the Protocols Additional to the Geneva Conventions, the legal status of many conflicts remains contested within and between states.[1]

Images of men in conflict center on the male as armed combatant, emphasizing the masculinization of the military and of war itself. Equally, images of women in situations of conflict abound. Such imagery is epitomized by the female refugee, the woman as mother, the woman as widow or experiencing loss, the aberrational woman as perpetrator, the woman as victim of sexual violence, and even occasionally, the woman as warrior.[2] The variance of images affirms the multitude of roles presented to or foisted upon women by the emergence of collective violence. This chapter seeks to map some of that complexity, expanding the conceptual framework for a broader analysis of gender and the post-conflict terrain set out in the Introduction. We emphasize that conflict creates both opportunities and setbacks for women. Paradoxically, it can be, in relative degrees, simultaneously a site of oppression and possibility. While conflict can act as a springboard for some women's emancipation,[3] this may merely be a short-term change in status. Once the "war" is over and the implementation phase is activated, such gains are easily lost as conventional conceptions of masculinity, femininity, and gender roles reassert themselves with vigor.[4]

Only relatively recently have the gendered dimensions of war, and of international law in general, been closely examined.[5] This analysis has been supplemented by consideration of the gender dynamics of ethnic conflict and internal conflict.[6] Despite some war-related opportunities, preliminary research in the post-conflict and transitional justice fields reveals that there are links between the destructive experiences of women during conflict and the exclusions that follow from peacemaking and transitional processes, some of which we have explored in the Introduction. There can be significant losses for women in terms of social and political autonomy during the post-conflict phase, as male elites seek to restore "normality" through the reassertion of traditional masculine and feminine role assignments. Sanguinely, we recognize that the assertion of "normality" has strong psychosocial pathways for societies overlapping with gendered role conceptions for women and men. Social flux and collective violence can create significant pressure to revert to tradition and the status quo ante across social, political, and psychological dimensions in post-conflict societies. In parallel, international actors impact women's roles, sometimes negatively and sometimes positively, as they implement economic liberalization and democratization schemes during the post-conflict reconstruction process.

This chapter explores the multiplicity of roles that women and men occupy in conflict and post-conflict settings. Section one starts by illustrating the tendency to essentialize women's roles in conflict situations. This sets the stage for the limitations that follow for women individually and has follow-on implications for society as a whole. We analyze women's roles as political and military actors, and underscore the importance of affirming and supporting the capacity of women to exert agency in situations of extremis. Section two follows with an exploration of the interplay between violence and gender in the context of war and postwar situations. We explore how experiences of violence are viewed in narrow ways, with a fixation on harms to the body and for women with a concentration on sexual harms. We identify the myriad of ways in which violence can be structured and experienced, addressing the need for broader and more encompassing assessments of structural harms. Section three examines the complexity of masculinities in the post-conflict arena. We undertake an assessment of the forms and impact of masculinities both during and after hostilities. Our broad interest in gender dynamics seeks a deeper engagement with the differing images of and realities for men in conflict and post-conflict processes, with a keen eye to how such positionality affects women sharing the same physical, legal, and social space.

Chapter 1 has explored the diverse social, economic, and cultural contexts that frame women's positionality in many societies before, during, and after conflict. Despite this multiplicity, women's complex and highly differentiated roles are often collapsed by the social and political dynamics of armed conflict and women are essentialized as victims only. The problem of essentializing women's experiences of war is increasingly being captured in multifaceted ways. The danger of essentializing women's agency, experiences, and outlook is present throughout any analysis looking at women's experiences of extremity. The problem with essentialization is that it fixes the perception of what "woman" constitutes in the location of analysis, assuming that there is one fixed form of action or perception that captures the experience of all women. Instead, gender analysis must be particularly attuned to the intersectionality of women's experiences, not only conscious of their gender but also of their race, color, religion, family status, and sexual orientation. Some feminist scholars have argued, based on the international court jurisprudence (particularly the International Criminal Tribunal for the former Yugoslavia and the International Criminal Tribunal for Rwanda), that the process of holding perpetrators accountable is focused on men who have committed crimes, including crimes of sexual violence. This negates "much of women's sexual and political agency during war,"[7] and the result may be "only [to] identify women as rape victims."[8] There is an evident distortion in seeing women as victims only and denying their capacity to exercise agency or to play a myriad of roles during violent conflict. This blind spot tends to produce policy and practice that views women as homogeneously powerless or as implicit victims, thereby excluding the parallel reality of "women as benefactors of oppression, or the perpetrators of catastrophes."[9] Some scholarly and policy analysis has sought to undermine this universalizing tendency to view women through the victim prism only. Such challenges give significant pause and require us to be extremely cautious as we set out global positions on the experiences of women in conflict. In traditional narratives, women's contribution to the activation, maintenance, and perpetuation of conflict and violence has been vastly underplayed. Such dearth of interest in fully probing and addressing the complexity of women's roles has had, we argue, a knock-on effect on the understandings of gender roles that pervade broader political and legal processes in ending conflict.

The category of women combatants (or even women as tacit supporters of violence) is one that poses particular quandaries for many post-conflict political and legal processes. Various scholarly disciplines are pervaded by the "assumption that women are generally more peaceful and less aggressive or warlike than men."[10] Generally speaking, the quantification of and rationale for women's political violence is grossly underresearched.[11] This paucity of research is tied to complex social assumptions that underplay the active roles of women in the military apparatus of the state, or any roles that women may play within nonstate structures in conflicted societies. Here also "the prevalent view of women as victims of conflict . . . tends to overlook, explicitly or implicitly, women's power and agency."[12] Moreover, women's active roles within national or ethno-national military organizations is defined by deep ambiguity linked to resonant debates about the identity of nation, the meaning of citizenship, and the complex interface between cultural reproduction and gender roles in any society.[13]

Studies of women combatants in a variety of conflicts, including the Tamil Tiger combatants in Sri Lanka, the IRA in Northern Ireland, and soldiers in Sierra Leone, highlight the empirical reality that women can and do engage in violent acts, and/or may actively support other women and men who carry out such acts in the context of ethno-national conflicts.[14] Women play a range of roles in facilitating violence not only as direct perpetrators—but as bombmakers, lookouts, weapon carriers, and protectors of those who carry out direct physical violence. It is estimated that female combatants may have composed as much as one-third of LTTE, the previously most powerful Tamil militant separatist group in Sri Lanka.[15] In Rwanda it is reported that twenty-seven Rwandan women received prison sentences for their participation in the 1994 violence.[16] Northern Ireland provides comparative, though more limited, examples of women's involvement in politically motivated violence.[17] Other ethno-nationalist conflicts, such as Afghanistan, Algeria, and Palestine, demonstrate similar patterns of women's participation, and women seem to have used and exploited local cultural expectations as a means to advance their military roles in these conflicts.[18] For example, they have worn traditional feminine garb to avoid detection when engaged in activities such as carrying weapons. Women appear more likely to participate as combatants in pronationalist movements rather than in institutionalized state settings. But these are not the only contexts in which the violence perpetrated by and for women arise; women serve as participants in regular militaries or as civilian perpetrators when opportunities arise.

We also need to address the complexity of women's support for extremist politics that undergird the resort to violence to achieve political objectives.[19] Acknowledging women's violence or support to violence has been a difficult process for many feminists. Reflecting on the involvement of women soldiers in the events of Abu Ghraib prompted Barbara Ehrenreich to say, "What we have learnt from Abu Ghraib, once and for all, is that a uterus is not a substitute for a conscience."[20] Recognizing that women can be violent aggressors challenges the stereotypes showing that "women are not monolithic in their outlook as a group and are not bearers of certain essential qualities such as kindness and compassion."[21] Moreover, a nuanced focus on women as benefactors or perpetrators of systematic violence ultimately helps us better address the causes of violence and prevent its recurrence.

Following conflict, women may not be forthcoming about their wartime roles, a self-imposed erasure that contributes to the failure to recognize these functions and their social, economic, and legal dimensions.[22] Women who self-identify strongly as political actors and wish to avoid being categorized as victims (despite experiences of harm), often choose not to appear before truth or accountability processes in post-conflict societies. If or when they do, they will not define their experiences as falling within the terminology of victimhood. Thus, across truth recovery processes, disarmament, demobilization, and demilitarization programs and other post-conflict mechanisms we find a marked absence of those women who have played significant political roles at the community/activist, military, or political level. These absences have complex causes.

First, while in some postrevolutionary societies "being part of the guerilla fighters has earned women significant social and political authority,"[23] this is not true in all post-conflict contexts. Instead, there is frequently a reversal of the increase in rights and participation that may have marked the revolutionary movement as a positive social space for women. With such reversals in play, articulating a female combatant role may not be a viable choice for women.[24] Second, many women recognize that in order to "fit" accepted social stereotypes their articulation of a combatant role must draw on victim or other acceptable narratives that do not adequately respond to their own perceived choices or circumstances. Finally, women's quick absorption back to traditional care and family responsibility roles operates to stymie any access to broader political or social platforms. As we explore at length in other parts of this book, one key element to understanding this dynamic is that in many conflict contexts, women's involvement (sometimes fully egalitarian, sometimes partial) is a temporary aberration in a time of extremity and does not represent fundamental social change.[25] Gender ideology does not disappear in times of war—it is merely suspended.

As we deconstruct women's roles during conflict, there is a danger of dichotomizing their roles and essentializing in other unconstructive ways. Are women fighters different from women who have not been involved in 'armed combat but who have experienced its effects? Are we simply assuming that women who are not active combatants are victims, or that women combatants cannot also be victims? Once conflict ends, female combatants are certainly survivors, and they may have been quite strong and visible actors during the conflict. Roles are not unidimensional or mutually exclusive. Women who performed in a combatant or political role may also have experienced harms in conflict, and those forms of harms/violence may not be heard, literally or metaphorically, within a truth-telling, accountability, or demobilization, demilitarization, and reintegration (DDR) context. For both men and women there may often be significant overlap between the victim and perpetrator categories, making post-conflict accountability and remedy a highly complex and sensitive terrain. Even as they fought, men and women might have experienced sexual violence, the loss of family members and livelihood, and the destruction or displacement of community.

VIOLENCE, WOMEN, AND VICTIMIZATION

Conflict and violence are synonymous, but violence for women in a conflicted society is a complex and multifaceted phenomena. There has been a demonstrable gap in acknowledging the depth and range of violence that women experience in conflicted societies, and only relatively recently has sexual violence been recognized as a crime subject to criminal sanctions. Though welcome, increased recognition for sexual violence does not in itself address the full range of violent experiences for women in conflicted and post-conflict societies. In this section we address the spectrum of gendered violence that women experience in situations of conflict, explore the adequacy of capture by international law, and address the other harms that women experience but are perceived to be of lesser consequence for accountability or remedy purposes.

Women experience violence in multiple forms in many societies.[26] Violence against women is prevalent both in the public and private spheres. Much feminist theory has rightly concentrated on bringing the sphere of private intimate violence into the public domain, and ensuring in policy terms that its "private" categorization does not mean that it is unregulated by the state.[27] In conflicted societies, women remain vulnerable to intimate violence but are also,[28] as has been extensively documented, the target of sex-based violence that is closely related to the methods and means of warfare used by combatants.[29]

Physical violence is consistently at the heart of societal experiences of conflict. What counts as physical violence for the purposes of classifying conflict in the controlling and overarching legal terms of international humanitarian law elevates and recognizes certain kinds of violence over others.[30] The legal classification of conflict is highly significant from a gendered point of view as it defines certain forms and manifestations of violence as relevant to the question of the legal status of a conflict (and thus what rules apply) and other forms of violence as not relevant. Generally what counts is public, threshold-specific hostilities between mostly state entities and between states and those nonstate actors who manifest sufficient control of territory and governance capacity to be viewed as quasi "state-like" entities. When violence is understood in specific and narrow ways,[31] to account for rape and the physical burning of villages, without also accounting for the inability to collect wood for stoves or to plant crops with the certainty of being able to harvest them, this affects broader understandings of what qualifies as "issues" for negotiation and mediation purposes. Arguably, the dual effect of such exclusions is to narrow the problems faced to a "male" conception of conflict and its effect revolving around allocations of power and territory. The matters that are framed as "issues" for resolution in the negotiation either in pre- or framework agreements toward transition may impact only peripherally on many women's day-to-day lives. They may leave untouched socioeconomic exclusions (which may themselves constitute violent experiences for women), and other forms of violence, which women may not see as compartmentalized into "conflict" and "non-conflict" related, but rather experience as a continuum, only partially addressed or not by ceasefires.[32] Moreover, the elevation of certain kinds of violence creates a clear bias in the outcomes of negotiations, most often demonstrated by the marginalization of those issues and experiences that are central to a gender-sensitive understanding of conflict resolution or intervention. Finally, it translates into a prejudice that is reflected in the form and substance of accountability that is intended to provide closure on the past experience of a conflicted or authoritarian society, and thus allow it to transition successfully.

There is a strong presumption that sexual violence in war is a thing apart, an experience capable of being parsed out from the "regular and normal" violence that accompany women's lives in many societies. In this calculus, the assertion of what is gendered violence in a time of conflict has a clear endpoint, usually a ceasefire agreement or a peace agreement. As this book explores in multiple ways, the experiences of women are not so neatly categorized. There is, we suggest, both continuity to ongoing experiences of violence for women in conflict, and parallel discontinuity to the scale, intensity, and forms of violence that women are subjected to. This conundrum is part of the complexity of fully seeing the gendered terrain of conflict and non-conflict violence, and how they intermesh. We recognize that there are conflict-specific differences, with scale and intensity variable across conflicts. Nonetheless, consistently across all conflicts, sexual and gender-based violence rarely conforms to the timelines of peace treaties and ceasefires but endures past them.

Continuities and disjunctions are often hard to disentangle in situations of conflict. Women may experience an ongoing level of background sexual violence in conflict, consistent with "normal" or accepted violence that occurs without armed hostilities between combatants in play. In tandem conflict also can produce a catastrophic discontinuity causing extraordinary pain, loss, physical damage, and despair, undoing the normative social order for women and rendering their capacity to restore their prior life exceptionally difficult.[33] We know that many conflicts bring additional or greatly intensified forms of violence and sexual acts perpetrated upon women. There is a layering on of violence, which serves as a form of entrenched "othering" and pervades the way in which women subsequently experience inequality, discrimination, and exclusion. These layers of violence are causal to why women do not experience full equality of opportunity before, during, and after conflict.

Many observers and commentators on post-conflict societies have asserted that there is a marked rise in the violence which women experience post-conflict.[34] Statistics in a number of post-conflict societies that measure such acts suggest, at least, a marked increase in reported violence. While there is insufficient empirical evidence to fully demonstrate such a trend, significant evidence points to the continued pervasiveness of violence for women when peace is theoretically won. This ongoing violence challenges a prevailing premise that the gains at conflict's end are experienced in the same way by women and men.

The legal mechanisms to address sex-based violence for women in war should rightly be found in domestic and international law norms and procedures. A core problem for domestic legal regulation of war atrocities is that it is highly dependent on the prevailing and codified international standards. As international law had historically avoided regulating such sex-based violence, the consequences and gaps of this absence were also reflected in limited domestic legal regulation. Because armed confrontation between and within states was carried out by male combatants, the laws of war were generally constructed from the vista of a soldier's need for ordered rules within which to wage war on behalf of the state. Consequently, women's interests fared notoriously badly when accountability was sought for the behavior of combatants. Significant augmentation of international humanitarian law and international criminal law now means that there is no doubt as to the augmented responsibility for acts of violence directed at women during armed conflict,[35] but problems still persist. These problems include the reality that typically persistent levels of violence against women may be the norm in many societies regardless of whether conflict exists or not. Women experience beatings, marital rape, kidnapping, terrorizing physical abuse, captivity as sexual and domestic slaves, and harsh physical labor as normative social behaviors and conditions. Law has historically done little to touch on these experiences by systemic deployment of legal sanction. To do so requires a broad multipronged effort across social, economic, health, education, and legal sectors to transform the normative reality for women.

Despite legal reforms and increased accountability, there remains a limited understanding of the forms and functionality of sex-based violence in war, peace, and transition.[36] Second, there remains ongoing intellectual and legal resistance to accepting the extensive empirical evidence that women's bodies have been specifically targeted to further military-political objectives, and that traditional categorizations of violence (and its appropriate sanction) are ill-fitted to deal with the pervasiveness of violence experienced by women in multiple forms across a wide range of societies. Finally, there has been little exploration of how the violence which has been grafted on to legal accountability norms (genocide, crimes against humanity, war crimes, serious and systematic violations of human rights norms) actually maps onto women's subjective experiences, and whether or not there are a range of other experiences which women would name as violence and for which they would seek accountability, but which are not legally categorized as such.[37] In this context, preliminary empirical research suggests that loss of a child, separation from children, and witnessing harm to children or family members are particularly viewed by women victims as primary harms to the self, often as or more egregious than a severe violation of their own bodies.[38] One firm conclusion for us as we reflect on the density of the relationship between gender and war is that extensive empirical work is needed to measure more accurately women's experiences of conflict violence and to measure the gap between existing legal categories and what women "name" as harms experienced by them in conflict and post-conflict situations.

Despite these substantial criticisms as to the adequacy of international legal processes in addressing violence experienced by women in conflict situations, substantial legal progress has been made in the past decade.[39] As Chapter 7 addresses, the Statutes of the International ad hoc Tribunals for the former Yugoslavia and Rwanda as well as the International Criminal Court (ICC) Statute specifically recognize specific forms of sexual harms as violations of the laws of war subject to their jurisdiction.[40] The ad hoc tribunals and the ICC have developed specialized victim support units, which seek to support and ensure the capacity of women to give evidence before the international bodies. These Tribunals and Court have issued indictments aimed specifically at prosecuting the perpetrators of sex-based violence.[41] There have been some successful and highly visible prosecutions for sex-based crimes that occurred both in the former Yugoslavia and Rwanda.[42] The Rwanda Tribunal's prosecution unit has produced an analysis highlighting successes and failures, in order to pass on "lessons learnt" to the International Criminal Court and other ad hoc bodies addressing sexual violation and violence against women.[43] An international jurisprudence defining the forms and limits of international humanitarian law's interface with sex-based violence has emerged, and despite valid criticisms of its scope, it nonetheless makes a substantial dent on the notion that impunity is acceptable in respect to sexual violence directed at women in times of war. A constructive pro enforcement approach has emerged that seems affirmative and capable of being sustained and expanded. We explore these positive developments in accountability in great depth in Chapter 7.

The chronology of greater accountability rooted in the range of harms experienced by women makes clear that gender-based violence and women's victimization are more squarely in the sights of international policymakers and states. However, it is also clear that a very narrow conceptualization of the forms and effects of such violence pervade state and institutional decision-making. Nonetheless the need for a wider and more systematic understanding of the nature and forms of gendered violence is still lacking implementation through accountability and enforcement sites, particularly in adequately addressing the harms resulting from the denial of economic and social rights.[44] Understanding properly what women face requires not only seeing the sexual violence and physical harms they experience but bearing in mind other interconnected harms also.

We remain cognizant that in this context, law itself also has the capacity to do violence as well as justice. Ethnographic work assessing women's experience of security in the post-conflict sites of Northern Ireland, Lebanon, and South Africa underscore the ways in which women view the law as doing violence to them in the post-conflict terrain.[45] There is a need for the insightful capacity to link the promulgation of laws that discriminate against and socially repress women and understand these as a form of structural violence to women, and as an enabler of more systematic forms of personal and communal violence.[46] This brings us back to a position of deeply engaging with the range of sites, experiences, and institutions that do violence to women. Recall that post-conflict transition often involves regression in legal status for women (sometimes from the pre-conflict context, sometimes from the positive practices that have been entrenched through decades of social flux and communal violence), as the social space opened up by conflict facilitating new social and economic order is quickly sealed off again.[47] This is particularly evident when part of the compromise with male elites at the negotiation table involves ceding legal issues of personal status to the sphere of customary and religious law.[48] In this, what emerges is that "the impulse to women's social transformation and autonomy is circumscribed by the nationalist project, which constructs women as the purveyors of the community's accepted and acceptable cultural identity."[49] Thus, concentrating more fulsomely on elucidating how women experience harm and the manner in which law can facilitate and compound extremities of social and personal experience is a starting point. More concretely, we need to look beyond harms to the body and think in broader and institutional terms. Only then can the full scope of violence experienced by women be adequately addressed in the post-conflict terrain.

MASCULINITIES AND CONFLICT

There are direct links between violence and conflict with the way that manhoods or masculinities are constructed.[50] If the essentialization of women's roles is one critical component in an examination of the gendered dimension of war, then an analysis of men is a complementary and critical aspect of our gender analysis. Conflict and the post-conflict environment are "vividly about male power systems, struggles and identity formation."[51] There may be an enormous flux in the male post-conflict fraternity both on an individual and communal level. Moreover, international organizations and institutions, typically headed by male elites, are arriving to reconfigure the society emerging from conflict. So men who were in power are losing power, other men (domestic and international) are taking their place, and, as is often the case when a conflict stalemate arises, international workers (generally culturally and politically differentiated other males) are coming into a society to fill a vacuum. As Handrahan has noted, this "international fraternity," the community of decision-makers and experts who arrive after a conflict on a mission of goodwill, holds the upper hand, morally, economically, and politically.[52] However, while the international presence is lauded for rescuing such societies from the worst of their own excesses, what is little appreciated is that such men also bring with them varying aspects of gender norms and patriarchal behavior that transpose into the vacuum they fill.[53] Moreover, despite an array of cultural differences between locals and internationals, internal and external elites share fundamentally similar patriarchal views, which operate in tandem to exclude, silence, or nullify women's needs from the transitional space.[54] Understanding the complexity of male roles and positions in the post-conflict environment is critical to fully mediating and addressing the needs and experiences of women.

A fairly substantial literature documents the forms of masculinity that emerge in times of armed conflict and war.[55] Theorists in diverse disciplines have identified organic linkages between patriarchy, its contemporary outworkings, and various forms of masculinity as they arise within societies and institutions, deepening our understanding of how masculinities are constructed and differentiated.[56] While the war literature has made significant use of the conceptual and practical consequences of the term masculinity, the term has been much less applied to and understood to be relevant in the postconflict context.

Masculinities study is a diverse and burgeoning field, which has significant insights to offer to the analysis we advance here.[57] Masculinity theorists and feminist analysis have not always worked in tandem, and it is only relatively recently that feminist scholars have sought to address what masculinity studies has to offer feminist theorizing.[58] In this vein, we start by asking the "man" question,[59] interrogating where and how men are situated in relation to the creation, perpetuation, and institutionalization of violence. In studies of masculinity scholars have described the centrality of hegemonic masculinity to male behaviors and motivations. This is described as the dominance of a certain notion of manhood in society, which is reinforced and perpetuated by men (and women), and from a feminist perspective has an indelible relationship with the operation of patriarchy.

In what ways does hegemonic masculinity work, and how do masculinities operate to benefit even those men who are at the margins of masculinity norms and practice? Even within the hierarchies of masculinity, subordinated masculinities benefit from the social construction of male privilege and value.

While an enormous amount of scholarship has been generated about the varying forms of masculinity and their effects, the concept of "hyper" masculinity is particularly relevant to the experiences of women in violent and conflicted societies. Hypermasculinity describes "a masculinity in which the strictures against femininity and homosexuality are especially intense and in which physical strength and aggressiveness are paramount."[60] Although other kinds of masculinities coexist with hypermasculinity, in situations of conflict and endemic violence, hypermasculinity plays an enlarged and elevated role, and is directly related to the way in which women are subjected to and experience violence. Its social traction is intensified when violence is endemic, and other social strictures are loosened, and the unloosening of these patterns and hierarchies is particularly fraught in the post-conflict process.

As societies transition from violence and more toward democratic or more liberal forms of political engagement, close attention must be paid to masculinities as part of the project of ending violence. Post-conflict societies present a unique and underanalyzed site of examination for masculinities. This lack of attention may result from the presumption that the post-conflict context is equivalent to peace, presuming that the masculinities caused by militarization have been "tamed" by the end of violent contestation. This presumption, however, fails to recognize the difficulties of unlearning socialization into the military and to account for the ways in which women experience violence both in conflicted and post-conflict societies. This lack of attention to masculinities results in a failure to respond to the myriad of ways in which masculinities transform, adapt, and reformulate in the post-conflict environment. Consequently, close attention to the forms and impact of masculinities in the post-conflict milieu is critical not only for women's experiences of the post-conflict domain but also for the success of the transition process.

The gap is narrowing between a conflict literature that recognizes the significance of masculinity as ordering phenomena, and a post-conflict literature that has not engaged in the same type of study. A number of scholars and policymakers have articulated the importance of paying attention to masculinities in the post-conflict context.[61] Harvard anthropologist Kimberly Theidon's work has engaged in ethnographic explorations of the disarmament, demobilization, and reintegration (DDR) process in Colombia and explored the forms of masculinity emerging and entrenching in the ending-conflict phase. In demonstrating the palpable effects of militarization "on the body" of the men she interviews (from their hardened faces, to the contours and shape of their torsos, to the reflexive actions that have been ingrained beyond consciousness), she reveals the enormous challenges of putting the "body" out of military usage and integrating it back to civilian life.[62] Former combatants explained to Theidon that joining a paramilitary group allowed the men "to feel like a big man in the streets of their barrios," to "go out with the prettiest women" and to "dress well," privileges they insist would not have been possible if they were not carrying guns.[63] In this exploration, the challenges that such men pose to the women and communities they return to are explicit.

Linked to the question of the emergence of certain kinds of violence in war is the underlying question of why men engage in violence? Violence may be deeply linked to men's assertion of social status and the value of the self in particular contexts. Violence may literally "make the man" in many societies, and not infrequently the site of the violence is a woman's body. Recognizing such deeply rooted links between the constructions of the masculine self, and the social acceptance of manhood, helps in understanding the difficulties in ending violence (as a formal legal matter). Ending violence in many societies is not a superficial engagement, but may require deep and difficult entanglement with the masculine construction of self. This requires asking the fundamental question of what does it mean to "be a man" in a violent society, when violence begets status and economic capacity? It means not only addressing egregious sexual violence in the context of conflict, but as explored above, addressing the underlying normativity of sex-based violence toward women that underpins the ordinary practices of many men in many societies. Increasingly, the theoretical and practical relationship between masculinity norms and violence are being explored.[64] Some international organizations have recognized that there is a pressing need to deconstruct and reduce the negative aspects of masculinity and to integrate men and boys into programs aimed at reducing violence against women.[65] But, policy analysis and practical implementation of such ideas is at an embryonic stage.

Research exploring the forms of masculinity that emerged in the former Yugoslavia identifies four compelling factors in the emergence of destructive masculinities. These include: (1) the lack of state authority leading to competition and promoting aggression, (2) fears that liberalization based on gender equality emasculated men when they took over jobs traditionally held by women, (3) the emergence of socio-cultural norms that associated women with the betrayal of the nation, and (4) the appeal of going to war for men without economic means as a mechanism to boost masculinity.[66] Other related causalities across multiple conflicts include economic and social insecurity; a lack of legal and political status particularly associated with group or ethnic identity; and the lack of opportunity for meaningful self-determination (whether external or internal) within the state. In multiple contexts, engaging in violence is a rational choice for men when few other opportunities may be provided to gain economic security (albeit that the participation in violence provides a highly tenuous economic existence or longevity), social status and value within their communities, and political security (again tenuous and fragile) for their families and communities. In post-conflict societies, the conundrums of addressing the confluence of violence and masculinity norms are compounded by the lack of other economic and social opportunities (besides war) available to men to assert positive masculinities, and to have practical and symbolic roles within societies that struggle on the economic margins and are deeply politically dysfunctional.

Critical therefore to understanding the forms of masculinity that emerge in violent communal conflicts is contextualizing the reality of economic fragility that men and women face in post-conflict zones around the world. Countries emerging from conflict are some of the poorest on the planet.[67] They have the highest number of refugee populations (who are predominantly female with child dependents) and internally displaced persons.[68] In this context, when one domain of status and economic subsistence is closed off (by the end of violent armed conflict) such societies struggle to replace the dysfunctional economy of war with a functional liberal economy of provision. The tools that for some men provided a means of survival in war are unreliable and may no longer be needed. Men and young boys who are under- or uneducated are at considerable material and other disadvantage in such settings. In this space of economic struggle, parallel economics of criminality may develop (or coexist), thereby allowing certain forms of masculinity to endure and to provide both status and material needs.[69]

It is particularly difficult to confront violent masculinities in social settings that have operated to seal off men spatially from women and children. In violently conflicted societies these patterns result from the gendered patterns imposed by widespread militarization, state detention and incarceration of suspected nonstate actors in internal conflicts, and the internal and external displacement of populations that frequently accompanies widespread violence. This is further compounded in societies that have deeply stratified gender roles, leaving little room for the enablement of positive masculinities in either the public or private sphere. The effects of such stratification are also intensified when one accounts for intergenerational transmission of violent norms, and there are few positive role models for boys and girls to observe and respond to intact and complementary gendered relationships. Furthermore, in societies where age stratification is intense, there is intense competition for economic and sexual resources, between younger and older men, and research suggests that inflexible social stratification can function to intensify the hypermasculinities that emerge in this context.[70]

Without addressing the causalities of masculine behavior and choices within a framework that integrates masculinities, we may fail to address the ongoing realities of how masculinities closely interconnect with post-conflict social, political, and economic outcomes. It is important to ask what happens to hypermasculinity when societies transition from violence and move toward democratic or more liberal forms of political engagement. Which men lose and which men gain in such contexts? Failure to account for and be cognizant of conflict-specific masculinities has a significant effect for women in particular, but generally on the success of the conflict transition process. As we discuss in Chapter 6, DDR programs in particular struggle with "what to do with the "morass of malignant male muscle." It seems obvious that men unable to positively manifest masculine roles may return to violent and destructive means of expressing their identities."[71]

Women often bear the brunt of the flux in masculine roles.[72] The theoretical gains made by women in status and legal protection during a transition are much more complex in reality. One female participant in a study of women's experiences of post-conflict security in South Africa has noted:

> I think, in as much as the law of the country allows women to be empowered, that is going to have a spin-off effect on men's behaviour and men's attitude towards women. In particular, those so-called empowered women. They'll always be the subject of abuse . . . everywhere you go . . . if you are perceived to be an empowered woman you are subject to a lot of abuse from society in general.[73]

The link between formal (generally equality) gains made by women in many post-conflict legislative and constitutional enactments conjoined with the political displacement of power for many men from the traditional routes provided during armed conflict creates a complex terrain.[74] It is upon this territory that women's gains and their intersection with masculinities in flux are played out. Maintaining any gender equality gained during conflict can, in our view, advance stability because in societies with significant gender equality, there is a generally noted pacifying effect on state militaristic behavior in the international arena.[75] Yet, as concrete realities expose the broader context in which those gains are negotiated and maintained, the scale of the challenge is evident.

The dominant images during conflict of men as militaristic and women as victims (or peacemakers)[76] simplify what actually happens in times of conflict. Men do exhibit hypermasculinity, but it is also important to acknowledge "men as agents of kindness" and affirm their agency in maneuvering around gender roles and refusing to engage in certain actions (despite substantial peer pressure).[77] It is also important to make visible the vulnerability experienced by men in war, and to view the deployment of certain methods and means of warfare as specifically directed at exposing men's vulnerability. In the aftermath of conflict, societies may reconstruct, on their own and with international help, their pre-conflict cultures, complete with traditionally gendered roles. Positive strategies forward for both men and women are essential to transforming the post-conflict terrain in ways that do not trap us into overly stratified assumptions about social roles or potentials. Integrated conceptualization and implementation is also necessary to pay much needed attention to the intergenerational transmission of violent norms, and to recognize the long-term effects of societal aggression allied with intimate violence on the children who experience the multipronged effects of a culture infused with violence and social inequality across all spheres. In this context, there is also transmission of violent behavior allied with deeply entrenched gender roles. Without attention to the factors that shape gender identity and ground the masculine and feminine notion of the self in conflicted and post-conflict societies, the patterns that collude to have an effect on the forms and experiences of violence will not simply fade with the conclusion of peace agreements. Rather, the method and means for reconstructing the masculine and feminine require close attention, mandating specific policy-oriented approaches and conscious attention to gender when negotiating specific measures across a range of arenas.

CONCLUSION

The crossing points between women, gender, and conflict are complex, and this chapter has only briefly touched upon some of the most challenging aspects of the interface. There is no easy shorthand that fully encompasses the range of conflict experiences for women, nor one totalizing narrative that fully integrates the varied nature and forms of conflict across multiple geographical and cultural settings. One thematic strand however is consistent, namely the varied nature of women's experiences and the variety of ways (both positive and negative) that women are subject to, interface with, or are causal to communal violence. Recognizing this multiplicity of experiences and contexts remains essential to developing a nuanced approach to post-conflict management and transition for women and ought to be a guiding principle for decision-makers, whether they are domestic actors or internationals. Placing women centrally in defining the problem(s) to be solved, the options that might be activated, and the application of those options in practice is pivotal to facilitating outcomes that value, address, and offer remedy and opportunity for women across the spectrum of post-conflict opportunities and needs. That central placement must, in our view, be guided by a substantive vision of gender equality and autonomy.

Close scrutiny of multiple post-conflict processes demonstrates that women's needs and concerns are gaining a foothold in a terrain that has largely excluded or marginalized them to date. Nonetheless, the policy positions outlined above combined with persistent anecdotal evidence from women activists, survivors, combatants, and victims underscore how fragile and precarious that foothold remains. The post-conflict terrain is contested territory, and the challenges to be present in key locales, to be heard and to have influence, remain ongoing for women.

PART TWO
Toward Peace

CHAPTER 3

The Significance of Security

Realizing Peace

In the immediate aftermath of conflict, security is critical to the possibility that refugees and former combatants will return home, that the rule of law can be established, and that the state in hostilities can move positively forward. The security situation in a post-conflict society is critical to preventing further conflict; within five years of the end of a conflict, some estimate that there is up to a 50 percent risk that the society will again become involved in violent strife.[1] Security issues are at the core of the reconstruction process for the local population, national leaders, and the international community, and they are central to the psychological notion of safety and well-being at the individual and communal level.[2]

Security is, however, capable of multiple and overlapping meanings.[3] In post-conflict countries, security definitions might range from the absence of armed conflict to the presence of well-organized civil and criminal justice systems that protect against individual and social violence.[4] Securing the peace could simply mean the absence of war—or it might also include the establishment of the conditions for social justice, human rights, nondiscrimination, and equality.[5] There is, then, a key distinction between negative and positive peace: the absence of armed conflict can be defined as negative peace, while positive peace can be conceptualized as the absence of both direct physical violence and indirect structural and cultural violence,[6] as well as the establishment of individual safety, in both public and private. The post-conflict context is a highly fraught terrain, not least because, as we have emphasized throughout this book, "post" conflict may be a euphemistic term. Hostilities may not be over, and violence may not end in sites officially proclaimed to be "post" conflict by other states, international institutions, and internal elites.

Frontlines of armed conflict may have formally dissipated, but violence may have moved to other social sites.

In the post-conflict context, international and local institutions and actors may narrowly focus on particular forms of physical violence to the person caused by state or armed actors in addressing security. They aim to deliver conventional notions of security such as demobilization, protection for soldiers to return home, clearing land mines, and new roles for security officers and former combatants. The focus is generally on official government actors, institutions and former militia members.

As a result, when post-conflict security discourse elevates the protection of and accountability for physical security and then narrowly defines what counts as physical violence (often conflating physical security with even more narrowly defined sexual security for women), this then elevates and recognizes certain kinds of violence over others, with decisively negative implications for women.[7] The marked emphasis on public acts means that private acts are neglected, inscribing a distinction that feminists have challenged between the public and the private. What generally matters is what occurred on streets, in public spaces, and in formal institutional settings. For violations occurring within the home, or close to private intimate spaces that women themselves describe as central to their experiences of vulnerability, lack of security and violation are deemed to fall within the "private" domain in most legal and social systems, and frequently outside the circle of notice and accountability. Thus, what happens within people's homes is not deemed important and is often entirely invisible.[8] We assert that, when violence is understood in specific and narrow ways, this limits broader understandings of what issues are open for negotiation, mediation, and reform purposes, and what kinds of institutional reforms ought to follow.

From the perspectives of the international actors engaging in reconstruction, the tasks of rebuilding infrastructure, delivering humanitarian assistance, and strengthening political and economic institutions all depend on a basic level of security. For persons displaced during war to consider returning to their communities, and even for those who never left, to begin feeling safe again, security-strengthening processes can provide some comfort. But, security has complex and layered meanings for displaced and local populations, often missed or ignored by external actors. International actors developing post-conflict programs may not develop policies and programs based on ascertaining locals' real needs and desires, but instead determine a policy objective (e.g., in the case of Bosnia, return of ethnic minorities to their prewar homes), and then create programs based around donors' levels of interest. When social scientists ask local populations what it would take for them to feel secure enough to return home, the answers are often not the donors' priorities, such as reconstructed houses, but being able to secure work, support their families, and send their children to school without discrimination.[9] Security for them means not just security *from* (harm, injury, sexual violence) but security *to* (care for one's family, work, thrive). All communities need basic guarantees that provide security not only to return home but also to reconstruct their lives. Indeed, a precise and agreed definition for the meaning of security by all the agencies, governments, institutions, and international organizations using it is still lacking. What is clear is that security reform is a broad concept which covers a multitude of relationships and sites.

Because security provides the foundation for post-conflict processes, we advocate an expansive meaning of the term. Indeed, as discussed in this chapter, narrow state-centric notions of security constitute part of the problem in addressing the exclusions and negative impact of change processes for women. The broadest possible consensus on the scope of security reform is vital to substantive gender parity and autonomy and is essential to the practical rolling out of security in post-conflict societies. This chapter first examines how gender is relevant to conceptions of security before exploring some of the differing meanings of security in post-conflict settings. It then unmasks the roles that gender and gendering play in security, showing how post-conflict security priorities accord with masculine conceptualizations of safety, and critiquing the state-centric approach which focuses on public violence. Finally, it suggests a new paradigm for future efforts at security that affects, and effects, equity between gendered concepts of how to manage safety.

IS GENDER CENTRAL TO SECURITY?

As an initial matter, consider why gender conceptions and sensitivity should be central to security issues. Security in the post-conflict setting typically emphasizes law enforcement and the military, although increasingly this mandate includes reform of the judicial, legal, and penal systems.[10] The centrality of gender—either masculine or feminine constructs—is not necessarily obvious to this paradigm. Indeed, centralizing gender consciousness, an awareness of potentially differing conceptions of safety from male and female perspectives, into rethinking security outcomes is an expansion that requires moving beyond substantive institutional changes within the ranks of security actors. Yet it is a necessary expansion: ensuring that gender matters can make a concrete difference by providing greater local ownership and more effective and efficient service delivery, and if done well, can actually result in taking the real concerns of women and men into consideration in the development of security post-conflict.[11] Consider the UN Gender Guidelines for Mine Action, which are designed to improve mine action programs by substantirely incorporating gender awareness. The Guidelines are exemplary in examining problems, providing solutions, and giving examples of successful programs.

Centralizing gender within any and all programs designed to enhance post-conflict security not only increases the chances that the programs will succeed in providing security for both men and women both, but also provides the best opportunity to recalibrate what it means to be secure, and contributes to the long-term viability of the transitioning society. Without consciousness of the need to include male and female perspectives, existing structures will "render invisible the gendered patterns and structures"[12] that accompany security reform. Identifying the pervasiveness of invisibility for women highlights the difficulties of implementing a transformative vision of security reform within a sector that has grown accustomed to asserting its own power.[13] In this context, it is worth recalling that the security sector is a prima facie masculine context, where hegemonic masculinity is always in play, and where women are typically excluded altogether and where gender concerns are viewed as marginal or irrelevant.

Strategies to rectify such exclusion require broad and transformative approaches addressing the social and cultural reality of women's obligations, the social actuality of women's inequality, and the violence that constitutes normality for many. Women's obligations typically include, for example, caring for children. Consequently, beyond the physical risks that all women face from sexual violence, there are additional security issues for women with children arising from their roles of protection and caring and as family caretakers. Only when such broader contextualization becomes part of the "fix," in step with microschemes and strategies to transform the security sector, will security be realized for the post-conflict society, not to mention the genuine realization of security for women. A consistent theme of this book is that societies that are not safe for women are not safe. Period. They are at greater risk for slipping back into disorder just as they are arguably more likely to become failed states in the first instance. In this framing, security for women is also linked to long-term strategies to contain and end cycles of violence and the perpetuation of intergenerational violence that accompanies conflict in many societies. Moreover, because of their vantage point in post-conflict countries, and because of the power of the transformative moment of postwar transition, women may be more likely to address socioeconomic issues that are critical to establishing security.[14] In brief, societies that are not safe for women are simply not secure in any broad and embracive sense of that term.

SECURITY REFORM AND TRANSITION

The reconstruction process imagines several immediate steps to providing basic levels of security as a society makes the transition from war to the absence of conflict. That is, combatants must be adequately demobilized and newly constituted security forces able to provide some assurance that former militants and refugees can safely return home. As an initial objective, the U.S. Institute for Peace suggests that:

> Armed opposition groups responsible for political violence have largely been defeated, subordinated to legitimate government authority, or disarmed and reintegrated into society. National security forces, increasingly operating lawfully under legitimate government authority, provide a safe and secure environment for citizens, assisted by a sustainable level of involvement by international forces (e.g. combat troops and police).
>
> STAGE II OBJECTIVE: National security forces, operating lawfully under legitimate government authority, maintain a monopoly on the legitimate use of force and provide a safe and secure environment for all citizens, without the operational involvement of international forces.[15]

Conventional notions of security also include goals that the peacekeepers behave appropriately, that land mines and unexploded ordinances be cleared, and that newly credentialed security officers understand their roles as critical to preserving the peace.

As these formulations show, security in a post-conflict country is often narrowly centered on "security sector reform (SSR)," which is focused on both official state actors, such as the police and military, as well as related actors, such as opposition militias, paramilitaries, and private security companies.[16] Such a state-centric approach, focused on certain aspects of armed conflict between (generally) male combatants, provides little opportunity for challenging alternative forms of insecurity.

Reformulating a successful and secure transition process for women requires examination of security sector reform, including a challenge to its potentially narrow focus. The term "security sector reform" first made an appearance in a speech by Clare Short, the British Minister for International Development, in 1997.[17] While the concept of security sector reform has substantial political and policy currency in Europe, it has generally received less emphasis in the United States. Despite this, the concept has permeated a number of international policy contexts in recent years.[18] Security sector reform has its roots in Western donor debates over how best to target and implement development assistance, thereby fostering a policy nexus between poverty and security debates.[19] In this context, security sector reform is asserted as an integral part of development assistance, especially in post-conflict societies, which are particularly prone to revert back to violent conflict.[20]

Security sector reform applies to repressive regimes, faltering or failed entities, transitioning states, and democratic states. In all these contexts, reform has concentrated on oversight and structure of civil-military relations,[21] the democratic control of the armed forces, and the integration of all the security agencies responsible for securing a state's internal and external integrity.

Generally, all these conversations exclude women, and women are not represented at the "tables" where such discussions take place. Indeed, consider that reforming the security system typically consists in conceptualization of practices that follow four macrosteps: ensuring civilian control; professionalizing and training security sector forces; demobilizing and strengthening the peace; and reinforcing (or reestablishing) the rule of law.[22] Examples of these types of reforms from the Baltics and parts of southeastern Europe include: new constitutions which establish that the military is subject to civil control; decrease in the size of the military; improved transparency; and changes in the judicial and police sectors.[23]

Even in its traditional context, security reform faces a series of challenges: the privatization of the exercise of force, the inability of some states to control their armed or military forces in part or in full, the capacity of armed and powerful remnants of totalitarian or extremist factions to exercise force, the parallel state-control mechanisms exercised by powerful criminal or terrorist organizations, and the capacity of technological developments to make traditional exercises of state force obsolete.[24] In this context, the major challenge to security sector reform is for the state to reassert its full control and authority over the exercise of force.[25] One such approach links security reform (whether in democratic or nondemocratic contexts) to funneling the security sector back to civilian control. Existing analysis, however, fails to engage with the patriarchies and exclusions that are reinforced (and/or invented) to re-exercise that form of control.[26] Thus an important conclusion drawn here is that the reformist mode of security sector reform contains an explicit modeling on Western security sector organizations with a compelling blind spot to the gender distortions inherent in these institutions and their subsequent export to other states. Compelling research undertaken on intimate violence experienced by the partners of military personnel and the socially constructed gendered nature of the military community in Western states demonstrates the evident contradictions inherent in exporting Western military models to transitioning states as presumed replicas of virtue.[27] The particular danger here is that the legitimization and external validation that accompanies strategies for successful security sector reform programs actually entrench gender-based exclusions and discriminations in ways that are extremely difficult to dislodge. In these contexts, the matters that are framed as central issues for resolution in transitional negotiations may only peripherally impact many women's day-to-day lives. Negotiators may leave untouched socioeconomic exclusions (which may themselves constitute violent experiences for women), and other forms of violence, which women may not see as compartmentalized into "conflict" and "non-conflict." Rather, women may experience forms of violence on a continuum, only partially addressed, or not addressed at all, by ceasefires that may focus only on formally recognized state and nonstate actors.[28]

This narrow vision of the parameters of security reform is coming under increased academic and policy pressure, represented by the views of the Commission on Human Security and others, which argues for a more inclusive and wide-ranging understanding of security generally and SSR in particular. The *Commission on Human Security* (2003) begins with the premise that achieving human security requires not only protection but also a strategy to empower people to support themselves.[29] The UN Millennium Goals inter alia focus on ending poverty and redressing socioeconomic imbalances and point to a more nuanced understanding by key states and institutions of the need for balanced relationships between, security, and peaceful coexistence.[30] Massive economic deprivation is now perceived as a potential security threat, particularly when those made most vulnerable as a result of such deprivations are women and children. Notably, a former UN Secretary-General has stated that the relationship between massive economic deprivation and violence needs to be more carefully considered in transitional processes.[31]

Alternatively, some literature in the field presents a view of security that is described as more cooperative in nature. This approach views the state in partnership with community and other societal groups to share responsibility for and capacity to exercise force and thus ensure (or repress) security. Such cooperative or community-based approaches also need critical assessment from a gender perspective. While they may be more informal, locally based, and communal in structure, this does not mean that they are gender neutral nor even positively disposed toward women's needs. In fact, quite the opposite can be true in practice. They may, in fact, be sites of significant oppression for women, functioning to reassert traditional modes of community decision-making and values, including deeply conservative views of women's roles that deny any capacity for women's rights or agency on their own terms. Critical probing of these cooperative models reveals substantial concern as to whether cooperative models actually seek to deliver shared (and gender sensitive) notions of security or whether the semantics mask equally problematic structural exclusions. If such models focus, for example, on encouraging the involvement of local stakeholders,[32] it is critical to ensure that those stakeholders represent the interests of all members of the community, and specifically women.

Both state and cooperative models present reform opportunities. In theory both could be sites for placing gender centrally in decision-making, law, policy, and implementation. Mixed state/communal structures, which include local and national actors, however, may in reality provide the most successful models both generally and from a gender audit perspective. A real challenge to national and international policymakers is to think through what this kind of mixed partnership would mean for the interests that to date have been dominant in security sector reform politics. This would also require identifying and then incorporating the individuals and groups most marginalized from the security reform process (mostly women, urban and rural poor, and ethnic/racial minorities) and ensuring their needs are articulated and subsequently met. While the traditional approach has been critical to post-conflict stability, security reform must acknowledge this much wider range of institutional and structural elements that cause greater harms to society as a whole and to women in particular.

Thinking forward we also stress that the dominant language of security, which emphasizes direct physical violence (generally specific to defined periods of conflict and only certain kinds of physical violence) and which is addressed through truth processes or political rhetoric, tends to exclude the broader relevance of the language of security for women. This means that the dominance of a certain understanding of security has a multiplier exclusionary effect for women in other transitional fora.[33]

CRITIQUE OF MAINSTREAM APPROACHES TO THE CONCEPT OF POST-CONFLICT SECURITY

There is a substantial body of general criticism concerning existing approaches to security reform.[34] Some have voiced concerns about the tendency of security reform to focus too heavily on "providing training skills, supplying resources and increasing organizational efficiency to overcome capacity deficits of the security system," at the expense of addressing more fundamental shortcomings, in particular the need to build up the integrity of the local security system.[35] Such integrity-promoting measures include structural reforms that discourage abuses (e.g., vetting, building institutional accountability, strengthening institutional independence, and advancing adequate representation) and ensure that the security system is actually responsive to and reflective of the communities it protects and operates within. But at preliminary analysis it is also clear that such reform-oriented criticism also suffers from a lack of gender perspective and integration. Thus, the strategies that are positively mooted to ensure transformation of security reform themselves fail to engage substantively or consistently with gender issues, or merely reproduce existing gender hierarchies.[36]

There is an inherent, and ultimately inevitable, structural link between security reform and confronting past abuses, specifically in conflicted or transitional states. The failure to acknowledge this dimension seriously undermines the extent to which security reform can be meaningful, long-lived, and transformative. Therefore, there is a need to think about security reform in the context of transitional institutional justice transformation.[37] In particular, there is a need to consider how the gender failings of past-focused accountability mechanisms have manifested themselves and how these failings have influenced current understanding of what role the past plays in security sector reform.[38] In particular, we need to be aware of the reality that individuals who have committed serious human rights violations, including violations directed at women, may continue to be part of the state police or military apparatus based on amnesty or other deals around lustration and vetting. We discuss these issues in greater depth in Chapter 8 but raise them here to point out the obvious intersection of security with other core transitional justice issues for women in the post-conflict setting.

Another clear (but marginalized) critique of security reform is located in the unwillingness of national or international policymakers and academics to address precisely "who . . . are the individuals who should participate in, take ownership of, and ultimately benefit from [it]."[39] Moreover, even those who advocate a deep concept of security sector reform run the risk of promoting lofty-sounding platitudes without fundamentally engaging with marginal voices.[40] It is also useful to reflect on the use of language by security reform insiders and the extent to which the terminology is exclusionary and sidelines gender. The focus on the language of leadership, control, containment of threats, and force assumes a particular understanding of security sector reform. The language also suggests a predetermined conceptualization of who the subjects of the discourse are. The discourse of security reform has a pervasive overlay of heteronormativity that pervades militarization, demilitarization, and security sector reform conversations.[41] This overlay is particularly relevant as we assess how intersectionality plays out in the security sector reform context and how problematic essentialist responses to the lack of gender-consciousness may be for women.[42]

Ultimately, existing notions of security are inadequate unless they begin to include gender-based concerns throughout the reform process, to use a broader notion of security to infuse the debates about security reform, and then address other structural exclusions and biases in order to bring about transformation. These concerns underpin our core mantra that women must be meaningfully consulted about the post-conflict processes that affect their lives, they must be adequately represented in the arenas from which reform and change issue, the outcomes that affect women must be legally and politically enforced, and there is a pressing need to benchmark and ensure that implementation follows, sufficient to address the inequality and exclusions that women experience.

IS SECURITY THE SAME FOR MEN AND WOMEN?

A basic principle in the interrogation of how gender is omitted from security is challenging the assumption that women's security and men's security are identical.[43] Rather, as research on women's security highlights, there are numerous obstacles in the post-conflict and transitional political environment to meaningful security for women. Such obstacles are based on a lack of political acknowledgment for the need to develop a wider and more embracive notion of security beyond a narrow militaristic and state-oriented approach. The result is invariably the lack of a secure physical environment, making it dangerous for women to function in any meaningful sense in the public sphere for fear of harm. In these contexts their vulnerability to sex-based violence is unchecked by the formal end of hostilities or the changeover in regime. In parallel, a broader approach to security could function to prevent or ameliorate the systematic emergence in many transitional societies of organized crime and racist or minority-targeted violence in the transitional phase.[44] So while the primary purpose of addressing gender security involves redressing the imbalance and distortion produced by dominant security discourses and the policies that accompany them, its broader effects may transform the post-conflict environment in unexpected ways.

We argue that genuine security goes far beyond those priorities imagined by peacekeepers and international workers transitioning a post-conflict country from peace negotiations to peacebuilding. Although gender consciousness has not yet been adequately integrated into post-conflict security discourse and practices, there are promising signs that gender issues are increasingly central to the discussion of conflict and post-conflict reconstruction, deliberations that are critical to notions of state and individual security. Some inroads are being made on the traditionally narrow and state-oriented view that security discourse belongs to and is only really about the state. We argue that the two—individual security and state security—are codependent. Further, we assert that improved understanding at the international level that mutually reinforced security for individual and community, one that encompasses physical, social, economic, and sexual security, is imperative. As our Introduction sets out, despite some limitations the UN Security Council's adoption of Resolution 1325 has resulted in significantly more attention to gender security issues in the context of conflict endings.[45]

There is an organic link between a lack of gender security and entrenched structures of inequality and discrimination.[46] There is an increasingly recognized connection between exclusions from economic, social, and political benefits and violence for women in conflicted and post-conflict societies, as Chapter 1 of this book starts to explore. In this telling, the spectrum of violence includes both public and private spheres. Research confirms that meaningful security and equality for women will not be achieved by simply placing barriers to state (or public) violence directed against them; rather, radical action against violence and its underlying causes in the private sphere must be part of the transformative project.

Security and the Peace Process

The absence of gendered security is experienced in all three phases of conflict ending, the preagreement, formal peace treaty, and implementation stages. In the preagreement stage of peace negotiations, massive and systematic violence against women may continue. While the modalities of bringing various actors and institutions into formal negotiations may abate the violence experienced by male combatants, it often has a much more limited effect on women's experiences of harm. In the formal agreement phase, ending violent hostilities has clear benefits for women. Nonetheless, when a conflict has been characterized by brutal gender-based violence, crossing normative thresholds of gender violation, even in societies in which women expect and experience regular violence, boundaries have shifted (for example, mutilation, gratuitous targeting of sexual organs, public and ritualized rape), and this affects the normative backdrop of societal tolerance for "acceptable levels" of violence to women. This is the context in which women have to negotiate what security means.

In the post-conflict implementation phase the absence of meaningful security (in both a narrow and broad definition) for women has direct and measurable effects on women's interest and participation in accountability processes. At the simplest level, if it is not physically safe for women to testify (whether before international, hybrid, or domestic courts or tribunals) by virtue of an insecure physical environment (and the barriers to women in this context will be higher than for men), then the absence of security will affect the narrative that emerges from the process of accounting for the past. This partial accounting then becomes the basis for broader societal reconfiguration and remedy, from which women may be excluded a priori. But at a deeper level, if we take security to encompass a wide range of markers, where women continue to experience high levels of "normal" sexual and physical violence within a transitional society, it becomes deeply problematic to expect women to make artificial distinctions between pre- and post-transition harms when the experience of harm may be continuous.

Security and Violence Against Women

Security has practical implications and numerous dimensions: many women remain concerned about their future security as they, and the members of armed groups, return home or face uncertain futures in new locales following displacement or removal. The overly masculinizing nature of the military and of nonstate insurgency/paramilitary forces will have had an impact on all associated with the conflict. As we noted in Chapter 2, it certainly impacts on the forms and experiences of violence in conflicted societies. Many women are survivors of conflict-related gender-based abuse, as well as gendered violence in the home that has generally not been viewed as conflict-related. Furthermore as we have noted above, many policymakers and academics have asserted that violence against women not only persists but "even increases beyond pre-war levels and sometimes even beyond wartime levels."[47] As a result of both sources of violence, women remain vulnerable to being potential victims of future abuse both from strangers and from intimate partners. While the overall evidence on post-conflict spikes in intimate and domestic violence remains inconclusive, there is an emerging consensus that closer attention needs to be paid to a society's general levels of violence and their effects on intrafamilial violence. One quandary raised by empirical assessments is the difficulty of collecting data during and at the end of the conflict, and evaluating how levels of violence have varied.[48] Domestic violence experienced by women during conflict may be more severe in its form because, particularly in ethno-national conflicts, the resort to external mediation of such violence (e.g., access to police) may have been entirely absent.[49] Thus, increased reporting at the end of conflict may not mean absolute statistical increases in violence per se. Rather, it may simply mean that reporting is possible where it was previously impossible, despite the fact that many forms of violence may remain unacknowledged. Regardless of how levels of domestic violence change post-conflict, however, violence remains an ongoing problem that must be confronted in the transition process.

Consequently, our focus on security begins with stability, but includes "domestic tranquility." Here again, security means safety in both the public and private spheres. In the aftermath of conflict, the instability that women have lived with does not inevitably dissipate. Indeed, rape and other forms of direct sexual violence may not end when the conflict ends, and women both want, and need, better protection from violence. In the eastern Congo for example, a four-year survey of more than 4,000 rape cases showed that the number of civilian rapes reported increased by a factor of 17, while the number of rapes committed by members of armed groups decreased dramatically.[50] The pervasiveness of violence against women during conflict may lead to post-conflict "civilian adoption of sexual violence."[51] This shift identified in norms and practices of sex-based violence needs greater tracking not least because it demonstrates the ongoing trauma and consequence of armed conflict for women, and the limitations of current paradigms to address sexual harms.

SECURITY REFORM MEETS PERVASIVE VIOLENCE AND DISCRIMINATION[52]

Security reform issues arise in all three phases that typically follow the end to violent conflict: first, the prenegotiation stage; second, the framework or substantive agreement phase; and finally the implementation phase.[53]

Starting from the position that women experience differential exclusions from peace processes generally (in all three phases), barriers to women's participation are further encountered in the specifics of security reform. As discussed in the Introduction, the exclusions persist despite the UN Security Council Resolution 1325 on Women, Peace, and Security, and more recently the adoption of UN Security Council Resolutions 1820, 1888, and 1889 on sexual violence and armed conflict.[54] Critical problems remain in implementing goals of inclusion.[55]

Security Reform and "Ordinary" Violence

Disaggregating conflict or repressive violence from intimate violence poses highly challenging conceptual and practical dimensions for transitioning societies. South Africa has been identified as the quintessential example of these challenges,[56] where the apparent spiraling of domestic violence rates postapartheid seems to challenge the notion that there is a clear distinction between preexisting gendered apartheid violence and experiences of domestic and random gender-based violence in the transition phase. As domestic and other forms of violence experienced by women are perceived to skyrocket, this peak of violence is not deemed relevant to security sector reform.[57] While the broader patterns of increase in (or greater reporting of) intimate and domestic violence for women in post-conflict societies requires greater empirical scrutiny, nonetheless there is significant anecdotal and other evidence to suggest that the end of conflict is not the end of violence for women.

Security sector reform has also consistently failed to engage with the "returning warrior" problem, the combatant who may be out of circulation for the purposes of public political violence but poses significant risk in the domestic private sphere. Here again the integration of ordinary and "conflict/regime" violence into security sector reform debates where regulation of violence is at the heart of the discussion is markedly absent. There is little acknowledgment in the general literature of the organic link between ordinary and extraordinary violence.[58] Moreover, there is a conceptual unwillingness to affirm that a failure to address that ordinary violence has long-term and structural implications for the success of any specific security reform efforts.

These observations suggest that transitioning societies in general, but those examining security sector reform in particular, should pay particular attention to the connections (or lack thereof) between ordinary and extraordinary violence.[59] There is a pivotal connection between the control of force that is sought by security sector reform (extraordinary and public) and a complete lack of systematic analysis of the ordinary private violence experienced by women, which is completely disassociated from the wider issues of control being exercised in society.[60] In this context, there is a need to challenge a militarized view of what constitutes safety and to bedrock violence against women as a central (ordinary) aspect of the security that needs to be created.

As we reflect what the concept of security means for post-conflict societies (and the relationship between ordinary and extraordinary violence), it is particularly important to probe the distinctions between de facto and de jure security. This requires meaningfully examining the security experience for women as opposed to conducting box-ticking exercises that check the utilitarian definitions of secure environments but do not actually test or ensure that security is experienced in practice by women.[61] A prime example of this gap between de facto and de jure security has been identified in the experiences of women in post-Taliban Afghanistan.[62] For example, contemporary empirical reports indicate that almost 90 percent of women reported experiencing some type of domestic violence.[63] Underscoring the relationship between women's status and their experiences of violence, women who were literate and women who earned their own incomes were less likely than other women to experience violence.

Locales and Representation

Representation constitutes a key element of re-engendering security in the context of security generally and security sector reform in particular. As many studies have shown, most of the locales where security is decided and implemented are decision-making entities that have a history of poorly (or not) representing women: women are not involved in the processes, nor is gender central to the entire project. According to a UNIFEM study of eleven peace processes, women constituted less than 8 percent of participants, and under 2.5 percent of peace agreement signatories.[64] On the other hand, gender security will not be assured by merely addressing the lack of women's representation in key security sector reform sites. As we have noted in our Introduction, it would be an elementary mistake to confuse representation with reform. Presence raises numerous complex issues concerning the assumptions built into the presence of women as representative in key decision-making contexts.[65]

Beyond the procedural package of issues raised by representation itself lies the further step of ensuring that women are meaningfully represented in decision-making positions and that there is a critical mass of women present so that divergent women's voices can emerge.[66] Achieving this outcome may require no less than fundamentally recalibrating the militaristic culture that defines the entities that presently make up the security conversation generally and security sector specifically. Consider also the multiple sites where representation itself must be advanced. We can conceive of four key entities engaged in security sector reform conversations:

❖ Governments
❖ The traditional security sector (including inter alia public militaries, nongovernmental militias and groupings, police, intelligence agencies, border guards, and private entities providing state or private security)
❖ Local stakeholders (including formally identified civil society groupings and identifiable social, religious, ethnic, and other groups who lack organization ability or formal recognition)
❖ External partners (including international institutions, regional and multilateral organizations, other states)

All of these sites are male dominated, with a notable dearth of women in key decision-making arenas. Engaging with gender security requires transformation in all these sites to prevent the phenomena identified earlier of patriarchies reinforcing one another in contexts that project as reform processes. If one moves beyond the idea of simplistic representation based merely on the idea that the presence of women (any women) constitutes gender representation in the security sector reform context, then a plethora of substantive institutional reform matters presents. These are relevant to all four of the entities identified above. Such strategies mitigate against the adoption of a specialized approach to gender security (i.e., just carving out so-called "women's issues") but emphasize the comprehensive set of contexts in which gender centralizing can operate and can be successful. They include recruitment, promotion, and transfer strategies; training agendas; discipline and grievance procedures; and axiomatically family-friendly working supports, as well as legal protections to entrench such advances. Fundamental issues of organizational culture and subcultures arise in all four sites as hegemonic masculinities and macho sexism are arguably endemic to these institutional structures. To underestimate the scale and depth of transformation required is to fundamentally underestimate the barriers that exist to meaningfully ensuring gender security, and ultimately to the project of conflict ending itself.

There are a multitude of intersectionalities that should be considered when defining post-conflict security. Men and women may have different notions of baseline requirements for feeling secure, families with children may have still different notions of security, and internationals' notions of security may well differ from those of locals. For example, immediate security needs from the perspective of local women concerned with preserving the family may well be that communal spaces such as markets and stores are patrolled and made safe, that food is readily available, that routes to and from water sources are secured, that schools are reopened and children are safe both attending them and on the way to and from school. Indeed, other intersectionalities, such as differences along the lines of class, religion, and urban/rural living, may also impact how men and women experience needs in the post-conflict process. In Afghanistan, for example, a woman's park provides a safe environment for women to unveil and learn to sew; women are often reported to be afraid to leave their homes for fear of fundamentalist groups.[67] These different needs, if queried, may be quite different from those identified by internationals whose primary objectives may include a safe environment for the operation of military and political actors. Those engaged in security reform must make at least basic assessments of these varying subsets of the local population rather than simply taking the input of the privileged (generally male) decision-makers. Such assessments require a degree of community and grassroots consultation that have generally been missing from the standard start-up of security sector reform in most post-conflict societies.

When all these practices are combined in a manner that elevates and affirms the experience and relevance of both genders, then a new vision of gendered security is achievable, one that is not "gendered" in an unjust, unequal, and distorted manner. In this view, gendered security can be seen as an umbrella that brings together a wide set of institutions and structures that guarantee security within the state. Here reform is linked to democratic transformation, a broader transformation that is based on equality and autonomy principles in multiple legal spheres and contains a redistributive economic dimension, as we discuss in Chapter 8 of this book. While these goals may seem wider than the narrow set of imperatives which have traditionally dominated post-conflict and transitional justice discourses, there is increasing recognition that a failure to address the broader demand for economic and political transformation can have profoundly disabling and limiting effects on the capacity for accountability and for broader societal advancement sufficient to prevent further conflict.

A NEW PARADIGM OF GENDERED SECURITY

Security issues are much broader than the security sector reform context and encompass security for the population to operate in their daily lives without fear. Gender-central reform must begin with an analysis of how security issues affect men and women differently, across intersectionalities. Only then can implementation proceed, with the need to ensure the reforms' effectiveness on all of the different levels. These range from disbanding existing structures within military organizations, to increasing female recruitment and retention within security sector actors, to making it safe to engage in the daily work of supporting one's family, to ensuring long-range educational and employment opportunities for all.[68] It involves assessing, at a local level, the various security needs of the population, which may range from the ability to collect firewood safely to the ability to report criminal activity to the police with an expectation of action. It then requires delivering security, creating new and more responsive institutional and individual actors who can manage the peace without masculinizing security, and who represent the community with a diversity of ethnic backgrounds and who are both men and women. Ultimately, rethinking security based on the needs of men and women who live in a particular society requires a social revolution, a retooling of pre-conflict attitudes and practices regarding the meaning of public safety. This process does not happen in isolation and must inevitably be linked to broader social and legal processes aimed at elevating the legal and political status of women in post-conflict societies. This section discusses the gendered implications of two recurring security issues: the masculinization of the security sector and necessity of accounting for both public and private forms of violence.

Masculinity and Reform

The security sector reform process raises significant issues about the interface between international masculinities as they connect with the societies experiencing transition. A central theme across much of the literature in this domain is the dominant narrative of masculinity pervading security sector reform policies and analysis. This metanarrative is also linked to a pervasive emphasis on what is deemed to constitute the core elements of the security sector. Typically the focus on certain providers of security (military, police, intelligence agencies, state security, paramilitary organizations, and border guards) continues to emphasize the public providers of security and fails to engage with the broader sites and causes of private violence experienced by women. An important general element to consider here is whether the bureaucratic, command control–oriented, masculine systems and structures which pervade the international community's interface with domestic security sector systems are actually structurally capable of accommodating change. A substantial challenge lies in identifying how to transform the masculine cultures dominant in this sector to deliver gendered security in practice, and how to create meaningful space for positive masculinity norms to emerge.

Moreover, what is seen as progress in security sector parlance may simply not respond in any way to the need for centralizing both genders and the needs of men, women, boys, and girls into security sector reform analysis. Thus, for example, some contributions speak positively to the advances made by integrating defense reform, police reform, and judicial sector reform under an integrated umbrella—instigating "a holistic approach to the provision of security, integrating all the relevant institutions and their connections"—but women's or other marginal voices are not integrated in any way.[69] Consequently, security sector reform in this traditional model could actually serve to perpetuate and extend structural patriarchies rather than undo and replace them.

Dealing with seemingly inherent masculinities involves multiple steps, starting with the conceptual recognition of the exclusive masculinities at play and conceding the harms that follow from hypermasculinity in conflict settings. The starting point in policy and lawmaking is a critical reframing that would then create the social and political space from which gender-sensitive training and policy reformulation could follow. All steps are premised on consultation and the meaningful inclusion of women and other marginalized voices who have an essential interest in security. Benchmarking and follow-up monitoring is also critical in the security setting to ensure that gender sensitivity translates into responding appropriately to gender-based violence. This patterning must occur from the multilateral, bilateral, and international state level out. It would then be replicated at the national, federal, communal, and local level in post-conflict states where security initiatives are taking place in multidirectional and multidimensional contexts (often simultaneously).[70] Partnering and interface among the local, national, and international levels is critical to long-term success.

Gender centrality involves commitment from all those involved in security, and it is composed of multiple steps. Reform needs to focus on the organization's mandate, actual practices, staffing, and transparency and accountability.[71] The following case studies provide several examples of this complexity and the need to act on various levels, and of processes for doing so.[72] First, gender consciousness must pervade any assessment of how to reform the security sector paradigm and how to define safety. In addition to assuring that the security assessment process includes men and women, boys and girls, there are a series of additional questions, such as the following:

What are the specific security needs of women and girls? How do women and girls cope with the absence or limitation of their security needs? Are women and girls legally protected from domestic violence and rape? Are these laws enforced? What services are available for women and girls suffering from domestic violence? Are women vulnerable to trafficking and sexual exploitation? Do the police have particular services for victims of sexual violence? How are victims of sexual violence treated by their communities? Do women have freedom of movement—for example, to leave the home or travel outside their district?

Specific security needs of men and boys: Where and how are men and boys experiencing insecurity? What support is there for men to change violent patterns of behavior and escape from violent environments? What economic and social opportunities do young men have?[73]

This series of preliminary questions involves recognition of the different threats to security and safety experienced by women, such as domestic violence and trafficking, and men, such as gun violence.[74] Such an assessment then provides a basis for rebuilding and training formal security sector actors, such as the military and the police, developing new laws, involving civil society entities, and modeling new approaches to public and private violence.

Second, developing and implementing security reform requires ongoing commitment throughout a society, as well as among international actors. States intervening and/or supporting post-conflict societies have started to operationalize gender-conscious strategies, providing useful models for this process. Liberia has, like other countries, developed a national action plan for implementing Resolution 1325; one focus is on increasing the number of women throughout the security sector, along with a variety of outputs and indicators of success.[75] An interesting dimension of this National Action Plan is its partnering dimension with Ireland, a Western state with a long history of peacekeeping in African states as well as direct experience of an ethnic conflict within its own territorial boundaries.[76] The partnership model also offers a means for post-conflict states to gain technical support and expertise, as well as forcing the partner state to examine its own security practices in multiple contexts, with learning occurring both ways. Even before the inception of the Liberian Plan, women increased their representation in the police force to 10 percent, with a target of at least double that number; a related initiative involved helping more Liberian girls finish high school, so they would be eligible to join the police force.[77] The police force also established a special Women and Child Protection Unit, which has become "an elite task force within the larger body of the police, in part because donor support has ensured that these police units are better equipped . . . Thus police officers want to be associated with gender-related work."[78]

While, as discussed throughout this book, simply adding women and stirring is not sufficient, it is one preliminary advancement strategy among many. Other strategies, such as formal recognition of women's equality, securing safety within communities, enacting laws concerning violence against women, and holding accountable perpetrators for conflict and post-conflict violence against women are discussed throughout this book and are the mainstay of long-term sustainable security for women.

Finally, one obvious caveat: as these examples show, security reform will take different shapes in each country, depending on the level of development and the strength of the governing institutions.

Violence Against Women and Reform

Key concepts in expanding our conceptualization of security and addressing specific harms experienced by women—both during and after the formal ending of conflict and the changeover of regime—are domestic, intimate violence and civilian rape. Providing protection involves both legal reform and practical strategies.

Box 3.1 GENDER MAINSTREAMING IN THE SOUTH
AFRICAN INTELLIGENCE SERVICES[79]

The Intelligence services of South Africa claim to have made great strides in gender mainstreaming:

In 2004, a Statement of Commitment was signed during the national celebration of Women's Day.

Transformational and emerging leadership programmes increased women's promotions.

A Gender Forum was established, which among other initiatives drafted a *Gender Mainstreaming Action Plan* that was finalised and endorsed in 2007. The *Gender Mainstreaming Action Plan* aims to create an enabling working environment that is free from any form of harassment, and to increase women's participation and advancement.

Gender issues were incorporated into the Civic Education Programme, which ensures adherence to the law and democratic norms.

A target was set of no less than 50% women at all levels of management by 2014.

A sexual harassment policy was implemented.

The establishment of a Women's Forum and a Men's Forum has been encouraged.

The number of women has risen significantly in most branches of the services as a result of these initiatives. For example, the percentage of female staff at the National Intelligence Agency rose from 25% in 2004 to 32% in 2008; on the National Intelligence Co-ordinating Committee from 27% in 2004 to 67% in 2008; and in the South Africa Secret Service from 21% in 2004 to 26% in 2008. Challenges that remain include the reticence to report sexual harassment and other rights violations, as well as increasing the percentage of women in management positions.

Source: Speeches by Ronnie Kasrils, Minister for Intelligence Services, Musanda, August 7, 2006, August 7, 2007, August 8, 2008 (available online).

First, legal reform must look both backward and forward: laws must clearly impose accountability and prevent impunity for conflict-related violence against women (as discussed in Chapter 7) and must impose stringent sanctions for post-conflict gender violence, ranging from domestic abuse to rape and including marital rape.[80] Law is thus an essential component of addressing and ensuring women's security needs. Women must be consulted about and involved in the design of new legal measures that protect against forms of violence in order to draw on their lived experiences and to respond to their needs. Changing domestic legal standards means advocating for the expansion and enforcement of the rule of law throughout the post-conflict state to increase provision of formal justice mechanisms, the monitoring of informal justice mechanisms, and the availability of health, education, and other government services. While in the short term many women will not have access to the formal justice system to advance protection of their legal rights, strong legal protection has both a persuasive and communicative effect in changing people's attitudes and perceptions. Over time, the foundation of identifiable rules and enforced sanctions provides an agitational space for women's advocacy. In this civil society space, women themselves can deploy law to become agents in establishing their own security. Such advancements create the broad kind of safety and stability endorsed by the Commission on Human Security.[81]

Second, security protection also involves practically grounded strategies that look forward, such as strengthening local authorities, establishing safe and secure locales, publicizing the availability of legal protections, and providing systems for emergency alerts granting the practical, resource, and geographical constraints that operate in many post-conflict societies. It means establishing media procedures to let women know (acknowledging the clear limitations of resources, geography, and the cohesiveness of the state's ability to provide) where they can go in case they are subject to an attack,[82] reassure them that help will be available, and make that genuinely available in a way that does not further stigmatize. This is, we recognize, ambitious in many underdeveloped post-conflict societies, for rural areas such as the highlands in Peru, or the African Great Lakes area, yet even in those areas, marketing social messages through maternity clinics or street plays can publicize issues surrounding the need not to tolerate further violence. Security extends more broadly to include measures such as the development of an independent media, which can publicize the availability of effective state and community-based initiatives and offer positive portrayals of women who pursue their rights.

For many women, the relationship between the physical violence experienced during conflict and the security of the post-conflict environment are not discontinuous realities but rather part of one singular experience that is not compartmentalized. Thus, accountability for violence may not have the same end point for women in the post-conflict transitional environment as it may have for male combatants or male political actors. This central insight profoundly redefines how we determine what constitutes security in the post-conflict environment, and whose securities are being advanced.

CONCLUSION

Gender security is a rich concept that extends beyond physical security to include civil, political, economic, and cultural security for men and women, boys and girls.[83] It includes formal and enforceable legal rights, as well as opportunities to participate in the economic and political life of the country. Some countries need safe (and passable) roads so that women can sell agricultural or other products,[84] protected marketing places, battered women's shelters, rape crisis centers and sexual violence counselors,[85] primary schools, and job opportunities for young men and women. In a weakened post-conflict state, women are fundamentally affected legally, economically, and physically by the state's failure to provide basic services, and as we argue in Chapter 8 of this book, women are challenged to a far greater degree by the elimination or alternation of those services than are men. Without access to the justice system and without laws reinforcing their status, women may be unable to assert their property rights, claim protection from domestic violence, or obtain credit. With a state unable to deliver basic education or health services, women's literacy rates decrease, and, when they seek maternity services or contraception, they have few options. All of these metrics in our view constitute part of a rounded notion of gendered security, which is beneficial ultimately to both men and women. Thus, it is important to remember that, notwithstanding the frequency with which issues involve a "gender" focus on women, gender (especially gender security) implicates both men and women.

The lived experience of women in conflicted societies suggests that the term "security" has much more territory to occupy than it has hitherto and that much work is needed to both ground and empirically quantify this fundamental difference of conceptualization. From that follows a hard-nosed examination of transitional processes, allied with a willingness to expand the narrow, masculinized band of public transition(s) that are viewed by many as transformative—yet consistently fail to take account of broader gendered transformations necessary to ignite genuine social revolutions in societies experiencing profound political and social change.

CHAPTER 4

Engendering International Intervention

Interventions in the affairs of states come in various guises, under various authorization schemes, with various constellations of actors. In order to examine the extent to which gender is considered and integrated into any part of the conflict-to-peace process, maintaining a specific eye to the protections in play for women, we view the post-conflict terrain broadly. We assess and outline the types of interventions implicating and involving a wide range of actors and institutions, loosely termed, and look at how women fare during the various scenarios and stages contemplated by interventions.

Terminology is key to this analysis. The typology of interventions assessed in this book include forcible military inventions (e.g., Somalia or Iraq), but focus primarily on the post-conflict involvement of international actors— interventions variously described as post-conflict reconstruction, humanitarian missions, transitional justice, human rights field operations, state building, international administration, and peacekeeping missions. We employ the term *intervention* broadly, in order to discuss all types and phases of international intervention aimed at political, legal, economic, and social transformation in which women have a stake. We also briefly look at some of the labels placed on certain types of interventions in order to unpack the extent to which gender is effectively addressed by any of these typologies.

Models of intervention differ; they occupy different (but overlapping) temporal phases, and the vocabulary employed to describe these models remains confused and subject to professional bias depending on the actors implicated. Despite differences, a few common norms emerge. First, for interventions to be legally justified, they need either the authorization of the United Nations or the consent of the receiving country. Such consent serves as a legal and political agreement between the sending and receiving states and other involved organizations. This is generally not an equal partnership, as the sending countries and donor organizations wield big sticks and substantial carrots. Additionally, the parties representing the receiving countries in the agreement are almost always local elites and bearing causal responsibility for the conflict which gave rise to the intervention. As such, "consent" in this context is partial or forced, frequently yielding a subsequent "lack of political will" on the part of domestic authorities to carry out even mutually agreed upon objectives. Second, sustainable peace is the stated objective of interventions, although this purpose sometimes goes off course in the buildup to negotiating the cessation of hostilities. Sustainable peace may also be undermined by the programmatic choices made by international institutions. Third, there will necessarily be overlap between organizational mandates in carrying out tasks related to intervention. Moreover, there may be overlap in the phases of intervention, as for example, humanitarian relief overlaps with peacekeeping, which overlaps with post-conflict reconstruction, which may overlap with transitional justice, both of which overlap with long-term sustainable development. Agency coordination is thus essential, and one entity must assume the lead in taking on that role. Fourth, effective implementation requires needs-based assessments to take place regularly and be continually recalibrated. Those identified needs must be defined in meaningful consultation with the citizens of the receiving country, and in this context, women must be effectively approached, listened to, and their needs taken into account in the formulation of each phase of intervention, from humanitarian relief through long-term development. Programs should be driven by the needs of the communities being supported and be assessed regularly. A model of intervention we endorse would support the development of political and social self-sufficiency so that affected communities can consistently articulate their needs in a way that evolves and deepens during the intervention phase.

This chapter sets forth existing modalities of international intervention in order to better identify points at which post-conflict intervention can operate to unpack and recalibrate gender roles and gender consequences, thereby improving the lives of women, men, boys, and girls in the post-conflict terrain. Specifically, this chapter will first briefly explore the legal basis and typologies of international intervention, addressing the gender limitations of each. Second, it will identify the international actors involved and discuss their roles as stakeholders in the outcome of the interventions, as well as the masculinities inherent in those institutions that may impact their roles and decision-making. Finally, it recommends some of the forms that gender-positive international intervention might take in order to capture the possibilities of the transitional moment to alter women's lives for the better.

For centuries, states, and more recently international organizations, have grappled with whether and to which extent they should (morally) or could (legally, politically, militarily) intervene in the affairs of other states. Indeed, one core premise for the United Nations was to mutually bind states in a treaty compact designed to prevent the "scourge of war," and to better address the inevitable refugee flows which emanated from them. This principle was, of course, bounded by another principle—the sovereign integrity and equality of states;[1] inevitably disputes have emerged over the scope and application of both principles in general and in application to particular cases.

The drawn-out demise of colonial regimes and the conclusion of the Cold War, both occurring in large part during the mid to latter part of the twentieth century, in different ways fostered the emergence of a number of new and newly independent states. The prospect of states being active or intervening in the political and economic transformation of other states captured the imagination of the international community.[2]

Legal Basis for International Interventions

The prevailing legal rules for international interventions are rooted in the UN Charter, although interventions come in many guises, based on many different types of legal authorization. In this chapter, we focus our discussions primarily around interventions sanctioned by the UN Security Council, although we recognize interventions may occur outside this framework. We note that there are differences in the ways by which interventions are sanctioned by the United Nations and the extent to which it is subsequently organizationally and structurally involved in those interventions. For example, the United Nations authorized forcible intervention in Somalia in 1993, with the United States leading a multinational force. In Kosovo, Bosnia, East Timor, and Eastern Slavonia (contested territory between Croatia and Serbia), it not only authorized intervention but also subsequently established and designated entities, including itself, as post-conflict international administrators. Other interventions take place on the authority (albeit highly contested) of different international organizations (IOs) (such as the bombing of Serbia by NATO in 1999 over its actions in Kosovo), or by states acting on their own authority (Iraq in 2003 by the United States and the United Kingdom). There are other differences, too. The interventions described above were forcible military interventions, but the term "intervention" can also describe nonforcible interventions, such as one state funding opposition parties in or imposing embargoes on another state, the latter also envisaged by collective action under Chapter VII of the UN Charter. Another type of nonforcible intervention is the peacekeeping operation (discussed at greater length in Chapter 5 of this book), which requires the consent of the host state, as well as authorization from the United Nations (through the General Assembly or the Security Council), under what has come to be known colloquially as "Chapter VI and a half" of the UN Charter.[3] Emerging practices have included authorization of nonforcible intervention by regional organizations (e.g., the African Union in Sudan) and the delegation by the United Nations of its enforcement powers to regional entities.[4]

The UN Charter envisages military interventions being sanctioned when breaches of the peace threaten international peace and security, and when other peaceful measures have proven inadequate.[5] The international community has also undertaken post-conflict reconstruction initiatives (with controversy) on the basis of UN Charter Chapter VII, which permits the Security Council to authorize international action, even without consent of the receiving country, to "maintain or restore international peace and security."[6] Though it addresses "threats to the peace," "breaches of peace," and "acts of aggression" rather than humanitarian disasters, Chapter VII powers have been used by the Security Council to authorize interventions in, for example, Somalia, Haiti, Rwanda, Bosnia, East Timor, Sierra Leone, and Cote d'Ivoire.[7] International interventions presuppose that a significant number of states, including at least some of the essential permanent Security Council 5, desire or are otherwise motivated to intervene. Since the end of the Cold War, intervening states have sometimes employed the language of "protection of the local citizenry" or "human rights" to justify intervening under the broad doctrine of humanitarian intervention, even when the primary motivation is self-protection or other economic or political interests. In more recent practice states have successfully invoked Chapter VII, convincing the Security Council that the intervention is necessitated by massive violations of human rights.[8] In this highly innovative approach to the definition of what constitutes a "threat" to international peace and security, the fact of systematic human rights or humanitarian law violations within a state alone have provided the basis for intervention.

The type of intervention initiated by the international community has typically been dependent upon many factors. Some factors center on the state in conflict, such as the type of political regime in the country in question, the cultural and social context of the hostilities, and whether the war was internal or crossed borders. Other factors center on the impact of the conflict on other states; for example, whether the conflict has sent refugees flooding across borders; the proximity of the conflict to first-world nations; the economic and political climate in the rest of the world; the extent to which other nations believed that they had something to gain by intervening (or something to lose by failing to intervene); and the willingness of one country or a group of countries to take the lead.

A fundamental question for feminist scholars, as we think about the practices of and rationale for intervention, is the extent to which gendered violations constitute part of the terrain of threat sufficient to activate international action; and if so, at what level.

Content and Rationale of Post-Conflict Interventions

As of 2009, there were fifty countries in which the international community was active in carrying out what could broadly be defined as "peace operations," not all of which were Chapter VII interventions and not all led by the United Nations.[9] Some of those operations, such as those in Central Asia and parts of the former Yugoslavia, focus on political and economic transition to shore up real or perceived weak states. Some are more traditional wartime operations, such as the operation in Afghanistan. Others, such as Sudan, Democratic Republic of Congo and East Timor are actively engaged in a combination of what some have labeled the modern approach to peacekeeping—a humanitarian mission combined with an expanded peacekeeping mandate emphasizing justice or human rights goals, promotion of democracy, establishment of post-conflict institutions, and infrastructure and economic development, rather than mere military-style prevention of hostilities.[10]

As we outline a broad view of what constitutes intervention, moving away from formally mandated military forces, a separate typology of interventions related to the role and function of states and institutions involved in rebuilding post-conflict societies comes into view. Many interventions (such as Iraq) fall outside of a clear promotion of reconstruction after mass atrocities, and we find it instructive to examine the post-conflict programs devised in those countries. It is also useful to consider programs undertaken by the international community before a country ultimately descends into communal conflict in order to assess whether and how the international community recognizes gender harms and inequity as having the potential to further destabilize the host country. It is helpful to look at these non–Chapter VII types of intervention because the transitional moment whatever its legal basis is one that holds the potential both for retrenchment or positive transformation for women.[11] From the perspective of the women in question, what matters is not type of or legal basis for the intervention, but that their concerns are recognized, heard, counted, and responded to.

TYPES AND PHASES OF POST-CONFLICT INTERVENTION AND THEIR POTENTIAL GENDER IMPACT

The type of intervention developed to respond after a state has failed is driven by many factors, with little mutually agreed upon doctrine concerning the actual components of international intervention. Common to all interventions, notwithstanding the label placed on the exercise undertaken, is the premise that by inserting itself into a conflict, its resolution, and its aftermath, the international community brings its own organizational, cultural, and national identities, preferences, and masculinities into the process. The post-conflict intervention phase can operate as a highly gendered sphere, one which is gendered predominantly masculine.

Even among post-conflict operations with similar labels (post-conflict reconstruction missions in Bosnia and East Timor, for example), the methodology undertaken to carry out substantively similar operations will vary widely. The differences in operations are sometimes undertaken for obvious reasons: cultural and political differences in the host country, differing and substantive legal understandings related to the factual circumstances of the intervention, and the extent to which laws and international agreements are accepted as binding by the various actors involved, to name a few. But, at other times methodologies differ for less obvious reasons. The driving actors in various interventions have tremendous control over how programs are undertaken. Consequently, the professional biases and opinion differences of the specific people employed in those missions will also greatly impact the methodologies employed and their outcomes.[12]

Scholars and high-level policymakers have attempted to define the specific phases of post-conflict peacekeeping, peacebuilding, and reconstruction,[13] but few such models have fully captured the overlap and ebbs and flows of the process. In some scenarios, for example, peacebuilding attempts begin during the peacekeeping phase (which can variously correspond with the simultaneous undertaking of preagreements, framework agreements, or implementation agreements to end violence). Here peacekeepers strive to integrate activities into their peacekeeping that look to long-term sustainability, for instance peacekeepers working on establishment of schools or job creation for the local population. In others, the core elements of the peacebuilding phase are constructed on paper during the peace negotiation itself (such as in Bosnia, where the core elements of the reconstruction process were set forward in the General Framework Agreement for Peace).

While it is clear that there is little coherence in the models used, some essential commonalities emerge: war is accompanied by some peacekeeping or other intervention, which focuses on security; signs that security is being improved lead to a stabilization phase that is often accompanied by humanitarian intervention in the provision of food, medical care, and care of displaced persons; stabilization allows for entry of more international organizations that tend to deem governance, democratization, and elections as a priority in securing local "buy in" and legitimatizing future reconstruction efforts, which will then be coordinated with domestic politicians. The governance phase tends to give way to the transitional justice paradigm wherein international actors work with new domestic authorities to determine both what to do with human rights and humanitarian law violators and how to secure the rule of law in order to continue to achieve sustainable peace and security. Then international actors seek to identify preexisting civil society structures to bolster or create it, in order to provide a strong local voice to counter and provide feedback to government. They also seek to build capacity toward long-term peace and security based in rule of law protections and a liberalized political and economic regime. Finally, international actors begin to secure economic institutions, having sought to liberalize the economy, and work on methods for eradicating corruption and securing long-term capital necessary to sustain stability. A key question is: where in these stages and processes are women visible or called into view?

The response is complex but we now turn to articulate some key intervention typologies and examine their interface with women and gender. First, the transitional justice paradigm. As a method and theory of post-conflict involvement by the international community,[14] "transitional justice" has much to commend it in particular for early recognition of gender complexities by its practitioners. Gender analysis figures significantly in transitional justice discourse and has greatly shaped the development and current state of the field.[15] In sum, transitional justice describes the overarching goal of correcting rule of law deficits in order that rule of law and justice systems address past human rights violations and secure future rights and institutional reform after a conflict or political changeover. In some contemporary analyses, transitional justice is viewed as a praxis of peacemaking and accountability, rooted in the notion that for a state to achieve sustainable peace after conflict, it must deal with the atrocities committed during the conflict. The starting point for a transitional justice model of peacebuilding is to ask questions, such as whether impunity, punishment, or amnesty is due the benefactors of war; how societies should deal with their violent pasts; and what remedies are due the victims of those crimes. In many of the conversations that follow, gender analysis in general and women in particular figure prominently. Increasingly, the transitional justice framework is being expanded to include institutional legal and political reform, as well as a plethora of social justice and economic redistribution issues. Often those employing the transitional justice model seek to determine which acts have the most transformative significance, understanding that the transitional moment, be it through war or political and economic evolution, is a powerful one, with tremendous potential for societal change. Because a number of transitional justice practitioners also consider economic and social justice, notably in arenas such as reparations and rule of law reforms to protect social and economic rights,[16] it can operate as a powerful post-conflict initiative for women—if women's needs are effectively considered.

"Post-conflict reconstruction," unlike transitional justice, describes the mechanics of achieving a stable, reconstituted, and sustainable society after conflict (which could include transitional justice initiatives). At its highest nadir, post-conflict reconstruction, because it is imagined as a comprehensive response to peacebuilding, could also be a means whereby individual rights (and women's rights in particular) are secured, protected, and sustained, and whereby the various communities that make up a previously violent and conflicted society become its most powerful voice and resource. In this approach, women and minorities would be protected and encouraged to emerge, find their public voice, and flourish. At its weakest nadir, however, post-conflict reconstruction can become the mere importation of the political, economic, and legal models of the intervening states, ungracefully parachuted into the country in question, and foisted upon its people.[17] Post-conflict reconstruction also has the negative potential to sidetrack, becoming primarily an exercise in political transition to procedural democracy or even a land grab wherein international and multinational companies empowered and supported by the economic liberalization projects of the intervening states, in the guise of carrying out economic transition, liberalization, and stabilization, limit communal benefit from or monopolize local natural resources. So structurally, this model, with its focus on democratic and human rights institution building, has the potential to capture the transitional moment in a way that is favorable to women and men. Recent post-conflict reconstruction scenarios have not manifested this promise.

We argue that gender analysis, norm creation, and norm implementation should become central to all of these emerging processes, in all of their stages, in all aspects of international intervention. Accordingly, it is crucial to observe that recent practice in devising post-conflict programs has yielded an unwillingness to create nuanced and cooperative spaces that might more fully ensure women's broad participation. Rather we observe practices more consistent with an overriding mandate of exerting control and maintaining security in its narrowest sense. For example, one type of intervention, state building, more accurately describes the process by which interested but external states determine the future political course of a burgeoning or floundering nation.[18] That the state in question is targeted and supported to become democratic with a liberal economy are key features of state building.[19] Of course many of those countries that states, policymakers, and aid practitioners persist in calling "transitional" are not in transition to democracy— and many, despite the language of state building, remain "turgid, often opaque, and rarely very democratic."[20] The sustained feminist critique of state building is relevant to our analysis here. State building is derided for its emphasis on the liberal legal framework, which, even within Western democratic states often exists contemporaneously with gender discrimination, exclusion, and high levels of violence against women. In one biting critique, the state-building model is celebrated for exporting a decisive public/private divide into weakened states as a way to bolster the state, but often at the expense of women's autonomy and social status.[21]

Another model of post-conflict intervention vulnerable to critique is international administration. Contemporary examples include Bosnia, Kosovo, and East Timor, where the United Nations took on or sanctioned the role of international "governor" in the region until such time as those countries were able to effectively govern themselves. Critics of international administration argue that the model is too heavy handed and autocratic. Partially in response to these critiques, a committee was tasked by the Secretary-General of the United Nations to discern best practices in relation to post-conflict reconstruction. The resulting report (the Brahimi Report) proposed in part that transitional administrations should place a premium on building local capacity, and should rely in as limited a way as possible on the international presence.[22] While widely applauded at the time of its release, the effectiveness of this so-called "light footprint" model has been put to the test in Afghanistan, with at best mixed results. The less autocratic style of international administration exercised in East Timor, which prioritized establishing a clear political endpoint, was also initially widely applauded,[23] but has also yielded mixed long-term results.[24] In fact, the exercise in East Timor revealed more clearly one large problem common to all post-conflict reconstruction exercises: the presence of the international community creates a falsely robust economy, which can collapse when it departs, bringing a new round of political chaos and insecurity. The two foregoing models operate with fairly narrow procedural definitions of democracy, and each is susceptible to critique that their emphasis on importing external political and economic models rather than on the development of inclusive, "bottom up" strategies generated from within the state in question is a recipe for disaster.[25]

None of the models described above, including transitional justice and post-conflict reconstruction, yet effectively deals with or fully integrates gender in the context of addressing war and its aftermath. In particular, despite the work of scholars to integrate gender into accountability discussions primarily through mainstreaming methods, there is still an enormous institutional gap regarding how to meaningfully centralize gender in the conversation about state structures and institution building in conflicted societies. If some have argued that we need a feminist theory of the state, it is evident too that we need a feminist theory of reconstructing the state from conflict.

THE ACTORS

The United Nations and its agencies have taken the lead in matters dealing with refugee flows and displaced persons since its inception subsequent to World War II. Since then, a multitude of other international organizations (IOs) and nongovernmental organizations (NGOs) have sprung up to fill gaps and provide expertise in the increasingly complex aspects of emergency relief, humanitarian relief, refugee assistance, peacekeeping, transitional justice, post-conflict reconstruction, and development. Ensuring that the mandates of these organizations are clear, that their actions are coordinated, and that there is little or no unnecessary overlap among them has been of primary concern to donors and scholars alike as international interventions increase in their complexity and costliness.

Among UN agencies, those most commonly associated with peacekeeping, security, and humanitarian (or prewar) aspects of interventions are the UN Department of Peacekeeping Operations (DPKO), responsible for securing and training troops and civilians for peacekeeping missions; the UN Office for the Coordination of Humanitarian Affairs (OCHA), responsible for dealing with the needs of people struck by disaster and humanitarian emergencies; the UN High Commissioner for Refugees (UNHCR), responsible for refugees and often all persons displaced by conflict; and the UN Office of the High Commissioner for Human Rights (OHCHR), tasked with undertaking human rights field operations to investigate human rights abuses. Some of these agencies, such as OHCHR, are more likely to be present after formal cessation of hostilities, while others, like the DPKO and UNHCR are more likely to be present before conflict has formally concluded. Some of these organizations will interface with states and nonstate actors through the prenegotiation, framework agreement, and implementation phases. Although the mandates of each organization operating within a mission are devised so as to overlap as little as possible, they still sometimes do, and their timelines of operation in the field have substantial commonalities. A perfect example of this mandate overlap plays out in the arena of gender mainstreaming, set out in the Introduction and Chapter 1. With regard to gender mainstreaming, each agency has been tasked to mainstream gender into its work. But where all are tasked, none bears responsibility, and so gender has not yet been effectively centralized into post-conflict work, although a new agency, UN Women, has recently been created with the expressed purpose to combine the gender work of all agencies, as described in the Introduction.[26]

In addition to UN agencies, a multitude of IOs have sprung up to handle the work perceived as necessary and attendant to conflict, but which the United Nations either cannot undertake, or would prefer to contract out. Organizations dealing with refugee needs, such as the International Rescue Committee, the American Refugee Committee, the International Organization for Migration, and the Norwegian Refugee Council, for example, work in the field alongside UNHCR in some cases, and in other cases act as an arm of UNHCR, serving refugees in places where UNHCR has only a regional presence. Other organizations, such as the International Committee of the Red Cross (ICRC), have mandates that specifically distance them from the work of the United Nations and other international organizations, so as to allow them to make their own bilateral agreements with the host countries, and thereby attain access, for example, to prisoners of war. Still other international organizations, such as Médecins Sans Frontières (MSF) also maintain independence from UN agencies and other IOs, in order to focus exclusively on health-related matters that inevitably accompany armed conflict and to make independent decisions about when to initiate their operations. Still other UN agencies, such as UNICEF and UNIFEM, have been active in conflicted and post-conflict societies, particularly when women and children are heavily impacted, typically setting up offices in the field only after formal cessation of hostilities.[27] It is obviously crucial that NGOs also be subject to any gender prioritizing mandates as they have enormous influence in the field.

Other IOs commonly involved in the post-conflict stages of intervention are the Organization for Security and Cooperation in Europe (OSCE), which focuses on political and economic transitions (be they driven by conflict or not) in Europe and Central Asia.[28] Finally, organizations like the World Bank, the International Monetary Fund, and the Council of Europe heavily influence intervention programming at all stages and in all their permutations, by establishing conditions whereby monies may be obtained or creating the benchmarks that must be achieved by transitioning states in order for donors to feel comfortable investing in the reconstruction programs as they develop.

Turning to the issue of gender representation introduced in Chapter 2, the gender profiles of such NGOs and other bodies must be measured for the representativeness of their staff. Male-dominated institutions and organizations are highly visible in the post-conflict field and may visibly compound exclusions and absences for women across the spectrum of intervenors. We do not equate representation with outcomes per se, but the absence of women or their presence in exceedingly limited number clearly affects substance. As feminist scholars have long noted, when masculine entities undertake masculine enterprises, women's interests can get lost in the process.[29] Given the profile and the centrality of these bodies to the experiences and outcomes for women in conflicted and post-conflict societies, codes of conduct including the requirement of gender representativeness should be developed for each of these organizations (including the nongovernmental organizations), specifically allied with the requirements of Security Council Resolution 1325.

The mandates of many of these organizations and agencies are often broad and vague. The risk in this is multifold: the organizations' conflict work and interests become self-perpetuating in that they define the problems for external donors and then morph to accommodate the funds which are then donated; the organizations consciously or unconsciously develop in response to available funding rather than by carrying out careful needs assessments; organizations skilled in one aspect (security, for instance) begin engaging in activities far outside their areas of expertise (education, for instance); the people who work in the organizations and agencies become accustomed to operating in emergency mode, and so fail to adjust to longer-term strategizing even long after the emergency phases have passed. In these matrixes women's needs rarely figure as a priority or a value, and thus we encounter another site in which gender is de facto excluded, compounding the factors of exclusion met in other locales.

Their Interests and Motivations

States or international institutions that become involved in international interventions as donors,[30] or by committing troops or civilian resources, are also stakeholders in the intervention and in its success. They are not uninterested parties. When probing the gendered dimension of these interests and calculating its effects for women in conflicted and post-conflict societies, similar patterns emerge as we have seen in other contexts. The paucity of women's representation at the highest levels of state and organizational decision-making leaves significant questions as to the capacity of such bodies to think about the gendered ramifications of their priorities and operation. Equally, if missions are not defined by the need to specifically address gender issues in both specialized and cross-cutting ways, then the measurement of what constitutes successful outcomes follow accordingly, and fail.

The presence of the international community is motivated by individual and collective interests, and those interests have multiple dimensions. The motivations leading to international interventions, like the interests driving them, can rightly be called self-interested or realist. In the period of post–Cold War optimism and multilateral enthusiasm, many states experienced a wake-up call after failures to intervene in Rwanda and Bosnia led to the massacre of hundreds of thousands of people, precisely the eventuality institutional and treaty structures sought to eradicate with the creation of the United Nations. Nevertheless, the motivations that ultimately lead nation-states to determine that they will join an international intervention effort are most often pragmatic or opportunistic. States become involved to quash regional instability, to explore and exploit new markets, to avoid refugee flows spilling over their borders, and generally in order to prevent other states from assuming too much power or accessing too many natural and other resources.

Nation-states are sovereign entities acting in their own interests that often neglect to look too far beyond their own cultural, political, and national biases when devising post-conflict reconstruction programs in other countries. For example, the OSCE, funded primarily by NATO states and led by a series of American (male) ambassadors in Bosnia and Herzegovina, focused on advancing political rights as their contribution to securing peace in the immediate aftermath of the war. The OSCE perspective was that the immediate political priority should be carrying out elections. Not only did those elections succeed in entrenching in office the people and parties responsible for the war,[31] they were rife with fraud and failed to accomplish the international community's (IC) goal of securing the return of displaced persons. The IC prioritized physical safety and political rights, clearing mines, rebuilding houses, and ensuring that people were able to vote. But they generally failed to effectively consult at the local level and so failed to discover that in order to return, displaced locals, the majority of whom were women and children, wanted assurances that their children could go to school and not be ostracized, that they could find jobs without being discriminated against, and shop without being jeered at.[32] What many displaced persons wanted in order to return to their prewar homes were essential assurances that the totality of their civil, economic, and social rights would be protected, not merely their political participation rights. This underscores the broader point we make about the need for gender centrality to start with deep and meaningful consultation with women about their needs. Here, women wanted their former homes to be meaningfully reconstituted as "home."[33] These needs were generally not recognized by the IC members because rather than assessing the real (and perhaps gendered) needs of the population of displaced persons, primarily women and children, the IC instead focused on replicating the political system it knew and understood.

Certainly the arena in which action is taken post-conflict is complex and the room for maneuvering is often limited. Even interventions which might fairly be described as somewhat compromised by the self-interests of the intervening states (Iraq, for example) may still be valuable, particularly for women, if their needs are properly assessed. At the very least we propose a conscious commitment to reassessing needs at various points on the intervention continuum. Among the many risks of self-interested intervention is that it becomes unreflective, built with no real discourse between international stakeholders and the citizenry whose lives they intend to impact. The most altruistic motives count for nil if they are not informed by the real needs, wants, and desires of the people who will be affected by those motives.

The caricature of the international male elite whose entire conception of the country in which he works is informed by his infrequent chats with his local male driver is a stereotype for a reason—it holds some truth. Similarly, it is insufficient for the male international actor to base his gender programs on the occasional chat with his female secretary and from those conversations presume to understand what women need in the host country. A more anthropologically driven inquiry into the views of representative groups of persons in which women are fairly represented, undertaken by the international agencies operating in the post-conflict theatre, would go some way toward ensuring that the programs prepared were actually useful and gender sensitive.

If international organizations were not driven to define security solely by political and civil rights, but were more amenable to creating programs directed at rights often designated by women to be critical, such as home, family, community, family care assistance, employment, and education, they might avoid this sort of pitfall. Of course, it is important to avoid stereotypes about "what women want." It is also important to note that we do not suggest that political rights are not important to women—they are, as we argue in chapters 8, 9, and 10. Yet one cannot help but think that at least with regard to the foregoing Bosnian example, if gender had been central in the creation of these post-conflict programs and agendas, it would not have been lost on the program designers that people want their children and communities to be meaningfully safe and secure before the family would consider returning home. The starting point for better outcomes for women post-conflict, no matter the motivation of the intervening states, should be a real and thoughtful assessment of what would be required to achieve sustainable security and peace from both women's and men's perspectives.

Colonialism, Paternalism, and Gender

Critiques abound that many forms of international intervention are dangerously close to colonialism by effectively engaging in "governance by fiat."[34] An example often invoked is the move by the High Representative in Bosnia to pass laws and oust elected officials from office when they failed to uphold the laws he passed.[35] This critique is sustained by those who endorse a minimalist role of the international community in enforcement. We take such an essentialist view to be overreaching when applied to lesser forms of intervention. Governance by fiat of course goes too far, but other types of intervention may be justified; there is a range of options open to states requiring assistance, and the dynamics of state interrelationships are too complex to be so reduced.

Another critique worth considering looks askance at preexisting, particularly colonial relationships, arguing that in this paternalistic paradigm of colonial relationships often reproduced in intervention settings, women can be at a particular disadvantage. The argument is that where preexisting colonial relationships drive post-conflict assistance (Belgium in Rwanda and France in Chad, for example), women's interests risk being sidelined as they were during colonial periods. In such settings, mutually reinforcing patriarchal interests of both local and international male elites operate highly effectively to exclude women. In many colonial settings, colonialist men colluded with certain elite local males ceding control of domestic and customary norms to these local elites (most often men) as a form of de facto compensation for their loss of control in the political sphere.[36] While no one makes the claim that modern international intervenors have been conspiring with local men to suppress the rights of local women, at least not overtly, internationals certainly do import their own, perhaps covert or subliminal, masculine biases in the creation of post-conflict regimes and institutions, often still to the advantage of male elites and to the disadvantage of women.

TOWARD GENDER-POSITIVE INTERVENTION

Sustainable peace, the common goal of all international interventions regardless of type and methodology, cannot be achieved by looking exclusively at what it takes to realize immediate security in the peace negotiation moment. We suggest four essential pivot points to consider when discussing peacekeeping, peacebuilding, or post-conflict reconstruction plans in order to advance the notion of placing gender centrally. First, establishing a process that assesses the situation of men and women and the role gender played in the prewar society and how those roles altered or played out during the war. Second, examining the role gender will play in the peace negotiation process and the structural recognition of gender bias and influence. Third, looking at the extent to which and how gender analysis is undertaken during both the conceptualization of the post-conflict reconstruction strategy and into each component of that strategy, even as each component continues to develop in the post-conflict continuum. Core to that must be a commitment to substantive equality and autonomy protections for women. Fourth, instigating the practice of measuring or establishing benchmarks for determining the success or failure of the undertaking as a whole and in its constituent parts.

There is clearly much more work to be done in formulating what will make for successful post-conflict reconstruction, what it hopes to achieve, for whom on what terms, during what time period, and for what ultimate purpose. Although those questions are beyond the scope of this book, it is important to understand that more forethought and long-term thinking must go into international interventions and post-conflict reconstruction in general in order to even begin addressing gender and women's needs. Here is an opportunity to revision the exercise altogether, placing gender central to the undertaking so that women might claim equal ground and opportunity in the aftermath of war. Because intervention takes place at the very moment when total transition—political, economic, social, cultural, and even gender transition— is most possible, at the moment when a nation could actually reconstitute itself in any image, it is very tempting to recommend that all preexisting means of formulating an intervention be scrapped altogether. Such a total overhaul is unlikely, but total overhaul may be reached incrementally and that makes it worth thinking in pieces about the endeavor. Within the framework of a sovereign nation intervening within another sovereign nation (or failed state), a typology can be conceptualized as generating short-, medium-, and long-term options, each of which could more effectively take into consideration the needs of women and look critically at how gender impacts programmatic, legal, and institutional success.

Reframing Gender as Central to Interventions

If overhauling the entire process is unrealistic, there are still recommendations to be made for future post-conflict contexts. When a woman is in a country undergoing intervention and transition, her initial needs may be highly contextual, yet often relate to ending violence, which is equally a priority for men and women. A short-term gender-sensitive alteration to current practice could be establishing security in its *broadest* sense (as we argue in Chapter 3), providing for basic social and economic rights (water, food, shelter), not primarily civil and political rights, and planning at an early stage for the sustainability of these rights. Imperative in all these short-term contexts, no matter what label is given to that context, is that women are not excluded and are actively centralized in deciding what short-term priorities constitute.

In the medium term, during the post-conflict phase in which accountability and justice are often deemed the priority (some semblance of gendered security having been ideally achieved), recommendations include moving beyond masculine bias as the basis for determining post-conflict allocations of territory and legal, political, and socioeconomic power, which are primarily based on masculine notions of "wrong" and "harm" and "violation."[37] Gender-central justice would emphasize accountability for violations of social and economic rights (discussed in chapters 8, 9, and 10), which, despite gaining increasing traction as hard law in many national and international contexts, are under-enforced and effectively treated as "soft" norms in many transitional contexts. Such prioritization would balance and complement the more commonly addressed civil and political rights violations. It would ensure that those negotiating the accountability process would enforce a more extended notion of what "harm" means to all persons within that society—women, as well as men, elites and non-privileged alike—when committing to a transitional justice agenda. Gender-central transitional justice would take a deeper view of harm, allowing for gender inequalities in the prewar society to be addressed through the transitional process, making better use of the transitional moment, and moving away from or at least acknowledging the masculine bias which entrenches gender inequality in the postwar context.

In the longer-term, the fact that doctrine is limited in describing what post-conflict reconstruction actually *is* may yield opportunity for making gender central in post-conflict reconstruction. At a minimum, gender-central post-conflict reconstruction should include the following: bringing in women, in sufficient numbers, as stakeholders to the peace negotiation table (here again proving that the groundwork for longer-term gains has to be made early); ensuring representation of women in the international organizations coordinating the reconstruction; imbuing each reconstruction project with a substantive gender equality premise tailored to that countries' needs, rather than seeking to tack gender onto preconceived programs; rethinking democracy and liberalized markets for their potential to enhance gender inequities (as argued in Chapter 10 of this book); taking full advantage of the gains made by women during the war and in the gender recalibration that can accompany the demobilization process in a way that is likely to enhance sustainable peace; and attending to de facto establishment of rights that have meaning in the daily quality of life for women, such as rights to education, family, employment, maintenance, divorce, inheritance, and physical integrity, rather than the single-minded focus on the procedural trappings of democracy.

Needs Assessments That Are More Holistic, Regular, and Gender Sensitive

Most intervention plans and their subsequent transitional administration structures are born of crisis, carried out by those who deal in military and foreign affairs, and carried forth under the auspices of the peace agreements written to quash the crisis. In its positive manifestation, this approach can yield flexibility and adaptability, which may be ideal in these post-conflict contexts when tailor-made solutions are neither possible nor advisable, and wherein the intervening states and international organizations do the best they can in suboptimal conditions when a crisis hits. Indeed, the capacity to adjust at a later stage and recognize the ad hoc nature of preliminary responses may be a sign of a maturity of approach to intervention. In reality, however, there is often simply not enough analysis and reflection undertaken by those on the ground in the action- and reaction-driven world of post-conflict reconstruction. And in this negative manifestation, internationals cannot expect to understand local women because they have considered only immediate security needs, often in the most limited sense.

Internationals cannot succeed in assessing needs, even immediate security needs, unless they consult with many people across many cross sections of the population, including women. The development world is succeeding somewhat in taking gender into account (as discussed in Chapter 11). Donors in the development context have experienced too many projects collapsing due to persistent failures to discuss the viability of the proposed project with both women and men in the host site. The result has been an increased willingness to more regularly consult so as to avoid wasting limited funds. Yet, donor agencies operating in the post-conflict reconstruction context continue to make the same errors based on inadequate needs assessments when it comes to working with women.[38] In Afghanistan, for instance, a market for women was funded and opened to great fanfare in 2007, but had no women in sight by 2009. The donors had picked a location for the market which attracted consumers engaged in construction, and who were not interested in purchasing nonconstruction goods from women. Furthermore, the women had difficulty in reaching the location.[39] The project failed.

There is often a vast incongruity between donor largesse and the actual needs of women in post-conflict societies. Needs assessments are not effectively undertaken, and donor interests, narrowly undertaken if at all and often based on what issues are "sexy" or "of the moment," inappropriately govern the establishment of post-conflict programs. Real assessments of the cultural, social, political, religious, or historical contexts of the failed state are not merely niceties of political correctness, but actions which might foretell whether prefabricated reconstruction programs will work within the particular setting at hand. This kind of analysis is also crucial to identifying the depth and breadth of women's cultural and socially based discrimination. They are also staples of practice in other professions involved in helping countries advance themselves (development and humanitarian assistance, for example). Yet these simple practices are rarely if ever executed at the outset of an international intervention or even in the latter stages of post-conflict reconstruction. Furthermore, needs assessments undertaken with gender central to the inquiry must be core to the establishment of post-conflict reconstruction plans, not tacked on as an afterthought. Internationals devising post-conflict programs must properly assess the needs of the local population, not base their programs on what they perceive donors will fund. Those assessments must take into account the entire population of men and women, adults, boys and girls, as individuals and as family units. Failure to so assess, as has been learned time and again in the development field, will inevitably lead to project failure and limited outcomes which ultimately doom the success of the overall project.[40]

Theory Informing Practice/Practice Informing Theory, with the Right People at the Table

The scholarship that informs and critiques peacekeeping, peacebuilding, transitional justice, and post-conflict reconstruction rarely makes it to the field. The personnel employed in international organizations are generally schooled in and rewarded for the skill of being able to function in emergency mode— "putting out fires," working in dangerous circumstances, under conditions of extreme stress. They are simply given no time and no encouragement to review, digest, and consider how or whether to implement the suggestions made by those with some objectivity or hindsight.

Furthermore, an enormous amount of the post-conflict reconstruction work done in the field is handled by lawyers, political scientists, and others with diplomatic or quasi-diplomatic backgrounds and, as peacekeeping expands (as will be discussed in Chapter 5), by the military. Meanwhile, the work of social scientists—sociologists, anthropologists, economists, and feminist scholars—is generally sidelined in policy and field considerations. Since the work is carried out by those with backgrounds in law, policy, and politics, the programs are formed through the lens of those professions, with those professional biases intact. Not only should those in the field be encouraged to take the time to consult the available scholarship in order to develop their programs and policies, but they should look at scholarship outside of their profession in so doing. Interdisciplinary learning must be integrated into UN, regional, and other programs.

Because there is a lack of doctrine in post-conflict reconstruction, what is imported into the transitioning countries' infrastructure is too dependent on what the importer knows best. Frequently a narrow range of representatives are at the table when programs are being devised (military men and diplomats developing the outlines of human rights programs, for instance), and so the least fluid models for governance, rule of law, human rights institutions, and so forth are imported. Unless broader and more representative groupings are included, from our point of view a diverse and multifaceted representation of women, asking the pertinent and difficult questions, and reflectively looking beyond what they know to truly see both the present needs and the desirable end goal, an ad hoc approach will generally continue to permeate post-conflict reconstruction.

The "theater" of international intervention is a highly masculine environment, with "theater" itself being the preferred term of internationals influenced by the military personnel populating the various international missions. In this setting, where most senior posts are held by international men while most of their administrative staff are local women, gender can never be properly considered if no one is even reading the recommendations made by those thinking about these issues from an objective distance.

Increasing Gender Equity in International Organizations

The ratio of men to women serving in senior positions in the United Nations and other IOs is dismal. The United Nations has recognized this as a problem and made some attempts to correct it.[41] Even so, while women's representation improved in lower-level posts, there were still few in senior positions.[42] One problem was that the goal of gender equity conflicted with the goal of geographical equity, in that "it is . . . often the over-represented countries from various regions that have a large supply of qualified candidates, including women,"[43] while underrepresented countries offered up no women for senior posts. The United Nations recognized a need to better incorporate women and by 1999 had corrected some of the problems relating to hiring women, but was again assessing why it could not *retain* women in midlevel and senior posts.[44] Their conclusion was that women were still not being promoted proportionately to men, in a system already plagued by infrequent promotions.[45] By way of positive comparison, the Council of Europe requires that to be considered for any judicial appointments to the European Court of Human Rights, each state *must* offer at least one woman candidate, and that if there is a suitable woman candidate, she will be appointed over a male of equal qualifications.[46] We endorse this gender affirmative action approach.

Equally of course, the mechanisms at the national level of diplomatic service which make women eligible for high-level international appointments generally involve a rotation of placements that are not family friendly. This means that many women may de facto opt out of such postings, so that reform is equally required at the national service level to influence and engage the international.[47] Sexual harassment, too, remains a large problem in international organizations, which often pair older international men with power, status, and a high earning potential with younger local women with low pay, status, and power (discussed further in Chapter 5).[48] The power differential is then exacerbated by the multicultural personnel and their differing attitudes toward gender parity and discrimination in highly fraught work settings.

Even with the closed nature of UN affairs and the lack of transparency in employment matters, a multitude of complaints have come forth from women who allege that they were fired for bringing sexual harassment claims[49] and from women bringing claims after being terminated, demoted, or refused promotion, ostensibly for inadequate performance.[50] The masculine culture of the United Nations has allowed senior male post holders to try to block sexual harassment investigations with claims of immunity,[51] and this appears to hold true in spite of and contemporaneous to its gender mainstreaming mandates. The importance of this is not simply with respect to UN practices, but in the interface of these practices with societies in transition, where women's gender inequality and exclusion are deeply entrenched—and not easily undone.

There are a few striking examples in which the faces of women do stand out in key roles in international interventions on the side of institutions created as a consequence of the intervention. In Sri Lanka, for example, women hold visible roles as police, border patrol, and customs officials and even in peace negotiations, and a Subcommittee on Gender Issues has addressed issues ranging over all aspects of reconstruction, not just those deemed traditional concerns of women.[52] In East Timor, too, a Gender Affairs Unit was created as part of the post-conflict reconstruction process; its role is to support the incorporation of gender into all post-conflict initiatives. These examples are less striking for what they depict about success in integrating women and more because of their stark contrast to other scenarios in which women are totally absent.

Women in key international intervention roles still stand out as anomalies, perceived as concessions to donor demands rather than real transformative moments and harbingers of times to come. The Sri Lankan Subcommittee on Gender Issues above, for example, only has authority to make recommendations, not to compel compliance with those recommendations. Too, there are legitimate fears that subcommittees and creation of units dealing with gender will compartmentalize so-called "women's issues," allowing those involved in international interventions to believe that such bodies are "addressing gender" despite their peripheral status. We acknowledge such concerns but view such institutional developments as representing legitimate attempts to give voice to women's concerns, often informed by consultation with the women that will be impacted by those recommendations.

While increasing the number of women in international posts within organizations attached to interventions would not single-handedly create more gender centrality in international interventions, it can certainly help. It is well established that the increased presence of women in missions renders those missions generally more gender sensitive, and increases the individual sensitivities of the men in the mission in relation to the host populations.[53] In stages, inserting more women into the institutions carrying out post-conflict work can make valuable short-term improvements in the success of that work, rendering missions more sensitive to gender concerns, more receptive to women's complaints, and more likely to create space for gender dialogue.

CAPTURING AND RETAINING GENDER EQUITY ACHIEVED DURING WAR

Each of the models of intervention presupposes that there are positive outcomes and opportunities to be seized from political, civil, and economic upheaval and even from war. The shift in political, civil, and economic realities offers opportunities to recalibrate the ordering and priorities of rights and remedies. In gender terms, women and men are confronted with opportunities to step out of prewar gender roles. "Rosie the Riveters" are created during war when women enter into the labor force and may find some social power and clout within that framework. Women often find voice through women's groups that are often the loudest voices for peace during war and for reconciliation after, even where they were relatively or wholly silent before. Women are often embraced into the military culture, when need presents itself, where they were not before.[54] In refugee camps, too, gender roles are often shifted and sometimes reversed as men are supplanted by aid workers as the "protectors," while women can find freedom to break out of prescribed gender roles by teaching, becoming physician's assistants and translators, and by assisting aid workers. There is also some evidence that reliance on women to distribute aid, take positions of authority, and incur community trust is likely to yield better dividends for international organizations, particularly in fraught political contexts. But identifying women as inherently trustworthy and men not can have a deeply negative effect on already challenged cultures of masculinity struggling in the post-conflict environment.

The transitional moment, as illustrated through the examples above, does not rest solely in the peace negotiation or in the aftermath of war. Rather, war and strife themselves create opportunity for women to emerge into the labor force and into more public spheres within society, as do the presence of internationals modeling different gender norms. So both men and women may be able to move out of their more socially, culturally, or economically defined roles in the postwar moments, when men are being decommissioned from war and women struggle to retain their more public roles. To the extent that women and men make gains that take them beyond traditional gender roles, typically in the realms of labor and public voice, those gains should be retained in the aftermath of war. Doing so with a gendered eye also requires being sensitive to the need to create positive roles and opportunities for men and undoing the cultures of hypermasculinity that have summited during violent conflict (discussed further in Chapter 5).

Commitment to capturing the full potential of the transition moment for women is a long-term proposition, most probably multigenerational. Structural changes imagining a massive overhaul in socially and culturally created gender roles are not going to be achieved overnight. To be sure, there are many shocking examples of the negative reassertion of social and cultural order on women in particular, as the caretakers of family values in the aftermath of war—Afghanistan being a case in point.[55] This means that donors and agencies committed to gender-central post-conflict transition must establish realistic benchmarks and a realistic time frame in which they can be achieved. Taking advantage of the opportunities in these transformative moments is slow work, the ultimate outcome of which might not be achieved for many generations after the war.

CONCLUSION

In reviewing the operation of post-conflict reconstruction enterprises, we propose a fundamental reordering such that gender is at the center of the decision to intervene in another state's affairs, is central in the peace negotiation process, central in the undertaking of post-conflict reconstruction, and central in all development contemplated toward a goal of long-term sustainable peace.

Capturing the political, economic, social, and cultural transitional space in order to render it as one which might advance the lives of women and men previously limited by their gender roles is a supremely challenging undertaking. Such an enterprise cannot even begin to be achieved in its most incremental and short-term steps, however, if the planning undertaken to develop the overall reconstruction strategy is not also sound, coherent, and carefully crafted to benefit the people it is meant to benefit.

The failure to understand and take into account the gendered aspects of war and peace undermines the ultimate success of post-conflict reconstruction programs. We propose that a paradigm shift in conceptualization and implementing such programs is required. International actors and states devising and enforcing various forms of international intervention, in parallel with domestic actors, fundamentally need to revise their conception of the work at hand, such that gender becomes central to the entire exercise at every stage.

The current manifestations of international interventions, in all of their various forms, are highly gendered affairs, even with the addition of gender mainstreaming to the mix. The gender dimensions in question still operate in broad stereotypes, with men negotiating the intervention and its various stages and manifestations, men having a voice in the process, and women, when dealt with at all, observed most often as victims of wartime atrocities. The masculinities of politics, diplomacy, and sovereignty are interacting with the masculinities of both the military entities sent to quell violence and the military masculinities they wish to negotiate with, dismantle, and suppress. At best, gender is mainstreamed (e.g., women and their needs are considered) in the transitional justice, accountability, and reconstruction phases of interventions. The intervenors feign attention to gender (e.g., the needs of women) in the reconstruction phases, but the entire intervention and all of its phases are so deeply masculine[56] that merely suffusing some of the stages of intervention with attention to the needs of women does little to create any sort of real gender centrality. Until intervening entities acknowledge how much of their programs, doctrine, philosophies, and plans are driven by the masculinities inherent in political and military regimes, those plans and programs will remain insufficient and unable to meet the long-term needs of societies of which more than 50 percent of the population are women.[57] Common to all of these missions and programs in each of their manifestations is the lack of engaged gender inquiry. Determinations at the very heart of the success of each of these programs—such as what is security, what is stability, and does it mean the same thing for all members within this society—fail to be undertaken. While men and women may well identify security in very different ways, just as elites and marginalized minorities may well differ vastly in how they define security and stability, these differences are not accounted for in developing the fundamental premises upon which every aspect of the interventions are founded.

In a truly gender-centered intervention inquiry, even the decision as to whether to intervene to prevent conflict would require an inquiry into the gendered affairs of the recipient nation and its citizens. How a peace agreement, through its various stages, is derived and with whom at the table it is to be negotiated, with attention to the gendered causes of conflict, and an understanding of the necessity for rendering gender equity in order to prevent future conflict is critical. Transformation must be substantial. In order for that to transpire, gender must not only be central to the programs created to assist a country in reconstructing, but to the entire philosophy driving the post conflict process.

CHAPTER 5

Peacekeeping

One of the most common forms of international intervention is the peace-keeping mission. The United Nations has deployed over fifty peace-keeping operations into conflict and post-conflict zones since 1948.[1] The goal of peacekeeping missions is to bring stability to a destabilized country by the (generally armed military) presence of representatives positioned by the international community. Peacekeeping was historically based on the principle that "an impartial presence on the ground can ease tensions between hostile parties and create space for political negotiations."[2] Accordingly, peacekeeping missions yield a perfect forum in which to elucidate issues of post-conflict gender concern and to analyze the gender inequalities and hierarchies that produce violence, discrimination, and exclusion, taking us further in exploring the patriarchal structures that are created and reinforced, rather than undone, in post-conflict settings.[3]

The United Nations and its member states are committed to peacekeeping as a means for preempting and stabilizing conflict, as well as securing peace in its immediate aftermath. Local populations, too, regularly state that the presence of international peacekeepers is absolutely necessary as a precursor to peace.[4] It is clear, therefore, that peacekeepers can serve as positive, stabilizing influences in conflicted societies. We broadly assert, however, that their role could be much enhanced if gender were made central to their mission—both by unpacking masculinities and addressing masculine behaviors that limit and undermine peacekeeping operations, and prioritizing awareness of and attention to the needs of women within the local host populations. Attention to gender, while not guaranteeing the success of these missions, should nevertheless serve to improve their effectiveness in establishing security and facilitating their relationships with the local population.

We address three primary components relevant to gender structures and roles within peacekeeping operations: First, the mandates of the peacekeeping operations; second, the training, discipline, and codes of conduct that peacekeepers must observe along with the types of sanctions imposed for breaches; and finally, the gender composition of peacekeeping missions. This chapter will discuss the types and current evolution of peacekeeping missions, the professionals who constitute them, the conditions of service, and the particular forms of masculinity that can arise or be compounded in the peacekeeping context. It will detail lessons learned from the successes of peacekeeping missions, as well as the multitudinous examples of negative peacekeeping, in particular gender-based abuse of local populations by peacekeepers.[5] Finally, we speculate on what gender-positive peacekeeping might look like by addressing peacekeeper accountability, including both "hard" law (jurisdiction of courts to try peacekeepers for crimes committed in service) and "soft" law (the development of codes of conduct and training materials for peacekeepers going to the field), and by increasing roles for women and expanding existing roles for men.

PARAMETERS AND STATUS OF PEACEKEEPING MISSIONS

The UN Charter, agreed to in 1948, expresses the hope that the establishment of the United Nations would "save succeeding generations from the scourge of war."[6] Peacekeeping, while not explicitly provided for in the Charter, has nevertheless evolved into one of the main tools used by the United Nations to achieve this goal.[7] When peacekeepers are deployed, the United Nations acts under color of international resolutions, binding the host countries to various commitments. The legal basis for such action is found primarily in Chapters VI and VII of the UN Charter.[8] Chapter VIII of the Charter also provides for the involvement of regional bodies and agencies in the maintenance of international peace and security.[9]

While peacekeeping operations have traditionally been associated with Chapter VI of the Charter, in recent years, the Security Council has adopted the practice of invoking Chapter VII when authorizing the deployment of UN peacekeeping operations into volatile post-conflict settings where the state is unable to maintain security and public order.[10] The Chapter under which a peacekeeping mission is authorized affects the scope of the mission's mandate, and may affect both individual peacekeeper's responsibilities and the overall effectiveness of the operation.[11]

Contemporary peacekeeping has undergone significant reevaluation based on varying factors, including scarce resources, state hesitancy about long-term external military commitments, concerns of mission creep, and increased apprehension for the safety of committed troops. Recent peacekeeping missions show a trend toward intervening in intrastate (rather than interstate) conflicts, which impacts both the willingness of sending states to provide troops and the complexity of the conflicts into which peacekeepers are being deployed.[12] As a result of some prominent peacekeeping failures, such as Somalia, Rwanda, and Srebrenica (in Bosnia and Herzegovina), the United Nations initiated a process of rethinking and retooling peacekeeping operations, seeking to disaggregate and set out the various kinds of UN support to and intervention in conflict and post-conflict situations.[13]

The United Nations has identified "[c]onflict prevention, peacemaking, peacekeeping, and peace enforcement" as potential elements of any peacekeeping mission.[14] This chapter, accordingly, employs the term "peacekeeping" in its broadest sense in order to discuss any aspect of peacekeeping operations that have a gender impact. Figure 5.1 depicts the UN view of some of these overlapping and expanding roles.[15]

Peacekeeping operations have become more complex and multidimensional, with peacekeeping troops made up of not only military personnel but also including civilians and police. Operations have also engaged in activities far beyond those originally imagined as within the core competencies of regularly deployed military personnel. Peacekeeping thus represents a microsite of the broader phenomena described in Chapter 4, whereby multiple professional roles are exercised in tandem in the post-conflict theater, with substantial effect on both women and men in conflict and post-conflict zones.

As the international community revises its approach to peacekeeping, it is also beginning to acknowledge the relationship between gendered roles and structures and conflict prevention. As discussed in Chapter 1, when the UN Security Council adopted Resolution 1325, it formally acknowledged the importance of women's roles in peacekeeping. Although Resolution 1325 has been influential in the effort to bring gender mainstreaming into peacekeeping operations,[16] it has not revolutionized actual practices in the field,[17] nor has it served to address women's needs or unravel the masculinities inherent in peacekeeping operations. This may in part be correlated to a broader

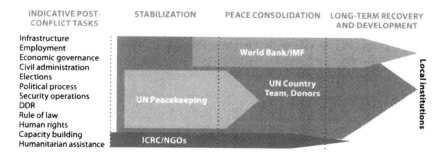

Figure 5.1:
The Core Business of Multi-dimensional United Nations Peacekeeping Operations

conceptual bias inherent in Security Council Resolution 1325, which mostly brings women into view as victims rather than as agents of transformative social change in conflict settings. Understanding how highly gendered structures underpin the social, legal, and political peacekeeping space gives us a sense of how much work needs to be done in this area to modify peacekeeping practices, to ensure that they become fully inclusive of women's needs and priorities.

IDENTIFYING THE PEACEKEEPERS

Peacekeeping contingents are made up of troops from countries willing to contribute to another country's stabilization, under the auspices of a UN mission, with a UN mandate. The United Nations spends more than $1 billion per year in peacekeeping operations, with about 100,000 people involved in these operations.[18] One troop-donating country will typically take the lead in the operation, a role often based on geographical proximity or prior ties, strategic interests in the region, or strong domestic pressure to contribute.[19] Because military units in all contributing countries are still dominated by men, peacekeeping troops are also generally male-dominated.

Because troops necessarily come from countries other than the host country, they often have different language skills, religious beliefs, and social and cultural practices than those of the local populations. There are very different understandings of gender roles among peacekeeping units and between peacekeepers and the local population. Furthermore, peacekeeping troops are sent from within the military structures of their own countries and have internalized various military strictures and valued qualities, skills, and characteristics that may interact in unexpected ways within the culture to which they are sent to function as mediators and intervenors. Peacekeepers may not have a unitary view of their roles. They could identify as UN staff, as military within the definition of their own national military culture and service structures, as humanitarian workers, or some combination.[20] Their role perceptions and loyalties could change over time and after interaction with the local population, or could be dictated or effected by the mandate under which they operate. In thinking about these questions, we need to pay particular attention to how perceptions of women's and men's roles intersect with these identities and loyalties. How these questions are answered by individual peacekeepers and whether they are addressed systematically, either by the sending countries or by the UN agencies deploying them, will have a tremendous bearing on the extent to which gender-based peacekeeper abuses can be reduced and eradicated. They also affect the extent to which women can and will be brought in as equal participants in conflict-prevention programs and processes.

Conditions of Employment

Peacekeepers can be either military or civilian. International staff working in peacekeeping missions can be hired directly by the United Nations, as permanent UN staff in the case of civilian positions, or *seconded* or on loan to the United Nations by the sending country (all military positions and some civilian positions). Seconded staff are governed not only by applicable UN rules, regulations, and Codes of Conduct, but also by any codes to which their sending countries wish to bind them.

Life during a peacekeeping mission can be quite stressful and dangerous. There are periods of extreme and life-threatening activity, followed by long lulls in which there is little to do. Peacekeepers lose their lives in service[21] and find themselves regularly working among the world's most traumatized people. They simultaneously operate under an expectation that traditional (albeit informal) masculine military approaches to trauma—facing it with stoicism and equanimity—will apply. The general likelihood that the peacekeeping missions are de facto gender segregated or with few women in their ranks also affects the conditions of deployment. Gender segregation influences the actions and attitudes of those on mission, as well as the culture of masculinity that pervades deployment. Under these conditions involving periods of high stress with little emotional outlet, interspersed with extreme boredom combined with gender segregation, ethical breaches have regularly arisen, as will be discussed further in this chapter.

MASCULINITIES OF PEACEKEEPING

Military cultures are intimately correlated with practices and cultures of masculinity. In war, stereotypical militarist discourses elevate men to "a world of arms and glory" and relegate women to the "world of birthing and mourning."[22] The longstanding "boys will be boys" culture has been used to explain the phenomenon of "camp followers," prostitution, sexual exploitation, and human trafficking that have accompanied international missions and military forays abroad.[23] Some scholars and activists have argued that military recruiters play on the promise of sexual adventure when they entice recruits with the image of travel to far-flung places, thus perpetuating the belief that sex tourism is an implicit benefit of military and peacekeeping service, and is therefore to be expected.[24]

Evidence suggests that international workers deployed abroad act in ways that they would never consider acting at home.[25] The sexual deprivation justification for sexually based crimes and exploitation, which has its basis in "biological essentialism" (that men are sexually exploitative because they need sex and cannot be deprived of it), is entirely insufficient in explaining this behavior.

Most men, whether "sexually deprived" or not, do not rape.[26] Most men are not violent. Most men are not soldiers, nor killers, nor do they assault.[27] The problem, therefore, must lie in the socialized masculinities of military culture in particular, and perhaps even more pointedly, in peacekeeping missions where the masculinities of military cultures and the culture of the host country interact in a forum of "perceived lawlessness" in the aftermath of war.

Peacekeeping is a deeply masculine and masculinized affair,[28] and the deep-seated masculine paradigm of the peacekeeper away from home, under pressure, functioning in the role of a savior,[29] must be squarely confronted if gender inequity and abuse are to be eradicated. The complexity of direct and subliminal messages about women absorbed by peacekeepers before deployment means that addressing the status and equality of women within the military hierarchy, as well as the appropriate attitudes of peacekeepers to the women they encounter in service, will be complex and multifaceted.

As we have set out in Part I of this book, we rely on—and generally assume rather than argue for—the claim central to the work of many radical feminists: that women as a group have been subordinated by the many cultures they function within. This includes the culture and context of peacekeeping by large international and imported male groups to conflicted societies. In this context, we assert that average peacekeepers do not understand gender issues to be a fundamental component of their work.[30] Peacekeepers who do understand that there is an expectation that they understand "gender issues" also acknowledge that this expectation makes them even more wary of the term. In this frame they associate "gender terminology" with added expectations thrust upon them, the value of which is not fully understood or accepted.[31] There is as yet no buy in.

Furthermore, to the extent that gender is taught as a component of peacekeeper trainings, it tends to be dismissed or forgotten in favor of aspects of peacekeeping deemed hierarchically important, such as military conventions and protocols, or caring for one's weapon or vehicle.[32] Peacekeepers view their role to be a military, or at least quasi-military, one. They are less interested in and often defensive of "soft" requirements thrust upon them which they perceive as distracting them from the business of staying and keeping others alive. Even trainings on international humanitarian law and the requirements directed by the Geneva Conventions have been deemed "out of touch with reality" by peacekeepers, who see the trainings as unrealistic[33] and as having little bearing on what they are in-country to do.

The power dynamics of peacekeepers vis-à-vis the local population is fundamental to the problems that have been identified in many peacekeeping missions, and an understanding of them is therefore integral to any future successes. The interaction between privileged, wealthy (even if only relatively), powerful, and largely male peacekeepers who carry weapons with the traumatized, poor,[34] vulnerable,[35] and relatively powerless local population is a dynamic which can be highly conducive to abuse. It also intersects with another powerful thread set out in our Introduction, namely the essentialist tendency to view women primarily as victims in conflict settings. Although most peacekeeping missions are more than 95 percent male, most of the local population interacting with peacekeepers is female.[36] This gender disparity, combined with the power differential imbued with its own culture of masculinity, gives rise to significant potential for gender-based inequalities and exclusions.

The interplay between power differentials and an accompanying colonial disposition, the latter informed by resonant notions of the exotic "other" female, creates a circular and negative dynamic which feeds on itself.[37] For instance, members among the local population in the Democratic Republic of Congo (DRC) and Sierra Leone observed that peacekeepers and other UN personnel "conveyed a position of authority and power over the host population."[38] Demonstrating the negative ramifications of this conflation is the example of a French mechanic, employed in peacekeeping missions in the Central African Republic (CAR) and DRC, and charged (in France) with rape, abuse of minors, and possession of pornographic material while on both missions, who attributed his crimes to having "lost all sense of reality," in a climate where "the colonial spirit persists. The white man gets what he wants."[39]

International troops understand that they would not be present if the host population could effectively govern themselves.[40] Further, many of the conflicts that peacekeepers arrive to quell contain elements of extremely violent gender-based atrocities.[41] The context and forms of gender-based violations during the conflict impact the behavior of the peacekeeping troops when they arrive, particularly where there has been a lack of accountability for or impunity with regard to those crimes during peace negotiations. The peacekeepers learn from domestic elites (who may themselves have committed gendered violations) that there may be historically permitted access to and little cost for committing violence against women.[42] The race, class, gender, and inherent power differences set up a simultaneous victim/savior dynamic, as well as a savage/savior dynamic, which carry with them the strong potential for abuse by outsiders, perpetrated on the victims for whom they have no sense of positive responsibility.

Cultural differences intersect with gender hierarchies as well, creating difficult interactions between peacekeepers and the local community. In Sierra Leone, for instance, reports indicate that some peacekeepers, offended by the bare breasts of local women, drove around local villages insisting that women cover up, justifying this response on the basis of the gender-sensitivity principles they had learned in their trainings.[43] Where religious and cultural practices differ between the peacekeepers and the local population, some research suggests that the peacekeepers tend to have less sexual interaction with the locals.[44] Where they are similar, there tends to be more sexual interaction.[45] Some sampling shows that peacekeepers have articulated the view that the abuse they inflict upon the locals can be rationalized by economic arguments.[46] Fatalistic and expatriate imperialist points of view can combine to allow peacekeepers to subconsciously feel that whatever they do could cause no more harm than the harm they have already encountered, thereby boosting practices of impunity.

POSITIVE AND NEGATIVE LESSONS LEARNED FROM PEACEKEEPING MISSIONS

While peacekeeping missions bring some semblance of security and stability to unsafe and unstable conflict zones, peacekeeping missions have also been associated with egregious human rights violations, including gender-based violence against and exploitation of women. If we are to transform the post-conflict terrain in order to positively address the needs and rights of women, then evidently accountability, remedy, and reform are also the challenges of gender-centralized peacekeeping. This section details some of the gendered positives and negatives associated with peacekeeping missions.

Peacekeepers as Stabilization Forces

By and large, male and female members of the local population view the presence of peacekeepers as a positive factor in creating and maintaining stability. They are especially grateful for additional humanitarian services offered by peacekeeping missions, such as access to medical services, construction of schools and public buildings, distribution of food, and gathering information toward prosecution and arrest of war criminals.[47] Peacekeeping missions have often played a constructive role in maintaining peace and security, and even missions deemed unsuccessful overall may have specific units or projects that succeeded in advancing microsecurity or reconstruction at a particularized local level.[48] For example, Australian troops in Somalia were credited with reassuring the local population by regularly driving out into the community and "aggressively patrolling."[49] Women in particular may benefit as the presence of peacekeepers has the potential to secure women's immediate safety and expand women's roles within their communities. For example, women may find more personal security in going about their daily activities and find a receptive audience to report crimes committed against them. They may also find some expansion of their traditional gender roles in accepting employment or financial incentives created by international presence.

The international presence has the potential to provide new pathways in modeling appropriate interactions between men and women. Take the Revised Gender Guidelines proposed by Mine Action, as an example. Recognizing that women hired to work on demining crews often suffered gender-based discrimination (being expected to cook for the men, for instance, which was not in their job description and for which they were not being paid), Mine Action monitored those behaviors and adjusted schedules accordingly, so that women took their meal breaks at different times than male crew members and could not therefore be expected to cook for them.[50] Further, recognizing that tribe and community affiliation dictates much of women's roles in a society, they recommend enlisting the support of the tribe or community as a whole to encourage women's participation. By way of further example, the report points to the solution in Afghanistan of married couples being hired to work together in teams.[51] In these ways, the presence of internationals, combined with the Resolution 1325 expectation that international organizations incorporate women, prompts creative gender solutions, drawn from broader worldviews, and thereby broadens the prospects for women within these societies at least for some period of time.[52]

POSITIVES AND NEGATIVES OF EMPLOYMENT AND ECONOMIC STIMULUS

A significant upside of the international presence is that it boosts economic opportunity for many. The UN Department of Peacekeeping Operations (DPKO), for instance, characterizes the presence of a peacekeeping operation as "an important economic force. . . . [with] the power to exercise a positive impact on women's employment opportunities."[53] Peacekeeping operations generate an economy very quickly, typically in countries where the economies have been destroyed by war, or overtaken by shadow economies of criminality and resource looting directly correlated to the perpetuation of violent conflict. Local people are hired as interpreters, drivers, cooks, housekeepers, and in most other administrative support functions. The private sector, too, gains a tremendous boost, supplying telecommunications, hotels, restaurants, and housing to the international workers. Attendant, however, is the danger of local dependency on employment created by the international presence–driven economy.

Some of the roles follow stereotypical gender lines: men are employed as drivers, interpreters, security, and administrative assistants; women find jobs as assistants, interpreters, housekeepers, and cooks. Some international agencies, however, are recognizing a social/structural opportunity and are beginning to specifically tailor their programs to hire women in a variety of roles despite traditional expectations that might otherwise preclude this.[54] In their employment, women may find some room to subvert local gendered labor norms that define what constitutes women's work, and these opportunities can provide transformative space for women, emphasizing our broader point about the unexpected capacity of conflict to shape women's lives in positive ways.[55]

These gains, however, are not without cost or complexity. Women may also be solicited for sex, either within their paid positions in the form of sexual harassment,[56] or outside of it, in the form of commercial sex.[57] The temporary economy created by the influx of internationals can be both helpful and problematic for a number of reasons. First, prices linked to international use, such as housing, restaurants, and hotels, are distorted and inflated. This can make it impossible for locals to make use of these services and commodities. To the extent that they can make use of them, they do so within a dual economy, whereby the same or similar services are offered on two pricing scales—one for internationals and the other for locals. Second, the peacekeeping economy that thrives in service to the huge influx of internationals with money can become an economic space in which women and girls are treated as commodities to be traded and haggled over by entrepreneurs doing business in this informal, but laissez-faire economy.[58] In its extreme form, women and girls are treated as chattel.[59] Third, many postwar economies are falsely propped up by the international presence. When the internationals depart, the economy can collapse or be considerably weakened. Gains made by women, economic and otherwise, may not survive the departure of the internationals. Finally, it is worth noting that the temporary economy accompanying peacekeeping may have little or no effect on the maintenance of shadow economies based on criminality and the ongoing asset liquidation that accompanies armed conflict in many parts of the world, and to which women also substantially contribute. As the shadow economy thrives in parallel, it continues to provide the basis for the cyclical resort to violence, fundamentally undermining the raison d'être of the peacekeeping mandate.

POSITIVES AND NEGATIVES ASSOCIATED WITH GENDER-CULTURAL INTERACTIONS

In the field, the DPKO is generally aware that cultural gender differences exist and that those differences should sometimes mandate, for instance, that there be no contact between male staff and local women where such interaction would lead to a violent interface. Nevertheless, the DPKO also properly understands that these cultural differences do not mean that UN staff should always "observe local custom to the letter";[60] some cultural interaction can in fact create space for both women and men to break out of their prescribed gender roles by observing the behavior of men and women in other cultures. This requires careful and considered balancing for the mission, judging its own best interest, as well as taking into account a broader responsibility to advance the equality and autonomy of women in post-conflict societies.

Disappointingly, sexual harassment remains a common problem in missions where the power differentials between the men and women employed within it are extreme. These power differentials are exacerbated in peacekeeping missions by cultural differences as they play out in the context of sex and relationships.[61] Local women often make up the bulk of the domestic and service-oriented positions within field missions, while men constitute the vast majority of the international positions of stature. The gendered power disparity can contribute to sexual harassment of the domestic women in a site where few mechanisms of reporting on sanctions are available.

SEXUAL VIOLENCE AND PEACEKEEPING MISSIONS

Despite the generally positive impact of peacekeeping missions within countries undergoing conflict, and in particular for women who make some security gains due to the presence of peacekeepers, multiple instances of sexual violence have been committed by peacekeepers. During missions in Africa in the mid-1990s, Belgian, Canadian, Italian, and Pakistani peacekeepers were implicated in crimes ranging from torture and rape to murder.[62] Peacekeepers inserted explosives into a woman's vagina after raping her,[63] bought and sold trafficked women,[64] and traded food for sex with young girls.[65] UN peacekeepers in East Timor were accused of offenses including child sex abuse, bestiality, and coercing women and children into prostitution.[66] Complaints of gender-based abuse by peacekeepers have emerged in Cambodia, Bosnia and Herzegovina, Macedonia, Mozambique, Sierra Leone, Liberia, Guinea, the DRC, Eritrea, and Kosovo.

Human Trafficking

Sometimes referred to as the peacekeeping economy (implying its inevitability), the influx of internationals into a conflict zone creates a demand for goods and services, including sexual services. The corresponding economic and social vulnerability of women in the country or in neighboring countries creates the supply.[67] As soon as peacekeepers arrived in Bosnia, for instance, traffickers began capitalizing on the collapsed economies in Moldova and Romania, promising girls and young women from those countries jobs as hostesses and nannies in Italy, but selling them as chattel in Bosnian markets to populate the brothels springing up to serve the internationals with financial means.[68] The brothels in Sierra Leone, too, are populated with refugee girls and women from Liberia who escaped years of being used as sex slaves by rebels are psychologically and physically traumatized, and who have no economic alternatives.[69]

Investigations into allegations of widespread sexual abuse of young girls and women in the DRC uncovered a practice of trafficking whereby young girls, aged eleven to fourteen, were "having sex with peacekeepers [as] a means of getting food and sometimes small sums of money. The boys and young men who facilitated sexual encounters between peacekeepers and the girls sometimes received food as payment for their services as well."[70] When girls, many as young as eleven, are provided by men to give sexual services to internationals, it constitutes human trafficking under the Protocol to Prevent, Suppress, and Punish Trafficking in Persons, Especially Women and Children, Supplementing the United Nations Convention against Transnational Organized Crime.[71] That such criminal activity is carried out by aid workers on the population they are sent to give support to is particularly egregious. Again, such practices underscore the forms of hypermasculinity that play out in the context of international military presence. The contemporary willingness of international organizations to positively address these behaviors is a small indication that times are changing and that constraints are increasingly being placed on peacekeepers to prevent sexual violations of vulnerable female populations in post-conflict settings.

The sex trade in post-conflict societies and the imperatives and economies that drive it demonstrate the complicated terrain that advancements in gender equality must navigate to succeed in substantively improving women's social, legal, and political status. When there is an extended presence of an international mission, the sex industry that arises to meet the demand tends to remain long after the departure of the internationals present as peacekeepers,[72] and the women who served in it are seen as "tainted," often unable to either reenter their communities or engage in any other form of economic activity.

Rape

Rape has been common in military ventures, both as a method and means of warfare and also ascribed to the "sexual deprivation" that purportedly accompanies the military man on mission.[73] Particular masculine characteristics valued in military cultures—dominance, assertiveness, aggressiveness, self-sufficiency, willingness to take risks—also correlate to rape propensity.[74] Some argue that the sort of group bonding necessary to build a cohesive and strong military unit can correspond to the propensity of men encouraging other men to carry out risk-taking behaviors, including raping women.[75]

In the DRC, girls as young as thirteen were raped by the UN Mission in the Democratic Republic of Congo (MONUC) peacekeepers. Other girls as young as eleven engaged in what was referred to as "survival sex."[76] Categorically an eleven-year-old cannot effectively consent to sex; sex with a young girl, whether or not in exchange for food for her daily survival, is tantamount to rape, particularly when the person with whom she is having sex is present under color of an international protection mandate. Persistent war-induced poverty, coupled with a lack of self-worth as a consequence of past gender abuse perpetuated in war, leads some women to "survival prostitution" to secure food and basic necessities.[77] Although the women are exchanging sex for money or goods, the fact that their very survival depends on it should mandate that peacekeepers refrain from all sexual relations with the local population. Survival sex, whether engaged in with minors or not, cannot be considered consensual and should therefore be tantamount to rape if committed by a peacekeeper.

In sum, while peacekeeping missions on the whole are considered to have a stabilizing impact on post-conflict societies, their presence can also impact women, for good and for ill. In order to augment the benefits and lessen or eradicate the harms, peacekeeping missions must squarely confront the complexity of their impact on women and men within the host countries.

WHAT WOULD GENDER-POSITIVE PEACEKEEPING ENCOMPASS?

The United Nations has taken some steps to mainstream gender in all its institutional dimensions, including issuing a Policy Directive on Gender Equality in 2006.[78] Field observers and gender advisors to field missions have begun making recommendations to address the problem of sexual exploitation by peacekeepers.[79] Although eradicating sexual violence by peacekeepers is an imperative, changes must go far beyond merely improving the response to sexual exploitation carried out by male peacekeepers on the local female population. Instead, the treatment of women in the local population and the overall behavior of the peacekeepers must be linked to the ability of missions to achieve their purpose—bringing about or maintaining peace and stability.

For example, appointing gender advisors is insufficient if the competencies and duties of those advisors are seen as soft or noncore functions—a nonessential add-on to the real duties of peacekeepers. As we have previously articulated, this grafted-on dimension limits the capacity of gender mainstreaming as an initiative to be truly transformative. It has the negative tendency to balkanize "gender" (code for "women") rather than centralizing and diffusing transformative policies that would affect the structural and social relationships between men and women throughout all aspects of peacekeeping operations. In some sense, this solution of adding on gender advisors to missions already operating for years (and only after reported gender abuse) indicates how poorly international organizations grasp the form and depth of the inequality and exclusion problems faced by women in post-conflict settings. It further demonstrates their limited appreciation of their own contribution to its maintenance.

Instead, an approach that places gender at the center of the deployment, organization, and role assumptions of peacekeepers would be more likely to yield results of substance for women. Going back to our core themes, it is a prerequisite that women are consulted about the design and implementation of programs and policies (including the deployment of peacekeepers and the tasks they assume) that affect them. Of necessity, women must be sufficiently represented both in the missions deployed and in the locals employed. Immediate, medium-, and long-term priorities set by peacekeeping forces must integrate gender at every nodal point, being aware that they interface with societies and cultures in which women frequently lack legal and political standing and are structurally excluded from social, economic, and political opportunities.

LEGAL ACCOUNTABILITY

As a starting point, the United Nations and states contributing peacekeeping troops must effectively deal with accountability of peacekeeper violations. The United Nations has no legal authority to prosecute peacekeeping troops sent to its missions because all sending nations retain jurisdiction over the actions of their own troops, no matter where they are posted or to whom they are on loan. The United Nations is the sum of its parts, the member states which comprise it. Not only have the member states that send troops to peacekeeping missions failed to develop sufficient consensus around prosecution of peacekeepers for their criminal actions on mission, but the doctrine of state sovereignty maintains great purchase in this domain.

Problems Associated with Lack of Accountability

The crimes associated with peacekeeping have been multitudinous. The accountability for those crimes is sketchy.[80] Not only does the United Nations have no accountability mechanism for its peacekeepers, but it has no real power to insist that either the sending country or the host country, the two sovereign entities that would have jurisdiction over the crime, prosecute crimes committed by peacekeepers.

The possible venues for prosecution—domestic prosecution in the sending country, domestic prosecution in the host country, and international tribunals—all have systemic problems associated with their execution. First, attempts by the United Nations to insist that sending countries prosecute such crimes domestically and report back to it regarding the outcome and punishment have received irregular responses. Few crimes are prosecuted, and those that are produce outcomes that at face value seem lenient by comparison to similar crimes in the home country. For example, when a Norwegian soldier killed a Macedonian minister and his family in a car crash in August 1999 after swerving into the wrong lane, probably intoxicated, he was immediately taken to Norway where he was sentenced to two months in prison.[81] The French mechanic accused of engaging in at least twenty-four sex acts with girls between the ages of twelve and eighteen while on mission in both the CAR and the DRC was ultimately sentenced to nine years in prison and ordered to undergo psychiatric treatment, punishment decried as far less than he would have been ordered to serve if the crimes had been committed in France.[82] Further telling was that the defendant said he was relieved to have been arrested because he was growing uncomfortable with his "attraction to African girls," which had been noticed for some time but not acted on by his superiors.[83]

After years of accusations by locals against peacekeepers, the United Nations finally took some action of its own. From January 2004 to December 2005, the United Nations investigated 278 peacekeeping personnel primarily based in Africa (DRC, Sierra Leone, and Liberia) on allegations of sex-based crimes.[84] These investigations, however, resulted merely in the *dismissal* of 16 civilians and the repatriation, on disciplinary grounds, of "132 uniformed personnel, including 7 commanders."[85] None were prosecuted by their host nations or sending countries, at least as far as the UN oversight apparatus is aware. Glaringly absent from the UN Investigative Reports, too, are the names of the peacekeepers and the countries from which they came, missing the opportunity to punish through shaming.[86]

While national militaries are accountable under the military codes of the state to which they belong, crimes committed during peacekeeping service often go unprosecuted. Even though Status of Forces Agreements,[87] the legal agreement binding the sending and receiving parties in peacekeeping missions, regularly include lengthy provisions regarding accountability for peacekeeper misconduct, meaningful accountability remains elusive. Moreover, the different categories of personnel, including civilian, military, and police, are governed by different rules and disciplinary procedures. As a result, the very persons sent to stabilize a host country and protect its citizens can rightly be viewed by the host population as having impunity for their crimes against it.

Where acknowledged, peacekeeper misconduct has often been responded to by merely dismissing the offending troops. Dismissal is insufficient, however, because first, dismissal alone—a punishment associated with labor and employment—does nothing to vindicate the victim, nor does it serve as a deterrent to others who would commit the same crimes with impunity. Second, it is still rarely used against those who have committed crimes during service. Placing the vindication of women's rights front and center of peacekeeping policy and implementation requires a commitment to pursuing impunity for gender crimes committed by peacekeepers, benchmarking the behavior of peacekeeping units, and penalizing states that fail to adhere to either requirement.

The second option, prosecuting internationals in the host country in which the crime has been committed, is also fraught with problems. First, due to the conflict that brings the peacekeepers and other internationals to the scene, the rule of law and judicial system are likely to be nonfunctioning or insufficient. For this reason, added to the backdrop of colonialist mind-sets and prejudices, the internationals are reluctant to allow their personnel to be subject to local justice. Accordingly, most of the bilateral Status of Forces Agreements whereby the host country has consented to the presence of peacekeepers and internationals contain provisions granting immunity and exclusive jurisdiction to the sending country.[88] Second, the host country is unlikely to want to anger internationals, who hold both the reconstruction purse-strings and the entry access into international and regional economic and political bodies, by prosecuting its soldiers.

Such lack of jurisdiction, followed by the typically internal and closed-door military prosecutions or no prosecutions at all, have led to a general sense that peacekeepers are largely immune and can therefore act with impunity. This diminishes their peacebuilding capacity and role in fostering security, particularly for women.

Prescriptions to Address Accountability

Peacekeepers who commit crimes should be held accountable for their actions. Such a core baseline is essential to the broader project of making women's needs and rights central to the discharge of a peacekeeping mission. UN policy formally confirms that peacekeepers are accountable for their crimes. The problem lies with implementation and the politics of implementation. There is a need to develop rules and systems of enforcement that apply consistently to all members of peacekeeping missions. Both are essential to transforming the post-conflict terrain when peacekeepers are the violators of women's rights.

Two recent attempts have been made to counter the United Nations' lack of power to demand that either the sending or host state prosecute offending troops. First, the International Criminal Court sought to assert jurisdiction over crimes committed by peacekeepers. This attempt was so bitterly opposed by some sending countries, and in particular by the United States, that it was believed by some to risk the future of peacekeeping missions altogether, as countries would simply refuse to contribute troops.[89] Despite this, a significant number of states have ultimately become parties to the International Criminal Court (ICC), acknowledging their willingness, at least in theory, to allow the ICC to bring proceedings against their peacekeepers should they be unable or unwilling to prosecute those crimes themselves.[90]

The second attempt to counter lack of accountability has been made by the United Nations itself, which has altered its Memoranda of Understanding (MOU), the document wherein sending countries agree to commit their troops.[91] The new MOU would require commanders to be responsible for the "discipline and good order of all members of the contingent." It also specifies that "discipline and good order" pertains to UN Codes of Conduct, not to sending countries' individual standards.[92] The performance review of commanders will also be based on how well they uphold this responsibility. This provision responds to recommendations made by investigators of sexual abuse in the DRC that it was commanders who must be made to accept their responsibility for the actions of their subordinates. Sending countries signing the new MOU would therein give assurances that every peacekeeper had received adequate and effective training before being deployed. The MOU also crucially contains explicit definitions of otherwise culturally ambiguous terms such as "sexual exploitation" and "misconduct." Because the revised MOU is a recent augmentation of deployment conditions, it is difficult to assess the potential impact on contributing states.

In 2007, the European Court for Human Rights (ECHR) decided a case involving two claims from civilians injured by peacekeepers,[93] holding that acts by peacekeepers in Kosovo were attributable to the United Nations and not the member states of which the soldiers were nationals.[94] That decision has significant implications and may inter alia undermine state obligations to fully train peacekeepers in conformity with their human rights obligations on UN missions and limit the extraterritorial application of human rights norms (including nondiscrimination) in peacekeeping contexts.

Regardless of potential momentum from the ECHR's rulings, the most viable option for holding peacekeepers and internationals accountable for their actions remains domestic prosecutions in the sending countries. Nevertheless, such prosecutions are rare, even after atrocious violations have been exposed. Whether this is due to the difficulties in securing evidence (much of which will be found abroad in the host country) or mere unwillingness to prosecute is unclear and likely depends upon the sending country and the specific elements of the particular violation.

Other compromises have been proposed as well, including one proposed solution to the immunity and jurisdiction problems—the use of on-site courts-martial, recommended by former Jordanian UN Ambassador Prince Zeid Ra'ad Zeid Al-Hussein, himself a former civilian peacekeeper. While such proposals have not been gender-proofed, they would in theory demonstrate to the local population that peacekeepers do not enjoy immunity and that their crimes do not go unpunished.[95] Alternative solutions include more forcefully and regularly utilizing the United Nations' power to repatriate culpable peacekeepers and instituting the power to blacklist those who commit crimes from being sent on future missions.[96] Finally, more work needs to be done on ensuring that contributing member states cede to the United Nations, through Status of Force Agreements or another agreed mechanism, at least the power to dismiss individual military officers involved in gendered human rights violations. Without at least dismissal for criminally culpable acts, impunity is likely to continue. Ceding such authority to the organization that has the greatest stake in successful peacekeeping might also create a greater social context in which the shame associated with such violations would affect the willingness of individuals to commit and states to tolerate these crimes.[97]

Even if legal accountability problems appear intractable in the short term, some of the most important prevention techniques may well be the simplest. For instance, inactive troops must be kept occupied with other activities. Peacekeepers who are trained for war but then have little to do, far away from home, get into trouble. Peacekeepers who have television access, movie nights, regular games, and competitive athletic events, and who are encouraged to pit their professionalism and unit reputation against those of other battalions in friendly rivalries, tend to get in less trouble with the local community and in fact tend to interact less altogether with the local community.[98] Demonstrating positive masculinities within peacekeeping units is a form of communication to the troops themselves and to the communities they function within, providing keen social and psycho-social markers on how men can behave in positive and valuable ways as they perform military functions.

TRAINING FOR PEACEKEEPERS

Most missions now require newly arriving peacekeepers to receive some gender-sensitivity training, ideally predeployment, as well as on site. The trainings, however, have been poorly prepared[99] and not always well received.[100] Nevertheless, providing trainings that address not only the particular vulnerabilities of women and girls in the post-conflict local population, but the attendant consequences to peacekeepers of exploiting those vulnerabilities, is crucial. Addressing such vulnerabilities without essentializing women in conflict zones as victims is a challenging task, but one that is absolutely necessary to avoid the probability that "gender sensitivity" merely reinforces peacekeeper assumptions about their role as saviors to victims in societies presumed "savage" or dysfunctional. Gender-sensitive training also requires paying attention to men and educating peacekeepers about the dangers of further compounding male vulnerabilities in post-conflict societies. This is equally fraught terrain, balancing the challenges of encouraging hypermascu-linities to reappear in varying forms in parallel with the tendency to infan-tilize and essentialize local men.

Problems Associated with Gender Trainings

Troops sent by contributing countries travel to the peacekeeping mission with all of the patriarchies seemingly inherent in military service intact. Superim-posed upon those notions are the cultural, linguistic, social, and legal differ-ences attendant to working in another country undergoing civil strife. The sending states are responsible for training their peacekeeping troops, and there is relatively little comparative data on the level of gender-sensitivity training they receive prior to deployment.[101] Once they arrive in-country, troops receive some additional training and, particularly in peacekeeping mis-sions with gender advisors, the quality of gender-sensitivity training included at that stage may be higher. When it exists, however, gender training will gen-erally be an add-on, and specifically focused on cultural interactions (between the host population and the peacekeepers), rather than being fundamentally integrated into the training process as a whole and conceived of as an integral and necessary component of peacebuilding.

There is little published material regarding what exactly goes into gender training that the peacekeepers receive in-country or predeployment. The DPKO generally addresses the challenges of training peacekeepers about gen-der issues with the following observation:

> Training on gender issues is difficult for a variety of reasons. By distinguishing between sex (the biological term) and gender (a social and cultural construct), gender training challenges traditional ways of thinking and uncovers common assumptions about women and men. Some personnel may find that discussing how culturally defined roles and responsibilities for women and men differ among regions and communities can be unsettling or even confrontational. It may provoke strong emotions by touching on deep-rooted, personal beliefs and family practices.[102]

The DPKO states that its "[b]asic training for peacekeeping personnel on gender issues generally consists of an awareness-raising course," which may be followed by more specific trainings on, for example, "combating trafficking in women and girls."[103] It is unclear whether the DPKO explicitly informs peacekeepers that other peacekeepers have been engaged in criminal activ-ities, which will not be tolerated and will lead to punishment, or just generi-cally raises awareness of the issues and leaves the conclusions to the particular incoming trainees. A large portion of the DPKO's gender training focuses on

HIV/AIDS, which indicates a certain passive-aggressive approach; peace-keepers are to be dissuaded from engaging in sexual activity with local women and girls not because it is inherently coercive and wrong per se, but because it may result in the acquisition of a sexually transmitted disease by the peacekeeper.

Prescriptions for Gender-Positive Peacekeeper Training

The presence of peacekeepers offers a multitude of possibility. Providing mas-culine role models and offering genuine opportunities for intracultural and social learning between peacekeepers and the local populations is a real prize in these contexts, one that has been systematically underappreciated. The value of these interactions can work both ways.

In order to capture the full positive potential of these interactions, peace-keepers must be effectively sensitized to the impact of their own gender roles with regard to the men and women of the host population they interact with. Gender training must be deemed as important to troops as knowledge of their weapons and vehicles. In order to avoid having gender training materials become just "another thing to put in your pocket,"[104] troops should be required to review the materials and undergo assessment based on what they learned when reading it in order to be permitted to begin their time in service. Peace-keepers should be regularly assessed on the material and taken out of active peacekeeping duty if they fail to pass the essential knowledge tests. If one goal of peacekeeping is to do more good than harm, then ascertaining a peace-keepers' knowledge of a code which expects him to respect the host country citizens is worth prioritizing—as worthy as punishing those same peace-keepers who violate it.

Most crucial is that there be "buy in" from the most senior among the peacekeepers, who then ensure the quality and regularity of the training and who are themselves held accountable for the misconduct of their subordi-nates. Superiors' benchmarks for success should rest in part on the ability of their subordinates to pass regular gender training assessments. Countries sending peacekeepers and the United Nations can begin enhancing their training programs to apprise peacekeepers predeparture of the issues likely to come up in service, including the need to respect and ensure women's rights and autonomy (including both women in unit and local women), so that they understand clearly how the stresses of the environment might affect them, as well as the punitive consequences of criminal behavior. To advance all of these goals, women must be hired as trainers and consulted on the content of the training. Men hired as trainers must be encouraged to view their role as pro-viding positive examples of masculine roles in the post-conflict environment, for both peacekeepers and the local population. Finally, benchmarks must be created to detail what outcomes are expected of gender training, to whom those benchmarks apply, and whether the outcomes have been achieved.

CODES OF CONDUCT

Most UN agencies have responded to a decade of horrific reports of abuse by internationals in the field by instituting their own field service Codes of Conduct. The Codes are an attempt to address the emergence of contemporary issues within a framework of developing new norms, given that existing norms generally found in national military codes and legislation fail to substantively address the peacekeeping context and the specific crimes that may emerge in post-conflict settings. While sexual abuse, crime, and exploitation continue, it is possible that Codes of Conduct will have some effect in addressing the attitudes and behaviors of soldiers mediating and supporting settlements to end hostilities between factions in post-conflict settings.[105]

While all UN personnel are subject to rules regulating their performance and actions, peacekeepers have their own Code of Conduct, known as Ten Rules.[106] These serve as a generic set of terms, more recently interpreted as holding peacekeepers to a "zero tolerance" standard. The Ten Rules state that peacekeepers are expected to conduct themselves in a disciplined manner at all times, to respect the environment of the host country, to respect and exercise awareness of local customs, to treat locals with respect, and to encourage proper conduct amongst their fellow peacekeepers. They are forbidden broadly to bring discredit to the United Nations, to "[c]ommit any act that could result in physical, sexual or psychological harm or suffering to members of the local population, especially woman and children," or to become involved in sexual relations which could impair their impartiality or the well-being of others.[107] The gaps between the rules allow for the existence of bona fide relationships between locals and peacekeepers.

The Ten Rules have no formal legal force, based on the sovereignty inherent in and maintained by the contributing country. The Rules leave it to the discretion of contributing countries to impose the sanctions for breach as they consider appropriate. Sanctions are based on the application of domestic military codes and regulations that are drawn in part from the legally binding Geneva Conventions and Additional Protocols.[108]

In response to particular allegations of peacekeeping abuses, some missions have instituted more specific codes of conduct, tailored to the circumstances of the mission. The mission to the DRC, for example, explicitly prohibited "sexual abuse and/or exploitation by all members of the civilian and military components" of MONUC.[109] It specifically defines sexual abuse in response to those particularized circumstances as any exchange of money, employment, goods, or services for sex, including sexual favors or other forms of humiliation, degrading, or exploitative behavior. It further forbids personnel from going to bars or nightclubs where "the services of prostitutes are available." Finally, and crucially, it spells out the legal consequences; violation of the rules results in summary dismissal. As often happens in peacekeeping contexts involving international organizations, goodwill is stymied by lack of implementation. Well into the year following the passage of the Code, it was still awaiting translation into French, in a predominantly French-speaking mission.[110] Within the two years following passage of the DRC-specific Code, hundreds of peacekeepers in the DRC were implicated in sex abuse, as described above.

Zero-tolerance policies, combined with clear and regular expectations issued by superior officers, can have a positive impact. For example, the Sexual Exploitation and Abuse (SEA) report from the UN Mission in Liberia (UNMIL) covering the period January to June 2008 identified only five allegations of sexual exploitation abuse being reported during the period. This is four less than the nine reported offenses against UNMIL personnel in the period from July to December 2007.[111]

Codes of Conduct must be written, tailored to local issues, and then observed and implemented.[112] Consistent with our emphasis on the importance of consultation throughout the post-conflict phase, local women need to be consulted and integrated into deciding what the "local" issues of priority should be. Prevailing masculinities of military culture, whereby superiors turn a blind eye to breaches that do not directly jeopardize the mission, or because they too breach the codes, must cease.[113] Breaches of these Codes of Conduct must then have real consequences. Breaches should result in both employment-related consequences (termination, repatriation, and blacklisting from future missions), as well as criminal consequences (dishonorable discharges and prosecution by contributing country) in order to have teeth. Other, more novel and extreme punishments should also be explored. For instance, UN staff violating prohibitions against sexual relations with the local population might be docked their subsistence allowance. The docked monies could be put into a fund to support the health of the women with whom they were involved and the children born of these liaisons who will be fatherless upon departure of the mission. Finally, a record of perpetrators of sexual abuse should be kept, and those on the list, as well as their superiors, should be barred from participating in future missions. Everyone up the command structure from a peacekeeper shown to have committed a crime should be barred from future missions. Peacekeepers must be required to report violative behavior of other unit members and held accountable for failing to report, as if they were accessories to the crime. Finally, Codes of Conduct should also be made widely available to the host country population.[114] Some missions have adopted hotlines for reporting by community members who have been violated, although these have been only minimally useful, most likely due to a combined lack of access to phones, intimidation at the thought of speaking with the offending organization, and lack of knowledge among locals about their rights.[115]

ADDED GENDER ROLES IN PEACEKEEPING

Although the DPKO has acknowledged multiple advantages to women's strong presence in peacekeeping missions, this articulation has not translated to greater numbers of women participating. From 2004 to 2007, women constituted less than 2 percent of personnel in military functions,[116] with that figure rising to 3.33 percent as of 2010.[117] Slightly more women were part of the civilian police component of peacekeeping missions,[118] the civilian international personnel,[119] and nationally recruited staff.[120] The Secretary-General has announced plans to increase that figure to 20 percent in police units and 10 percent in military units by 2014, but acknowledges that it will be impossible unless sending countries offer women troops.[121] The largest number of women (albeit still very few) is found in professional civilian positions within DPKO missions, and many of those positions are devoted to gender-advising roles. Furthermore, the more senior the position, the less likely a woman will be the post holder.[122]

Just as controversy surrounds the call for women to become part of domestic military structures, debate continues about women serving as peacekeepers, based on pacifist and anticolonial sentiments.[123] Nevertheless, studies have shown that the presence of women in military units is generally positive for women—both the women in the local community and the women in the military infrastructure.[124] In peacekeeping missions, the presence of women improves access and support for local women, makes male peacekeepers more reflective about their own roles, and broadens the skill sets and style of peace negotiation and conflict reduction practices.[125] The United Nations deployed its first all-female peacekeeping unit in Liberia in 2007 and expressed plans for another to Haiti.[126]

Of course, there is also evidence to suggest that at present life for women peacekeepers manifests many complexities and practical difficulties. Evidence of gender-based sexual harassment and tension alone would make service unpalatable to the very women whose presence might significantly alter the tenor and form of the peacekeeping experience. In part as a consequence of exclusionary and discriminatory practices, in most peacekeeping operations there are few, if any, women,[127] despite the UN-wide call for fifty-fifty gender balance across professional posts[128] and despite the DPKO goal of gender mainstreaming.[129] The low numbers of women can also be ascribed to the fact that the vast majority of peacekeeping personnel are supplied by sending countries which control the percentage of women based on their internal military rules regarding women in service.[130]

To ensure greater and varied representation of women in multiple institutional sites in post-conflict societies, increasing women's participation in the peacekeeping setting is vital. The UN High Commissioner for Human Rights, for example, argued that the success of the UN Observer Mission to South Africa (UNOMSA) was due in large part to the fact that it was led by international women and was gender balanced.[131] Further evidence more broadly suggests a correlation between missions deemed successful and the presence of women in that mission: the mission to Namibia had 60 percent women, South Africa 53 percent, and Guatemala 49 percent women.[132]

Increasing "gender" roles in peacekeeping missions, however, is not limited to increasing the number of women peacekeepers. It should also, as argued above, contemplate creating space for men to effectively engage as gender trainers, setting examples by offering expanded notions of "masculinity" to peacekeepers and the local population. Equally, it should also contemplate ways for peacekeepers to liaise with locals in gender-sensitive ways, and provide roles for local women in peacekeeper programming. In some missions, for example, the complaints of local women regarding peacekeeper behaviors are addressed by a "peacekeeper–local woman liaison."[133] The expanded roles for both men and women can serve to challenge the stereotype of male-only protectors and women solely as educators on gender issues or in need of protection.

Gender roles must be created for locals, as well as peacekeepers. Some members of the militaries sending peacekeepers understand that when women in the host country are marginalized, "the nation takes on the testosterone-laden culture of a military camp or a high-school boys' locker room."[134] To counteract this, internationals responsible for post-conflict reconstruction tasks associated with peacekeeping have been adding programs directly aimed at enhancing women's status. These include, for example, increasing education opportunities for girls, believing that girls who are educated and eventually able to join the labor force will have a strengthening effect on the society as a whole. Mine Action, for example, has prepared Gender Guidelines that delineate extremely specific tasks and programs designed to integrate women and gender awareness into all of its activities. Identifying cultural customs and societal expectations that prevent women's involvement in the work of demining, they recommend the following: using visual images of women carrying out mine action on the vacancy announcement; holding open days for women and families to see and check the location of the work; and employing staff closer to the area of operation so that women do not need to be away from family and households, thus increasing personal security and reducing the need of chaperones.[135] These specific actions are an excellent example of how organizations involved in peacekeeping work could first identify the benefits to women's participation in their work; second, identify the obstacles to increasing that participation; and third, seek solutions to overcome those obstacles. A parallel balancing act also requires identifying positive roles and opportunities for men to undertake. This is especially valuable as regards demilitarized combatants potentially unlocking the gendered paradigms that have perpetuated cycles of violence and contributed to cultures of violent masculinity in post-conflict societies. The paradox is that while internationals can recognize that the integration of women, even the focus on women, is essential for the development and stabilization of the host country, they still often fail to apply the same principles to their own organizational dynamic. Although the United Nations should be cautious about placing women in positions that would lead to dangerous interactions and would be otherwise ineffective,[136] it should not use that caution as an excuse to exclude women per se.

CONCLUSION

Peacekeeping remains a committed function of the United Nations and other regional organizations, and is likely to remain the response to stabilizing fragile and violent states by the international community, to a greater or lesser degree depending on political circumstances. As such, states and international institutions engaged in peacekeeping must devise their programs, in consultation with local women, and with an understanding of how gender impacts the success of those programs.[137]

Following are our recommendations:

1. A complete reworking of the notion of peacekeeping to include not only a set of military priorities but involves the maintenance of peace and security, and social and economic stabilization in a broad sense, vastly increasing the number of civilian peacekeepers with expertise to carry out these roles.
2. Integrating a gendered notion of security into peacekeeping, driven by meaningful consultation with local women.
3. Cross-jurisdictional gender training that is consistent among multinational troops and contributing states, and which is benchmarked for gender-positive results.
4. Making peacekeeping gender-friendly, specifically to augment women's participation by attending to rotation, staffing, and civilianizing of the operations.
5. Accountability for peacekeeping deficits, at the national level (enforcement at the hard end of the military justice system) as well as internationally, through the ICC.
6. Making the failure to meet gender-specific objectives result in a financial penalty for states (to be taken from the funds they receive for peacekeeping activities).
7. Revising the relevant laws of war to account for humanitarian law responsibilities for soldiers deployed in peacekeeping contexts.

8. Prioritizing the inclusion of local women equally with men into all program development discussions, as well as in all local hiring, and ensuring the possibility of implementing the gender parity by attending to the gendered dimensions of daily life (such as childcare), in creating those discussions and jobs.

UN agencies and other programs operating in the post-conflict peacekeeping environment are beginning to put forward positive suggestions for addressing gender constraints limiting women's employment within peacekeeping operations. These should be implemented and emulated.[138]

Programs can[139] and must be designed with conscious attention to the goals of bringing women into a range of peacekeeping activities, ensuring that no measures harm women due to failures to properly consult, and that those negative masculinities inherent in military-related activity are recognized and dismantled where possible. Where peacekeeping missions employ locals, those projects must specifically aim to hire women as well as men.

More women must be incorporated into peacekeeping missions, within both the civilian and military structures, both internationally and locally, to allow for greater flexibility in respectful interaction between internationals and host country populations. More men must be inserted into gender-training roles in order to counter gender stereotypes and to provide positive gender examples for peacekeepers and the local population. Gender reform that offers expanded roles for both men and women is essential to allow both host nations and troops to view positive masculine and militaristic behavior that demonstrates the capacity for kindness, social contribution, and egalitarian interaction with women.

The mission and goals of peacekeepers must be firmly understood as respecting, including, and being engaged in upholding the rights of women. The laudable goals of including women into all discussions, programming, and hiring—both local and international—must be suffused into all aspects of the work. Only by specifically establishing criteria to attract women to peacekeeping roles and by addressing their needs will women seek to be included in substantive ways allowing them to avail themselves of the opportunities that arise directly as a result of international presence.

CHAPTER 6

Disarmament, Demobilization, and Reintegration (DDR) Programs

Consider this: at one of the DRC's disarmament camps, an interviewee reported there was one woman who was placed "in the special women's quarters at our site. As she was there all by herself, we decided to put some disabled male combatants who had been injured by mines in her quarters . . . There was no need to adjust [the disarmament] activities to her specific needs."[1]

Contrary to the epigraph with which this chapter begins, there is a need for disarmament to move away from a focus on male combatants and to recognize that a gender focus requires paying attention to female issues. The disarmament, demobilization, and reintegration (DDR) of former combatants has become a critical element of most peace agreements and often predates formal pacts or treaties as part of the conditions to be met prior to entering formal negotiations.[2] DDR is that part of post-conflict security building and security-sector reform designed to stabilize fractured states by encouraging members of armed groups to give up their weapons and enabling former combatants to go home again.[3] And yet, as the introductory quotation illustrates, even when those who design DDR programs understand the need and benefit to include women in DDR, it is not immediately clear to those who implement such programs how best to translate existing guidance into practice.[4] A gender lens reveals how situations and constructs appear neutral, but in practice, the men are effectively overprivileged; the failure to effect equality between/among genders itself then constitutes a security problem.

This chapter examines a series of issues implicating disarmament, as well as gender relations and constructs. It begins with an overview of the basic forms of DDR programs before turning to a discussion of the potential power of integrating gender perspectives and practice into the DDR process. It then examines challenges to the development and implementation of DDR programs and the conceptual limitations of applying gender practice and theory in this fora. Finally, the conclusion suggests how to improve DDR and ensure the centrality of gender issues in development, implementation, and monitoring. DDR programs should be utilized as a tool that can effectively enable women to access economic, political, mental, and physical security in the postconflict environment.[5]

DDR PROGRAMS: WHAT HAPPENS?

DDR programs do not follow one template, but they are typically discussed during the early (preagreement) peace process and initiated after the framework peace agreement has been signed, as one of the first components of peace process implementation.[6] These discussions in the preagreement phase are typically dominated by elites and military actors and convened by intergovernmental delegations, mostly made up of men, rendering them distinctly masculine and unreceptive to gender-sensitive infiltration. The multilateral agencies funding these programs generally agree that DDR should only be undertaken with certain conditions guaranteed.[7] These conditions include a peace accord that establishes the framework for DDR, a general sense of confidence in the peace process itself, minimal levels of security, ownership of DDR by all relevant stakeholders, and basic guarantees of information and transparency.[8] Given the fractured nature, form, and implementation of peace agreements, however, these conditions are rarely met.[9] Successful DDR processes depend on broader developments toward a peaceful environment and are subject to frequent disruptions; they seldom proceed in such a linear fashion.[10]

Traditional DDR programs have conceived of combatants voluntarily entering reception centers to turn in arms, thereby beginning the demilitarization process.[11] They assume ideal—and rare—conditions, imagining DDR as a set of technical interventions to assure, for example, effective containment of armed groups, collection and destruction of weapons, division of former combatants into those who will remain in or join the country's armed forces and those to be demobilized, and then the effective reinsertion, reintegration, and rehabilitation of those demobilized into their communities of origin.[12] The calibration of emphasis among these three goals tends to vary significantly between sites, but demobilization and demilitarization are generally emphasized over rehabilitation. Expansive visions of DDR understand its utility in serving as a broader basis for post-conflict development and healing,[13] and explore its impact on the surrounding society.[14] It is within these broader visions that an understanding of the power of challenging gendered roles and constructs takes its place.

Where armed conflict has reigned, DDR is a central component of ensuring the conditions that enable grassroots security at the community level. But DDR also has top-down instrumental and policy goals. When undertaken early in the conflict-ending process, DDR functions as an important preliminary step in ending or limiting violent conflict and effectively facilitating control over armed forces, be they state or nonstate actors. Indeed, there is an important and increasingly acknowledged relationship between disarmament and security, when security is defined broadly to include the meaningful ability to live in one's community, free from harm and with equality of access to employment, schooling, and political and social voice.

THE POWER OF GENDER AND DDR

Gender perspectives, in particular examining the role of masculine conceptualizations and constructs, are important to the analysis of DDR programs and the development of new models for numerous reasons. First, as Chapter 2 shows, armed conflict affects women and men differently. These differences need to be taken into account throughout the processes of demobilization and demilitarization. Second, under many existing programs, women and men have unequal access to resources following conflict. This is compounded by the gender biases and inequalities inherent in most societies, and is heightened by a DDR focus on male combatants. Third, DDR is one component of security-sector reform, with a goal of achieving both short- and long-term peace. While "peace" remains elusive in most post-conflict arenas, failure to incorporate both genders into any security initiatives undermines the objective of achieving long-term peace.[15] Finally, to effectively dismantle individual and collective wartime behavioral patterns and mentalities requires focusing specifically on men and issues of masculinity.[16] While DDR programs already evidence some gender consciousness, this operates within the context of reforming or remaking masculine structures. We recognize of course that for DDR interventions to succeed, they must be designed in the context of each country's special circumstances, but maintaining general consciousness of gender effect is critical from the inception of any initiative.

Correspondingly, DDR has the potential to enable women to undo the dominant conflict script of their victimhood, making possible articulations of accountability for sexual harms and enabling women's access to economic distribution and political representation. DDR also ideally recognizes the multiple roles that women play during the conflict, as combatants, those otherwise associated with armed forces (WAAFs), such as cooks and sex workers, dependents—and victims. Even when women do not actually bear arms, the failure to consider them as combatants can be seen as an attempt, with both positive and negative possibilities, to depoliticize their role.[17] And, as this section also discusses, DDR provides an opportunity to diagnose and address the issues of masculinity that are often intertwined with the military presence.

The power of DDR programs generally rests with the incentives provided to recipients to hand in their weapons. As discussed above, the requirement to disarm combatants frequently constitutes a core element of transitional processes.[18] In practice, much less emphasis has been placed on the reintegration element of the DDR mantra, and funds from donors have flowed accordingly. There is a growing recognition, however, that this focus is underinclusive. Instead, recognition that just as war has effects beyond the engaged combatants, DDR processes benefit from acknowledging that dependents and others who may not have been directly involved in the fighting are nevertheless impacted by it.[19] Reintegration in Afghanistan, for example, has helped wives and family members of former combatants by funding literacy programs and vocational training projects, as well as deworming for children.[20] Here, the mandates of DDR programs are beginning to apply a much wider mandate in who might be covered by and included by programs and support.

If the purpose of DDR is to encourage those engaged in violent conflict to return home and be peaceful, then those incentives ought to be offered to a wider group who provided material and direct support to the militants. Notably, of course, the emphasis on those engaged in active and narrowly defined combat has excluded women and girls who historically have been involved voluntarily or forcibly as camp followers, cooks, home keepers, and sexual slaves. And, if the purpose of DDR is in part to provide psycho-social support to all those damaged by communal violence who would be unable to return to their villages and effectively and peaceably integrate with their families, then those services should also be offered to this wider group who supported the militants.[21] Indeed, as discussed in Chapter 7, because Article 7 of the Statute of the International Criminal Court defines crimes against humanity to include "enslavement," "sexual slavery," "enforced prostitution," and "any other form of sexual violence of comparable gravity," the wider role of women and girls in the operation of militias and militaries is under greater scrutiny internationally. The International Criminal Court has now begun to prosecute persons for the crime of sexual slavery.[22] Increased legal accountability for such crimes provides a stark contrast to the lack of recognition given to the victims when women have not been deemed eligible for rehabilitative DDR benefits.[23]

There has been some general recognition, too, that "gender consciousness" must be integrated into DDR programs. But the gap between rhetoric and reality in mainstreaming gender into DDR practice remains vast. Parallel to the lacunae in outcomes for gender mainstreaming is the danger that feminist goals lose their substantive content in the conversion of transformative outcomes to bureaucratic goals. This pattern has been well documented in the development context and is a potential hazard in the DDR context.[24]

Moreover, while acting instrumentally to facilitate control over armed forces (both state and nonstate), less obviously, DDR can create extraordinary vulnerabilities in societies where guns are "both a threat *and* a source of security."[25] Recognizing that communities may find it difficult to reintegrate former combatants, that civilians may be resentful of special programs that benefit those combatants, and that women may be expected to provide care for injured and disabled ex-soldiers can help in ensuring that DDR programs are effective.[26] An inevitable hazard created by demobilization, demilitarization, and reintegration of former combatants in a gender-sensitive manner is the challenge it poses to the production, control, and maintenance of masculinities in conflicted and post-conflict societies.

As Chapter 2 shows, the military is closely tied with manhood, and, indeed, militaristic actions are supported by an ideology of male toughness.[27] By the time combatants enter the DDR process, they are deeply enmeshed in this cultural vision of manhood. This specific site of male status allows men to have access to economic opportunities in societies that have few such opportunities for men. It also includes access to female sexuality as a reward for their perceived social and military status, and a set of privileges that confirm and support a particular form of hypermasculinity. When these practices of masculinity become embedded in social and economic pathways for a society, undoing them is an arduous task. As a result DDR programs struggle with what to do with the "morass of malignant male muscle . . . Men unable to positively manifest masculine roles may return to violent and destructive means of expressing their identities."[28]

Masculinities appear in several different ways throughout the DDR process. First, socialization into male roles, as both a traditional head of household and then, as a result of the conflict, into the assumption of violent roles, may be difficult to undo. Thus, a highly complex issue that arises in the context of identifying and managing the forms and facilitators of violence in many transitional societies is the relationship between disarmament and intimate violence. Second, men and boys may also have been victimized throughout the conflict, possibly by abduction, indoctrination, and sexual violence. Disarmament, demobilization, and reintegration planning need to develop special counseling and training programs addressing the complexity of men's roles post-conflict.[29] As we have discussed in Chapter 2, this requires acknowledgment of and response to men's particular vulnerabilities as exposed or created by violent conflict.

Using a gender perspective that analyzes the impact of social constructions of the masculine and feminine, a number of issues emerge concerning the fundamental purposes of DDR programs. First, what constitutes disarmament sufficient to satisfy a ceasefire requirement in the politico-military sense may not in fact entail the removal of all such weapons from the public, nor, and more importantly for women, from the private sphere.[30] An obvious linking issue, then, is how to measure the success or failure of demobilization from a gender perspective. The international community and donor agencies are understandably interested in developing benchmarks to determine whether DDR programs are successful. But successful toward what end? We argue that any benchmarks must hold DDR programs accountable to meeting the real needs of both men and women. This benchmarking for success through a gender-sensitive lens is markedly absent through many of the programs that are heralded as success stories by the international community.[31] Second, demobilization generally fails to address the deep imprinting of violent masculinities in former combatants and the effects of a militaristic culture on the civilians that surround them in the transitional and post-conflict context.[32] We find that the underlying psycho-social dimensions, which in a conflicted society have supported the resort to violence and the elevation of particular forms of masculinity that accompany it, are not in any sense deconstructed or addressed by the formal demobilization process. Thus, a key issue to be addressed concerning violence is what is meant by the term "ending violence"? In the parlance of ending public violence or internal conflict, this conversation revolves around decommissioning weapons and getting armed insurgents to swap violent confrontation for peaceful debate about contested issues. However, this kind of discussion rarely engages with the fundamental requirement of changing deep-seated social attitudes toward the use of violence.[33] Where discharged-but-not-disarmed combatants return to their homes and families with their weapons, the sites of violence may simply move from the public to the private sphere.[34] These framing issues provide the context for exploring the flaws in implementing DDR programs so that they affect gender equality rather than reflect the privileging of masculinization. Reflection allows for the capacity to construct programs which better focus on how disarmament and demobilization could truly result in demilitarization of minds, communities, and culture.

DECONSTRUCTING DDR PROGRAMS

On the most basic level, DDR programs have been flawed by narrow approaches to the process of demilitarization, including the definition and eligibility of the groups targeted for services, the types of services offered, and the parameters of the reintegration process. The programs are focused on the demobilization of weapons, not minds, and do not address the modalities and socio-psychological pathways that have created, and then continue to perpetuate, violence. Instead, DDR programs are typically evaluated based upon the numbers of combatants demilitarized or the number of weapons collected,[35] rather than broader measures of the levels of violence or the numbers resettled.

While women play a variety of roles in the armed forces, they often play a combat support role and have no weapons to turn in. Consequently, they are often overlooked and unable to benefit from resettlement allowances or training programs conditioned upon turning in a weapon.[36] The percentage of participants in the DDR process who are women and girls is dramatically lower than the estimates of how many are actually drawn into the armed forces; for example, while female combatants constituted approximately 12 percent of all combatants in Sierra Leone, only 8 percent of those who participated in the DDR process were female.[37] In Liberia, while women and children constituted 38 percent of the armed groups, only 17 percent of those who participated in the DDR program were women, girls, and boys.[38]

Women may not participate in DDR for numerous reasons. First, if they served in noncombatant roles, they may be formally excluded from the terms of the program,[39] particularly if the program is centered in a "cash for weapons" plan.[40] In the Congo, for example, one of the four criteria for DDR eligibility includes "possession of a weapon."[41] Even if they were combatants, women may find it difficult to prove their status, and deeply entrenched social understandings of a woman's role may make the task doubly difficult.[42] For example, while the Burundian government allowed women to participate in DDR, it excluded pregnant women.[43]

Second, although women may have stepped out of constricting gender roles during conflict, once hostilities end, they may feel pressure (internal and external) to return to their more traditional roles in the household, and so may simply melt away from their armed groups. This is a broader phenomenon we describe throughout this book of the transitional moment sometimes contracting political and social space for women rather than expanding it. So, while conflict sometimes results in the expansion of women's roles (into the military or the labor workforce, for example), post-conflict transition can result in the constriction of women's roles and the stigmatization of women associated in any way with the armed forces, unless there is explicit attention to managing those perceptions. Moreover, if women were forced into combat, then they may want to escape its strictures as soon as possible, understanding that substantial social stigma may attach to these roles and thereby bypassing even monetary incentives.[44] Finally, they may simply fear further personal violence in the DDR process, particularly if they were involuntary members of the armed group and are placed in close proximity to other group members.[45]

Through DDR programs, ex-combatants may receive significant amounts of cash, particularly when one considers the per capita income of the targeted nation. In Sierra Leone, for example, where the per capita annual income is less than $200, ex-combatants were paid $300,[46] as was the case in Liberia.[47] In the Democratic Republic of the Congo (DRC), the total amount of the Transitional Subsistence Allowance, given in three apportionments, was approximately $350.[48] Although the Afghanistan program began by giving former combatants $200, the money was later integrated into other reintegration support as evidence emerged that some commanders used violence to extort the money from their subordinates.[49]

This focus on giving male combatants money is integrally linked to the broader themes explored in this book—women's exclusion from social capital and their lack of legal status. Indeed, Chapter 8 shows a comparable problem with reparations. Studies have repeatedly shown that men and women spend money differently, and in ways that matter to social and communal well-being. Studies in Angola chart the alcohol and drug binging impact of disbursing de-mobilization monies to men in a DDR program. The program failed to anticipate the likely spending patterns that would follow and the immensely negative effects on the discharged combatants, as well as the communities who absorbed them.[50] Infusing this kind of money into communities without adequate planning can engender a significant number of social problems, compounding rather than loosening the hypermasculinities of the conflict period, and failing to grasp a significant opportunity to genuinely integrate men back into the families and communities in positive and enriching ways for all.

There are many ways to improve the basis of traditional DDR programs. One fundamental weakness involves giving monetary incentives to combatants as individuals rather than to their families[51] and communities.[52] Second, as discussed above, in focusing on combatants with weapons, as opposed to those playing a combat support role, the programs essentially operate in an exclusionary manner compounding gender stereotypes and entrenching those assumptions into the post-conflict legal and political order. A third weakness is the tendency of DDR programs to emphasize economic reintegration, rather than psychological and social rehabilitation.[53] Reform of DDR programs has included a focus on providing food, allowances, and skills training, which are valuable additions, but they generally continue to overlook the need for assistance with post-traumatic stress, domestic violence, and other psychological ailments that arise from war.[54] This parallels a phenomena we have identified in other areas such as security sector reform where the reformist response to post-conflict challenges still fails to be fundamentally transformative to the gendered dimensions of the conflict. Challenging these underlying premises shows the tremendous scope for such programs to support the emergence of positive masculinities in the post-conflict terrain. Transformative programs can encourage men and women to play a wide and diverse range of roles, undoing not only conflict harms but making inroads on broader gender exclusions and stigmas in the process.

RECONSTRUCTING DDR PROGRAMS

There exists a tension in DDR programs between security issues—disarming combatants—and humanitarian concerns—disarming and rehabilitating society.[55] Best practices for DDR programs recommend that they move beyond simply taking away guns and include changes in social roles, in particular, directly involving women in the process.[56] UN Security Council Resolution 1325 specifically "[e]ncourages all those involved in the planning for disarmament, demobilization and reintegration to consider the different needs of female and male ex-combatants and to take into account the needs of their dependents."[57] As we have discussed in the Introduction to this book, the snowball effect of Resolution 1325 has prompted significant change at the United Nations, including the establishment of a Task Force on Women, Peace, and Security and further Security Council Resolutions concerned with conflict, gender, and sexual violence. While the jury is still out on the overall effects of Resolution 1325, and there is some evidence to suggest that its effects have not been as robust as had been predicted, there is still long-term potential that these structural provisions may have positive effects on the approach to DDR.[58]

Incorporation is not, of course, enough. Gender-sensitive theory and practice, taking account of both the needs and vulnerabilities of men and women, must be *central* to the DDR process, from initial planning stages through final evaluations, as lessons from the field clearly demonstrate. That means equity of treatment for men and women, recognizing the inherently stratified gender structures of DDR programs regardless of whether "women's issues" are formally considered. To date, the United Nations as the key actor in the disarmament process still largely views gender as a matter of specialized focus, as "an issue requiring special attention" rather than being made foundational and definitional to state or institutional processes involved with DDR.[59] The limitations of the gender mainstreaming agenda in the DDR context are instructive. While gender mainstreaming has opened up some opportunities in some specific post-conflict settings, it suffers from the general weaknesses of a lack of commitment by senior managers, poor resourcing, lack of expertise, marginalization within the implementing institution, and a failure to translate its content into action.[60]

In some literature, there is a positive emphasis and recognition of the role of female soldiers and the female dependents of male combatants.[61] Moreover, much has happened at the United Nations since Beijing and the Security Council's adoption of Resolution 1325. Different UN agencies have made varying amounts of progress in their funding priorities and policy implementation. The DPKO now has a Gender Advisory Team at its headquarters and is giving advice in the field. The Team has developed guidance materials and is advising all mission components on implementation. Other programs, including Mine Action, which has historically been dominated by men, now include women and girls as beneficiaries as well as practitioners. Gender balance in staffing has also improved substantially. Such progress should be lauded, but we stress that consistency in gender-sensitive consultation, planning, policymaking, and implementation is patchy and despite the best intentions of some committed policymakers and states, mainstreaming remains limited in its effects when translated to the sites of post-conflict operation. At the heart of this problem for DDR is a lack of gender centrality in this policy context.

To make real and sustained progress, we suggest the following. First, gender centrality must pervade all aspects of planning and implementation, beginning with the process of negotiating the peace process and agreement. Second, gender consciousness does not require gender neutrality; it requires awareness of how both men and women may be differentially impacted by programmatic choices. This means, for example, that DDR programs and policies must work harder to unravel the masculinities produced by or complicated during war, just as they must fully incorporate women and families into the reintegration components of DDR. DDR programs have a unique capacity to address the hypermasculinity that frequently accompanies violent hostilities between groups. An approach that centralizes gender necessitates a focus on addressing those masculinities during DDR processes and making a priority of advancing positive models of masculinity. Finally, indicators of success must include the program's responsiveness to both men and women, individuals, and communities, rather than merely counting weapons.

Gender Centrality in Planning and Implementation

The processes involved in establishing and operating DDR programs must be gender-aware. This means thinking through the various stages that lead to the end of hostilities and ultimately produce formal agreement(s) to end violence. Ensuring that the prenegotiation phase and formal negotiations are gender conscious provides an important (but not sufficient) basis for DDR gender sensitivity. As we have noted in our Introduction, preliminary arrangements concerning DDR are often central to precursor agreements, and this is the phase in which women are least likely to be included for a number of structural reasons. To make DDR programs work for women, increased cooperation in the planning process is required among governments, nongovernmental organizations (NGOs), and civil society institutions that are engaged in security and development. Planning should ensure the inclusion of both genders by, for example, evaluating early on the differing needs of males and females associated with armed groups.[62]

While including women in peace negotiations is not necessarily related to ensuring women's participation in DDR, being structurally and procedurally gender-sensitive at this point provides the foundation for recognition of gendered needs throughout the process.[63] Indeed, women who participate in peace negotiations frequently suggest different priorities and bring alternative perspectives on the conflict into the room.[64] As discussed in Chapter 2, we cannot essentialize women as peacemakers and assume that their presence will make a difference for women. Women have played pivotal roles in maintaining violent systems, nationalist movements, and divisions. Nonetheless, women's voices can have a positive and different impact when they are based on women's experiences during wartime and expectations of what will happen when they return home. Indeed, increased coordination and support of local women's organizations that focus on disarmament and peace could effectively address gender issues that might otherwise be neglected.[65] Moreover, providing a place at the peace table for women soldiers and women who served in noncombatant roles may ensure the inclusion of their specific concerns.[66] For example, the inclusion of women's groups in Liberia was critical to encouraging women and girl soldiers to agree to undergo DDR. While initial estimates were that only 2,000 women would participate, women's groups organized themselves as the "Concerned Women of Liberia," and worked with DDR administrators to develop an awareness campaign; almost 25,000 women and girls were disarmed and demobilized.[67] The example illustrates how women can serve as positive role models and as representatives for the voices of their all-too-often silent sisters.

General Programmatic Issues

Various reforms can be implemented throughout the DDR process to improve its responsiveness to the gendered dimensions of conflict and combatants.[68] These reforms must also be connected to other aspects of the society's post-conflict transformation; changing the DDR processes, priorities, and procedures alone does not guarantee nondiscrimination or socioeconomic rights, and all these elements must be integrated with other gender-centrality programs. Basic recommendations include independent assessments of the DDR process with a mandated gender analysis; expanding the definition of those eligible for DDR to include those who were members of the armed forces in a variety of roles; making payments available to families of combatants and their communities, rather than to individuals; increased collaboration with youth groups and networks in order to facilitate community acceptance of stigmatized victims; and a greater focus on psychological and social recovery.[69]

The rhetoric of DDR programs concerning gender inclusion has certainly improved; however, problems with applying gender equality in programming remain. One background concern is that an emphasis on gender is often equated with highlighting gender-based violence in general and rape in particular. Such emphasis often ignores the social and structural contexts, specifically a lack of equality in the contexts from which violence occurs. On the more general concerns with equality, examples abound. For example, while the Multi-Country Demobilization and Reintegration Program (MDRP)[70] for the Great Lakes Region requires among other gender-specific requirements that benefits for male and female combatants at demobilization centers be equal,[71] a strict adherence to the rhetoric could be counterproductive. If, for example, with respect to special reintegration kits,[72] the practice meant that where men receive condoms, women would receive female condoms,[73] or both men and women would receive sanitary supplies. Such a focus on providing "equal benefits" overlooks real gendered needs.[74] Similarly, a decision to provide childcare at camps technically provides equal benefits to both fathers and mothers, but as women are typically the primary caretakers, the childcare is more likely to help them. Our position requires importing a genuine and situated understanding of difference into the provision for equality, in a way that reflects biological, social, and material needs.

Equality necessitates accounting for the different needs that men and women face, rather than merely requiring equal provisions. Unless gender is central to conceptualization, planning, and implementation, equity is a redundant concept. In recognition that male combatants typically have dependents—and that women are more likely to spend money on the family than on themselves—some portion of the DDR cash benefits should be paid directly to wives or families.[75] To ensure transparency and accountability, DDR administrators might involve female family members—wives, mothers, adult daughters—in the disbursement process and in any budgeting training and discussions.[76] To ensure that this does not foster violence by the ex-combatant, it should ideally be explained as standard operating procedure by the relevant intervenor, obviating the view that it constitutes a selective process targeted at particular men. One potential structural benefit of this approach is that by augmenting women's access to resources and by giving them access and control, one starts to subtly (and slowly) change societal judgments concerning women's worth, producing a potentially more radical and transformative change over time.

SPECIAL ACCOMMODATIONS FOR WOMEN AND GIRLS

In light of their roles before and during the conflict, women and men may have different psychological, economic, and developmental needs. The vulnerabilities that women have experienced during war are perceived to fall within the private domain in many legal and social systems, leaving them beyond the circle of notice and accountability. These vulnerabilities often include the psychological consequences that follow from physical insecurity and sexual violence, as well as the internal and external consequences of, at least temporarily, acting outside of gendered role expectations. Women who have participated in the armed forces, paramilitary groups, and insurgent forces may be stigmatized not just because, like men, they have been involved in the conflict, but also because they have failed to conform to gender-role expectations.[77] DDR programs could be designed with gender centrality by actively seeking to prevent the application of gender stereotyping in skill and job trainings, or ensuring adequate health facilities (including separate bathrooms and maternity clinics) for female participants. If and when money is distributed, programs should determine whether women have access to banks or credit institutions to ensure the safety of their funds, and if necessary premising the availability of funds generally on the necessary legal changes to allow women to access such payments.[78]

Women may need special counseling if they have been victims of gender-based violence. Reintegration camps must be safe so that women are not threatened by sexual violence during the DDR process, and security issues will differ for men and women, boys and girls. If women are responsible for cooking, cleaning, or childcare, then they must be able to collect fuel safely, to gather water and wash clothes in a protected place, and to place their children in a facility with which they feel comfortable.[79] Security must also include attention to private and intimate violence in such spaces, so that not only is externally perceived harm being attended to but also the ever-present threat of partner and proximity violence for women.

While all DDR program staff need training on gender sensitivity, given our emphasis on representation it is important to ensure that the staff is gender-integrated. Gender-balanced representation will assist women in feeling more comfortable, particularly when it comes to health care and related issues.[80] Greater female representation may also transform incrementally how men in the process of being decommissioned from military and paramilitary organizations address and respond to women in authority.

While the gendered DDR toolkit may be perceived as having a Western bias and may therefore be received as partial or imperialist, the post-conflict moment is, nonetheless, an opportunity to improve women's lives. The more complex question here is the interplay of the intervenor with local cultural norms. A critical and complex question is whether the DDR facilitator "encourages" women to maintain the independence and autonomy that conflict-related roles may have generated without fully understanding the costs or the compromises women make. Equally complex is the lack of substantive support offered to autonomous role assertion by local women in post-conflict sites as intervenors bring their own patriarchal bias with them and operate their mandate as facilitating a return to "normality," including more traditional roles for women.[81]

Reintegration of Female Combatants

As we have discussed in Chapter 2, women combatants occupy a complex role in conflicted and transitioning societies. This social and cultural complexity may explain in part the difficulties with recruiting women to participate in

DDR programs. These difficulties range from the stigma attached to being a member of the armed forces to requirements that weapons be exchanged for entry. Thus it is clear that programs must develop strategies to ensure women's inclusion in all aspects of the process. Recruitment outreach[82] could be done through health centers and maternity clinics, particularly because women's literacy rates may prevent them from accessing written information. We accept a role for specific quotas[83] to ensure that women are included as eligible combatants. When it comes to reintegration, programs must be sensitive to cultural dynamics concerning women's roles, while nonetheless supporting women. Programs must also be inventive in reaching out to women who have "melted away" after combat to avoid the consequences of being identified publicly as combatants. For example, rather than providing credit only to men, who may be listed as property owners, women need access to credit as well. Equally, rather than simply providing training on how to care for traumatized children based on the assumption that women will be the primary caretakers, providing women with educational and market-based opportunities to further their own skills and livelihoods is an important transformative capacity for DDR programs.[84]

ATTENTION TO MASCULINITIES

One of the central quandaries for the DDR process is how to undo the masculinities learned, heightened, or intensified during wartime. We have addressed the general intersection of masculinities with the post-conflict setting in Chapter 2 but now turn to reflect on its particular challenges in the context of DDR. Where discharged combatants return to their homes and families, the sites of violence may simply move from the public to the private sphere. From the gendered critique of accountability mechanisms, what we learn is that truth processes may examine the prior violence in the public sphere but will not engage in any way with the continual violence that is facilitated in the private sphere by non-rehabilitated former combatants. This disconnect between the operation and scope of core transitional justice mechanisms and the intimate and everyday realities of living with a former combatant for women could hardly be more starkly contrasted. This gap of understanding has been graphically identified in such transitional societies as South Africa.[85] Here the perceived escalation of domestic violence rates postapartheid have raised deep concerns about the relationship between preexisting apartheid violence and its spill-over to a transitional society. The complex dynamics of violence continuums between conflicted and post-conflict societies remain understudied, and a dearth of empirical data is evident. Nonetheless, we are conscious of a broader phenomenon well identified by scholars and activists in which the reassertion of violence in the private sphere during the transitional phase may constitute a form of compensation for male combatants, for their loss of public status and hegemony.[86] This is graphically shown by the psychological phenomena of the returning warrior who has, through conflict, normalized the use of violence and views the home as another site in which to exercise power and control through physical force on his partner and his children.[87] We also acknowledge that women combatants may also return to the home front deeply damaged by the experiences of conflict and that the intergenerational transmission of violent norms and social dysfunction may be part of their reality and legacy.

Given the complexity of the masculinity terrain in post-conflict societies, it is important to recognize that in seeking to equalize the terrain of DDR itself, it may follow that men may perceive themselves to lose out in their only route to material gain in a post-conflict society. We have previously asked what it "means to be a man" in a violent society, and this challenge is also directly faced in the DDR context. Undoing the discriminations and exclusions inherent in DDR programs should ideally occur in a context of broader social and equality-driven transformations. In reality, this is rarely the case, and we recognize the difficulties of DDR alone engineering broader changes in gender status, stratification, and value in any society.

Thus, the link between formal (generally equality) gains made by women in many post-conflict legislative and constitutional enactments, conjoined with the political displacement of power for many men from the traditional routes provided during armed conflict, creates a complex social and legal terrain. It is upon this territory that women's gains and their intersection with masculinities in flux are played out. Formal gains for women may, in fact, be nullified or significantly constrained by the reality of social and community context, in which the accommodation of men's deeply entrenched social status may outweigh the enforcement of formal legal norms in practice.[88] Moreover, the social realities that women confront in highly patriarchal societies are propped up and perpetuated by masculinities in action—limiting in subtle and crosscutting ways the reach of law.

DDR programs can help to separate manhood from its violent and military meaning by providing positive, nonviolent role models and means for achieving status. Former combatants in Colombia expressed being "tired" of combat, and observers suggest that "DDR [could] make more explicit what these men gain in the transition from combatant to civilian."[89] In the Congo, for example, the DDR program is collecting information on how programs that involve men can dissolve gender stereotypes.[90] Offering vocational education and creating employment opportunities in both the public and private sectors can serve to channel aggressive energy into more productive uses.[91] It is also evident that the integration of men more positively into their family and parenting responsibilities offers some means to redress the complex roles that men must manage in the post-conflict context. Here, relatively simple moves, such as ensuring that families and children are integrated into the DDR process, can operate as positive transitionary measures to support both men and women and open up spaces for social transformation. Another important and related move is to extend and broaden the categories of combatants for the purposes of DDR programs, ensuring that women who have provided support roles to military or paramilitary forces (as well as women who have been involved in direct hostilities) are included and fully integrated into DDR programs.[92] This would assist both in ensuring that women combatants are not doubly marginalized by their involvement in military and paramilitary organizations, and that the opportunity is provided to affirm the status of women combatants (who frequently languish and suffer the post-conflict stigma of nonconforming gender roles as society returns to "normal"). It would further include women fully in the benefits that flow materially and otherwise from demilitarization.

Resocializing men requires integrating the information known about the effects of hypermasculinity into the planning and delivery of internationally constructed and supported DDR programs. It means moving the emphasis away from merely handing over guns to neutral arbitrators and instead integrating psychological and reflective counseling into the demilitarization of combatants. It requires a commitment to gender integration for DDR programs, literally bringing the wives, partners, and children of combatants where possible into the demobilization space. These approaches utilize the social connectedness of men to their families and children to affirm individual and group capacity for a different and positive masculinity. It mandates modeling for such men—bringing into the demilitarization space men who have the capacity to act as accepted role models, and who offer a different life perspective, functioning in a post-conflict and perhaps still violent society. Ultimately, and far more difficult, it requires providing other economic and social opportunities for men to express masculinities in ways that are not socially and politically destructive. As a result, there is a significant overlap between the reconstruction of violent masculinities in post-conflict societies with the provision of meaningful economic opportunities for men (and women).

Attention to Male Victimization

It is also important to acknowledge that men and boys may also have been victimized throughout the conflict, possibly by abduction, possibly by sexual violence, as well as the violent ritualization that frequently accompanies male initiation into predominantly male military fraternities. As is generally noted in the context of sexual violence experienced by women, underreporting is rife in this regard. We do not have a deep understanding of the form, dynamics, and scale of sexual violence that men experience in times of conflict. There is some nascent literature that suggests a link between sexual violence of men by men and deeply rooted practices of feminization.[93] In this telling, sexual violence experienced by men is a direct playing out of wider social (and violent) practices that are generally directed toward women. For many men who experience rape, the result is to undermine their own masculinity in fundamental ways and put in doubt their sexual identity. Moreover, this literature also links to a greater appreciation for men's vulnerabilities in situations of conflict and the utilization of sexual methods and means of warfare. Sexual violence experienced by men is, we know, significantly underreported, although empirical proof other than anecdotal evidence is difficult to establish. The statistics of the Peruvian Truth and Reconciliation Commission (TRC) suggest that men may underreport (even as the statistics illustrate that women are the most prevalent victims of sexual violence). Of the 538 cases of sexual violence reported to the TRC, 527 correspond to women and only 11 were attributed to male victims.[94]

Equally evident in this context are the unique vulnerabilities of young men and male children who have been conscripted into militias, insurgent groups, or paramilitary forces. As the initial indictments from the International Criminal Court illustrate in relation to the harms visited upon child soldiers, acts of sexual violation were intentional and systematic, clearly intended to break bonds between children and their families or communities of origin and force relationships of dependency and shame into the paramilitary organizations.[95] These practices are also intimately connected to the perpetuation of intergenerational violence and the escalation of criminality and social dysfunction in post-conflict sites. All of these multiple contexts of male victimization (made more complex by the victims' parallel roles as perpetrators) require melding into the programmatic structure of DDR programs. In particular, DDR programs need to develop special counseling and training programs addressing the harms experienced directly and more broadly, forcing difficult conversations about men's roles post-conflict.[96]

Male victims may feel caught between the hypermasculinization of war and their own feelings of vulnerability and stigma.[97] Recognizing that gender-based issues are not merely instrumental goals for the benefit of women can help in developing programs to aid this population. These programs might include specially trained counselors, targeted educational opportunities for boy soldiers, and specific health care measures. Like others undergoing the DDR process, they too will benefit from forms of economic empowerment that may help them resolve their feelings of victimization. Ultimately, the result may be the construction of societies in which cycles of violence can be ended and new pathways molded to advance nonviolent contestation.

Ensuring that DDR programs meet these goals requires mandatory commitments to gender centrality in the body of peace agreements. They require agreed upon formulas to advance such agreements, as well as a recognition that DDR is only one component of larger peace and security efforts.[98]

Integrating DDR with Accountability

If DDR programs are to contribute to long-term peace and stability, they must take a holistic approach that is integrated into the larger post-conflict reconstruction process. Critically, DDR programs must integrate a justice component.[99] Without doing so, meaningful societal transformation is unlikely.[100] The relationship of disarmament to accountability for human rights violations is complex, not least because in some contexts successful disarmament may be premised on political compromises that exclude or deny the possibility of accountability. If we accept that a link exists between past accountability and meaningful reform, as well as on the capacity to deliver and make DDR successful, then the nexus between these issues is further highlighted. The compromises made during peace negotiations, mostly made by influential locals supported by internationals, often fail to engage with the particular vulnerabilities created for women by partial or excluded accountability. These vulnerabilities are critical to the creation (or lack) of real security for women.

For example, if individuals who are perceived as having committed egregious human rights violations or war crimes are rewarded with money and skills, tensions will naturally develop between them and noncombatants who do not receive such assistance and who do not see human rights abuses being punished.[101] They will return to their homes, safe in their impunity. This section considers four methods of reconceptualizing DDR to include accountability. Not surprisingly, each method has benefits and drawbacks.

The first method favors equality over stability. The International Peace Academy (IPA) suggests, for example, "[o]ffering reintegration benefits directly to the communities in which ex-combatants (as well as other displaced populations) are to be reintegrated" rather than to the ex-combatants themselves.[102] On the positive side, this serves to mitigate tensions that may have developed between ex-combatants and noncombatants. It also serves to tie ex-combatants into their community and may allow them to be seen as providing benefits and compensation to the community for previous human rights and humanitarian law violations. On the negative side, as the IPA concedes, "since idle ex-combatants pose a serious threat to peace and security, they must indeed receive special attention."[103]

A second method is a hard and fast rule of denying reintegration benefits to anyone who has committed serious and systematic human rights or humanitarian law violations.[104] Positively, this serves the dual purpose of signaling to community members that violations will not be rewarded. It may also have the side effect of increasing funding in certain circumstances, as international donors are increasingly likely to fund projects incorporating human rights and, increasingly, those that address gender-based sexual violence.[105] Such an approach does have associated limitations. Foremost, the scale of human rights violations in many of these conflicts is so widespread that to enforce such a norm may be unrealistic and counterproductive. Indeed, adherence to such a norm would mean there might be very few to reintegrate. One possibility would provide for partial benefits to be paid, but placing the remainder into a fund for victims. Such an approach could be tied to lustration (discussed in Chapter 9), which sets out a range of disqualifications for persons who have committed serious human rights violations from holding public office or public service positions. The enforcement of lustration has been broadly limited to Eastern European states, and its successful export to other sites is an uncertain journey given the specificity of the tool and its limited institutional application to date.

A third approach would be to screen all ex-combatants for human rights and humanitarian law abuses yet only deny reintegration benefits to those responsible for committing truly egregious violations unlikely to be prosecuted by the International Criminal Court (ICC) or local criminal process.[106] Positively, such an approach is a realistic modification of the previous approach and strikes a balance between community concerns and disarmament requirements. In practice it is the contemporary approach of the United Nations and other states supporting peace agreements forward.[107] Several drawbacks are associated with this method. First, such an approach is difficult to implement and may be beyond the means of many fractured and fragile nations emerging from decades of conflict.[108] Problems are also associated with implementation of the screening process. Challenges range from ensuring that the vetting is done as neutrally as possible and in a manner that protects the procedural due process rights of alleged perpetrators, to protecting the security of groups that engage in the identification and vetting process, to establishing standards for who will be screened out of the DDR program. Although many victims know their perpetrators and may have identified them to local NGOs or authorities, due process is needed to guard against false allegations. A possible solution could entail using reliable and well-established civil society groups that can verify the names on their lists, as well as collecting information from local prosecutors, court systems, and the military justice system (to the extent that such institutions and records exist), where victims may have attempted to file complaints. Many NGOs engage in rigorous data collection and could provide invaluable assistance for purposes of DDR screening.[109]

Particularly because ex-combatants will challenge their identification as perpetrators, not only should this list-based approach place a high bar on reliability, but human rights norms may require that the ex-combatant receive an opportunity at a later stage to clear his or her name.[110] This screening process requires painstaking record-keeping, a task that many countries emerging from conflict may find difficult, although there are models in other contexts from which to draw practice. Already, there are emerging norms in international law with regard to data collection.[111] Moreover, the international war crimes tribunals have also developed jurisprudence concerning the right to confront witnesses,[112] an important step in the types of procedural protections that should be offered to the ex-combatants. Finally, lustration laws, designed to screen public officials based on past abusive acts, have also dealt with sensitive data.[113]

A second potential weakness is that soldiers may not participate in a DDR program in which they will be subject to screening and possible prosecution. Such criticisms are generally misplaced. DDR offers the lure of money and skills training. Such incentives may, for many former combatants, be so great that they would be willing to risk the probability that they would be identified as having perpetrated a war crime. Indeed, given, for example, that most Congolese survive on less than $2 per week, a promise of more than $300 is a significant incentive.[114]

A final approach would be to condition full participation in DDR programs on confessions to crimes and then reduce any subsequent sentencing, or simply require the combatant to testify fulsomely in front of a Truth and Reconciliation Commission.[115] Positively, there are reasons to believe that many ex-combatants would support the truth-finding process as a requirement to DDR.[116] Negatively, such an approach may not go far enough for many victims, thus hindering reintegration—and some ex-combatants will not participate. Moreover, these procedures must be aligned with the country's more general amnesty policies applicable to past crimes and may not be severable from such broader political agreements. Whichever of these approaches is implemented, for meaningful societal transformation to take root, DDR programs must incorporate a justice component.[117]

CONCLUSION

A DDR program's success can no longer be measured by counting weapons turned in by former combatants. Instead, accounting for the needs of both men and women might additionally assess how many noncombatants were processed; how many combatants completed gender-sensitivity trainings; how many DDR staffers were female; and how many family members were included in the DDR process. It might also examine reports on violence that occurred through the DDR process, paying specific attention to gender-based violence. Until DDR programs and their implementation are based on a new calibration that makes gender central to their conceptualization, development, execution, and assessment, DDR programs will fall short of the goal of facilitating short- and long-term peace and stability. For many societies, DDR has become a cyclical experience where violence stops and starts, weapons are episodically turned in but subsequently repurchased or accessed, and hostilities are inevitably reignited. To prevent the human, social, economic, and cultural costs of enduring war, the mechanisms to end it have to be radically rethought, and DDR programs provide an evident starting point.

CHAPTER 7

International and Local Criminal Accountability for Gendered Violence

Criminal accountability is increasingly a central component of the peacemaking process that accompanies the ending of entrenched violence between and within states. This chapter addresses the extent to which post-conflict accountability mechanisms including international criminal law norms and institutions attend to women's experiences of violation, and how they can be improved by acknowledging and responding to women's actual harms and injuries. In doing so, and corresponding to the increased emphasis on criminal accountability for violations of international human rights and humanitarian law norms, we focus on the enforcement of sanctions for sexual violence and other forms of sex-based violation. We acknowledge that there is an extraordinary tension inherent in the creation (and sometimes imposition) of international accountability and highly Westernized modes of legality in post-conflict societies. The bodies are often devoid of any interest or strategic support to buttress or rebuild domestic legal systems that may be in considerable disarray. We affirm the importance of investing material and capacity-building resources into domestic legal systems, using the spurs provided by international criminal process.

The concentration on accountability for sexual crimes has both positives and limitations. It demonstrates the significant strides made in respect of gender-based violations in international law but also exposes some significant biases in the kinds of harms for which remedy is offered and received by women. Section one outlines how norms prohibiting and sanctioning sexual violence came to be incorporated into humanitarian law, identifying advances made. In tandem, this section also addresses a range of normative accountability gaps for women. We argue, as we have done throughout this book, that post-conflict processes have a bias toward the violations of civil and political rights, of harms "to the body," and often fail to capture the full panoply of violations which women experience and define as harmful to them.

We are particularly attuned to the dangers of overemphasizing sexual and penetrative violations of women's bodies, and the lack of attention to emotional harms, harms to the home and personal spaces, and harms to children and those to whom women are intimately connected which may constitute direct harm as experienced by women in times of conflict.[1] Even when sexual and reproductive violence is addressed, accountability processes often fail to attend to the variety of effects that women experience. These harms include depression, low self-esteem, insomnia, anxiety and shame, vaginal and reproductive tract problems, sexually transmitted diseases, difficult births, and sterility. If acknowledged at all, these are generally viewed as merely secondary harms. Existing norms further fail to address violations of social, economic, and cultural rights, and thus have little purchase over core aspects of the conflict landscape and its aftermath. We argue that this disproportionate attention to physical harms not only has a tremendous effect on women's lives, but may also undermine the long-term sustainability of the peace—the primary goal of post-conflict reconstruction. Section two of this chapter is directed at the rules of evidence and procedure operational in the existing ad hoc international courts and tribunals, and underscores their importance to the successful pursuit of criminal accountability for crimes against women. We also posit that these procedural devices undergird broader autonomy and equality advances for women. Section three is focused on local initiatives to address a variety of crimes committed during conflict. Given the limited capacity of international courts and their concentration on prosecuting those most responsible (often those exerting command and control responsibility), restorative justice has emerged as a focal point of alternative accountability. We tackle its gendered benefits and limitations.

SEX-BASED VIOLENCE AND ACCOUNTABILITY IN INTERNATIONAL LAW

Women experience violence in multiple forms in many societies.[2] Violence is experienced both in the public and private spheres. Much feminist theory has rightly concentrated on bringing the sphere of private, intimate violence into the public domain and ensuring in policy terms that its private categorization does not mean that it is unregulated by the state.[3] In conflicted and authoritarian societies, women remain vulnerable to intimate violence but are also,[4] as has been extensively documented, the target of sex-based violence that is closely related to the methods and means of warfare used by combatants.[5]

International law had historically avoided regulating such sex-based violence. Because historically armed confrontation between and within states was carried out by male combatants, the laws of war were generally constructed from the vista of a soldier's need for ordered rules within which to wage war on behalf of the state. Consequently, women's interests fared notoriously badly when accountability was sought for the behavior of combatants. There is now no doubt as to the augmented accountability for acts of violence directed at women during armed conflict,[6] but problems of enforcement still persist.

First, despite legal reforms and increased accountability, there remains a limited understanding of the forms and functionality of sex-based violence in war, peace, and transition.[7] Second, there remains ongoing intellectual and legal resistance to accepting the extensive empirical evidence that women's bodies have been specifically targeted to further military-political objectives, and that traditional categorizations of violence (and its appropriate sanction) are ill-fitted to deal with the pervasiveness of violence experienced by women in multiple forms across a wide range of societies. Finally, there has been little exploration of the extent to which the violence which has been grafted on to legal accountability norms (genocide, crimes against humanity, war crimes, and serious and systematic violations of human rights) actually maps onto women's subjective experiences, and whether there are a range of other experiences which women would describe as violence but are not legally categorized as such.[8] We stress the need to draw on wider social and empirical research that affirms the connected harms women experience and the way in which trauma is differentiated for women and for men.[9] Drawing on Robin West's analysis of women as "intimately connected" from bearing, delivering, and caring for children in ways that men are not, and extending a theory of connection to the experience of harm, we are convinced that harms to women in conflict contexts cannot simply be reduced to sexual harms to the female body.[10] We suggest that much greater empirical and policy attention needs to be paid to charting the range of violations that women themselves define as central to their individualized experiences of violation and harm. Often such harms are sidelined as being secondary in nature, particularly when they constitute emotional or psychological harms, and are the product of direct harms to others—children, partners, and family members to whom women are connected or in a relationship with. Neither domestic nor international legal systems do a good job in recognizing such harms as necessitating legal accountability in the criminal sphere. Empirical evidence suggests that there is a distinctly gendered aspect to the articulation of harm and that women and men perceive, experience, and process harms in different ways.[11] This suggests that there is much work to be done in naming and translating a gendered notion of harm into law.

We conclude that extensive empirical work is needed to measure more accurately women's experiences of violence and to determine the gap between existing legal categories and what women identify as harms experienced by them in conflict and post-conflict situations. Here, we must be more attuned to the need for a feminist methodology that listens to what women say about what harms them and to understand that a woman's construction of harm may be structurally and substantially different from that of a man. We affirm the value of consultation with women about the forms and nature of harms experienced, and encourage that advocacy for the expansion and enforcement of international criminal law be fully grounded in women's lived experiences across multiple cultural and social settings.

It is also evident, as we have explored in other chapters, that systematic violations of social and economic rights accompanying violent conflicts, which may be pivotal to their ignition, are generally ignored or sidelined by post-conflict criminal accountability mechanisms. This raises a number of unresolved issues. First, where socioeconomic deprivations have been causal to the discrimination and exclusion of groups and minorities, there is a grave risk for the future stability of a conflicted society to leave distributive justice matters entirely unresolved in the post-conflict phase. Token criminal trials of select leaders in the post-conflict phase may entirely sidestep the necessary confrontation with inherited stratified social and economic systems. Some policymakers and scholars argue persuasively that it is imperative to tackle horizontal inequalities resulting from the systematic violation of social and economic rights in order to prevent conflict.[12]

We suggest that international criminal law has an underdeveloped role to play in this regard, and that creative and innovative application of the crimes against humanity category is an important tool. Article 7 (Crimes Against Humanity) of the Statute of the International Criminal Court (ICC) includes such categories as enslavement, deportation or forcible transfer, and other inhumane acts of a similar character intentionally causing great suffering or serious injury to the body or to mental or physical health. In all these groupings, we see significant potential to address deliberately created inequitable and systematic economic harms, many of which have particularly corrosive gender effects in conflicted and post-conflict societies. Second, the failure to address systematic violations of socioeconomic rights such as deliberate starvation, blockade, and destruction of food and water sources as crimes to be viewed under the microscope of crimes against humanity and/or war crimes does a disservice to the champions of accountability and to the victims of such violations. The victims fully understand what the act and the intention in such violations may have been, no less than the violence of torture or extrajudicial execution. Women are the most observable and visible face of these harms in many societies given gendered care and nurture roles (added to their responsibilities when combatants leave the home and or fail to return). Failure to account for social and economic violations is failure to render visible the violations that women experience most profoundly and with the most effects throughout conflicts. Innovative and creative thinking about the application and expansion of criminal law norms is required. But equally, criminal law sanction is not always the sole and most effective means to address gendered harms. A more nuanced and contextual approach is needed to balance criminal accountability with a variety of other social, governance, economic, and political initiatives outlined in Part III of this book.

THE LEGAL JOURNEY TO CODIFY GENDERED
CRIMES IN ARMED CONFLICTS

In order to understand how far we have come and how far we have to travel, we reiterate that the lack of comprehensive legal sanction for sexual violence during warfare has taken decades to expose.[13] As accounts of systematic sexual violence against women emerged from the former Yugoslavia in the early 1990s, there was ongoing academic and policy debate as to the international legal status of violence against women, and specifically that of rape, under the laws of war.[14] Those debates can be traced back to the Nuremberg Tribunals and the paucity of accountability for sex-based crimes that occurred during World War II. Prior to Nuremberg, rape and forced prostitution were enumerated offenses in the War Crimes Commission of World War I,[15] although lack of a worldwide consensus that an international tribunal could hear such charges halted any actual prosecutions.[16]

Though the Charter of the International Military Tribunal at Nuremberg (IMT) included innovative new charges such as crimes against humanity, rape was not enumerated in the Charter. Some crimes against women were prosecuted at Nuremberg, particularly sterilization and forced abortion,[17] but even there because the crimes were often subsumed within the prosecutorial category of genocide the focus lay on the nongendered aspect of the violations. Evidence from the Nuremberg transcripts reveal reported instances of forced prostitution,[18] including such practices at certain concentration camps. The transcripts disclose that rape and other forms of sexual assault were rampant during the Nazi regime, and that these rapes often preceded murder, the latter being the only crime for which perpetrators were actually held responsible.[19] Control Council Law No. 10 included rape in the list of crimes against humanity, but the lesser status of the Council Laws left unresolved the status of rape as a serious violation of the laws of war in its own right.[20]

The Tokyo Trials provide an important example of some accountability for Japanese practices of forced prostitution and rape during World War II. Indictments specifically incorporated rape under the heading of conventional war crimes and crimes against humanity.[21] Despite this, a significant limitation on accountability was that the International Military Tribunal for the Far East (IMTFE) Charter only had jurisdiction over individuals for war crimes and crimes against humanity if they were also charged with crimes against peace. Some scholars have credited the inclusion of specific rape charges in the IMTFE indictment to the presence of women in the prosecutorial team, a historical precedent that reinforces our call for the inclusion of women at all stages and all relevant post-conflict institutional settings.[22] Evidence from the IMTFE transcripts reveals that the tribunal specifically recorded the extent and effect of the use of rape as a weapon of war by the Japanese.[23] The raping of Chinese women during the Japanese invasion of the city of Nanking was so widespread that the offensive itself is historically referred to as "the Rape of Nanking." Women were raped in front of their families,[24] often until they required hospital care,[25] where they could be raped again, a pattern that has been revisited in numerous conflicts since.[26] The tribunal was also unusual in that there is some evidence of care by the justices at the IMTFE to prevent offensive cross-examination by defense attorneys on the issue of rape.[27] Regrettably, and indicative of both the shame as well as the cultural and social context of the violations, not a single victim was called upon to give evidence before the IMTFE; rather, witnesses to the rape of others testified.[28] As regards forced prostitution, there is now extensive knowledge of how rampant and widespread forced prostitution was during World War II. Estimates on the number of Korean, Chinese, Filipino, and Indonesian women forced to provide sexual services for the Japanese army vary between 80,000 and 200,000. While evidence of forced prostitution was available after World War II and was even articulated in the IMTFE transcripts, it was not prosecuted as a crime. A variety of reasons have been adduced for this, including the destruction of evidence by the Japanese in the period between surrender and the administration of the peace agreement, the role of collaborators in the recruitment and operation of the "comfort" women system, and the reality that until relatively recently, few survivors of the comfort stations were willing to come forward to discuss their ordeals.

The specific international legal prohibition for the crime of rape in situations of armed conflict is found in the Fourth Geneva Convention,[29] and at Articles 76(1) and 85 of the First Protocol Additional to the Geneva Conventions.[30] Its prohibition under the Geneva Conventions defines rape as an offense against honor, rather than an offense of a distinctly violent and sexual nature. This tells us that not only have all-encompassing sexual crimes against women been historically excluded from legal prohibition under the laws of war, but when included they have been facets of a male status violation.

What then (and still now) concerned many observers is that the status of prohibition for sexual violation was low within the hierarchy of humanitarian law offenses.[31] This meant that ensuring accountability for the atrocities committed against women in any conflict would require creative interpretation to allow crimes of sexual violence to fit the category of "grave breaches" or serious offenses, which give rise to international jurisdiction under the Geneva Conventions.[32] The establishment of an ad hoc tribunal for the former

Yugoslavia partially forced legal and policy conversations as to whether rape could be read into the Hague Regulations and Geneva Conventions.[33] Clearly, in the real world of conflict, this interpretative position seems to have little effect on the perceptions of criminality for combatants and their superiors. An "interpret in" approach would have achieved little. As states moved to create international criminal tribunals in the former Yugoslavia and Rwanda, it was vital that such tribunals, as the inheritors to an incomplete Nuremberg and Tokyo legacy, acknowledge and incorporate the gravity of sexual offenses into their substantive law. Subsuming female-centered violence into existing categories was not enough, as that would fail to concede the specific nature, effect, and rationale of these offenses.

Despite these birthing concerns, the statutes of the ad hoc tribunals for the former Yugoslavia (ICTY) and Rwanda (ICTR) explicitly recognize specific forms of sexual harms as violations of the laws of war and subject to their jurisdiction. Equally, both Statutes in their general provisions leave room for crimes of a gendered nature to be read into their diffuse categories. For example, Article 2 of the ICTY Statute confirms that the tribunal can prosecute grave breaches of the 1949 Geneva Conventions.[34] Torture and inhuman treatment are prohibited under Article 2(b).[35] Both have been applied to include crimes of sexual violation. Importantly, there is an ongoing debate as to whether there is an inherent value in prosecuting sex-based crimes under the specific title of sexual harm or whether there may be benefits to the victim and the capacity of the prosecution to garner conviction by utilizing more diffuse categories, specifically by prosecuting sexual violations as torture.[36] Article 2(3) of the ICTY Statute also proscribes prosecution for "willfully causing great suffering or serious injury to body or health." Article 4 of the ICTY Statute is concerned with the prosecution of the crime of genocide. For the first time, the relationship between violent sexual acts directed at the women of a national, ethnic, racial, or religious group, and the destruction of that entity was recognized. This provision constitutes legal acknowledgment that sexual violence in war serves a functional purpose in destroying an opponent's culture by defiling an essential component of society,[37] its women (as symbolic of cultural and bodily integrity) and its childbearers (as its future). The provision created grounds for the prosecution of genocidal acts where serious bodily or mental harm was caused to members of the group,[38] and where measures were imposed to prevent births within the group.[39] Article 5 of the ICTY Statute endorses the position that rape constitutes a crime against humanity.[40]

The ad hoc tribunals were the starting point in a much greater imprint of accountability mechanisms on conflicted and post-conflict societies generally. The follow-through was the establishment of hybrid tribunals in a number of sites where systematic human rights violations defined the conflict context, including the Sierra Leone Tribunal. In ongoing and future conflicts, the International Criminal Court will be a critical site of accountability for gender-based violence.

The agreement by states on a Statute for the International Criminal Court, the requisite number of ratifying states, and the appointment of a prosecutor issuing indictments, confirms a trend that in the main seems positive and capable of being sustained and expanded.[41] The Court is based in The Hague and in a relatively short period of time has demonstrated its capacity to advance legal engagement with conflicted and post-conflict societies.[42] The Statute expands the definition of crimes against humanity and war crimes to recognize rape, sexual slavery, enforced prostitution, forced pregnancy, enforced sterilization, and trafficking.[43] Of particular interest in terms of post-conflict accountability is Article 7 of the Statute, which defines crimes against humanity.[44] For women, Article 7(g) sets out the full list of sexual crimes—rape, slavery, forced pregnancy—that could anchor a crime against humanity designation. Article 7(h) specifically sets out gender as a ground on which a claim for persecution can be based. Its substantive provisions and its rules of procedure and evidence demonstrate considerable learning from the gendered aspects of the ad hoc tribunals' work, though it is still too early to tell what kind of practice and jurisprudence it may generate.[45]

Each of the ad hoc tribunals developed specialized victims support units, which support and ensure the capacity of women to give evidence before the international bodies. This has also been replicated by the Rome Statute system.[46] At the ICTY, Rule 34 of the Rules of Procedure and Evidence creates a victim and witnesses unit set up under the authority of the Registrar of the Tribunal. Its responsibility is to provide counseling and support for victims and witnesses. In particular, it is charged with providing this support in cases of rape and sexual assault. The ICTR also established a victims and witnesses support unit under Rule 34 of its Rules of Procedure and Evidence,[47] though as the Registrar to the Court has noted, particular challenges have been faced by victims coming to this court (location, the poverty of the Great Lakes region, and the general unwillingness of states to commit to the resettlement of particularly vulnerable witnesses from the area).

The creation of specialized support services is vital to the successful prosecution of gendered violence. The experience in many jurisdictions is that women frequently underreport sexualized violence,[48] not least because of the perception that the legal process is a hostile and unsupportive environment within which to press their claims. Even when the environment is supportive, empirical assessments of victims' experiences show that the disclosure of traumatic experiences may be beneficial to some victims but harmful to others. The latter data belies broader claims about the presumed psychological benefits of testimony at both the individual and collective level.[49] Vanessa Pupavac has powerfully argued that the "international therapeutic paradigm" and the increased popularity of war trauma studies obscures the material needs of survivors, pathologizes war-affected nations, and authenticates the political and social imperatives of powerful states cultivating essentialized and deeply problematic notions of the victim. Given these complexities, at a minimum we underscore the need for meaningful and fully resourced victim support given the consistent nexus between protracted conflict and the politicization of sexual violence against women.

The horrors that many women experienced during conflict are augmented by the insight that their cultural and social mores were as much the target of sexual violation as their physical bodies. The knowledge that it is not only a woman's body that is targeted, but the body politic she represents, assists in understanding the prevalence and forms of sex-based violence. It also helps to explain the public and ritualized experiences of rape for many victims. Perpetrators understand (as do the victims) that public sexual violence is a form of communication and power, not only a sexual act. It plays out in graphic form the kinds of hypermasculinity we have discussed in Chapter 2, where men communicate to other men their relative positions of power and helplessness. It also demonstrates the continual hold that the notion of female purity has and the value it exudes in communal settings. It confirms the double victimization that many women experience once violence ends. Victim support units are a start to affirming on an international level the premise that fair legal process is not simply achieved by utilitarian utilization of the subjects of violation by formal legal proceedings establishing the guilt or innocence of alleged perpetrators. Instead, the process affirms its own responsibility to the victims by seeking to aid the restoration of balance and some normality in their lives. This occurs directly through the facilitation of resources that individual victims might not otherwise have access to and remains attuned to the material and concrete needs of victims.

There is a vital link between accountability and remedies—and the need to broadly assess what kinds of harm merit recompense. Moreover, criminal accountability in the absence of material recompense to victims appears very shallow justice when the material needs of victims are overwhelming. A broader sense of victim obligation is made more cogent by the fact that the ad hoc tribunals generally arose from the identification of wider goals by the international community, the drawing of an international bright line on unacceptable behavior during war. The women witnesses and victims, prepared to allow their stories to fill the spotlight of scrutiny, are the facilitators of that line-drawing. They are particularly vulnerable given cultural and social elevations of women's purity and virtue in many societies. Correspondingly, the international legal process must be cognizant of the additional burdens that extraterritorial legal scrutiny places upon women and respond accordingly. The creation of the ICC Trust Fund for Victims as an integral part of the Rome Statute system is a valuable advancement on making the reparative and the prosecutorial operate in tandem.

Significant indictments have been issued by ad hoc tribunals and have been aimed at the perpetrators of sex-based violence.[50] Those indictments bear some scrutiny. Though a small number of cases have produced substantial jurisprudential advancements for gender equality, it has required enormous advocacy to achieve these outcomes. For example, in the *Akayesu* case, it was (arguably) as a result of the amicus curiae brief submitted by the NGO Coalition for Women's Human Rights in Conflict Situations to include sexual violence in the indictment that the Prosecutor amended the original charges.[51] The International Criminal Court has charged Thomas Lubanga Dyilo with the offenses set out in Articles 8(2)(b)(xxvi) and 8(2)(e)(vii) of the Rome Statute (focused on the conscription of child soldiers in hostilities). In May 2009, the legal representatives of the victims in the case filed a joint application asking the Trial Chamber under Regulation 55 of the Court's Rules to add to existing charges. They specifically sought to add the crime against humanity of sexual slavery, the war crimes of sexual slavery, and the crime of cruel and/or inhuman treatment. In July 2009, the trial chamber agreed but, at time of writing, the addition is under appeal to the Court's Appellate chamber. The legal wrangling in the case underscores the point about the difficulties in grafting on sexual violation charges and the procedural obstacles that confront women in accessing redress.[52] The difficulties of pursuing accountability for gendered violence at the International Criminal Court underscore the fragility of prosecuting gender-based crimes generally. In the case of Jean-Pierre Bemba Gombo (who was the alleged president and commander in chief of the Mouvement de Liberation du Congo), Pre-Trial II of the ICC refused to allow the prosecutor to bring multiple charges of sexual violence to address the full range of harms experienced by rape victims. At the heart of the Pre-Trial's reasoning is the assumption that the two charges sought by the prosecutor to address crimes of sexual violence—torture and outrages upon sexual dignity—are, in essence, the same as the single charge of rape. The Chamber reasoned that the counts of outrages and torture were "fully subsumed by the count of rape." This decision is a further and pointed illustration of the challenges that full accounting for gendered violence face in international institutional contexts.

Doris Buss has persuasively argued, based on close empirical analysis of tribunal indictments, that there is a significant gap between indictments for sex-based crimes and other crimes.[53] It appears that comparatively—based on the estimated number of sex-based crimes in the former Yugoslavia in her study—the number of indictments may be disproportionally lower relative to other crimes and other charges. Moreover, while sexual violation or sex-based crimes may be initially charged on indictment, there appears to be a significant drop-off from indictment to prosecution. Tally this with the demographics of participation in tribunal proceedings, demonstrating the low percentage of women witnesses appearing, and we have troubling evidence of the limited participation of women, which clearly exacerbates the extent to which gender crimes are being prosecuted. These patterns require greater empirical analysis but demonstrate what we know already from the domestic legal context: that for a variety of entrenched structural reasons, sex-based violence faces built-in barriers to prosecution. The practical effects are evident: Fewer violations that directly affect women appear before the courts, less jurisprudence is generated, and the stigma associated with sexual violation is perpetuated. Accordingly, we caution that the perceived advance for the prosecution of sex-based crimes in international courts is still in its infancy and not inevitably bound to success in adequately responding to the violations of women's rights.

Positively, there have been successful and highly visible prosecutions for sex-based crimes that occurred during the conflict and genocide in the former Yugoslavia and Rwanda.[54] These tribunals adjudicating war crimes committed on the territory of the former Yugoslavia and genocide plus other crimes in Rwanda have traversed unique thresholds since their creation.[55] They are the first international ad hoc tribunals since the Nuremberg Trials and the first comprehensive criminalization of acts of violence committed during internal and external war deemed sufficiently abhorrent to warrant international regulation. In the process of more general accounting, the tribunals have sharpened the boundaries of international humanitarian law and cast light on the murky shadows of sexual violence during warfare.[56] In particular, the Yugoslav conflict is mooted as exceptional because of the way in which violence to women was widely exposed as a method and means of warfare, not ancillary to military objectives but innately linked to them.[57]

Both ICTY and ICTR tribunals demonstrated that when significant political and lobbying energy was directed at engendering substantive definitions of criminal offenses in the statutes of the tribunals, the gravity of rape and sexual offenses against women could be acknowledged.[58] Gravity suitably affirmed—in parallel with domestic courts grappling over centuries with the precise legal definitions of what constitutes the act of rape, international courts also struggle. The tribunals have gone some way toward adopting a broad definition of the term. So, while penetration remains a central doctrinal aspect, there has been willingness to view a slightly wider array of acts as fitting within the sanction.[59]

Both ad hoc tribunals have produced an international jurisprudence defining the forms and limits of international humanitarian law's interface with sex-based violence. Despite valid criticisms of its scope, the jurisprudence nonetheless makes a substantial dent on the notion that impunity is acceptable with respect to sexual violence directed at women in times of war. Significant cases, such as the *Celebici* trial, adjudicated offenses committed in a detention camp in Central Bosnia in 1992, and found that the act of rape may constitute torture under international humanitarian law.[60] In the *Celebici* trial, the accused was found guilty as a co-perpetrator of torture and for aiding and abetting in outrages on personal dignity, including rape. Here, the tribunal also held that a witness who had been forced to watch the repeated rapes of another was a victim of torture. The ICTR in its landmark decision *Prosecutor v. Akayesu* (above) affirmed that rape can be a constitutive act of genocide under international law.[61]

The prosecution of sexual violence during wartime is crucial to restoring the dignity and integrity of individual women who have experienced a deeply personal crime and seek acknowledgment and punishment of the perpetrator. Moreover, punishment of sexual violence is linked to removing the stigma of sexual violence for women and shoring up women's stature and value in a transitioning society. We caution, however, that the range of violations and harms experienced by women are not yet effectively and consistently addressed by post-conflict accountability mechanisms and procedures. Prosecuting crimes of sexual violence alone will not remedy the harms done to women during conflict. A more transformative and structural response will be required at both the domestic and international level.

The June 2010 Review Conference of the Rome Statute conducted a stocktaking exercise on the impact of the Rome Statute system on victims and affected communities.[62] The exercise did not differentiate between victims, and thus there was no distinct gender focus. Key points have emerged nonetheless, including the specific problems faced by women in their daily lives and the stigma that women experienced when returning to their communities after conflict when they had been victims of sexual violence.[63]

Some experts hold out considerable hope for the capacity of the ICC to advance international humanitarian law's ability to genuinely respond to the plight of ordinary women who have been subjected to violent and debasing sexual violation. Judge Patricia Wald has articulated the view there may be room, through the long-term jurisprudential work of the ICC, to directly address the broader political, social, and economic exclusions and discriminations that women face in multiple societies.[64] In particular, she notes that the hold of the crimes against humanity category which, unlike genocide, does not require a nexus to armed conflict but can include state-ordered and tolerated regimes of discrimination that violate the fundamental rights of women can be extended. Arguably, conditions of extreme social and political inequity could amount to the discrimination that is a vital element in the underlying crime of persecution, which can qualify as a crime against humanity. Even the agitational capacity of such offenses works to put pressure on governments when they join the treaty regime and force consideration as to whether their domestic practices are conforming. Perhaps of equal and underappreciated value is that the very existence of the Rome Statute allows women to mobilize nationally and transnationally and use legal standards instrumentally to force deep and meaningful social change at the local level. Notably, the Review Conference placed particular emphasis on the role of the Trust Fund for Victims established under the Rome Statute system as a means to provide physical rehabilitation, psychological assistance, and material support.[65]

EVIDENTIARY RULES AND SEXUAL VIOLENCE

As well as affirming the value of augmented legal definitions and jurisprudence, the ad hoc and hybrid tribunals have made significant inroads on the structural limitations of charging and prosecuting sexual violence. They have done so by creating a body of procedural and evidentiary rules which are critical to advancing gender-central criminal accountability. These are the Rules of Evidence and Procedure facilitated by Article 15 of the Statute of the Tribunal of the ICTY, Article 34 of the Statute of the ICTR, and Article 96 of the Sierra Leone Tribunal.[66] The ICTY and ICTR Rules affirm that the Chamber shall not be bound by national rules of evidence.[67] This affirmation is a persuasive statement that the tribunals viewed themselves as capable and competent to institutionalize new approaches, a trend that the ICC appears in the main to follow. In general, less attention has been paid to the radical changes wrought by these rules to the criminal adjudication of sexual offenses against women in the international legal arena. We stress that substantive legal recognition of sexual offenses in their own right would have achieved very little if the procedural mechanisms which apply to the conduct of criminal cases had not been subject to drastic reevaluation. The reform (and in some parts radicalization) of rules of evidence facilitating the prosecution and trial of sexual offenses illustrates a chink of international recognition for the significance of process in the institutional treatment of gendered violence. They are also related to a restorative process in ensuring that the adjudication of sexual violation affirms the positive capabilities of women in post-conflict societies and becomes part of a legal transformation that places women's experiences centrally, affirming the equality and status of women. In so doing, accountability processes advance and affirm women's agency and equality.

Existing rules of evidence regulating the conduct of criminal trials concerning gendered violence have been subject to vocal and persistent criticism in many jurisdictions for their perpetuation of unstated social understandings regarding female and male sexuality.[68] Rape and sexual assault trials have been marked by the lack of female perspective in the courtroom and the application of a male standard. Edwards notes: "It is in the rules of evidence and procedure that we find the reproduction of the precipitating construction of female sexual behavior that makes a charge of assault by the complainant difficult to sustain."[69] Such constructions are reflected in traditional doctrines of defense, including that the woman should fend off violent attack "like a man" or be considered unchaste and thus unworthy of legal protection for violation. It is reflected in the "fresh complaint" doctrine, the myth that the truly vitreous woman would immediately complain of any sexual violation. The operation of these doctrines has contributed to women publicly fearing the prejudice, hostility, stigma, and disbelief that follow from criminal process whether domestic or international in form. We suggest that reframing the criminal process when prosecuting sexual crimes is an instrumental means to address broader societal inequalities and assumptions around women's sexuality and status, and may propel deeper transformative effect.

The Rules of Procedure and Evidence of the ad hoc tribunals are exceptional to the extent that they are more "victim friendly" than most parallel domestic criminal codes.[70] Strong nongovernmental lobbying throughout the process of their creation largely produced this outcome. The rules relevant to the investigation and trial of sexual offenses can be divided into three broad categories. First, the rules related to the protection and support of victims and witnesses. Second, general rules of evidence presentation which envisage and take account of the specialized demands of sexual offenses. Finally, those particularized rules pertaining to the adjudication of sexual offenses. In all contexts, the procedural changes work to reframe what ought to be standard practice at the domestic level (recalling that post-conflict societies invariably experience sharp legal reform in parallel to accountability), and constitute part of the legal reform endeavors that also accompany international oversight of post-conflict societies.

The ICTY and the ICTR statutes both identify the need to appoint qualified women to the staff of the Victims and Witnesses Unit.[71] This requirement parallels a broader need in our view to ensure adequate gender representation on these courts.[72] This coincides with and supports the establishment of quotas to ensure fair numbers of female representation in international settings and specifically as judges to international courts, tracking the Convention on the Elimination of All Forms of Discrimination Against Women (CEDAW) Article 4 requirement of temporary special measures to address systematic inequalities faced by women.[73] The existing ad hoc tribunal rules do not include a quota requirement for female representation, only the inclusion of a consideration requirement.

The responsibility to protect victims in post-conflict societies is critical to ensuring the integrity and the security of the accountability process. It is a sine qua non for women's participation in criminal accountability. This duty is affirmed under Rule 69 of the ICTY Rules by allowing the court to order the nondisclosure of the identity of victims or witnesses at risk.[74] Unresolved tensions in the former Yugoslavia, comparable to the reality of most post-conflict societies, including the lack of free access across the four political entities recognized under the Dayton agreement, made safety a priority for women.[75] Nondisclosure of identity is particularly significant to victims of sexual violence. In the former Yugoslavia, for example, the failure to implement the provisions related to the return of refugees and the continuing liberty of large numbers of indicted war criminals foreordained that many witnesses and victims feared giving evidence in open court.[76] In post-conflict situations, women will often be reluctant to come forward with testimony. Some will wish to obliterate the experience from their memory, while others feel degraded and ashamed by the incident(s) and fear social exclusion should their experiences become public knowledge.[77] This is particularly true in societies where a high social premium is set on women's purity—commensurate in a metaphysical sense with the purity of the nation. Evidence suggests that women victims have felt exploited by media and international experts who seek their stories but have little sensitivity to the trauma that additional publicity may bring to them.[78] Thus, legal process must not become another site of trauma for the victim.

Ensuring that giving testimony is not a form of secondary trauma for victims has been and remains a critical concern in post-conflict settings.[79] To address this issue, Rule 75(c) of the ICTY Rules of Procedure and Evidence hold that the chamber shall, where necessary, control the manner of questioning to avoid any harassment or intimidation of witnesses. Sexual assault cases are frequently characterized by aggressive cross-examination of the female complainant, a means of withholding validation of the woman as a credible witness. We need to be attuned to the heightened vulnerability of women giving evidence in a post-conflict setting and to the trauma effects that such courtroom processes may incur. Consideration should also be given to the effect the conduct of trials may have on a wider community of victims and their willingness to come forward. We know that the telling of sexual assault under the potential distortions of cross-examination may turn the woman's violation into a pornographic vignette, with deep traumatic revictimization resulting. International courts and tribunals have the means to ensure and set a baseline for the way in which sexual offense trials can be litigated that offers a model for domestic legal systems to do better. In this approach, the key is that the trial is not focused on the conduct of the victim, thereby becoming a trial of female accountability rather than male responsibility.

For many victims of sexual violence in times of conflict, the question of how to fully establish the heinous and aggravated nature of the violations experienced is a vital piece of the accountability matrix. Procedural rules have the capacity to advance this end. For example, ICTY Rule 101 outlines sanctions following successful prosecution for offenses listed in the ICTY Statute. The rule allows that when determining a sentence, the trial chamber shall take into account any aggravating circumstances that accompanied the perpetration of the offense.[80] Given the empirical information available both in the former Yugoslavia and other conflicts, aggravated elements have increasingly accompanied acts of sexual violence in war. These include public and ritualized violation, forcing family members to violate one another with threats of violence, and particularly harmful sexual violation using objects. Explicit in these acts is the simultaneous defiling of both woman and community.[81] Particularly harmful is the long-term trauma experienced by women when rape takes place in front of family members, including children and spouses.[82] In many conflicts, including the former Yugoslavia, women were held in prolonged detention where they were repeatedly assaulted and sexually violated. Women impregnated by sexual assault were kept in detention until their pregnancy was so far advanced that they were unable to seek abortion services had they so desired. All these contextual circumstances evidently constitute aggravating circumstances to the sexual act itself. Proceedings, procedural rules, and sanctions need to be in sync to ensure appropriate redress for the extremity of violation experienced by women during the conflict. Crucially, we suggest that these "additional" factors are perceived by women as being just as harmful as the primary act (for example, rape) that international criminal law captures. Recognizing this should encourage deeper and reflective thinking about the extent to which criminal sanctions sufficiently encapsulate the harms which women themselves define as most egregious.

Procedural rules across the ad hoc tribunals and the ICC give specific consideration to evidentiary management of sexual violation offenses.[83] The first significant departure from the domestic practice of many states is that no corroboration of the victim's testimony is required by the ICTY and ICTR Trial Chambers.[84] In many jurisdictions, the evidentiary distrust of female complainants is illustrated by the established norm that the victim's testimony be corroborated in order to support a conviction.[85] It is often accompanied by admitting prior sexual conduct of the victim in open court.[86] The relevance of a woman's sexual past has been as controversial as the corroboration requirement in many jurisdictions.[87] As the most private of crimes, rape and sexual violence rarely generate a public audience (though evidently some practices of ritualized public violence in conflict departs from this). Thus, corroboration historically concentrated on the evidence of force, resistance, identity, and character of the victim herself. The formal commitment to noncorroboration and the exclusion of a cautionary requirement is a significant advance by the tribunals. It confirms a formal international norm of equality between the sexes.[88] It validates the principle that formal definitions of crime are not sufficient to ensure accountability for infraction. The reformation of these rules in an international forum may prevent the victims of gendered crime experiencing violation a second time. Equally, it may intensify a reevaluation of domestic evidential standards. There is also the faint hope that such rules will assist in the creation of generally accepted international standards on the adjudication of sexual offenses. We strongly support this broader endeavor, as we outline further below in our analysis of the International Criminal Court's potential for women victims of violence in war.

The punishment of rape in warfare could be thwarted by the importation and validation of strategies whose goal was to make the victim defend her past behavior, circumventing scrutiny of the sexual violation itself. Arguably, in the context of armed conflict where threat and coercion are omnipresent, the notion of consent is highly controversial. The anecdotal and empirical evidence available suggests that in most conflicts, women are assaulted and raped by men they knew, by neighbors and acquaintances. In this context, there is perceptible danger that the proximity of prewar relationships gives defendants intimate knowledge and capacity to exploit their victims' prior relationships as a means to justify their own behavior.

In regards to the defense of consent, Rule 96(ii) of the ICTR and ICTY Rules of Procedure and Evidence outline the parameters under which consent may be raised as a defense to the charge of rape or sexual assault. The consent defense has been reproached for facilitating a loophole whereby legal emphasis is placed on what the man thinks rather than what the woman does in the circumstances of sexual violation. In these contexts the rule started from the premise that consent cannot be a defense if the victim had experienced or had fear of violence, duress, detention, or psychological oppression.[89] It remains to be seen whether the fact of ongoing armed conflict is sufficient per se to establish such fear or oppression, a key future question for the ICC.

In sum, the advancement of accountability for sex-based violations of human rights and humanitarian law is not solely progressed by strong substantive norms naming gender-specific violations. Critical and often overlooked is the detail of the rules of procedure and evidence that underpin and structure the manner in which substantive violations are processed in court.

OTHER ACCOUNTABILITY MECHANISMS—RESTORATIVE JUSTICE AND OTHER PRACTICES

Some argue that as a result of a degradation of confidence in the rule of law generally and/or in the enforcers of law during a conflict, traditional criminal accountability mechanisms are not appropriate for legal enforcement post-conflict. Given the political consensus necessary to drive criminal prosecutions, as well as increasing costs of international justice and partially allied with a desire to engage in broader society-wide accounting, there has been an escalating resort to a variety of accountability mechanisms.

Increasingly visible in post-conflict conversations and practices about accountability are restorative justice mechanisms. We now turn to evaluate its possibilities as one of the alternatives being mooted to the formality and cost of international criminal accountability.[90] Restorative justice measures emerged as highly developed and imaginative conceptual and practical approaches from academics and policymakers. They have been identified as a means to address regulatory lacunae with particular groups, or to address lacunae in policing and criminal justice in divided societies.[91] While not seeking to devalue the overall contribution of restorative justice approaches to fraught rule of law restoration and processes of reconciliation, we believe that it is also necessary to address the problems and limitations of restorative justice when applied to gender violence. We also raise some general concerns around the use of restorative justice measures in post-conflict situations for women.

Typically, restorative justice is characterized by apologies and other forms of direct victim confrontation with perpetrators, allowing victim and perpetrator to share a (safe) space, allowing the perpetrator to acknowledge the "wrong" committed and the victim to articulate the hurt or damage done to them as a result. External and internal facilitators should not underestimate how difficult the return to "normal" may be, and thus how problematic the application of restorative justice principles and practice may be in the context of communal or interethnic violence. As Deepak Mehta and Roma Chatterji note, "Taken-for-granted notions regarding community solidarity become deeply problematic when it is one's neighbors who are the perpetrators of violence. . . ."[92] Psychological literature on violence and atrocities confirm this profound difficulty.

This is particularly true where victims continue to live in and occupy the physical spaces in which violation and hurt took place. For these victims there may be little or no separation between the "past" of the incident(s) and the hurt of the present. Thus homes, streets, shops, neighborhoods, which post-conflict, to the external observer, seem a bustle of ordinary and routine activity, may contain deep reservoirs of memory associated with violence, prohibition, exclusion—an ensemble of past and present in one continuous collision.[93] In this context, restorative processes can serve to complicate and further heighten the confrontation for the victim rather than alleviate it.

Importantly, a number of commentators suggest that when assessing how women victims feel about the legal process, particularly when the violation has been a sexual or reproductive one, the key issue for positive therapeutic outcomes lies with the quality of esteem and respect they experience during the proceedings.[94] This notion of restoring dignity is exceptionally important in rape trials, whether domestic or international. It enables shaking off feelings of complicity and self-blame, and in societies where honor and virtue hold particular social importance for women, may enable restoration of these values to the self. It remains entirely unclear whether restorative justice mechanisms enable this recalibration.

We accept that restorative interfaces may serve useful purposes, especially where the alternative may be no legal or public acknowledgment to the victim, or where alternative community responses may inflict serious human rights violations in their own right on the perpetrator without any due process.[95] However, some serious reflection is required when restorative justice mechanisms are proposed as a panacea to law-enforcement gaps when no other rule of law building is undertaken and reparations may not figure as part of the process of accounting. Most particularly, we have serious concerns as to how appropriate a restorative process of confrontation may be to respond to the accountability needs for women and girl victims, and specifically those who have suffered intimate violence.

Gacaca Courts as a Site of Restorative Justice Practices

One version of restorative justice implemented on a mass scale has been the *Gacaca* courts in Rwanda. They were created as a pragmatic response to the paucity of legally trained personnel left following the 1994 genocide, and the sobering reality that thousands of imprisoned individuals for crimes of varying severity related to the genocide were languishing in inhumane prison conditions.[96] *Gacaca*, Kinyarwanda for "justice on the grass," is a judicial process in which the Rwandan public was to try and judge those who wished to confess or had been accused of genocide crimes.[97] While lauded by many as a success story, the gendered impact of *Gacaca* courts has been less subject to stringent scrutiny.[98]

Preliminary analysis suggests that women who experienced sexual violence fare predictably badly in the proceedings.[99] The intimacy of the hearings—usually in a village setting to which the victim and perpetrator both have a connection—has meant that few women have given public testimony about their experiences of rape and sexual violation. Moreover, commentators have noted that villagers attending *Gacaca* sessions are more than mere spectators to the proceedings, and that their accounts and testimonies play an integral role in the procedure.[100] Importantly, villagers' descriptions and reports regarding the defendant and the complainant directly affect the sentencing administered by the presiding judges. A pause to the gendered dimensions of such interactions in the context of intimate sexual violation should raise questions about how secure an environment this would be for a woman testifying to rape or other forms of sexual assault. When such testimony is given, there is no victim or other psychological support systems available, and no special training was given to the facilitators of the *Gacaca* courts to address and manage the particular challenges (and power inequities) that arise when examining sexual violence. There is also some evidence that witnesses have been afraid of their central role in the *Gacaca* process—anecdotal evidence of witnesses being threatened with harm by the family and friends of the defendant abound. For rape victims, the fear of close and effectively unprotected confrontation with their violators may in itself be a significant bar to participation. Compounding the difficulties of confrontation, there is a significant lack of testimonial and medico-legal evidence in Rwanda impeding the investigation and prosecution of sexual violence. The chaos of the genocide meant that medical examination of rape victims and preservation of evidence was not possible. Many women raped during the genocide did not survive the genocide or have since died of HIV/AIDS or other causes.[101] During the genocide, Interahamwe, or soldiers, frequently raped women and girls after they had killed their family members in their presence. Human Rights Watch has reported following numerous interviews with survivors in the context of testifying to rape in *Gacaca* sentiments such as: "I thought about it, but in *gacaca*, it is easy to deny sexual abuse because there are no witnesses."[102] These testimonies depict an erasure of sex-based crimes from communal consciousness and from the oral histories constructed about what happened in all its depth and difficulty to Rwandan society.

There have been modifications to the *Gacaca* laws since their inception. A revised law adopted in 2004 enhances the protection for victims of sexual violence in order to facilitate reporting and testimony.[103] Under the new law, a rape or sexual torture victim may choose among three alternatives: testimony before a single *Gacaca* judge of her choosing; testimony in writing; or testimony to judicial police or prosecutorial personnel, to be followed by the complete processing of the rape case by the prosecutor's office. This is an improvement, but still leaves much work in the implementation phase to protect the security and confidentiality of the victim. That is still very much a work in progress.

Ultimately, we stress that a confrontation in *Gacaca* (or any restorative justice mechanism) may constitute a continuation and extension of the violation rather than a point of closure. Interaction with the perpetrator may underestimate the cost of social expose to victims of sexual violence in societies where sexual violation either is un- or underacknowledged and thus lacking meaningful support systems for the victim and her family. Human Rights Watch has noted in its extensive work on barriers to justice for rape victims in Rwanda that there is a "general societal tendency to minimize the incidence of sexual violence against adult women."[104] Alternatively, in societies where sexual violence is pervasive and "normalized," it may also serve to negatively single out one experience of sexual violation from a host of experiences that the victim (and others) undergo on an ongoing basis. The other sobering point to reflect upon is that any form of criminal accountability, whether formal or restorative, may shift attention away from the urgent material needs of women in post-conflict societies. These needs include food, shelter, health care, and education for themselves and for their children. As Human Rights Watch reminds us:

> For rape victims, particularly those living with HIV/AIDS, medical care and counseling are essential, but they . . . face formidable obstacles to obtaining those services. They lack information about access to care. Fearing stigmatization should they be diagnosed with HIV/AIDS, they do not seek HIV testing or

treatment. They lack funds to pay for health care and for transport to treatment facilities. They frequently do not have family members to assume nursing, child-care and household responsibilities. Many do not have enough to eat, which impairs their health.[105]

This narrative reminds us that criminal accountability is generally an important and central piece of the post-conflict matrix, but it is not sufficient per se to meet the fundamental needs of victims.

CONCLUSION

The augmentation of legal standards defining sexual and sex-based violence committed in war as crimes, combined with the creation of international tribunals and courts, has substantially advanced recognition that sexual violence in conflict is not merely marginal but central to addressing the causes of conflict. Gender-sensitive rules of procedure and evidence, combined with direct support to victims and vulnerable witnesses, have also been a major advance in reinforcing the appropriateness of expanded categories related to legal responsibility for sexual violence in warfare. The lack of legal pedigree for the prosecution of such acts in international law[106] made it imperative that the ad hoc tribunals and now the International Criminal Court continue to view the successful prosecution of sex-based violence as a priority. But even where there is a well-disposed international mechanism of accountability, it will only catch a very small number of particularly horrendous violations that take place in any armed conflict. The perpetrators coming to such courts and tribunals are merely a fraction of those who have committed violations of domestic and international law. More often than not, criminal accountability is neither sought nor supported by the international community and the internal elites who broker the deals that make peace.

It is also evident that criminal prosecution alone does not solve all the issues of accountability and need faced by women victims of sexual violence. A cogent example of this dynamic is evidenced by the treatment and compensation that should be given to women victims and witnesses who have developed HIV/AIDS, transmitted as a result of rape during genocide or systematic sexual violence. In the Rwandan context, scholars have been critical of the ICTR's unnecessarily restrictive approach toward compensation generally and the tribunal's failure to provide antiretroviral (ARV) treatment to victim-witnesses, in stark contrast to the provision of ARVs to defendants in tribunal custody.[107] While the policy was changed in 2004, it illustrated the harsh issues at play in our understanding of justice in such contexts and the broader challenge in providing continuing care to victims once the tribunal ends its work.

Relying on tribunals and courts alone will never close the capture problem we have identified in this book, namely the gap between the harms women actually perceive as being most harmful to them as a consequence of war and the appropriate remedy to respond. Another part of this tapestry is the broader legal reforms and post-conflict reconstruction programs that should, in our view, accompany the criminal accountability process and ideally precede it. These institutional pieces are vital to initiating the complex social and legal work of elevating and valuing women, without which the piecemeal work of a court or tribunal may have little long-term effect nor any domestic institutional support to maneuver it through the local terrain.

Despite the criticism of international criminal accountability, its task is doubly important given the equal lack of credible domestic practices to draw upon in ascertaining and implementing sensitive trial and trial process in adjudicating sexual violence.[108] International action has a double effect. It affirms the importance to states of holding perpetrators accountable for sex-based and sexual violence. Equally, setting international standards that move away from domestic defects may have a knock-on effect, which filters the international standards back to the domestic courtrooms of observing and participating states, thereby remaking practice at the local level.

The lack of international interest in acknowledging that violence against women is pervasive and extensive heightens the significance of adjudicating violence in conflicted and post-conflict societies. While the Convention on the Elimination of All Forms of Discrimination Against Women (CEDAW) and UN General Assembly resolutions have moved issues of violence onto the agenda of the United Nations, female-centered violence is still a peripheral matter to most states, and admonition for its perpetuation has negligible effects. It seems that each small step is a leap as far as the articulation of female-centered violence is concerned. Taking gendered violence out of the feminine arena of the CEDAW Committee and placing it high on a general agenda of international accountability goes some way toward heightening its profile and affirming its seriousness. The danger is that being placed on the agenda does not confirm its place on the hierarchy. One lesson from Nuremberg is that while rape was not charged, sexual forms of torture including rape were presented at the trials, as they were at Tokyo, but little or no international memory was created about the gravity of these acts as an organized and logical part of the conduct of war. Sexual violence has had a history of omission in international law. Most often it is absorbed as a part of the cluster of violence that accompanies the waging of aggressive war, and its particular identity obliterated. Part of the challenge that faces those interested in the realignment of international humanitarian law to account for the persistent recourse to violence against women is to constantly reassert the centrality of law in confronting such violations. This means not only moving to have the positive prohibitions reflect the inclusion of gendered violence, but to have the supporting structures reflect the same prohibitions. This necessitates prosecutorial mechanisms that both respect and protect the defendant's rights while simultaneously correcting gender bias. The long-term success of international criminal law for women rests on the willingness of the international community to ensure that it has defendants to try, witnesses to hear, and victims to listen to. The long-term success of post-conflict reconstruction rests upon understanding what women truly perceive as broadly harmful to them and remedying those harms in the broadest possible sense.

In assessing the influence and value of international and domestic criminal accountability for violations experienced by women, it is also important that we acknowledge law's limits. In doing so, we recognize the symbolic and practical importance of criminal accountability. However, we remain convinced that only a synergy of such mechanisms allied with embedded gender-focused policymaking driving at the deep inequalities and disadvantages experienced by women will fundamentally transform women's lives in post-conflict societies. We caution that feminists should be suspicious when law only addresses a fraction of transgressive sexual acts and fails to engage its powers to compel and to sanction toward engendering equality and nullifying discrimination. Both are central to changing women's lives.

CHAPTER 8
Remedies

This chapter examines a range of legal and quasi-legal remedies in post-conflict societies offering alternative or parallel mechanisms to retributive justice processes. These remedies are typically advanced as multifaceted enablers to address the needs of victims, as well as providing some form of accounting for violations perpetrated during armed conflict. These remedies serve a dual purpose by framing a political and social narrative to the conflict just experienced. They can also function as one of the principle means of economic redistribution utilized to address victims' material needs in post-conflict settings.

Accountability and remedy processes vary considerably across conflicted and transitional societies.[1] We note that methodological differences in such mechanisms and the variance of societal responses to the demands for accountability make it necessary to inject caution into any comparative analysis, such as the one we offer here.[2] A related problem is that the experience of women for cultural, social, and political reasons is varied both within particular transitional societies and across transitional societies. The status of women prior to a conflict, as well as specifics such as educational opportunities, health, and reproductive access and rights, may make a substantial difference to the overall experience of women and the kind of demands for remedy which may then be articulated in the post-conflict phase.[3] Other matters such as intersectionality of violence, due to factors such as religion, ethnicity, sexual orientation, age, and disability, affect any gender analysis of accountability and remedies broadly defined. From our starting point, a key element is the extent to which any measure offers a means to further or deepen women's equality and autonomy in societies emerging from conflict.

We start with a focus on truth commissions and truth recovery processes and then move to discuss reparations, lustration, and other mechanisms that facilitate redressing harms experienced during conflict. Section one addresses truth processes, examining a range of issues, including the gendered dimensions of truth processes, the ways in which women are substantially disadvantaged or excluded, and the manner by which a gendered analysis could be conceptualized and implemented. Section two turns to reparations, addressing their organic link to truth processes and exploring the ways in which such repairs can function to compound rather than undo inequalities. Section three gives attention to lustration as a means to institutionally address systematic human rights violations, exposing the ways in which it has generally operated without reference to or reflection on gendered harms.[4]

TRUTH PROCESSES

In societies transitioning from conflict, the construction of truth matters, both abstractly in terms of identifying "who did what" and concretely to define "who gets what" in the aftermath.[5] Truths are usually excavated by examination and accountability for the past, specifically by structured assessment of serious human rights violations. Many view this backward-looking approach as central to the capacity for damaged societies to transform, thereby rebuilding political and social trust.[6] It is also directly relevant to confronting "social injustice and patterns of inequality, discrimination and marginalization that were underlying causes of a conflict and that inflicted major suffering and victimization on vast swathes of a population."[7] Truth is then poised on the precipice of past and future, deeply contested but essentially unavoidable as a political matter. It also has utilitarian and practical dimensions that profoundly affect the inclusion or exclusion of individuals and groups.

Because of this emphasis on "dealing with the past," the morality and law of holding human rights abusers accountable at the point of societal change has been central to transitional justice discourse in conflicted societies.[8] It makes sense therefore that trials, courts, truth commissions, amnesties, and the degree and form of punishment and remedy to victims should all be the primary focus of interest. But missing has been any substantial and sustained analysis on how and where gender fits within this institutional scheme.

Some societies, or more accurately, the political elites within them, make strategic choices not to engage in discussions about the past and thus to avoid any substantive engagement with the thorny questions of remedy in the process of political accommodation.[9] In doing so, they are represented as making the political calculation that the "peace is too fragile" to be endangered by raking up difficult issues, and that the most pressing need for a society experiencing violence is to bring hostilities to an end.[10] Because men generally dominate peace deals, such calculations are generally made by male political elites from both sides of the hostile factions. Consistently when engagement with the past is a part of a political negotiation toward transition, a number of similar features generally tend to be present. This chapter explores these commonalities and their gendered dimensions.

We examine the functions, structures, and problematics of truth process from a gender perspective. It is important to stress that the issue of gender is not simply a question of illustrating women's experience in times of conflict in a particular narrative space. Rather, demonstrating the differential experiences of men and women is a means to show how conflict "creat[es] specific kinds of subjects."[11] In undertaking this kind of evaluation of truth processes, one can see how conflict operates to limit the opportunities for all—but in different ways for men and women.

Features and Assumptions Concerning Truth Processes

The conditions in which truth processes are established vary from country to country. The context of peace negotiations have a clear bearing on what will be included within a truth commission or truth recovery's terms of reference or mandate. For example, if amnesty figures prominently in the agreement to end hostilities, there is a clear impact on the form (if any) of truth recovery that follows and what crimes a truth process may be empowered to examine.[12] Working on the presumption that truth processes and reparations matter to women emotionally as well as practically, commitments to a truth process and the terms of that process are important to assess in a gender-sharpened viewpoint. The terms of reference for a truth process are particularly pivotal to understanding where gender fits into the frame of accounting, if at all. Historically these terms of reference have been narrow and aimed at addressing violations of political and civil rights. In our view, a genuinely transformative process of truth recovery must be broadly concerned with patterns of inequality and marginalization. Linked to this is the need to ensure that truth-telling is not seen as a costly luxury in highly resource constrained environments, but is integrated into rebuilding all aspects of social, economic, and political life.

Truth processes, and particularly truth commissions, emerged to some extent as a compromise between the inflexibility and formality of criminal legal processes[13] and/or because of unwillingness to pursue any form of criminal accountability for human rights violations which occurred during periods of conflict or authoritarian rule. Using amnesty as an inducement to end hostilities between combatants also figures prominently in the trade-off between advancing criminal accountability or truth process in a post-conflict setting. As we have noted in Chapter 7, gendered violations are generally obscured in the political horse-trading that accompanies amnesty negotiations. This pattern of accountability losses for women in post-conflict institutional mechanisms is also to be seen in truth process creation and operation.

Policy analyst Priscilla Hayner identifies five essential goals for a truth commission that we broadly endorse. These include discovering, clarifying, and formally acknowledging past abuses; responding to specific needs of victims; contributing to justice and accountability; outlining institutional responsibility and recommending reform; and promoting reconciliation and reducing conflict over the past.[14] Thus, the stated aims of truth commissions, as a means of delivering accountability, are to provide a detailed account of patterns of abuse and create an accurate record of a society's past. Across truth processes there is a general consensus that the aim of a truth commission is not criminal prosecution,[15] but rather to build a picture of what happened on a systematic basis in order to prevent recurrence. In this frame, the goal is to move from individual acts or crimes to the broader context in which harms were committed.[16] A truth process is often intended to represent a break from the past, not only by drawing a line under a history of human rights abuses, but by providing a symbolic gesture to overarching political accountability, thereby facilitating the rebirth of political legitimacy within the society. Truth processes therefore carry a greater social and political weight than is immediately apparent, and this further heightens the need to pay close attention to the gender biases that accompany them. Truth processes are also critical to setting the terms upon which reparations occur.

Truth commissions are lauded because they provide a more flexible approach to dealing with a history of human rights abuse than trials do.[17] While trials are characterized as legalistic and narrowly focused on individual perpetrators, truth commissions are regarded as a means of placing the victim at the center of the process and dealing with abuse at a collective or societal level.[18] The role of a truth commission has been described as the mechanism by which "a new public space in which people (often those previously liminal in the context of political transition, such as victims) are allowed to debate the past, to exchange information and perspectives, to externalize grief, loss and anger, and to try to reach some form of consensus as to a way forward."[19]

It follows that a persistent claim made in favor of truth processes in general and truth commissions in particular is the central role played by the victims of human rights violations in the proceedings. In this way, some view the difference between trials and truth commissions as located in "the nature and extent of their attention to victims."[20] In theory then, truth commissions focus on victims, and consideration is given to a "broad array of testimonies when analyzing and describing the greater pattern of abuse."[21] The effect of this, according to Hayner, is to "give victims a public voice and bring their suffering to the awareness of the broader public."[22] Undertaking a gender-centralized review of the success of truth processes reveals that the extent to which this victim-centered identity is meaningful is highly questionable. We argue that for women, the experiences of truth processes may, by contrast, result in greater marginalization and a lack of recognition for the specific experiences of their victimhood. We critically probe the extent to which truth commissions deliver on their promises of victim-centeredness for women.

Truth commissions are further vaunted for facilitating historical or communal narratives on the past experiences of a society, thereby enabling broad political and social outcomes through a politically driven change process.[23] However, this broad focus is not as expansive in practice as the rhetoric that accompanies it suggests. Specifically, the broader picture refers only to the political context in which such acts were undertaken and is usually not intended to probe intersecting, and perhaps more compelling, narratives related to economic and social deprivations of rights.[24] In general, truth processes have rarely or successfully addressed underlying practices of discrimination, exclusion, and marginalization that are intimately linked to the ways in which violence is triggered and then experienced during violent communal conflicts.[25] Identifying these patterns is essential to seeing gender as a relational construction, and not merely to utilize gender as a term to justify uncovering the experience of women in truth recovery processes. Instead, attention to broader and deeper patterns of economic and social exclusion would enable truth processes to advance a more considered understanding of how differently men and women experienced life in a conflict zone. It would also demonstrate how gross human rights violations impacted men and women differently.

Truth commissions and truth recovery processes are capable of fairly and fully addressing such intractable problems, and there are increasing examples of ad hoc bodies doing so effectively.[26] We assert that thin narratives operate to the detriment of truth telling generally, but particularly limit what truth commissions will say about women's experiences. This then affects the broader landscape of legal reform and financial remedy that are inextricably linked to truth recovery processes. If gender and with it social and economic inquiry is left out of the narrative that shapes the change process, then the legal and political transformations that follow are gender deficient.

THE GENDERED DIMENSIONS OF TRUTH RECOVERY

It is now generally accepted that truth commissions and truth recovery processes have lacked a gender dimension.[27] Some recent inroads have been made on this pattern of exclusion, though the fundamental absences and silences experienced by women persist. A number of quite specific features across truth-telling processes are critical to the experiences of women. First, the encounter in the truth recovery setting is one between "victims" and "perpetrators." Both of those terms are not straightforward and require further interrogation. Victims are often defined in relation to acts experienced, though the status may also be conferred by reference to social group, ethnic origin, or minority status.[28] Group status and harms may dominate in the rationale for the establishment of such fora, and this can function to obscure gendered experiences for women, as well as the complex relationship between women's equality and the political goals of key minority, ethnic, or social groups. As a result of the complex relationships between gender and group status, women's harms end up being downplayed or subverted to the perceived wider needs of the group or minority in the truth-telling and reconstruction process.

A growing literature in transitional societies has identified a distinct hierarchy of victim status that emerges in many post-conflict or transitional situations.[29] This hierarchy elevates certain privileged victims, those whose experiences parallel a particular political narrative of the conflict, or whose individual circumstances have strong symbolic resonance for larger national or ethno-political narratives. Left out by such maneuverings are those whose victimhood may be complex or compromised and whose story may serve to "complicate" the narrative rather than giving it the linear coherence that broader political objectives may demand. Women may often fall into this category. Brandon Hamber and Steve Kimble's analysis of the South African truth commission shows a failure to identify women as victims, even though others have documented how women bore the brunt of the oppression experienced through apartheid in its daily and multiple manifestations in homes, streets, and communities.[30] They emphasize the particular need to focus not only on "vertical violence" (between black citizens and security forces) but also on "horizontal violence" (between neighbors and communities).[31] Because apartheid (and similar conflicts) created systems of privilege, exposing those who benefited even as they also experienced victimhood is important and deeply challenging. In South Africa, hierarchical privilege between whites, Indians, "coloreds," and blacks was an important aspect of the apartheid project, which confirms the more nuanced forms of victimhood and the multiple categories of "victim" present in the apartheid era. This particular dynamic of "victim-perpetrator" narrows the interpretation of "victim" to a highly essentialist understanding, undercutting what we learn about the complexity of violence. These complexities have particular purchase for how we place and understand women's narratives. It is important to look past narrow categories of acceptable or "appropriate" victimhood for women, and the stereotypical roles which women are then required to assume within tolerated but predefined boundaries of victim status.[32] Thus women combatants, women perpetrators, women who fail to conform to accepted social stereotypes, and women whose activities or choices involved them crossing ethnic, religious, and social lines are often viewed as being outside the acceptable and elevated categories of victim. The point is not merely descriptive; these women then lose out on the ascribing of status that gives access to remedy, material support, and economic benefits.

Second, the harms for which accountability is sought and remedy is given are invariably violations of civil and political rights, and certain kinds of rights violations have a higher status than others. Most often, the process of transitional accountability and redress restricts itself to examining a narrow band of civil and political rights violations, generally those related to direct physical violation of the person's bodily integrity. These frequently map directly onto those rights considered non-derogable by international human rights law treaties.[33] This process has been described as an inherent "bias" of transitional justice accountability mechanisms.[34] This will "catch" some of the violations which women experience, but not all. They exclude the broader social and economic deprivations that women and their children routinely experience in situations of conflict and which evidently contribute to real harms to the body, such as hunger, lack of access to maternal and reproductive care, and broader health damage. Including these harms within the framework of truth commissions would challenge existing conceptions of the nature and experience of the conflict for both men and women, highlighting the differentials and creating a more reflective basis from which legal and political change (and restitution) follows.

The emphasis on particular kinds of physical harms also avoids engagement with more complex emotional and psychological harms for men and women in conflicted and post-conflict societies.[35] In this vein, some feminist literature suggests that traumas are not externally located but rather are most acutely felt in how "violation came to be incorporated into the meaning and feeling of structures in relationships between husbands and wives; between mothers and sons; and between women themselves."[36] When violation is thus internally incorporated, it is neither time-specific nor singular in effect. Rather, its effects can far exceed the original moment of the violence itself and may not become evident immediately.[37] This issue is particularly relevant given the paucity of women attending and giving testimony to truth commissions and the literature suggesting that women process post-traumatic stress disorder (PTSD) and other forms of trauma differently from men. Truth recovery processes tend to have short and limited time frames, and if one does not "come in" and self-identify as a victim in the given time frame, then there may be no other opportunity to do so.[38] When harms count as violations are then inevitably narrowly constructed. Moreover, when there may be social and psychological differences in how women respond to traumatic experiences truth processes in their current configuration may effectively function to exclude women in multiple and overlapping ways.

Evidence suggests that sites of violation are not external and may not (for women) be experienced in the myriad public or institutional spaces that have overwhelmingly defined the locales of violence for public male actors.[39] Rather the spaces of violation are the private contiguous spaces that women consistently inhabit out of public and legal sight, and unnoticed by the legal processes that frame the transition in many societies.[40] This insight is critical to pinpointing the chasm of differences that may exist between a man's version of what meaningful accountability and remedy constitute and a woman's perceptions of the same process. This means that truth commissions need to widen and deepen their sites of inquiry. It requires consulting with women about what the focus of inquiry should be and opening up a broader array of sites to analysis and understanding of harm and reparation.

A third feature of the truth commission formula is that there is a marked emphasis on public and not private acts for the purposes of recording, as well as constructing a societal narrative.[41] What generally matters is what occurs on streets, in public spaces, and in formal institutional settings.[42] Violations within the home or close to private intimate spaces that women themselves describe as central to their experiences of vulnerability, lack of security, and violation are deemed to fall within the "private" domain in most legal and social systems, and frequently outside the circle of notice and accountability. Thus, what happens within people's homes is not important and often entirely invisible.[43] Moreover, shattering the security of the home space is not an isolated act, but one that for many women is a continuous presence, whose influence lingers literally and emotionally.[44] When truth commissions fail to widen their examination of the narrative of conflict to violations that take place in "private" spaces, they limit a deeper telling of the gendered nature of a violent conflict and its differential impact on men and women.

Some preliminary examples of this public focus are useful to bear in mind here. Across truth-telling processes certain public space violations have a higher status than others. Thus, for example, street confrontations such as the Soweto Riots in South Africa or the Civil Rights Protests of the 1960s in Northern Ireland have attained symbolic even mythic status, whereas violations in the home across jurisdictions fail to have the same kind of preeminence. This commentary is not to suggest that accountability and remedy for street violence are not necessary or that the effects of mass public violence on communitarian identities (male and female) should be dismissed. However, the absence of similar social and political prominence to home-based violations, often the most consistently experienced form of community and family violations which occur in conflicted societies, evidences a profound lack of understanding for events which are absolutely devastating for women. Research has demonstrated that the placing of the home as the center of family life and the lived lives of women within them is considered by women and children as the most humiliating and destabilizing aspects of a rupture with the state. For example, contemporary research in Northern Ireland by Campbell and Connelly indicates that in Northern Ireland, house searches and the manner of their conduct were critical to political radicalization in Nationalist communities.[45] In South Africa, it is also clear that the use of terror tactics by the police and army to violate the homes of "problematic township residents" constituted deliberate and premeditated state policy. Research consistently notes that the "entrance of violence into the home means that political action is everywhere, and no one can ever relax."[46] Thus the violation of the home and familial space can, and is recognized as such by the perpetrator of such acts,[47] constitute a devastating act generating ongoing insecurity at the deepest levels of human and social need. When women gave testimonies to the South African Truth and Reconciliation Commission (TRC), their stories were firmly located in specific time and place most often associated with their domestic roles.[48] Violations in these spaces are deeply bound up with a violation of the location where women usually exercise the most control and mark a fundamental disruption of all which has been ordered and predictable. The loss of security in the family and home is a metaphor for the wider societal chaos but often is missed as such by truth-telling processes. Violation in these locales is understood both by the perpetrators and the female victims to make women feel particularly inadequate, showcasing their failure or powerlessness to protect loved ones, thereby disrupting the moral and community order in a fundamental way.

A number of consequences for any gender analysis follow. First, the general emphasis that works its way through the terms of reference and operation of truth recovery processes affirms the age-old public/private distinction that feminist theorists have so long sought to dismantle.[49] It tells us that despite the rhetoric about transitional justice and truth commissions as transformative structures for a society, they are often narrowly constructed transformative events tailored to specific political needs.[50] More specifically, they are events which predominately seek to fold the experiences of the prior regime/conflict into a narrative that, from a gender perspective, has a consistent patriarchal undercurrent. Essential to centralizing the gendered dimensions of truth processes is the necessity that their mandates include the responsibility to identify underlying practices of social injustice, marginalization, and exploitation that were responsible either directly or indirectly for the violent conflict or crisis or that could weaken the ability of the society to resist further conflict in the future if not redressed. Finally, as a result of defining harms in particular and narrow ways, the narrative being constructed by the truth recovery process is generally one that excludes the home, the family, and the relationship between these entities and the state from the ethno-national project whose legitimization is being serviced by the truth-telling process.

Truth and Gendered Testimony

Truth processes are intended to open up spaces of narrative and voice. A particular feature of women's testimony to these fora is that many victims are literally unable to articulate the harms they have experienced to the audience.

Some women who appeared before the South African TRC were silent in the formal public hearings, unable to give "voice" to their pain.[51] Instead of vocalization, what was heard was silence. As Motsemme argues, such silences should not be dismissed but rather understood as "part of a range of language of pain and grief [which] narrate often hidden but troubled elements of their recent past."[52] It is also important to understand the highly Westernized notions of agency represented by the speech act,[53] which may not map onto the dominant modes of expression in non-Western societies. She also usefully documents the extent to which at TRC hearing women's contributions were defined by "pre-linguistic states of crying, whimpering and inarticulate screeching, which all form part of bodily expressions that are framed outside language."[54] The silence of women is a key component of both a gendered theory of articulation and of the differences between men and women in describing their individual experiences of pain and violation.

Public silences are a persistent feature of women's testimonial presentations in truth-telling contexts. Those silences should not be read as nonstatements about the experiences of women. The problem is one of how we mark the significance of communication (in law as well as in narrative forms) and what weight those listening give to both verbal expression and silence. Thus, scholars such as Venna Das have argued that the failure to understand silence as expression is a denial of both the pain experienced and an act perpetuating the violence experienced.[55] Das has also argued that silence can be a powerful choice for women, an act of agency that is conscious and not passive and should not be understood to regulate the woman's choice of expression as a further act of victimization.[56] Much therefore depends on the sophistication of the listener—in the case of truth processes, the men and women chosen to mold a collection of narratives into a collective expression to mark a divide between past and present. Thus, as Fiona Ross reminds us, we need to be careful, as "diverse ways of telling have different qualities, and silences are not neutral or homogenous or uniform in their effects."[57] A final matter to be addressed in this context is that identified by Ross based on her assessment of the South African TRC. She highlights that women giving evidence generally spoke about the experiences of men with whom they were emotionally or biologically connected (sons, husbands, and family members), while men talked primarily about their own experiences.[58] This externalization of experiences and a lack of voice to women's own experiences evidences the limits of the truth-telling process in their current configuration.

Such insights require us to reflect on what a feminist truth-telling process would look like and what values and mechanisms are best utilized to give women full agency, as well as to wholly and creatively listen to the ways in which women's harms and experiences may be articulated. Here we stress that neglecting or making invisible gendered patterns of harm and abuse entrenches impunity, distorts the historical record, and undermines the capacity of the post-conflict state to be genuinely transformative for women. A feminist truth process would devise and implement a means to fully account for gender-based violations, address the material exclusions and deprivations that define women's lives in times of conflict, and fully report on how gender inequalities underpin much of the violence that occurs, as well as address the broader social, legal, and cultural inequalities that prevail pre-, during, and post-conflict for women.

HOW CAN TRUTH RECOVERY MECHANISMS CENTRALIZE GENDER?

Truth processes need not fail women. They have the symbolic, institutional, and structural capacity to articulate women's experience of conflict, define such experiences in the language of human rights and humanitarian law violations, and create the moral and legal basis to require redress in measures such as reparations that often follow truth processes. UN Security Council Resolution 1325 has created pressure to ensure that the establishment of truth recovery processes give greater attention to design, incorporating women in ways that advance women's representation, presence, and the gender substance of the issues addressed. This creates some momentum to change, particularly as national action plans of implementation are being developed in states that support Resolution 1325. We encourage and support such developments.

Usefully, the International Center for Transitional Justice has produced an effective manual that outlines various mechanisms and practical measures for those creating truth commissions to utilize in centralizing gender.[59] The design element mandates addressing both the internal and external dimensions of truth recovery processes. At the heart of any design process must be meaningful consultation with women. Such discussion must address the processes' terms of reference, their methods of working, the protection and support of those who come to give witness, and attention to the gendered consequences that follow in linking truth with reparations. Substantial and not tokenistic representation of women on truth commissions is critical, as well as gender diversity within the professional staff discharging the day-to-day work of such bodies. Gender-sensitive training for all staff from an early point, as well as the inclusion of and substantial funding to victim support and follow-up, is essential. Procedural requirements include a broad and inclusive mandate that affirms the centrality of gender to the process of truth inquiry, linking social, economic, and cultural rights deprivation with the gendered dimensions of conflict experience and flowing gender through each dimension of the inquiry.

Public outreach to the most vulnerable victims and those who have the least capacity to attend such processes without financial and other assistance is vital. This includes rural women, women with childcare responsibility, women with care functions, women with marginal socioeconomic status, and women whose violations create stigma for them within their communities and families. A good example of this positive approach is provided by the Peruvian TRC, which is viewed as more gender friendly than earlier truth commissions in the region such as those in Guatemala and Chile. The Peruvian model adopted innovations in working methods and give weight and space to gender in its final report.[60] The Peruvian TRC report recommends that the state put in place a comprehensive plan (PIR) whose objective would be to "repair and compensate the victims of human rights violations as well as the social, moral and material losses or damages suffered by victims as a result of the internal armed conflict."[61] This broad approach is a good comparative reference point, although regretfully the TRC report listed rape as the only act of sexual violence identified for reparations through the PIR. As a result, victims of other kinds of sex-based violence are not included within the mandate of reparations provisions. Moreover, the TRC recommended that the reparations program be implemented with five crosscutting foci, including the promotion of gender equality, regretfully, the follow-up body to the TRC, with responsibility for drafting the reparations program, did not take up this recommendation. The Peruvian report demonstrates both innovation and limitations and shows how far we still have to travel in ensuring that these processes genuinely and fully compass women's experiences and then create the bridge to action in the post-conflict and reconstruction phase.

Finally, benchmarking and measuring the outcomes of truth process in terms of their attention to gender issues and their particular capacity to respond to women's needs is an important accountability requirement. In this context, substantive advancements in acknowledging and supporting women's equality and autonomy across a range of transitional mechanisms and institutions are critical.

REPARATIONS[62]

Reparations are increasingly part of the package of measures that accompany post-conflict legal remedy and reform.[63] They are also organically linked with truth processes and other mechanisms that identify "victims" of conflict, offering financial and other types of support to them. Those processes of identification are often deeply contentious and politically divisive, as the recognition of victimhood is viewed as a micro negotiation about the nature and causality of the conflict itself.

Reparations have moved to the center of discussions about remedy in post-conflict societies based on a recognition that transition requires not only doing something to address the actions of perpetrators, but also to specifically address the needs of victims. Reparations come in multiple forms, ranging from individual financial compensation to more innovative forms of group and community compensation of material, social, or financial benefits. Some reparations have no financial component but are symbolic, demonstrative, or memorial in nature. Complicating recognition is the reality that the dividing line between victims and perpetrators in many conflicted societies is a murky one. This complexity layers the negotiations that surround political and legal agreement on victim status and the obligations that follow. The essentialization of women in many contexts as victims tends to obscure engagement in multiple fora around their role as perpetrators or supporters of violence. This pattern also persists in the context of reparations, where a highly essentialized notion of both male and female victimhood tend to dominate and operate to deepen the essentialist narratives of men's and women's behaviors during armed conflict. These essentialist notions often fail to match women's experiences of conflict, and the emphasis on penetrative sexual violence as the epitome of victim status for women has meant that women will actively choose not to be placed in the victim category for social and cultural reasons.

Beyond a narrow utilitarian set of goals and outcomes, reparations can also support states in the process of liberalization or democracy consolidation by recognizing victim citizens as equal rights holders.[64] More radically, reparations are a means to tap the transformative potential of remedy, having "a capacity to subvert, instead of reinforce, preexisting structural inequalities."[65] The root of that enablement lies in the economic dimensions of reparation, which allow the victim the potential for social advancement and the accrual of means in societies that have few such opportunities. Doing so on an equal basis means that reparations can make social and economic equalization possible in ways that criminal accountability and other transitional mechanisms are structurally unable to facilitate. This capacity for transformation is critical and complex for women and, like other post-conflict processes, can advance women's equality in multiple spheres.

Reparation can also inversely operate to stymie or limit women in unexpected ways. When we ask the seemingly simple question of "what do we repair" for women, and if we bring that back to the status quo ante (where the woman figuratively was before the harm took place), in many societies preconflict, women were not treated as equal rights holders but were subject to systematic violence, discrimination, and exclusion. Unless we embed into reparations a means to unsettle preexisting gender hierarchies and undo the structural harms that may, in many cases, be causal to the actual violence and harm experienced during a conflict, we do little to repair for women. We may in fact undo some of the social unsettling that the conflict itself will have produced. As Professor Ruth Rubio-Marín so cogently reminds us, reparations promise a means to link individual rights to a broader political project, "namely, one that may require the transformation of a pre-existing order when it systematically subordinated certain groups."[66]

The trend to incorporate reparations is confirmed in the jurisprudence of regional human rights' bodies and by the practices of states as diverse as Argentina, Chile, Northern Ireland, South Africa, Guatemala, and Peru. The United Nations has produced general guidelines giving guidance on the appropriate support for victims. In 2005, the General Assembly produced the *Basic Principles and Guidelines on the Right to a Remedy and Reparation for Victims of Gross Violations of International Human Rights Law and Serious Violations of International Humanitarian Law*.[67] While the attention to reparations across judicial systems and in UN human rights operations is to be welcomed, the move toward "engendering transitional justice" has by and large had little influence on the conceptualization, design, and implementation of reparation programs on the ground.[68]

Rubio-Marín elaborates an agenda for such "engendering" with three specific criteria:

[1] avoiding formal gender discrimination in the design and implementation of such programs . . . [2] looking for ways of ensuring that patriarchal norms and sexist standards and systems of values are not leaked into reparations . . . [3] optimiz[ing] the . . . transformative potential of reparation programs so that they serve to advance toward the ideal of a society altogether free of gender subordination.[69]

Some of the practices encouraging such transformation include linking reparation to legal reform (particularly with respect to women's rights to hold real property), asking women what forms of reparation best meet their needs, assessing and supporting the women in the context of the community they live in or have to return to, and viewing reparation as a means to give agency to women rather than as confirming the status of passive victims.

There is some evidence of an emerging practice of engendering reparations in well-established human rights tribunals. For example, in November 2009 the Inter-American Court decided the *Cotton-Field v. Mexico* case, which is the first international human rights decision to recognize the nexus between reparation and a situation of structural discrimination. Here the Court found that reparations should aim at reforming the general gendered context in which the violation occurred, thus aspiring to restitution but also to correction.[70] The Court ordered that the investigation into the deaths of a number of women specifically include a gender perspective to fully understand the social and cultural context in which sexual violence occurred. This approach points to the potential for the transformation of reparations practice not only in the specific context of transitional justice but more broadly applied to human rights violations. The Nairobi Declaration on Women's and Girls' Rights to a

Remedy and Reparation is also evidence of the gathering international pace on the importance of reparation to women's rights as victims but more broadly to the use of remedy to undertake deeper corrective and equality-focused transformation.[71] Section 3 of the Declaration thus outlines

> That reparation must drive post-conflict transformation of socio-cultural injustices, and political and structural inequalities that shape the lives of women and girls; that reintegration and restitution by themselves are not sufficient goals of reparation, since the origins of violations of women's and girls' human rights predate the conflict situation.

As outlined above, reparation comes in many forms. For example, it includes apologies, dedications, financial compensations directly to the victim, communal reparations, building social infrastructure, and providing health care and other needs on a group basis. While all of these options for repair need to be evaluated on their own merits and in the context of the harms in question, it is also globally desirable that the gendered dimensions of any proposed reparations program be evaluated in the societal context of recovery and rebuilding. Public apology, for example, may be limited as a form of reparation to victims when it ignores the structural dimension of the harm in question.[72] Apologies do little to address fundamental structural inequity and may in fact mask its ongoing perpetuation in the form of institutional revision and/or creation. In this context, the form of reparation and its effect on addressing broader issues of structural inequality and deprivation can only be fully addressed by the core mechanisms of consultation, gender-sensitive design, and implementation, as well as transparent and gender-informed benchmarking.

In many post-conflict programs and structures, gender has not been systematically included in reparations design and execution. First, reparations programs do not adequately "count" or include the harms that women experience, leaving out rape, sexual violence, reproductive harm, sexual mutilation, forced domestic labor, forced "marital" unions, forced impregnation, forced abortions, forced sterilization, and deliberate infection with sexually transmitted diseases and/or HIV/AIDS.[73] Some of these fault lines are inherited from their reliance on truth processes as a means to adequately define the universe of victims to compensate. Some are self-made by failing to recognize the gender-stratified and discriminatory universe into which reparations judgments and remedies fall. Second, reparation programs are often underinclusive in their design (comparable again to the biases of truth processes), relying primarily on what are presumed to be the most serious human rights violations: torture, murder, disappearance, and other violations of physical integrity including imprisonment and due process violations. In the Peruvian reparations program, for example, where violations were ordered on a scale of severity, rape was at the bottom of the list because it was concluded that rape did not end victims' lives, nor affect the capacity of victims to generate income.[74] Such an approach reveals an extraordinary masculine bias in the assessment of what constitutes irreparable harms[75] and how those harms play out over a lifetime, particularly in societies where women are valued for their childbearing capacity as well as their perceived purity. While some reparations processes have compensated by "interpreting in" sexual violations to the more general categories of serious harms,[76] this approach is inadequate. Reparations must provide explicit recognition to female-gendered harms. When this occurs, women gain the material benefits of reparation, and thus reparations fulfill the broader mandate of enabling full democratic citizenship for women, by operating as a mechanism to enhance and extend social, economic, and cultural status.

A third structural bias of reparation, which coincides neatly with the same phenomenon for truth processes, is the emphasis that reparation follows from testimony to the harm experienced. Requirements of public process, often allied with requirements related to proof of harm, significantly disadvantage women from receiving reparation benefits. As we discussed in the context of truth commissions, the combination of stigma in attesting to certain harms allied to strict time limits that fail to recognize the difficulties for women in coming forward to attest to sex-based harms in the aftermath of conflict, are enormous structural barriers excluding benefit from the material compensations that reparations bring.[77] There are ways to surmount these issues. For example, in addressing the issues of time lag and its relationship to gendered harms, the truth commission in Timor-Leste (East Timor) recommended that the reparations program consider victims who have come before the commission, but also allowed a two-year lag for other potential beneficiaries to be identified.[78] Finally, when reparations themselves are structured in ways that fail to recognize existing legal barriers to women, they then compound rather than subvert inequality. In societies where women cannot own property or are limited in the capacity to access material wealth through customary law rules, lump-sum monetary payments, for example, may simply be absorbed and spent by men. Thus, the form of reparation matters and can compound existing inequalities.[79] It is patently evident that the reparation may be negatively affected by structural discrimination within communities or may be subject to manipulation or vulnerable to interference by paternalistic ends.

The design of national reparations programs may require rethinking, particularly in societies where there are limited economic means and individual reparation may not be economically feasible—specifically by thinking through balance between individualized and communal measures. Reparations may be able to go "above and beyond the immediate reasons and consequences of the crimes and violations" and "address the political and structural inequalities that negatively shape women's and girls' lives."[80] Collective material and economic benefits are a key aspect of thinking forward. If the stigma associated with rape or other crimes prevents women from accessing or wanting to access the individual reparations, should the repair mechanism then accrue to the community (even if the community is essentially perpetuating the stigma, i.e., rewarding them for their views)? Should financial compensation be awarded to women based on culturally defined harms such as virtue and reputation? These are difficult questions as they value the very assets, such as virginity and purity, that are instrumental in patriarchal societies to the causes of violence for women in the first place.[81]

Looking forward, a basic requirement for the design and implementation of reparation programs ensures that they do not perpetuate or enshrine discrimination.[82] While this means that they must recognize gendered harms such as rape, reproductive harms, and the transmission of HIV/AIDS, a broader question is whether they should address society-wide gender-based discrimination.[83] Some reparation programs include innovative solutions that not only address the violations which women experienced during a conflict, but promise a route to confront the systematic and deeply entrenched violations that women encounter as part of the day-to-day reality within their cultural and jurisdictional context. They do so by focusing on the range of harms that women experience, without a singular focus on sexual penetrative violence and by offering some material security to women to undo the vulnerability that creates a perpetual cycle of inequality and exclusion. An additional positive feature of some recent reparations efforts, in recognition that resources are meager in many post-conflict societies, has been to expand and concentrate reparation on broad material benefits such as education, health care, and housing rather than on lump-sum payments to specific individuals. In parallel, thinking broadly about forms of reparation that can be interlinked to material supports, individual acknowledgment, apologies, and public recognition may be offered. However, the material emphasis lies on providing physical and mental health care, pensions, provision of education, skills training, and microcredit. These broad social goods are also tailored and prioritized to those groups who are deemed most vulnerable in the post-conflict environs, such as women and children, war-wounded, and widows. The provision of these goods corresponds to the anecdotal evidence that suggest that these immediate, medium-, and long-term provisions are more valued by women in the post-conflict phase. For example, the Sierra Leone TRC has recommended that the family members of survivor victims be included among the potential recipients of medical services including physical health care and psychological support.[84] This is an important precedent in establishing that family care (usually carried out by women) is accepted as a category requiring support and recognition through reparation programs on its own merits. In Timor–Leste (East Timor), the Commission for Reception, Truth, and Reconciliation (CAVR) specifically defined the categories of most vulnerable victims it would give priority to, and these included people with mental and physical disabilities, victims of sexual violence, widows and single mothers, and children affected by the conflict. Morocco's Equity and Reconciliation Commission has recommended that reparations to female victims should be systematically larger (10–20 percent) than to their male counterparts for the same kind of violation, in recognition of the differential effect of violence on women and men.[85]

While there has been significant emphasis on holding individual perpetrators accountable, much less attention has been paid to how "gender considerations could be integrated into measures for redress."[86] Even in the context of accepted violations of a woman's sexual and physical integrity, there are limitations in conceptualization and enforcement of remedies. Specifically, sexual and reproductive violence not only undermines basic integrity rights, but also violates a number of other substantive economic, social, and cultural human rights. As a result, sexual and reproductive violence must be understood as a form of structural violence "whose far-reaching political, social and economic effects influence the countries' long-term chances for recovery and development."[87] In this view, a gendered understanding sees not only the physical violation, but understands its connection to a range of other social, emotional, and economic capacities. Repair based on this conceptualization would compensate not only the direct physical harm but the other connected harms.[88] Thus while sexual violence has been at the forefront of advocacy for reparations, it should not serve to obscure or limit engagement with wider discrimination. Exclusions create the conditions conducive to women's inferior social status and their heightened economic, social, and cultural vulnerability. In this view, sexual violence becomes an important lens to view other harms, make them visible, and repair more broadly and deeply.

LUSTRATION, VETTING, AND GENDER

A final practice in the newly developing range of remedies that have come to the fore in post-conflict societies are lustration and vetting, which serve as "processes for assessing an individual's integrity as a means of determining his or her suitability for public employment."[89] Lustration and vetting constitute tools to address the structural deficits of legal and political institutions and acknowledge systematic human rights violation.[90] The end result of such procedures may be to exclude or purge officials of prior regimes and/or human rights violators from public office. This form of accountability is administrative; generally, it has little direct involvement with victims. Its strength lies in signaling the values of new state institutions, and it can have punitive consequences for human rights violators by taking away their state employment and their status as policemen, military officers, or state officials.

In general, vetting and lustration have been far less studied than other measures such as prosecutions, truth-telling, and reparations. This institutional reform aspect of vetting has been mainstreamed by international organizations involved in post-conflict societies, thereby increasing its political currency and impact. Countries in which lustration has taken place include Argentina, El Salvador, Greece, South Africa, Bosnia and Herzegovina, Poland, Hungary, the Czech Republic, and East Germany. Lustration and vetting are rarely integrated with gender-centered accountability and remedy. We argue that there is a high value in such incorporation and in thinking through the use of lustration to address gendered harms by state officials.

The emphasis in states that have implemented or considered vetting and lustration processes has been on addressing violations of civil and political rights. Within this broad framework there is a clear hierarchy of violations being seized upon as particularly important—generally torture, violations of the right to life, and occasionally serious violations of due process rights. Particular violations experienced by women are generally absent, and sex-based violations have not figured prominently in the discourses surrounding the implementation of lustration or vetting procedures. Moreover, little attention has been paid to how more generalized violations may have been experienced differentially by women and men.

Institutions in transitional societies exert considerable capacity to transmute and reinvent themselves in hasty fashion when threatened with externally driven change. Post-transition political influence is generally directed at self-protection and avoiding or minimizing the ouster of officials from public office regardless of what human rights violations they may have committed, including serious crimes of gender violence. These insights reveal the importance of addressing institutional makeup and the need to reinvigorate such institutions post-conflict with gender centrality as an imperative.

Formulas for vetting vary. In El Salvador, vetting included "total vetting," "direct vetting," and "indirect vetting." Total vetting implicates the complete abolishment of an institution, direct vetting is generally explained as explicit vetting that evaluates the personnel of an institution and determines who should be separated from it, and indirect vetting refers to institutional reform measures that require personnel to undertake new selection procedures in the future.[91] The Greek transition involved "differentiated vetting," in which a form of variable treatment was applied to various aspects and agents in the state apparatus who were involved in serious and systematic human rights violations.[92] The variability concept emerges from the central tension between fairness and responsibility in the transitional moment. Other states (Argentina as an example) have rolled out practices of implicit rather than explicit vetting. These informal practices show that one response to a lack of formal mechanisms in numerous countries has been "indirect" vetting processes, whose activation largely depended on the agitation of victims themselves and the nongovernmental sector more broadly.

Lustration is invariably a function of the political context and political compromise which dictate the pace and form (if any) of vetting. Timing and political environment are a significant part of lustration conversations. Various country studies illustrate different models. Argentina, for example, presents the face of gradualism. Here the state sought to avoid an immediate and all-out purge of officials suspected of gross human rights violations, but implemented a more phased form of official removal—with the consequent effect of undermining the conditions that make full rehabilitation of institutions and officialdom possible.[93] El Salvador illustrates the limitations of improvised vetting instruments allied with selective multilateral political pressure and the challenge of vetting in a context of extreme instability.[94] South Africa illustrates how a lack of any formal vetting can still allow for practices like vetting to emerge in institutional practices de facto, specifically through policies of rationalization and affirmative action.[95] While officially sanctioned vetting processes generally garner the headlines (and prove most contentious) and are perhaps least efficient,[96] forms of de facto vetting emerge as the most interesting study. In all the cases involving lustration, the gender component of the violations giving rise to administrative action were at best subdued, at worst invisible. The post-conflict lustration conversation is one in which women struggle to be heard and have structural impact.

One difficult and underassessed arena is the extent to which individual country approaches to lustration conform to broader international standards concerning impunity and accountability for human rights violations, including standards of nondiscrimination on the basis of sex. With this general concern is our broader assessment that, by and large, lustration and vetting processes are rarely informed by the experience of gendered harms. Specifically the decision to apply administrative sanctions will never be based on the scale and extent of sex-based harms. Moreover, there is also little if any attention to the necessity of addressing structural impunity for gendered crimes, and the patriarchal institutions and attitudes that create an environment in which gendered violations take place are tolerated and perpetuated. If gender harms were more broadly defined to include a range of women's experiences, lustration might function (with truth processes and reparation) to play a wider role in embedding equality practices and use institutional reform as a platform for wider gender redress.

Vetting is not a one-stop process. Instead we conceive of a vetting continuum whereby lustration and/or vetting may emerge over time as a key long-term element of institutional reform. In tandem, the success of administrative justice is grounded on the foundation of accurate information and processes of information management, as well as transparency and fairness in the execution of any such process. The technicalities making for successful administrative practice are very difficult to implement in conflicted and post-conflict societies, and they encounter specific roadblocks when gender-based violations are in play. For lustration to have meaningful effect, it must be connected to broad and deeply transformative political and legal processes. Lustration embarked upon without other transitional mechanisms in play is unlikely to have deep institutional effects on the management and military cultures that created and sustained massive human rights violations within conflicted states. But, considered as one of an array of mechanisms operating on multiple levels it may function to embed broader institutional values that become central to the state's new dispensation. In this way, if we think of remedies in broad ways, lustration and vetting cannot be viewed as sites apart from criminal accountability, truth processes, and reparation but rather as equally necessary to the integration of deep and lasting structural changes that have crosscutting effects in post-conflict societies.

CONCLUSION

Truth recovery, reparation, and lustration are often viewed as more holistic solutions to the violations that have taken place in highly complex and intractable conflicts than criminal trials, because they offer a broader and more flexible menu of accountability to societies struggling to reestablish the rule of law. They are also frequently promoted because of their apparent informality, as options that allow for seemingly open-textured procedures, making them ostensibly more suitable for the variedness and complexity of the transitional legal landscape. Despite this external appearance, such mechanisms in practice often mimic (unwittingly or otherwise) the kind of procedural formalities and biases that are to be found in a formal legal proceeding.[97] To some degree, these procedural formalities may be part of the institutional DNA that is activated once legal form and method enter the seemingly informal process in any measure.[98] Equally, all of these mechanisms, despite their departures from the restrictions of ordinary criminal norms of accountability, reflect many of the same biases of exclusion to women's experiences that are present in the more formal processes of the criminal law (whether domestic or international). These biases and exclusions have an obvious bearing on the efficacy of these processes and solutions in remedying women's experiences of the violation.

Fundamentally, the pragmatics of informal justice in transition are no less gendered than their formal counterparts, despite the casualness and flexibility of operation which might, at face value, lend itself to assumptions about gender neutrality rather than emphasizing masculinized priorities. Moreover, as has been surveyed elsewhere, informal processes have a greater risk of susceptibility to discriminatory factors, as the very lack of formal due process means that subjective (and often biased) factors can enter the deliberative context. As we have consistently articulated, the liberal critique of the justice component of transition has frequently overlooked a key reference point: the gendered nature of "justice" in the transitional context with a sustained analysis of what "wrongs" are accounted for and which are not.

Institutional sites such as truth processes, reparation, and lustration for officials (and consequent reform of institutions) are an important battleground for women's rights and profoundly shape the new dispensation and the functioning of the state that emerges post-conflict. They are the preparatory sites for transformation, but if bounded or limited in the notion of what is to be transformed, there are clear winners and losers. Women are far too often on the losing or minimal side of the transformation equation. By reconceiving these sites as places of feminist activism, much may be gained for advancing a broader notion of what is to be remedied in the transitional context, the result of which may be practical gains for women and girls. The goal is to enrich the transitional justice project with mechanisms that are broadly framed to account for socioeconomic rights and needs, and maximizing the material gains that women can make through conceptions of remedy that are grounded in and draw from the lived experiences of gendered harm.

CHAPTER 9
Law Reform, Constitutional Design, and Gender

New laws and constitutions are increasingly part of the standard package of legal and political revision that accompanies the end of violent conflict in many societies. Agreements on principle, as well as specific and detailed provisions on law reform and new constitutional arrangements, constitute a core element of multiple peace agreements. Law's expansion as a substantive site of peacemaking offers significant possibilities to advance women's rights and to address women's needs in numerous post-conflict settings.

This chapter concentrates on rule of law, constitution making, and constitutional enforcement. We are concerned not only with what laws and constitutions do *for* women, but also what they do *to* women; even where laws and constitutions may appear neutral, they often impact disparately or differently with respect to gender.[1] Legal reform is critical in post-conflict societies. Legal reform places the mantle of legitimacy on the nascent post-conflict government, providing alternative routes to the resolution of differences that may have previously given way to violence. Legal reform is often the way for a new post-conflict government to prove its bona fides with the watchful international community. Legal transformation is also essential in societies where women face formal and entrenched discrimination and where access to law is limited for, or excludes, women. As outlined in Chapter 1, violent societies, poverty, and the status of women overlap; consequently, the post-conflict rule of law must be wielded to address the status and autonomy of women in order to move beyond violence and poverty toward peace and equality.

In parallel, constitutions are an important tool to advance substantial legal transformation. Constitutions are valuable because they frame the prospect of a fresh start for a community; for places that have been deeply and intrinsically violent, constitutions have tremendous symbolic importance. Moreover, constitutions may provide the mechanical instruments to harness political impulses, transmuting violent action into more constructive dispute settlement. For women, constitutions may have a more pragmatic and immediate function by offering a route to address direct discrimination and formal legal barriers that may have limited their status and capacity before and during conflict. In this chapter, we posit that constitutional creation and reform in conflicted societies is central to broader peace process negotiation, arguing that one cannot fully understand or explore women's constitutional and legal advancements in a post-conflict setting without fully theorizing and understanding the overlap between rule of law, constitutions, and peacemaking.

Section one of this chapter examines rule of law initiatives and their effects on compounding, rather than undoing, existing inequalities for women. We address the longer-term implications of inadequate and ill-conceived legal reform in societies that have been deeply violent. We follow by assessing rule of law rhetoric and initiatives in multiple post-conflict societies, exploring their value and limitations for women and offering a set of pragmatic suggestions on ways to undertake legal reform that would place gender central. Section two turns to constitutional revision and enforcement and reveals the low priority and attention given to women's full membership in the constitutional and legal community. A critique of the "gender-neutral" citizen infuses our analysis, exposing the limits of this concept in post-conflict settings. Section three analyzes peace agreements as constitutional texts. It examines the constitutional dimensions of pre-agreement, framework, and implementation agreements, along with their implications for women. This analysis is concerned not only with equality (both formal and substantive) for women but also with equity and agency, the latter including access to and effective participation in decision-making.[2] Section four scrutinizes the tendency to focus on the rights-bearing portions of a constitution as *the* route to addressing women's rights. We argue that concentrating on constitutional rights provisions alone is insufficient to fully capture the way in which power is structured in post-conflict societies and can miss the broader and negative impact of constitutional changes for women.[3] We broadly address transitional constitutional design and the ways in which the arms of government relate to one another and with what consequent effect for women. We emphasize the importance of social and economic rights and view them as an important structural vehicle to bring about transformative effect in transitional societies. Section five addresses reproductive rights for similar reasons, drawing out an emphasis on the importance of autonomy for women in post-conflict settings.

GENDER AND THE RULE OF LAW IN POST-CONFLICT SOCIETIES[4]

This section briefly explores how gendered and problematic dimensions of rule of law discourse and practice can intensely emerge in post-conflict societies and how that impacts (or fails to impact) women. In focusing attention on gender deficits, we hope to sharpen and reorient rule of law discourses by bringing gender into view. There is no one-size solution to rule of law reform across multiple violent societies. Rather, we start from the premise that women need to be factored into legal reform from the outset, that they be meaningfully consulted about the priorities for reform, and that their needs and rights are integrated at every relevant opportunity. Most challenging in this regard has been the blatant sidelining of gender in rule of law initiatives across multiple states, based on the premise that the rule of law itself is a neutral concept. We start by undermining that essential premise. Situating our analysis is the idea that the rule of law movement gains cachet from being a defining and motivating cog in the transitional process. It is also a highly influential movement with significant buy-in from international institutions and states invested in conflict zones, politically, militarily, and otherwise. Yet, such transformation can be selective, both in its spheres of influence and in its masculinity. While transformation may occur, the pivotal question we raise is: for whom?

There is a need for further empirical research mapping causality between rule of law initiatives and gender-oriented goals (particularly given the methodological challenges presented by measuring rule of law gains or losses).[5] As we have set out in other parts of this book, what may appear to be a moment of opportunity for women can become a moment of retrenchment. Such retrenchment, at least from a feminist perspective, is arguably located in the core private/public division that accompanies the rule of law in theory and practice. Moreover, despite substantive advances in dismantling the public/private divide in many Western societies, Western states—in part, through rule of law proselytizing—can entrench the operation of this divide in transitional states.[6] The goals of rule of law reform are often unclear. Indeed, "reliance on the rule of law as the harbinger of greater gender equality might be over-optimistic, if not misleading."[7] We agree.

In crude terms, the "rule of law" is an assertion of law's preeminence: its autonomy from and superiority over fallible politics and other potential tools for post-conflict transition. Enthusiasm for the rule of law by development experts, security analysts, and human rights activists is driven by "a desire to escape from politics by imagining the rule of law as technical, legal, and apolitical."[8] This caricature, however, underplays the complexity of modern governance and administrative regulation.[9]

Law is not a panacea for ending violence; indeed, law can serve to "validate and facilitate oppression and violence, whether by the state directly or by private actors with tacit state approval."[10] This systematic pattern illustrates the barriers faced and the extent to which a more somber set of expectations concerning the rule of law's impact might strengthen rather than weaken women's positions. Such minimal conceptions lack any emphasis on the substantive outcomes and, in terms of gendered results, are often satisfied by procedural reforms (rules written, courts in operation) rather than any fundamental assessment of transformation in the quality and substance of law delivered by such institutions. A key element in this matrix is the international community's demand for the rule of law in post-conflict societies. Minimal conceptions of the rule of law imported to post-conflict societies can negatively impact the advancement of substantive gender goals in at least three ways.

First, formal or procedural understandings of the rule of law contain an implicitly conservative bias. The rule of law in its narrowest vein is viewed as generally unconcerned with the content of rules and is in many formulations "compatible with gross violations of human rights."[11] In this formulation, the rule of law agenda does not lend itself to resisting values embodied by the state, and its transformative reach is potentially (and in many of its current configurations) stunted. In this light, rule-of-law-infused transitions can arguably sustain, without contradiction, persistent discrimination against women, systematic and normalized private violence, and immovable barriers to equality in the public sphere. Self-evidently, when one takes onboard an international human rights law corpus that includes the pivotal Convention on the Elimination of All Forms of Discrimination Against Women (CEDAW), some legal frames may hold significantly better outcomes for women than others. The distance between "rule of law" and "human rights" discourses is reduced when thicker and more substantive understandings of the rule of law are invoked (notwithstanding also that human rights rhetoric can equally shortchange substantive gender goals). Nonetheless, the essential point is that rule of law frames for transitional societies offer potentially splintered and pared-down transformation, but in the guise of substantive change. One way to articulate this difference may be to distinguish between reform and transformation. Both offer movement forward from the status quo, which in a deeply conflicted or violent society is a positive outcome when mass atrocity, undeniable suffering, and uncontrollable violence are all variously at play.[12] But for those stakeholders who seek transformative change, the rule of law paradigm may always fall short.[13] The challenge for feminists and those concerned with the advancement of women's interests in the context of social transformation is how to capture some of these mechanisms and bend them more systematically to women's needs, if outright reform is unlikely.

Second, and following from its inherent conservatism, rule of law formalism—as "universal rules uniformly applied"[14] entrenches the invisibility of the private sphere through its implicit orientation toward the value of autonomy. Law generally does not recognize the gendered subject as different, but seeks instead merely to guarantee a level of individual autonomy from interference by the state or from others.[15] We find this to be insufficient.

Accepting that dichotomies of sameness and difference provoke their own reactions from feminist scholars, the inability to structurally acknowledge and address the compounded exclusions and harms experienced by women in transitional societies means that they are implicitly disadvantaged by the status of the autonomy value. Elevating minimalist rule of law values can therefore sustain a public/private divide in which (domestic and international) law's "proper" role is merely to police the boundaries between autonomous, self-regulating individuals. As Hilary Charlesworth has aptly pointed out, "[h]istorically, the formation of the state depended on a sexual division of labor and the relegation of women to a private, domestic, devalued sphere. Men dominated in the public sphere of citizenship and political and economic life."[16] The creation and maintenance of these boundaries has been facilitated and legitimized by a rule of law discourse, within which presumed neutrality is a central plank. What Western policymakers and political observers are overlooking in their enthusiasm for the rule of law as a response to troubled transitions is that movement from a state of weak or absent rule of law to the achievement of the rule of law involves far more than getting judges trained, putting modern police equipment in place, and reprinting and distributing legal texts. It is a transformative process that changes how power is both exercised and distributed in a society and thus a process inherently threatening to existing power holders. It also involves basic changes in how citizens relate to state authority and also to each other in the public sphere and in the private sphere of home and family. Grasping that transformative potential is critical to ensuring gender centrality in rule of law initiatives. Honing into this aspect of rule of law transformation is absolutely critical for advancing women's rights and prioritizing their needs.

The implications for women of the public/private divide have been well documented by feminist scholars over the decades.[17] Law's oversight of the private domain is purposely constrained, and it remains effectively out of regulatory bounds. This, in turn, ultimately translates into structured inequality and exclusions being validated to the social, legal, and economic detriment of women. We argue that this rule of law blind spot becomes particularly manifest in transitional reform initiatives. The nub surprisingly is that despite inroads made on the public/private division in many Western democracies, its reestablishment in the context of transitional societies represents a marked feature of the rule of law paradigm. New beginnings can paradoxically facilitate a retreat to the private domain while celebrating the reconfiguration of the public. There is increasing evidence that transitions with thin conceptions of the rule of law produce adverse or limited gender outcomes. Moreover, given the inherent rule of law biases outlined above, it is not clear that substantive rule of law application fundamentally changes outcomes for women.

The third potential consequence of elevating rule of law formalism is that in the desire to "reestablish normality" during the transitional period or to enhance the legitimacy of legal transplants, rule of law interventions may actually encourage and reify "traditional" cultural practices and structures that are ultimately harmful to women or that reentrench women's prior exclusion. This approach or deference-led legal reform by intervenors lends itself to becoming allied with traditional authority structures that oppress women. Moreover, and highly problematic for women, international actors will frequently cede control of customary law to local entities with negative impact for women in order to secure agreements with local elites.

Law and Legislation

Law reform priorities rarely impinge upon those legal strictures that most limit women's equality and protection in conflicted societies. Thus, commercial rules frequently emerge ascendant; it is no accident that such reforms facilitate the opening up and functioning of markets.[18] Criminal accountability is frequently at the forefront of the rule of law project, and we concur that accountability is a priority. Nonetheless, as Chapter 7 on criminal accountability reveals, this accounting is selective and decidedly gendered, exposing the limited willingness and capacity to address the full range of harms experienced by women in these societies.[19] Criminal prosecutions generally emerge for a narrow range of sexual violations, and the dearth of prosecution sought and successfully achieved is striking. Administrative law reforms rarely engage wholesale with the private sphere and generally strike Faustian bargains with religious institutions, which oust from the regulatory frame those matters which affect the private lives of women and their capacity to participate meaningfully in the public spheres. The exclusions range from contract reform, inheritance, property ownership, divorce, and a range of legal status matters.[20] All of these significantly impact access to legal opportunity structures for women.[21] At a minimum, reconsidering the rule of law as inclusive to women requires a reordering of priorities, listening to constituencies that include women in shaping the priorities of law, and implementing change that reflects more equitable gender parity.

Notwithstanding the limitations of much rule of law reform efforts, some of those reform efforts have engaged in substantial institutional work that address the role of women in transitional contexts. The Office of the High Commissioner on Human Rights has developed a set of practical reports/toolkits for post-conflict states.[22] These practical resources cover a range of areas—truth commissions, prosecution initiatives, vetting, mapping the justice sector, the legacy of hybrid courts, monitoring legal systems, and reparations programs. For example, the reparations report argues that newly established reparations mechanisms should afford women significant input into identifying the rights that would trigger reparative benefits, allow for more complex conceptions of reparation (beyond merely material compensation), and ensure that women have a significant role in the distribution and control of compensatory redress.[23] The toolkits demonstrate two things: (1) a conceptual recognition of the need to bring women into the frame of transitional societies across a range of dimensions; and (2) concrete suggestions on how to address the absence of women in meaningful and practical ways. Nonetheless, without a radical reassessment of the implications of existing mainstream approaches to conflict resolution and governmental transitions, we remain profoundly skeptical of the capacity of broader systematic change.

Even in those transitional states where the rule of law reforms have included a gendered dimension, some telling patterns emerge. The first is the gap between the rhetoric of equality transformations and the lack of enforcement measures on the ground. This underenforcement problem for gender equality has been identified in places as diverse as Northern Ireland, South Africa, and Afghanistan.[24] The site of the gap is most evident as we measure the lag between the powerful equality-driven rhetoric of transitional constitutions and their subsequent interpretation and enforcement in specific contexts. Second, peace agreements often contain gender equality language, driven by the requirements of supranational legal obligations of UN Security Council Resolutions 1325 and 1820, 1888, and 1889. Close examination of these agreements reveals that gender inclusion lacks grounding in principles and practices of equality and autonomy that might be achieved by linking treaty provisions to specific mechanisms of enforcement or measurements assessing success or failure.

There is virtue in starting with a more circumspect view of the benefits that rule of law brings for and to women in transitional societies. In recognizing the corrosive effects that the legal production of certain kinds of rules have for women in transitional societies, we may at least start to take remedial steps. The first of those is grounded in slowing down the rule of law importers and exporters. Pause and reflection may be the start of a more thoughtful way forward, where women seeking justice do not merely get law, but also get a commitment to and enforcement of equality.[25]

CONSTITUTIONAL TRANSFORMATION
AND POST-CONFLICT PROCESSES

The theory and practice of constitutions and constitutional design differs in conflicted and transitional societies from historic constitutional settings.[26] A key feature of many post-conflict negotiations has been agreement on constitutional principles, as well as the inclusion of "constitutional-like" arrangements, within peace agreements themselves. While constitutional agreements rarely ever constitute a utilitarian mechanism to end the violence between political adversaries, they typically include a range of measures that impact legal and political structures within the state in conflict, with the goal that these structural changes will have transformative effects on the causality of violence. The importance of substantive and structural legal reform is understood as so central to the short- and long-term cessation of hostilities that while the agreements to end conflict are often described as "peace treaties," they regularly also constitute core constitutional agreements, contain elements of such agreements, or even fully incorporate regional human rights instruments as the basis for the post-conflict constitution.[27] The dividing line between traditional constitutional documents, whether constitutions per se or Bills of Rights, may be elided by the reality that in practice the two may be collapsed in the course of ending violent contestation between various political actors.

While this section examines the constitutional elements of conflict endings, it is important to understand that there is often no clear blue water between the constitutional "piece" and the wider set of agreements to end violence. Nor is there a clear sense as to how the constitutional elements will be practically and effectively implemented when post-conflict institutions have yet to be established. What we now also better understand is that most new constitutions fail, and with them, most new democracies.[28] As a result, it becomes particularly important to play close attention to how constitutions are crafted in post-conflict settings, particularly when such documents may be one of the bridges to ending violence and advancing peaceful coexistence over the short, medium, and long term. The process by which documents are agreed to and implemented is also decisive to how women are incorporated into or excluded from constitutional processes and agreements.

In charting this gendered territorial overlap between peace agreements and constitutional agreements, this analysis focuses on three aspects: (1) the negotiation process that leads to the inclusion of constitutional norms in peacemaking deals; (2) the substantive constitutional conversations and content that accompany the deal making, with particular emphasis on equality provisions, as well as the grounding of agency for women in institutional design; and (3) the enforcement of constitutional content, as it affects and implicates women's interests and needs. Throughout we pay particular attention to women's exclusion from the process and substance of norm creation and enforcement, yielding close attention to violence and to the gaps between design, substance, and enforcement.

Much of the problem in addressing gender deficits in constitution making lies in the continuing belief in and adherence to the concept of the "gender-neutral" citizen during moments of transition. The fallacy of acting on behalf of the gender-neutral citizen allows those drafting the constitution and negotiating its content to mask the extent to which women are actually not the beneficiaries of constitutional change or incur only marginal advancement on the issues that affect them most. A representative sample of the gender blindspots of transitional constitutions is found in a 2009 report surveying a sample of 599 of the roughly 800 constitutions put into force since 1789.[29] While there is partiality evident from the survey as to what "counts" as a transitional measure, on its own terms it notes that relatively few constitutions specifically address transitional justice, only 1.3 percent in their sample mentions truth commissions, and only 2.2 percent contain provisions regarding crimes committed by prior regimes. The survey contains no mention of either gender provisions or socioeconomic redress. The fact that the report does not mention gender reflects a broader structural bias as to what constitutes transition-generated change in a post-conflict or postrepression society.

PROCESS: PEACE AGREEMENTS AS CONSTITUTIONAL DOCUMENTS

The tripartite classification of peace treaty forms and processes which we have drawn on throughout this book[30] shows the variety of contexts in which women are visible and included—or invisible and excluded—in post-conflict constitution making.

Gendered Constitutional Implications of the Prenegotiation Phase

Prenegotiation phases are generally concerned with broad context or principle setting and seek to set terms enabling the cessation of violent hostilities between combatants. Importantly, these principle-setting mechanisms tend to have an intense focus on military and political values (ceasefires, amnesty, political representation) and ignore broader social, economic, or redistributive ideals; they also tend to exclude women from the negotiations. Notwithstanding its focus on military and security outcomes, this phase has constitutional impact, with key and lasting constitutional arrangements following from the principles set at this stage. Accordingly, women's absence from this phase is an egregious omission.

For example, in the Northern Ireland context, the 1993 Joint Declaration on Peace (Downing Street Declaration),[31] which was the political precursor to military ceasefires by domestic paramilitary organizations and predated the broad framework agreement, outlined a series of principled positions agreed to by the Republic of Ireland and the United Kingdom governments.[32] Women were markedly absent in this principle-setting phase. While formally lacking binding legal status, these political agreements essentially set forth the legal and political framework (and legal principles) governing the conflict's end and the new political dispensation.[33] In South Africa, thirty-four overarching principles were agreed to by a multiparty negotiation process in 1993, prior to the election of the National Assembly that formed the drafting committee for South Africa's postapartheid constitution. Again, a highly masculine process with limited female representation framed the substantive agreements that would follow. The principles were incorporated into an interim constitution and drawn on for guidance in the drafting of a final constitution. In East Timor, some observers have suggested that the final constitution was largely based on a 1998 draft document that had been prepared in advance by Fretilin, the dominant political party in the country. Arguably women's attempts to participate in the constitutional drafting process had little impact on the final document because it was driven by previously set internal political dynamics and within a highly closed and masculine space.[34]

In some post-conflict constitution-making sites, women have sought to eschew the closed nature of these early preagreement deals by anticipating that constitution making is likely and setting their own agenda in advance of such processes, seeking to foreclose the exclusion they would otherwise experience. Colombian feminists, for example, operated in a highly anticipatory way by securing advance engagement in the Colombian Constitution process in 1991, and organized early and with sufficient voice to impact the formal and informal processes.[35] In Rwanda, in advance of the constitution drafting and parallel with closed processes involving only elite political actors, a seminar organized by the Rwandan National Assembly, the Forum for Women Members of Parliament, was convened with the assistance of international actors to consider ways in which the constitution could be more gender friendly.[36] Women were organized, recognizing that without input at this stage, long-term exclusions were likely to be compounded and entrenched.

In Iraq, where the gender provisions of the constitution were keenly watched and scrutinized nationally and internationally, an international nongovernmental organization (NGO), Women for Women International, met in Jordan in June 2005 and produced a report, *Our Constitution, Our Future: Enshrining Women's Rights in the Iraqi Constitution*, which concluded with a list of ten recommendations for constitutional provisions. While tracing cause and effect on the final shape and content of any of these constitutional/peace agreement documents is difficult, there is a general consensus among policymakers and scholars that without early input, outcomes for women are negligible or far more difficult to secure in the implementation phase of an agreement. Anticipatory and early action by women's organizations on the constitutional dimensions of peace agreements is critical to advance women's interests from the inception of negotiations—formal and informal—to end violent contestation. Ideally, women should be included at the prenegotiation table; the foregoing examples demonstrate that parallel action by women's organizations is required both to bring attention to women's particular needs and to force the recognition of gender needs and women's presence by the local and international elites negotiating.

Gendered Implications of Constitutional Design in Peace Agreements and the Effect of UN Resolutions Attempting to Mainstream Gender

The second phase of peace agreements are "Substantive/Framework" agreements that "aim to sustain ceasefires and provide a framework for governance that will address the root causes of the conflict."[37] These documents are generally ambitious and far-reaching, tackling matters such as demilitarization, prisoner release, amnesty, and the military's status, but also addressing legal and political reform, social and economic reparation and reform, as well as institutional reform. They set out, as constitutions typically do, a framework for the exercise of power and lay the groundwork for government policies across a range of social, economic, and political dimensions. They sometimes include specific constitutional manifestos, setting forth the procedural basis and timetable for such constitutional matters.[38]

Framework agreement phases are more likely to include women in at least some minimal and public form, even if the agreements themselves fail when it comes to gender centrality. Women's involvement often, but not exclusively, results from the oversight of international actors and agencies as they support a peace process, and empirical evidence suggests that UN involvement at least affects the terminology of framework peace agreements so that they more frequently reference women.[39] Whether resulting from the involvement of international actors or from the trickle-down effects of UN Security Council Resolution 1325, local actors are typically under significant pressure to include women in order to legitimatize the negotiation process, even if women are not actually given the opportunity to articulate effectively on issues that affect them.[40] For example, in East Timor, the UN Security Council established the UN Transitional Administration in East Timor (UNTAET), which was formally committed to and worked with local women's groups to bring about women's participation in the transitional administration and in constitutional drafting processes.[41] The medium- to long-term effect on women's status and equality remains unproven, not least because we are not far enough away from the conflict with the application of consistent legal and political indicatives on women's rights to make a judgment, but a presence requirement has at least been met. In parallel, East Timorese women's groups played a decisive role in pressing forward gender issues. To foster women's participation in the transitional processes, the women's civil society network (REDE) sponsored the First Women's Congress in June 2000.[42] The full cause-and-effect relationship here needs further study, but a correlation between international presence and greater civil society activism by women illustrates some of the positive benefits of international entanglement in post-conflict societies for women.

Furthermore, international pressure and attention may also create domestic political opportunities for women. Rwanda again provides an interesting example in which women were able to utilize the political rhetoric of the ruling Rwandan Patriotic Front (RPF)'s commitment to gender (to comply with international donor pressure and the knowledge of international attention fixated on the jurisdiction) and translate it into actual presence at the constitution-drafting table.[43] Three of the twelve appointed constitutional commissioners were women. The mere presence of women was not, however, sufficient in itself to ensure a substantive role in constitutional negotiations. It required the combined presence of women with the external pressure generated by women's organizations and informal political networking to enable a greater set of gains than might otherwise have been possible. The capability of these grassroots organizations was significantly augmented through domestic and international support, such that they were able to cast themselves as central rather than peripheral stakeholders in the transitional process. They managed to successfully frame gender as a strategy for national development and security in the context of an ethnically torn society.[44] A key element to women's success in Rwanda was the speed and strength with which women's associations grew in the post-conflict period in Rwanda, supported financially and otherwise by the UN Development Fund for Women (UNIFEM; now UN Women) and domestically by the Ministry of Gender and Promotion of Women's Development. This pattern of growth is, we note, generally at odds with what happens for many women's organizations in post-conflict societies, when civil society often collapses from a lack of longer-term external economic support and from the drain of key actors to the public sector.[45]

As illustrated throughout this book, while UN Security Council Resolution 1325 "urges UN Member States to ensure increased representation of women at all decision-making levels . . . for the prevention, management and resolution of conflict," this requirement alone may not be sufficient to address deeply seated gender inequalities.[46] Empirical assessment of the effect and implementation of Resolution 1325 remains indeterminate on whether the requirements of the resolution necessarily deliver "better" outcomes for women. Comparison across peace negotiations and agreements raises warning flags about the efficacy of Resolution 1325 in practice.[47] As we have stressed throughout, the presence of women in decision-making contexts is a necessary but not sufficient condition to ensure transformative outcomes with gender as a measure.

Even if women are appropriately represented in the framework agreement phase, as mandated by Resolution 1325, and even if that mandate is occasionally carried out as is arguably the case in post-conflict Rwanda and East Timor, women are more typically marginalized or absent from key conversations in highly gendered ways. There is also a gap between the rhetoric of the constitution and the subsequent enforcement of gender provisions. For example, as we have illustrated in the context of security sector reform in Chapter 3, while security is central to the change process in post-conflict or postrepressive environments, women, by virtue of their historic absence from military, police, and paramilitary forces, are rarely involved in or have the capacity to be central in these conversations.[48] The same fundamental dynamics are in play in post-conflict constitutional settings.

The very process of deciding which groups are critical to enabling the end of conflict (generally which military actors will be included in or excluded from the negotiations)—a decision made by local and international elites—determines the crux of the substantive negotiation process and often its outcomes. These process decisions on inclusion then directly affect the perception of whose needs should be kept on board and what compromises are worth offering to maintain the presence and inclusion of certain key groups over others. These compromises are often then worked into the core principles from which the processes of constitution making and enforcement follow. Women as a group never hold this privileged status as the dealmakers or enablers, not even under Resolution 1325–prescribed inclusion. As a result, there is a clear predetermination as to status, inclusion, and compromise of the negotiators that sees women inevitably sidelined, again subsumed by the pretense of the "gender-neutral" citizen. If and when women work strategically to use the division between other political groupings as a means to advance the needs of women (as well as broader compromises that may not be politically exclusive), such initiatives are often framed as being in the general interest, rather than in terms of advancing women's interest per se.[49]

For example, during the course of the Northern Ireland substantive peace negotiations, a women-only political party, the Women's Coalition, worked strategically to advance broadly applicable provisions on social and economic rights protections. The economic and social rights agenda made up a significant part of the negotiation landscape and constituted an integral part of the final agreement. As a result, there is now a specific political commitment in Northern Ireland to this broader concept of equality, which has been given a statutory footing under Section 75 of the Northern Ireland Act of 1998. That broader duty to ensure equality of process and outcomes falls to government and public bodies to implement. This legislation imposes a statutory duty on public authorities to "promote equality of opportunity" between "persons of different religious belief, political opinion, racial group, age, marital status or sexual orientation"; "between men and women generally"; "between persons with a disability and persons without"; and "between persons with dependents and persons without."[50] Regrettably, resonant with our broader concern here about the gap between principle and practice, these requirements have been interpreted in practice by the UK government to focus primarily on process and not outcome, limiting the truly transformative potential of measures which might address differential impact of state action on particularly marginal or vulnerable groups and individuals. An important and relevant dynamic of the Women's Coalition position was that their positions on equality measures were not couched in terms of addressing women's evident needs, but rather as a means to avoid and/or utilize sectarian splintering between opposing Nationalist and Unionist political parties.[51] The example keenly demonstrates that in order to have women's needs addressed, women strategically elect to characterize those needs as "universal" or generally applicable in order to have them included.

Another limitation of Resolution 1325 is that while it prescribes the inclusion of women, it does not mandate gender auditing of the peace treaty/constitution *as a whole* to assess if women's interests are best served by the final agreed-upon document. Some attempts at benchmarking Resolution 1325 are taking place,[52] and periodic reviews have been provided for the resolution within the UN infrastructure.[53] Despite this, evaluation of the impact of the resolution on women's lives remains concentrated on case studies, and little systematic analysis has focused on key sites of women's equality, autonomy, and status to test the depth and effect of change.

PEACE AGREEMENTS, CONSTITUTIONS, AND CUSTOMARY LAW

Constitutional documents have a heightened importance in legal systems where the rule of law has been absent, denigrated, or manipulated to corrosive and authoritarian ends. In such contexts, there is a high degree of overlap between women's poor social, economic, and political standing and the legal apparatus which gives little value and meaningful protection to women.[54] Lack of attention to women in constitutional contexts has powerful representational and practical consequences. Moreover, in societies where rule of law is fragile or absent, customary institutions and practices clearly survive when formal legal structures collapse (especially in rural settings).[55] A broad swath of research on the status and protection for women in customary and communal settings indicates real problems of equality, fairness, and entrenched gender bias.[56] Constitutional negotiations and peace agreements constitute one means to address this deficit. Consequently, secular constitutional documents play an important mediating role in providing a legal space in which customary and religious laws concerning women can be contested in a structured, rule-driven forum.[57] Secular documents may facilitate the creation of a contested legal space in which the values of equality, tolerance, and nondiscrimination have legal potency and can be articulated to respond to other culturally relativist values which invariably limit women's rights and opportunities. Constitutional norms should be valued not only in terms of their substantive content and their instrumentality, but as a means to open up a substantive space of contestation for women.

A further complication, which we have alluded to throughout this book, is that the point of transition may not necessarily mean transformation for women, but rather may have retrograde elements that negatively impact gains that women have made in their status and personal lives through the course of a conflict. In the transition phase, "the impulse to women's social transformation and autonomy is circumscribed by the nationalist project, which constructs women as purveyors of the community's accepted and acceptable cultural identity."[58] The point is most cogently illustrated by study of the complex role that women have played within the Palestinian Liberation Organization (PLO) and in the ongoing struggle for Palestinian statehood. In 1965, the PLO established the General Union of Palestinian Women (GUPW) with the stated aim of creating more robust opportunities for women in social, political, and economic life.[59] This was supplemented and extended by the establishment of women's committees by Fatah and other nationalist and socialist parties in the 1970s. In addition, a wider and generally secular women's network emerged through the creation of civil society NGOs and research centers throughout Gaza and the West Bank. Yet, in the face of long-term occupation, related violence, economic insecurity, and political infighting, instead of seeing a robust role for women in the public sphere, in recent years Palestinian society has witnessed a reactionary retrenchment of traditional gender roles.

As Wong and Kassim's study of Palestinian women and the constitutional developments since the Oslo II process reveals, there can be a Janus-faced dimension to constitutional developments for women.[60] An examination of the Basic Law of Palestine, for example, an evolutionary document intended to become a final constitution once the state of Palestine is formed, illustrates a set of highly fragmented and contradictory developments for women. Positively, both the Basic Law and the Draft Constitution set out general human rights' clauses applicable to both genders. They also contain some gender-specific provisions,[61] but underscoring the analysis advanced here, the Draft Constitution also places all personal status matters, including women's rights, under the control of one of the religious institutions in Palestine.[62] Compounding the contradictions, in the wake of the transitional government's failure to secure peace, adopt a constitution, or establish a unified government, cultural backlash and political divisions have brought the gender-equality agenda to a near standstill.[63] As the national identity struggles continue, the thorny situation of women continues, hemmed in between an ongoing conflict with Israel (including border closures, unemployment, chronic poverty, and violent incursions) and the strong assertion of patriarchal norms within Palestinian society—a product in part of what some have termed a "crisis of masculinity,"[64] in which religious mores play a central role in defining women within the Palestinian nationalist discourse. In this framework, religious leaders have ample scope to argue that "religious laws [are] the only authentic statement of pre-occupation and pre-colonial law,"[65] and thus personal status regimes which require women's obedience (rather than guaranteeing their equality) become part of the "hard irreducible core of what it means to be a Muslim."[66] This is part of the landscape of retreat in which success and failure of constitutional protections have to be judged for women.

Constitutional compacts that follow protracted conflicts need to do more to engage with the fundamental social and cultural contexts that support, create, and protect such discriminatory and exclusionary practices; without a transformative social and economic agenda to accompany the rhetoric of impermissible acts, it is debatable what fundamental change is likely to be engineered. They must address substantive as well as formal equality for women, no matter what the legal formula for advancement may be. Substantive equality encompasses positive programs to ameliorate disadvantage. It entails both positive and negative rights. When women's agency and equality are addressed, women's inclusion, access to, and effective participation in decision-making, both in the political-legal sense and with respect to one's person, can also be tackled.[67]

GENDERED DIMENSIONS OF CONSTITUTIONAL DRAFTING IN IMPLEMENTATION AGREEMENTS

The third phase of agreements identified by Bell's paradigm are "implementation agreements" which "take forward and develop aspects of the framework, fleshing out their detail."[68] The inherent and "constructive ambiguity" of peace agreements is often the means to ensure that vastly opposing political entities agree to sign on to them.[69] This means that much of the difficult work of real compromise is left to the implementation phase, where both genuine opportunity and pitfalls continue to exist for women.[70] As we have noted in the Introduction, implementation agreements are often deeply contested and are viewed as a site in which compromises and agreements previously made can be undone or effectively renegotiated on better terms for some military and political parties.

There are significant examples of the implementation phase as the context during which constitutional norms and legal outcomes are more evidently advanced than in either the pre- or framework negotiations phase. Northern Ireland's ongoing negotiation of a bill of rights and the South African Constitution,[71] for example, each involved a lengthy period of public consultation and engagement. Part of the political settlement in Northern Ireland was a substantive commitment to the augmentation of human rights and equality protections in the jurisdiction. The human rights dimension infused the Good Friday/Belfast Agreement and continues to dominate many of the post-conflict political and legal conversations. It is evidenced by the establishment of new institutions, revisions to the criminal justice system, and policing, as well as in the striking centrality of economic, social, and cultural rights to the overall shape and tone of the agreement. Following the acceptance of the peace agreement by all parties, domestic legislation, the Northern Ireland Act 1998, established a national human rights institution, the Northern Ireland Human Rights Commission (NIHRC), to advise the government on human rights issues and in particular on the creation of a bill of rights for Northern Ireland.[72] Within the process of proposing and consulting on what the bill of rights should contain, there has been a particular focus on social and economic rights.[73] The women's sector in Northern Ireland has been part of a highly visible Human Rights Consortium which continues to lobby for an expansive bill of rights, illustrating the benefits of a wide and deep consultation process in the implementation phase for rights protection and legal reforms generally. Time and inclusive process can be very effective in developing "buy in" as multiple constituencies not only connect to the mechanics of constitutional engagement (constitution making as a process), but are also deeply involved in the contestation over what kind of social contract is sought and agreed upon by a society experiencing transformation. Where public consultation is deep and meaningfully ordered, and women's organizations have the supported capacity to cast themselves as central rather than peripheral stakeholders in the process of negotiations, impact on constitutional outcomes is possible.

The tightrope that women walk in the negotiation and postagreement context is that the political space they occupy can be essentialized by utilitarian political capitalization holding out women as being predisposed to forgiveness and reconciliation or certain kinds of political and social arrangements over others. The Northern Ireland negotiations, for example, illustrate both the capacity of women to cast gender as central to the agreements (by using the momentum toward final status political agreement to create a women's political party, which was included in the core of the negotiation process), but equally illustrates the extent to which in order to "keep" negotiations on track, the Women's Coalition became the de facto facilitator between the warring ethno-religious political factions largely dominated by men.

As articulated elsewhere in this book, timing is key in this phase, as international actors are still operating in emergency mode throughout the peace negotiation phase and often well into the implementation phase. This impacts constitutional drafting where women's issues tend to fare poorly, in part because security issues and political rights (without gender-central consciousness) are prioritized. Economic and social rights implementation, which affect women most heavily, tend to be set aside while urgent (often military) matters are undertaken. This view of what is urgent is extremely shortsighted, and in our view has long-term effects on the substance of the peace negotiated and its ultimate capacity to support and enable social change.

The end of public violence creates significant economic and social pressures for women, manifested in different ways in differing contexts. Financial and economic stresses significantly limit the capacity of many women to remain engaged in post-conflict implementation negotiations. In the Northern Ireland context, this point is illustrated by the creation of a separate and wide-ranging review of policing (the Patten Commission); a disconnected review and reform process for the criminal justice system; a fractured set of initiatives to address the needs of victims spread out between 1998 and 2011; and the ultimate devolution of criminal justice to local government. All of these microprocesses were highly politically charged and extraordinarily time-consuming. Engagement in any one process, whether policing or victims' needs, required significant amount of legal and policy capacity and the ability to direct that one issue with concentrated focus. Such broad and consistent political capability was simply not possible in the women's sector. Thus, the practical inability of an underfunded women's civil society initiative to stay involved in all of these conversations illustrates the point that implementation phases can be the most challenging to women's interests and needs.

Although we argue above that women's parallel activism is key to bringing women's issues to the fore during constitution making, civil society organizations (of which women's organizations form a key component) experience significant setbacks and challenges in the post-conflict context specifically impacting implementation.[74] These include the withdrawal of funding by international and local donors on the basis that, because the "war is over," the funding can be better spent elsewhere. For example, in East Timor, funding to civil society (including women's organizations) was dwarfed by the overemphasis on acute peacekeeping concerns at the expense of developing long-term civil society capacity. The underfunding was compounded by the decision by UNTAET to phase out the humanitarian and rehabilitation pillar (which supported civil society)[75] in 2000. This lack of material support coming in the context of ongoing public violence and broken governmental institutions meant that women's hopes of security, social empowerment, and political participation languished. Further, the loss of specialized personnel within civil society who move into new "post-conflict" institutions creates brain drain within women's organizations.

In practice, while the implementation stage continues to press ahead with enormous political and legal changes—many with a constitutional hue—women's organizations are often less well-prepared than either political entities or other civil society groupings to address and impact on the process and are most likely to be excluded. If we abandon the notion that the key constitutional challenges or changes are neatly held within the scope of one document or one singular process, we gain a more nuanced understanding of how women's needs and issues are likely to be left out of constitutional conversations in post-conflict societies and the scale of the effort needed to maintain their presence.

CONSTITUTIONAL GENDER CENTRALITY—SUBSTANCE AND EXPORT

In whatever form the constitutional elements of a political settlement are configured, it is critical to assess whether the substance specifically addresses the particularity and totality of women's membership of the political, economic, and social communities of the state. These elements need to be assessed across the principle-setting stage, in the formal agreements context, and in implementation arrangements. Making gender central in all these settings requires more than mainstreaming approaches, but instead requires starting from the women's point of view and making a vision and practice of gender equality a central benchmark of successful outcomes.

In general, there has been a tendency to scrutinize such documents (where they are scrutinized at all) only with reference to provisions that deal specifically or generally with sex equality and/or the prohibition of sex discrimination.[76] Other versions of this equality-oriented approach include limiting classifications based on sex or protecting the class of women per se, reaching to private discrimination as well as discrimination by the state, guaranteeing affirmative rights to the material preconditions for equality, and setting out broadly aspirational norms as well as judicially enforceable norms. These are all useful and pragmatic guidelines. Nonetheless, this approach has some limitations.

The first is that such foci tend to assume that rights-conferring provisions are the only means through which to view a constitution's impact on gender. Rights must be included,[77] but feminists and policymakers need to pay close attention to other matters as well. The other matters start with the definition of citizen, the impact on women of major architectural choices such as the models of government (federalist, parliamentary or presidential, theocratic or secular),[78] the form of representation (such as the use of quotas),[79] and gendering the institutions (by minimally ensuring the adequacy of representation and access) that adjudicate on the constitution (notably its constitutional court). Analyzing and advocating for particular kinds of constitutional structures and constitutional mechanisms have not been fully internalized by feminist and other commentators as central to advancing how women are treated under new constitutional arrangements and sidelined in analyses and advocacy.[80] Women need to pay close attention to the effects of the separation of powers (including the nature of the executive, the structure of the legislature, the independence of the judiciary), federalism, and the electoral system for them and for advancing issues that particularly affect women in the society in question. Women need to advocate on these structural issues and be politically sensitive to the effect of structural choices on women. We are careful to note that structural benefits and disadvantages will vary from one society to another and there is no "one size fits all" that works for all women in all political varieties of political systems. Rather, the key is attentiveness to substance and effect across a range of arenas. Other critical contexts include the role of the courts and judicial review, the incorporation of international human rights law into the domestic legal system, and states of emergency.

For women, the constitutional question is in part whether the constitutional moment (however constructed) actually promises a gender-neutral capacity for transformation on equal terms. More pointedly, constitutional negotiations allow for the redress of systematic and historic discrimination and exclusion by positive measures.[81] A key issue here is gender quotas. The evidence on the matter is generally clear: "to achieve even remotely equivalent number of women and men in national legislatures, formal equality with respect to voting and running for office is not sufficient."[82] In the post-conflict constitutional moment, there is a unique capacity to address the lack of gender parity in democratic constitutionalism. For example, in the South African context, women's organizations forced the African National Congress (ANC) to adopt a one-third-quota system prior to the first set of democratic elections post apartheid.[83] In East Timor, local women's organizations sought a 30 percent political gender quota in the Constituent Assembly, but several key UNTAET officials balked, stating that gender quotas would impair free elections.[84] This is despite the fact that the UN Development Fund for Women (UNIFEM) had previously stated that social "obstacles need to be acknowledged by policymakers, lawmakers and electoral authorities when they determine the conditions of free and fair elections."[85] Notably, UNTAET's authorizing resolution specifically endorses the Convention on the Elimination of All Forms of Discrimination Against Women (CEDAW) position that states should take "appropriate measures to eliminate discrimination against women in [. . .] political and public life." East Timor illustrates the complexity of the interface around equity in representation and the challenges of international (and gendered) views meeting local articulations of need and equality, the results of which sowed significant confusion and dispute at the local level.

One model for gender benchmarking and oversight is a constitutionally mandated entity created through a transitional negotiation process that oversees and enforces broad compliance to gender equality and inclusion across all segments of the negotiation and implementation phases. Given the cyclical and protracted nature of many conflicts (and the repeat player problem), such an entity may need to be anchored into the long term. This means ensuring an institutional presence past a transitional phase and into a normalization phase for a society seriously prepared to engage with making sure gender equality survives transition. Section 181 of the South African Constitution provides for a Commission for Gender Equality accountable to the national assembly, whose functions include promoting "respect for gender equality and the protection, development and attainment of gender equality." The Commission has specifically designed powers under the constitution to monitor, investigate, research, educate, lobby, advise, and report. While its impact has been limited,[86] and a full exploration of its operation is beyond the scope of this analysis, it is unusual precisely because of its constitutional identity, portending how innovative constitutional design can anchor gender benchmarking and oversight central in political and social discourse.

Throughout this book, we have identified the tendency for post-conflict interventions and responses to be myopic in terms of their foci and definition of the problems to be resolved. Such narrowing, we argue, fails to capture the variety and complexity of women's experiences and is ultimately detrimental to the protection of women's rights and interests broadly construed. A particular deficiency is the emphasis on the protection of the civil and political dimensions of the presumed gender-neutral citizen, and the limited engagement with a broader set of substantive protections, namely social, economic, and cultural rights. As a result, formalized equality may be satisfied by including provisions on nondiscrimination, but may fail to advance women's status substantively.

Again, by way of example, in the East Timor constitution, while the language of the constitution is strong, rhetorical strides are not accompanied by robust enforcement provisions. So, although the constitution establishes an ombudsman to investigate human rights complaints against public bodies, the office only has the power to recommend that "competent organs" take action within the relevant sector of government.[87] In the absence of specific constitutional provisions that address discrimination in employment, education, family law, and criminal justice, women must rely on the enactment and enforcement of domestic legislation. Moreover, the backdrop to any advancement for women in East Timor is significant socioeconomic disadvantage compared to their male counterparts. Women suffer higher rates of malnourishment than men, are more likely to die from maternal-related exposures, have primary responsibility for childcare and domestic work, and 65 percent of East Timorese women are illiterate.[88] The UN Development Program reports that "women receive less food than men and one third between the ages of 14–49 are malnourished; fertility rates are high, as are the rates of death in childbirth."[89] As both the Commission for Reception, Truth, and Reconciliation (CAVR) and others report, East Timorese women "continually stressed the need for justice to encompass their ongoing [struggle for] economic and social rights."[90] This background of socioeconomic insecurity, which hardly surfaces in the constitution, is primarily what impedes women's full inclusion and political and economic participation.[91]

Women and men in transitions are not necessarily or always opposed when it comes to what interests are prioritized in the negotiation process. Men and women have many interests in common in determining enforceable outcomes of change processes. For instance, the implementation of legislation and programs on human rights, including citizenship rights and democratic participation in the exercise of state power, are especially crucial to previously excluded groups. But normatively, women are persistently the most excluded people within these groups and stand to profit most from any redistribution of state power and benefit gained in negotiations, provided these benefits are fully enforced. The lack of protection for economic, social, and cultural rights in post-conflict societies affirms the breadth of obstacles faced by women in asserting the need for economic provision and redistribution of resources.[92] Christine Chinkin makes the link between the failures of economic reform and the limitations of the traditional spheres of transitional justice:

> It is our contention that failure to deliver economic, social and cultural rights through national legal frameworks in accordance with international standards undermines the sought-after stability and human security post-conflict (including food, health, gender and physical security), which in turn lessens the ability or willingness of victims and witnesses to participate in the formal processes of post-conflict justice.[93]

Connectedly, as conflicts end we are increasingly seeing the emergence of violent street protests and riots in countries that are technically post-conflict.[94] Significantly, post-conflict tensions and violence often arise out of the very same types of socioeconomic grievances that caused earlier periods of political violence and human rights violations. This is cogent validation of the need to address broader social and economic disparities, inequities, "structural violence," and structural inequality.[95] Social and economic factors can be "powder kegs" that "if left unaddressed threaten to blow up peace initiatives."[96] The constitutional process (as well as transitional processes more generally) needs to be cognizant of the causal connection between prior socioeconomic inequalities and conflict eruption and conceptualize reform accordingly. This requires centralizing the conversations about inequities and redistribution at the core of the constitutional compacts that are advanced in post-conflict societies. In turn this means promoting and strengthening participatory mechanisms for constitutional negotiation that address conditions of historical exclusion contributing to political marginalization.[97] However, as others have documented and as we discuss in Chapter 10 of this book, participation without the capacity to affect and influence political and economic agendas is futile and may be counterproductive. It may create expectations that are not met and fails to address the lived realities of social and economic disenfranchisement on the ground.

A final piece of this substantive overview is terminology. Gendered words matter and constitutions are rife with them.[98] It is unlikely that the use of the feminine pronoun is ever intended to embrace the masculine,[99] and as other feminists have long noted, it is not by mere accident that "he" has been employed to cover all individuals, both in legal instruments and general written and spoken discourse. In some transitional contexts, the use of language has starkly reversed assumptions. For example, in the South African drafting, an executive decision was made by Cyril Ramphosa to employ "women and men" throughout, even for example in the appointment of the national commissioner for police service.[100] This is not merely cosmetic, but subtly acknowledges that constitutional language itself functions to reorder and reconfigure society.[101]

Making gender central and going beyond the acknowledgment that women have particular needs requires transformative action across multiple spheres that have consistently been most resistant to legal regulation (including social and economic enforcement as well as in customary law). It also, in our view, requires inclusion at all levels, starting at the constitutional norm apex and working its way down through legislative and policy routes. Including women in the conversations that establish the norms in the first place is absolutely critical to engendering the process. Addressing equality, discrimination, and social status through the process of institutional revisions and constitutional enforcement, thereby encompassing both procedural and substantive equality, means that constitutional enforcement looks and feels radically different in terms of its weight and punch for women in transitioning societies.

REPRODUCTIVE RIGHTS

This section addresses reproductive rights in constitutional conversations because they are critical to the transformation of women's lives. Without essentializing women's reproductive and caring roles, these experiences are nonetheless central to many women's lives and legal realities across cultures.[102] Gains in social, political, and economic equality are critical for women in conflicted societies, as too often their substantive structural inequality determines the scope and extent of the harms they experience in times of conflict restricts their ability to construct lives post-conflict. Women's equality and their capacity to exert reproductive choices are deeply intermeshed in most societies, and we address that nexus here.

Reproductive rights are important for a number of reasons. First, as Chapter 8 has explored in relation to accountability and remedy, even though sexual violence directed toward women is a consistently overwhelming facet of protracted conflict, access to legal remedy alone may be less intrinsically valuable to women than access to reproductive choices and reproductive care. In addition, guaranteed and safe access to reproductive health will inevitably increase women's political and social choices over time.[103] Second, as our comparative data reveal, women's low social and political status is invariably connected to their capacity to exert any autonomy over their reproductive choices.[104] In this way, as has often been noted, the female body remains the ultimate site of social and political control. The inclusion of reproductive rights in post-conflict legal and constitutional documents can be a crude but effective measure for assessing how integrated women have been to the negotiating process, the extent of gender-specific protections included in agreements to end conflict, and the specific and tangible legal gains women have made during the negotiation process. Finally, reproductive rights are a measure of the extent to which a constitution values women's agency. Agency—the ability to act, to enjoy autonomy, to play a part in decision-making, and to exercise power—is critically affected by the manner in which women experience reproductive freedom.

Constitutional changes in a number of societies have offered formal advancements for women, although these rhetorical victories may be simply that. South Africa is sometimes regarded as the touchstone in this regard, as no other existing constitution addresses the full range of issues related to reproductive rights. A highly focused and well-organized set of interventions by women's organizations and other supportive civil society organizations led to inclusion of reproductive autonomy in the constitutional framework. In its formal equality provisions, the South African Bill of Rights includes pregnancy within the impermissible grounds of discrimination. Under Section 12 (Freedom and Security of the Person), it provides inter alia that "Everyone has the right to bodily and psychological integrity, which includes the right (a) to make decisions concerning reproduction; (b) to security in and control over their bodies. . . ." Concerning duties and responsibilities of the state, under the heading of health care, food, water, and social security, it provides in Section 27.1 that "Everyone has the right to have access to . . . health care services, including reproductive health care."[105]

While this provision seems exemplary, it, too, is not without practical difficulties in implementation. These constitutional protections for women's reproductive autonomy must be understood in the context of the tension between the women's rights movement and the antiapartheid movement.[106] Moreover, the gap between the enforcement of reproductive rights and in particular access to abortion may arguably have widened in the postapartheid era despite the formal legal guarantees available to women. This is because in practice, and for obvious reasons of resource limitations, reproductive health and choices cannot be guaranteed to women at the same depth and quality across a resource-strained economy. Moreover, much of the advocacy that delivered the constitutional provisions was generated by women with access to the political channels to secure the constitutional language, but was divorced in practice from the grassroots experiences of most women and from the socio-cultural context in which a right of access to reproductive choice is exercised and becomes meaningful. In short, without also undertaking the grassroots work to enable women to access reproductive choice without stigma and social repercussion, its meaningful effect for many ordinary women struggling with the sociological expectations of women's roles will be limited. The challenge is also compounded by prevalent and deeply entrenched practices of intimate and domestic violence, undoing in itself the theoretically won freedoms of reproductive autonomy contained in the constitution.[107] The lesson is once again that paper guarantees are a necessary but not sufficient assurance for the meaningful enforcement of women's rights in the constitutional context. Despite this and the hard work that lies ahead for South African women, the constitutional provisions are strong barter to start the process of enablement.

Another cogent example of the gap between theoretical gains and enforcement in practice is Afghanistan, where women's advocates made specific gains in the post invasion constitution.[108] The Bonn Agreement stipulated women's inclusion in all Council meetings and in the interim administration. Women made up 12 percent of the Emergency Loya Jirga. The Final Afghan Constitution of 2004 includes specific provisions for women's rights. Article 22, for example, guarantees the equality of men and women.[109] Female parliamentarians in Afghanistan say, however, that men who oppose gender equity have systematically dominated the country's powerful lawmaking institution.[110] This point connects with our previous discussion that representation alone may not be sufficient to undo the pernicious social and legal exclusions experienced by women. Moreover, the constitution does not include other forms of economic rights such as a right to health, any type of reproductive rights, nor guarantees of personal autonomy. Notwithstanding a lack of provision for economic and social rights, since the end of Taliban rule, conditions for some (though mainly urban) women in Afghanistan have improved. They have seen increased enrollment in schools for girls and guarantees of electoral seats for women political representatives.[111] For most women, however, the litany of formal guarantees hides a far more depressing reality.[112] We are not suggesting that the protection of reproductive rights would instantly undercut a complex set of social and cultural interactions that are coalesced around the legal status and capacity of women in Afghan society (or any other). However, ignoring the centrality of reproductive rights, capacity, and care to women is to fundamentally disengage from the core rudiments of women's lives that predict the quality, status, and autonomy of that lived life from girlhood through maturity to old age.

The Convention on the Elimination of All Forms of Discrimination Against Women (Article 12) is a useful guide to constitutional drafting on reproductive rights.[113] However, we stress that the provision of reproductive rights in any constitutional context is limited and the force of their impact speculative in terms of short-, medium-, and long-term outcomes for women. What we do know is that women who experience early, frequent, and repeated pregnancies are most at risk for serious and long-term health outcomes. Childbirth remains a risky medical experience for many women, and maternal deaths are still a significant feature of the world's mortality demographics.[114] All of these facets are heightened in violent and conflicted societies, where pregnancy and violent sexual assault overlap and where access to any form of medical intervention for the trauma of rape, pregnancy, childbirth, and postchildbirth complications, including fistulas and female genital mutilation (FGM) complications, will be exceptionally limited. In addition to the broader rationale for the inclusion of reproductive rights in new constitutional dispensations, such pressing prior histories point to the relationship between constitutional settlements and the broader restitution that takes place in violent communities. They speak particularly to the unique perspective that women may exercise in terms of what constitutes adequate restitution for violations of their personal and bodily integrity.

Thus, one important litmus test for women's broad and substantive equality and inclusion is the ability to include reproductive rights and freedoms in the constitutional zone of protection.[115] Conversely, autonomy related to reproductive capacity and access to maternal and reproductive care for women greatly increases the meaningful realization of a range of other rights that may broadly be made available by the transitional process.[116] In sum, reproductive rights capacity and access is one of the core benchmarks that we suggest requires consistent inclusion to measure the full and transformative effect of transition from conflict to peace for women.

CONCLUSION

Legal reform has become embedded in the framework that is broadly applied to conflicted societies, viewed as an indispensable element of facilitating the end of hostilities by creating social and political conditions conducive to peace. However, it remains very unclear if the rule of law is a prerequisite to a successful transition or the consequence of it.[117] As Pistor, Haldar, and Amirapu argue, "reliance on the rule of law as the harbinger of greater gender equality might be over-optimistic, if not misleading."[118]

In crude terms, the rule of law is an assertion of law's preeminence—its autonomy from and superiority to fallible politics. As such, it is deeply attractive to places where politics are deeply discredited and where the promise of neutrality seems essential to the advancement of liberal (in contrast to violent) politics. Despite the evidence that the rule of law industry's global ambition is motivated in part by its profit potential,[119] and whether despite, or because of, these dynamics, the "rule of law has become integral to the aesthetics and cartography of 'transition.'"[120]

The rule of law can be distinguished from what Duncan Ivison terms "negative constitutionalism" or rule by law.[121] Thin, minimalist, formal, or procedural rule of law theories are often contrasted with thick, maximalist, or substantive theories. The former—focusing on qualities such as openness, impartiality, certainty, and prospectivity—are rarely disputed as being key to law's capacity to stabilize behavioral expectations, and thus create a baseline for reciprocal interaction and conduct.[122] They are in theory positive for both men and women transcending gender boundaries. Such qualities are evidently central to the rehabilitation of law in conflicted or repressive societies. We clearly endorse the value of law's rehabilitation and the importance of reestablishing clarity, order, and predictability in legal and political systems. Our concern lies not so much with the abstract, but with its outworkings for women and the failure to fully grasp (by well-intentioned internationals as well as local elites) that the importation of certain rule of law models is deeply fraught for women and may not advance their social and political well-being in a substantive and sustained way.

As we have outlined in opening this chapter, the public/private distinction sustains and confirms women's oppression on a global level, and it is also a part of the legal export between states and from internationals and interested states to elites in transitioning states. Gendered biases are implicitly carried into the rule of law mantle. Across transitional societies, rule of law praxis reveals copybook priorities: judicial reform, constitution writing, legislative enactments, legal infrastructure, and security sector reform. All in theory open up the possibility of gender engagement—few if any deliver. Most tellingly, however, is what gets left out. The high priorities generally sidestep domestic violence (seen as unrelated to public and political violence), legal inequalities (for example, equal rights to property ownership for men and women), religious law (and its regulatory capacity in the private sphere), socioeconomic protections specific to care responsibilities, and meaningfully mandated equal access to political representation. Seeing the ways in which rule of law language and its attendant institutional mechanisms reaffirm and reinforce existing inequality and exclusions for women is an important starting point to reconfiguring and rethinking standard rule of law deployment in post-conflict settings. We have advocated that the same kinds of tools utilized by Western feminists to expose the bias and limitations of these systems for women should be applied with equal force to societies that are the export recipients of systems discredited in other settings. The starting point is consistent: consult with local women, identify their needs and priorities, integrate such requirements in policymaking and institutional reform, and benchmark globally to ensure that women's equality and autonomy are being consistently advanced.

In parallel, contemporary constitution making in post-conflict settings requires critical probing in its conceptualization and delivery. As we have set out above, constitution making has a significant overlay with peace negotiations, and the peace treaty itself is often the vehicle for the advancement of constitutional norms. Such constitution making involves a number of dimensions and has some unique aspects. First, post-conflict constitutionalism engages a broader set of documents across preagreement, formal agreements, and implementation involving various degrees of formality, negotiation, and civic participation. Second, it often occurs in the context of ongoing violence and thus necessarily prioritizes acute short-term security concerns over the kind of chronic economic and social issues that disproportionately affect women. Third, it often advances the rights and role of minority groups in ways that tend to sideline gender and divide women across geographic, ethnic, and social class lines. Finally, it must often strike compromises to balance competing pressures to (a) the international community's advocacy of provisions guaranteeing women's rights and equality and (b) local constituencies' advocacy of provisions protecting customary and religious laws (particularly against the broad backdrop of colonialism) that codifies inequality for women.

A speculative exercise involves asking how the constitutional piece of legal reform might be reconstructed to fully account for and value women's lives and needs.[123] It would be a mistake, in our view, to focus overly on a particular constitutional form or model to apply across the multiplicity of conflict and post-conflict contexts where constitutional intervention is initiated. Rather, to engender transformative changes, legal measures may require combination with broader public education process, economic reconfiguration, and a more skeptical and critical engagement with legal tools themselves as the primary means to resolve deep-seated inequities.

The negotiation and creation of constitutional documents in conflicted and post-conflict societies is not neatly contained in one phase of the negotiation. Rather, depending on the conflict and the site at play, it may fall across multiple stages of the negotiation process and may appear to variable degrees in all three. Increased recognition of the multitude of arenas in which the constitutional conversations take place illustrates both opportunity and challenge for women. Despite the lofty goals outlined for the transition from conflict to peace, institutional change through constitutional principle and agreement remains elusive. It remains even more deeply contested territory for women.

Meaningful transformation requires a more sophisticated conversation that enables a deeper understanding of how institutional resistance encompasses gendered, social class, and other "identity securing" systems of privilege.[124] As a starting point, paying due attention to the outcomes when we fail to account for gender would allow us to see what is at stake and why transitional societies sometimes "fail" to move forward positively. This view shows that the presumed benefits of transition do not apply equally to all.

With this improved understanding, we see the importance of ensuring that gender is central to the entire process that results in constitution-drafting, the substantive provisions, and the resulting legislation that implements constitutional guarantees. It is equally central to thinking through what the rule of law priorities are for states and in what order they will be addressed and supported. In both contexts, auditing and benchmarking for gender from the inception of the process is essential to securing genuinely transformative outcomes for women. In this guise, a gender-centered constitutional process and rule of law programs might go some ways toward transformative change for women in conflicted and post-conflict societies.

PART THREE

Reconstruction and Development

CHAPTER 10

Gender and Governance

Governance is viewed by many key actors as one of the lynchpins of post-conflict reconstruction. As international actors become more heavily involved in post-conflict environments, states and multinational institutions have extended the intensity of their interest in and commitment to governance language, policies, and institutions by installing it as a specific component within peace process implementation.

An elusive term, governance has been said to describe the "application of rules and processes through which authority and control are exercised in a society, political decisions are made, the rules for the scope of action of state and society are structured, and resources for economic and social development are administered."[1] As with other aspects of post-conflict reconstruction, there is no agreed-upon doctrine about what constitutes "good governance," although the phrase is widely employed.[2] In the post-conflict context, governance embodies the notion that the state has either lost (or never had) an effective political administrative structure, and strategies must therefore be devised to build or reconstruct it after conflict.

More importantly for the purposes of this book, the post-conflict phase presents the possibility of entirely new conditions and systems of governance, and governance programs provide the possibility of radical transformation regarding the place of women in the society's political processes.[3] Transformation is not inevitable, of course, because the transitional state is not a tabula rasa. The political and economic direction the emerging state takes will be heavily influenced by its previous form, the influence of its elites, and its pre-war and wartime power structure. For all of these reasons, the state may also be unable to disengage from embedded gender inequalities and exclusions, which may limit its transformative potential for women. Thus, as we have outlined in our Introduction, post-conflict transition processes may trend retrograde rather than forward-looking and transformative for women.

While a multitude of contexts and opportunities arise for the infiltration, and advancement of women in the post-conflict governance context, one consistent and specific solution offered in post-conflict governance processes (or in constitutional drafting and rule of law as it relates to political structures and processes, as discussed in chapters 8 and 9) is that women be considered for elected office and even placed into elected office via the use of quotas, whenever the international community has had enough leverage to insist upon it. This is considered the "go to" remedy for spearheading political change for women. For many governance programs, this has meant setting quotas for women within formal political structures (parliament and ministries, for example) and within political parties (on party lists, for example).[4] But what actual impact does augmented representation have on the possibility of sustainable peace? And more importantly, do greater numbers of women inserted into positions of governance pursuant to internationally mandated quotas lead to any real gains in advancing women's substantive equality? While we ultimately conclude that quotas can serve a useful purpose, as discussed below and in earlier chapters, we propose that a precondition is the commitment to a practice of establishing and implementing civil, economic, social, and cultural rather than solely political rights to institute and maintain women's gains in post-conflict processes.

This recommendation is made in part because the gendered terrain of governance goes far beyond formal political structures. When the consequences of gender stereotyping and gender inequity are examined, it becomes clear that post-conflict governance must also include the private sphere, civil society, and identifying the locus of political power that effects change in ways that positively and substantively impact women's status.[5] We are not convinced that advances for women will come through the greater visibility of feminist ideas in legal-institutional space alone.[6] As this book demonstrates, changing social and economic structures to ensure that post-conflict societies are reimagined as spaces of equality for both women and men proves challenging and elusive.

This chapter will discuss how "good governance" is conventionally defined in the contemporary post-conflict reconstruction context, detailing the components of typical post-conflict governance programs, including elections, institution building, and civil society, and the extent to which these programs actually centralize gender. Second, it will look at the role of international actors in determining that democracy and economic liberalization are necessary components of post-conflict governance, interrogate that proposition, and look at some of the gender consequences for women of that determination. Finally, it will consider engendered governance frameworks that would emphasize substantive rights, access to labor markets, and demonstrated gender equality over procedural rights and gender quotas.

When hostilities between combatants halt, international actors typically arrive to assist domestic actors with the reestablishment of their governance systems and infrastructure. As we set out in Chapter 4, the timing of their multiple forms of intervention is variable. Given the immediacy with which international actors generally attend to governance issues post-conflict, it follows that international actors view governance as instrumental to security. Equally, given the attention paid to governance in the longer term, international actors also seem to view governance as a bridge between post-conflict reconstruction and development.[7]

As we have noted elsewhere, the international actors involved in the development and implementation of post-conflict governance programs may have already been actively engaged with the conflicted society. The parameters of the postwar assistance, therefore, may be prefigured by earlier international engagement, prior to any preagreement, framework agreement, or implementation phases. Because post-conflict reconstruction programs have largely been funded, driven, and dominated by Western (generally democratic) actors who have a stake in their successful outcome, they have tended to prioritize the construction of a democratic form of government as a central component of immediate post-conflict security, reflecting evident partiality toward their own political systems.[8]

Post-conflict governance programs typically focus on what are conventionally seen as the three primary building blocks of governance: (1) free and fair elections, (2) strong central and local legislative and executive institutions, and (3) the creation of a healthy civil society. Not all these imperatives are equally weighted and prioritized; in practice, there is a notable emphasis on the first and second dimensions. Although governance programs ostensibly contemplate the incorporation of women more centrally into each dimension (through UN Security Council Resolution 1325 mandates), practice on the ground demonstrates that where gender is dealt with at all, it is done in governance programs by (1) encouraging women to vote, (2) inserting women into legislative and executive structures via quota requirements, and (3) assuming that women will find their voice within civil society, while men maintain their traditional dominance of the formal political systems. Thus, the systems remain gendered to men's advantage, though obviously elite and privileged men gain more than men already marginalized within the political economy of a postwar society. We concur that independent, fair, and accessible elections, institutions, and civil society are all elements to be included in post-conflict governance programs. However, they are not the only building blocks to transformative ends, nor are they the building blocks most likely to open up male-dominated political and administrative systems, creating an enabling space for women.

Governance programs, even those now required to "mainstream gender," trend toward securing formal political rights within official political structures and institutions.[9] Existing programs in general try to slot women into new or reformed institutions and secure women's de jure political and civil rights, reflecting our general critique of gender mainstreaming as being grafted on, rather than being initiated from, an organic assessment of what women want and need. We propose that this model be turned on its head. Governance programs should begin by placing gender central to the enterprise of political transformation and regulation. Instead of grafting women's concerns onto preconceived post-conflict governance programs, international and domestic actors engaged in post-conflict governance should be asking the following questions: What would it take—within formal and informal political structures, within both the public and private sphere—to secure women's fully emancipated and empowered place in the reconstituted society, to unpack the masculinities inherent in the political process, and, most importantly, to assess and reflect what women really want and need? A consultative assessment is thus the starting point of reinvigorating externally driven governance reform to fully and meaningfully address women's post-conflict needs.

If undertaken, the foregoing inquiry would bear out the conclusion that elections and institutional political reforms alone are insufficient to deliver peace and stability to post-conflict societies,[10] and what constitutes good governance for women should lead to a far greater policy emphasis on the private sphere and on economic, cultural, and social rights. Such a practice of "engendered governance"[11] stands a credibly better chance of prioritizing issues that would reflect the articulated needs of the female half of many post-conflict societies and moreover have transformative effects for men.

The effectiveness of a post-conflict governance program, as measured by international actors and the benchmarks they currently employ, will be determined by many things: the situation before the war, the strategic engagement of the state emerging from conflict, the way in which peace was negotiated, the "buy in" of the domestic actors and post-conflict governing elites, and the capacity of the post-conflict state to secure the economic and bilateral interest of key states. Undoing existing gendered hierarchies and creating new and transformative gender discourses is not integrated or factored into these core imperatives, not least because Resolution 1325 fails to address the fundamental inequalities and exclusions which give rise to women's particular vulnerabilities in war.

THE GENDERED COMPONENTS OF POST-CONFLICT GOVERNANCE PROGRAMS

With the injection of gender mainstreaming into post-conflict programs under Resolution 1325,[12] the actors establishing governance programs have been (in theory) required to deepen their multidimensional approach. One useful characterization of these multiple governance dimensions describes them as (1) "security governance," (2) "political-administrative governance," and (3) "socioeconomic governance," all of which are interconnected.[13] To date, most post-conflict governance programs have focused overtly on the second dimension, political and administrative governance, and building the systems, processes, and infrastructure of government. They tackle the first dimension, security, through programs such as disarmament, demobilization, and reintegration (DDR), rule of law, and peacekeeping, and practice illustrates that the third dimension is largely ignored, with the important exception of economic liberalization, which will be discussed below. The emphasis reflects a hierarchy of priorities that we view as invariably exclusive of and potentially discriminatory to women's needs and priorities.

Democratization

Democratization has become the transitional governance norm in post-conflict reconstruction and international interventions.[14] While honed during the so-called "third wave" transition, when a multitude of countries were transitioning politically from authoritarianism, fascism, or socialism, all post-conflict reconstruction operations now contain a strong democratization component.[15] When the international community is involved, post-conflict governance structures can be imported as replicas of institutional elements in the Western states supporting the reconstruction.[16] In spite of the fact that such deeply gendered political institutions may not even deliver positive gender outcomes in their own nations, internationals involved in post-conflict reconstruction regularly import institutions and policies—adding a dash of gender-oriented policy to satisfy mainstreaming requirements. In such importation, consultation is absent, and few structural assessments are made as to whether programs and policies would actually provide local women with voice, agency, and power commensurate to men.

One problem lies with presuming the overall benefits of democracy as a political system. Particularly for those with weaker political leverage in a polity, the assumption that procedural democratic protections produce substantive democratic outcomes is one that has been interrogated and found wanting.[17] Inadequate democratization may operate instead to weaken genuine democratic impulses and strengthen the autocratic tendency by lending it the veneer of process.[18] In other words, while democratization is promoted in all post-conflict reconstruction processes, it may not actually produce the desired "democratic" outcomes in all post-conflict situations.

Democratization enterprises are primarily concerned with procedural democracy—elections and the establishment of electoral systems—and implicitly presume that holding elections advances stability,[19] even though studies consistently reveal that elections and electoral systems have little real impact on inviting women and minorities as stakeholders in the power structures of a transitioning state, as will be discussed below. Proponents of democratization counter that living up to democratic standards is merely consonant with already existing international customary obligations for states.[20] They would argue that proof of the democracy's legitimacy as the political standard bearer in the modern world order is the fact that "non-democratic states, with a view of strengthening the legitimacy of their government, try to portray their political regime in a democratic fashion rather than choosing to dispute the role that democracy plays in the international order."[21]

But critiques of democratization-centered post-conflict reconstruction abound. First, even if democracy is the goal, democracies are not created instantaneously. The international community has been reluctant to step back and let democracy slowly unfurl, when it does so via the mistakes of uneducated, corrupt, nationalist, or self-interested but nevertheless elected officials.[22] An obvious and related critique is the clearly undemocratic nature of the internationally led processes that produce "democratic" regimes and the unresponsive and unaccountable ways in which international administrations administer some territories, as discussed in Chapter 4.[23] Some critics go so far as to describe international administration as the "new Colonialism."[24] Preliminary evidence suggests that legislative measures and regulations imposed through international administration do not hold, and short- or medium-term gains are nullified by longer-term reversion to instability.[25] A third critique, addressed below, is that elections are idealized as a vehicle for instant democracy when they can in fact inadvertently operate to exacerbate conflict.[26] The inability to harness violent factions or the favoring of certain groups over others in the process of producing electoral outcomes means that elections may be merely a pause in the return to violence. Fourth, the process of rendering or requiring democracy can be rightly perceived as deeply paternalistic, reinforcing patterns of patriarchy that are antithetical to women's interests.

None of the foregoing critiques, of course, imagines substantive equality for women as an objective. Thus, we affirm a broader critique of democratization-centered post-conflict reconstruction, taking issue with the emphasis and prioritization of elections and superficial procedural identifiers of democracy, often at the expense of achieving substantive indicators of democracy (primarily equality).[27] Democratization alone fails to achieve gender equity.[28]

A gender-central approach to democracy in post-conflict societies would start from the conceptualization ably advanced by feminist political scientists distinguishing between procedural and substantive democracy, emphasizing and valuing the latter.[29] As we have outlined in Part I of this book, what drives the concept of gender centrality is a principle of substantive equality, which in this context promotes and makes central the primary substantive characteristics of a democracy—equality of participation and representation. This requires not merely replacing the rhetoric of democracy with the rhetoric of equality, but advancing principles and practices of equality that address women's concerns: including women, promoting women's equality of participation, equality of political voice, equality of representation, equality of opportunity (within the political sphere, but also in employment, education, and law), equality of outcomes, and equality of agency. This approach goes beyond a traditional liberal emphasis on civil and political rights and presupposes the relevance of social and economic conditions to delivering the substance of women's equality in the political realm. This approach would also be more beneficial to ensuring long-term and sustainable peace than shallow democratization, with its contemporary focus on civil and political rights, electoral systems, and political institution building.

Elections

Free and fair elections are considered the foundational element in establishing a democracy,[30] and equal participation in the political process is a concept enshrined in international law.[31] However, the UN Special Adviser on Gender has now acknowledged a multitude of factors present in post-conflict countries likely to impact negatively on women's participation in electoral processes. These include the (false or overtrumpeted) expectation that elections will secure peace; the unstable security climate; massive displacement that disproportionately impacts women, who are unlikely to carry identity documents; the fact that political campaigning takes place in the public sphere where women are often disadvantaged or even unable to participate; fraud and corruption, which make it harder for women to participate; partisan use of state resources, which entrenches the status quo; the disproportionate percentage of women who are illiterate; and the fact that post-conflict work is donor driven and that donors do not prioritize "women's issues."[32]

Despite these acknowledged obstacles, the participation of women in elections and the increased, if not equal, representation of women in elected office have nevertheless been identified by the United Nations and its member states as primary components of gender mainstreaming.[33] Various strategies have been developed to achieve this goal. Without decrying greater representation for women, we conclude that it is a necessary but insufficient practice to ensure women's greater access to and opportunity from political process.

Clearly, there are a multitude of procedural impediments to genuinely incorporating women into post-conflict electoral processes. Laws may need to be drafted, changed, or implemented to ensure women's ability to participate, due to women's differing needs, ranging from inability to read ballots or become easily educated about candidates[34] to election security and actual capacity to vote where women's safety is not secured.[35] In many instances, women more than men will be new to voting and will need to be educated about the relevance of elections to their lives, informed about the candidates and parties, and encouraged to register for and participate in the election process. Registration itself may be more difficult for women who often face legal obstacles in proving their identity, having lived largely within the private sphere and without formal legal rights often attached to voting. Moreover, women must sometimes be assisted in the most mundane and mechanical aspects of elections—getting to their polling stations and actually voting without the undue influence of male relatives—particularly in instances where illiteracy risks making her individual vote meaningless when a male relative "assists" with casting her ballot.[36]

When elections are undertaken in the early days after peace negotiations as part of the implementation phase, the elections themselves may be problematic. In a setting of physical insecurity and safety concerns, massive internal and external displacement, and ongoing economic fragility, the ability of women to participate effectively in elections can be difficult to meaningfully protect.[37] Because wartime elites remain the most visible and vocal individuals within a society, elections can serve to entrench those same wartime leaders, but now in a democratically sanctioned postwar government.[38] Post-conflict elites may have been complicit or previously responsible for human rights violations, including serious and systematic violations of women's rights. Accordingly, the apparent commitment to democratic values is undercut by de facto impunity for wartime atrocities when those who committed those atrocities may be conferred legitimacy, having been elected in internationally contrived and condoned elections. While wealthy Western democracies believe that elections will transform poorer countries into stable societies, this is often an unrealistic expectation,[39] particularly given that elections can so easily be separated from more fundamental and necessary reforms, such as transparency in government, meaningful development, involvement of the civil society sector, and a literate population able to understand participatory governance.

Although important, attention to women's participation in government must not begin and end with electoral reform. Such a myopic approach fails to see and address the broader set of social, customary, and familial limitations that operate to constrain women's participation in the public sphere. Even when legal changes are made to electoral laws, principles expressing the desire to involve women in elections often fail upon implementation.[40] The reasons for this are multiple but are rooted in the broader social status of women and the layers of constraint that affect their lives, including access to political and social capital and access to information.

Ultimately, voting is a start, but alone does little to secure the actualization and enforcement of rights for women. As a consequence, elections alone and elections too early are rarely useful to the enterprise of securing democratic governance within a post-conflict society, let alone sustainable equality. In fact, though some post-conflict "deals" may work for and enable minorities to participate in a procedurally protected and meaningful way (e.g., Kurds in Iraq, Catholics in Northern Ireland), they may come at the expense of women or overshadow women's needs and rights in the deal-making phase. A complex feminist space emerges as women in such minority groups may actively agitate for benefits to the national or social group at the apparent expense of their own interests. With the possible exception of these minorities who secure specific electoral benefits during the peace negotiation phase, ethnic minorities and women (as minority political stakeholders, if not quantifiably a minority as women) rarely benefit from early elections. Without connecting elections to more fundamental reform in the legal and political structure, they will rarely provide the outcomes that would transform women's legal and social standing.

More challenging, and involving a deeper inquiry about the sources and forms of inequity and discrimination in the state's culture, there may need to be significant social revision before women meaningfully access the legal right to vote. This involves ongoing recognition that transition is potentially a far more long-term endeavor for women than for men, though both sexes face challenge and change in the process. In order to achieve positive outcomes for women with regard to governance in general and elections in particular, the starting point is one of consultation with women on the ground in post-conflict societies. This is hard and time-consuming work. It requires overcoming the social and cultural restraints (as well as providing translation, care, and access capacity) to directly canvass and incorporate women's views on such matters as (1) when elections should best be held (time of day, day of the week, month of the year); (2) what kinds of structures would best enable women across multiple social, economic, and familial constraints to participate; (3) where voting locations should be placed to enable women's attendance; and (4) training local women to act as election monitors, judges, and overseers to break the culture of masculinity enveloping voting infrastructures in many societies. The information elicited must then crucially be implemented in practice, in a gender-sensitive way, seeking continually to modify and recalibrate practices through ongoing consultation and negotiation with women.

Quotas

In virtually every post-conflict scenario since the early 1990s, quotas have been established for women's participation in government.[41] Quotas may be imposed with regard to elections (e.g., requiring that women constitute a certain number of candidates or a certain proportion of the electorate) or with regard to political and administrative institutions (requiring that women hold a certain percentage or number of leadership positions). Quotas can succeed in bringing more women into positions of power,[42] which creates the possibility of change as women and men both then bring their distinct perspectives to bear, in the political sphere.[43]

A concern with quotas, as with elections, is that quotas alone might be deemed sufficient to satisfy the gender component of post-conflict governance. The institution of quotas does not, by itself, answer the question of whether women as a group, and women within particular cultural, religious, economic, race-based, or family subgroups, make any real gains in establishing a political voice. There is a real risk that the post-conflict transitions may generate a focus on the level and numbers of women in positions of formal political power and use those numbers as indicators of the achievement of gender equality without further interrogating substantive gender outcomes.[44] For instance, through international intervention and quota development, women in post-conflict East Timor secured 27 percent of elected constituent assembly members; in Rwanda, women captured 49 percent of parliamentary seats in the 2003 elections; and in Afghanistan, women officially occupy 27.7 percent of lower parliament seats.[45] However, one need only look at the present state of women's equality in Afghanistan to understand that holding seats in office alone does not equate to gender-conscious governance.

Of further concern is that it is not clear that women voted or placed into elected office or governance institutions through quotas actually increases the likelihood of legislation, laws, and policies that improve women's lives.[46] Nor is it clear that women in elected office should be responsible for, required to serve as, or be interested in being spokespersons for women's concerns per se. Even if women are placed as candidates on an election ballot, for example, they (a) may stand little chance of being elected, (b) once elected might not actually help improve conditions for women, and (c) perhaps should not, in a strictly democratic system, be expected, just because they are women, to use their position to improve conditions for other women. These conundrums reflect the wider issues of women's complex intersectionality in conflicted and post-conflict societies and are generally not in the vision of those intervening or overseeing post-conflict governance programs.

Arguments concerning quotas as a means of securing women's participation in government can be summed up as follows:[47]

PROS	CONS
Quotas are empirically the most effective way of achieving a better gender balance.	Quotas distort the idea of representation and work against women.
Quotas can circumvent conservative party leadership.	Legislated quotas benefit the wives, daughters, sisters, cousins, etc. of traditional male politicians, not women who have developed constituencies of their own.[48]
Once some women are elected, they serve as role models for other women.	Women elected through legal quotas are less respected and have no real power. Many women therefore [do not] want to be elected via quotas.
If women are represented in the legislature, they can help remove some of the structural barriers that prevent women from being elected.	Quotas result in less competent legislatures.
Quotas are not discriminatory but rather compensate for an already existing discrimination.	Quotas are discriminatory against men.
Rather than limit the freedom of choice, quotas give voters a chance to elect both women and men.	Quotas take the freedom of choice away from the voters.
Quotas that deliver greater procedural equality of representation may over time deliver substantive equality outcomes.[49]	Quotas are directed primarily at women and do not necessarily address the cultures of masculinity that pervade political life.

The pros and cons of quotas set forth, we accept that a wider presence of diverse women in multiple settings articulating a variety of political views is an important element of undoing gender stereotypes and changing perceptions in the public. Indeed, no country has managed to reach levels of female representation surpassing 25 percent without some type of explicit quota.[50]

We now turn to address the specifics of how we believe quotas can be most effectively employed in changing women's daily lives.

Quotas can be instituted at multiple levels of post-conflict governance, both local to federal levels and within elected and appointed positions.[51] One mechanism for employing quotas involves increasing the inclusion of women on party lists during the electoral process. Most countries have electoral systems based on either majority vote or proportional representation; more women tend to be elected under the latter system.[52] In proportional systems, political parties present lists of candidates, and voters must choose among competing party lists. Parties receiving sufficient votes are allocated a certain number of seats in proportion to their share of the vote, and the members at the top of those parties' lists are elected. Those favoring the use of quotas in proportional systems assert that there is a greater incentive for parties to draw up a diversified list of candidates, including women, in order to appeal to a wider base of voters. If women are placed high enough on the party lists, in which candidates are ranked in order of party preference, they will probably win seats in parliament.[53] In proportional systems, party lists may be open or closed. Open lists allow voters to mark their preferences for individuals on a list, while closed lists require the voter to select the entire list in the order in which it appears.[54]

In sum, there is evidence that the practice and policies of greater women's representation can contribute to the goal of opening up democratic processes to women and to the wider benefit of the political system.[55] When quotas are implemented, more women secure positions within political parties and for-mal political institutions. But it is also clear that there is a "tipping point"; effective quotas require a substantial number of women and not merely a tokenistic gesture toward equality.[56] One way of using quotas more effectively is to think again in terms of short-, medium-, and long-term gains from using the post-conflict process to reconfigure gender roles in order to make gains for women. For example, while in the short term women may be elected for rea-sons of their connection to important elites (or male relatives), their partici-pation nevertheless at least serves the symbolic purpose of heralding greater social and political change. In the medium term, there may well need to be a goal of reaching a "tipping point" of women's representation, such that real gains for women will only accrue when, for example, 30 percent of elected or appointed officials are women. In the long term, placing women in positions of power via quotas can help begin to address the need to transform the cultures of masculinity that pervade and define political life in many jurisdic-tions. A transformative gender-sensitive governance process would make it possible for men to articulate different needs for themselves and for women, thereby shifting the responsibility of women's issues to both men and women—and creating different conceptual and practical pathways for the consideration of gender issues in politics.

INSTITUTION BUILDING

In the post-hostilities phase, a clear goal for international intervenors and supporters is the creation of a functioning government infrastructure at the central, regional, and municipal levels. In some societies, such structures existed before the war and require only reconstruction. In others, they never existed and must be constructed or reconfigured to align with the international (and ideally agreed domestic) conception of stable governance structures. Often this work begins with constitutional drafting, as discussed in Chapter 9 of this book. There are two types of post-conflict institution building as it affects women: (1) building municipal, state, and national governance structures which might incorporate women and become responsive to their concerns, and (2) building ministries and other human rights and equality-focused entities which directly or indirectly impact women's rights.

The first type of institution building focuses on bringing more women into formal political structures.[57] As discussed above, we believe that quotas can be useful in securing representation for women in these formal political institutions,[58] but cannot serve as the sole means for fundamentally and inclusively addressing gender issues and securing better outcomes for women.

The second type of post-conflict institution building that may be viewed as directly addressing women are ministries focused on human rights or women's rights. This second type of institution building deals with creating the infrastructure to address the substance of human rights and, ideally, women's rights; for example, the creation of a Prime Ministerial Commission on Gender Equality (East Timor).[59] Other institutions created post-conflict to deal more generally with human rights and equality issues could also be said to have the potential to address women's issues, although the ever-present risk is that even within human rights entities, women's issues will not be prioritized.[60]

In thinking about these two types of post-conflict institution building that might begin to address issues of concern to women, a broad and important query arises. Do specialized women's institutions really do more for women than would integration into the broader political spectrum? There are several factors suggesting they may not. First, an open question remains whether the specialized women's rights entities are compliant with the Paris Principles governing national human rights institutions.[61] Second, these entities tend to be seriously underfunded. Finally, they tend not to have legislative, subpoena, or other accountability powers, making it very difficult for them to do much more than rhetorically address women's rights.

In conclusion, democracy-oriented governance programs that focus on creating "women's institutions" risk using these institutions as a sort of talisman for gender equality in governance. Representation and the creation of institutions should be viewed as only one element of a package of measures whose overall goal would be the advancement of women's equality and non-discrimination. Representation matters, but it will only be effective when allied with a package of legal, policy, and social measures designed to work in concert to centralize women in the decision-making process and to effect outcomes that measurably improve and value women's lives.

Civil Society

One key part of the post-conflict governance program package includes fostering the creation or bolstering of civil society. Civil society is a complex, multifaceted phenomena in most societies linking together a variety of formal and informally organized social and political groups in ways that intersect with social and political agendas and interests. It serves to interact with and push back against top-down forms of government and can create a bridge between the private sphere and public political systems. This can be important for conveying private sphere concerns to formal political power holders and can generate support for human rights and democracy norms from the bottom up. Many governance specialists assert that political liberalization works best, and therefore a post-conflict society becomes most secure[62] when it encounters a vibrant and well-organized civil society that can push policymakers toward a substantive rights regime.[63]

Nevertheless, in the post-conflict reconstruction world, civil society is rarely viewed as essential to security, but rather is viewed as a component of long-term sustainability and capacity building, almost as a development concept. It is therefore rarely prioritized for support in the immediate post-conflict phase where governance is being attended to and is often therefore adversely affected by loss of international and bilateral funding on the basis that the "war is over."

Not all relevant actors are convinced that augmenting and supporting civil society capacity is the right approach for women. In the aftermath of hostilities, civil society space risks being constructed as a dumping ground for women, minorities, and other inconvenient groups seeking to gain access to the formal political sphere. A considerable risk of overemphasizing civil society post-conflict is that the existence of civic space may undo the need to bring a wider and more diverse group of actors and groups in formal political processes. Women's organizations and structures are not always fully integrated into and valued even within broader civil society structures. Is civil society as bias-free as some assume with respect to women's equality and inclusion on equal terms? Despite civil society's status as outside government and power structures, it too may also manifest patriarchal hierarchies of victimhood, status, and significance. Furthermore, if civil society promotion masks an assumption that women operate best outside of formal power structures in the world of nongovernmental organizations (NGOs) and community work, then this essentializes women's roles in highly problematic ways.

Feminist and human rights scholars also have been justifiably skeptical of grassroots approaches that celebrate "community,"[64] as "community initiatives" may in fact mask patriarchal and gender-biased structures and require significant revision in order to operate fairly and to women's benefit. The community can be just as masculine and patriarchal as the formal political arena.

Moreover, when civil society thrives and projects a public voice, its most prominent proponents can be drawn "up" into the posttransition formal power structures. This pull can be seen both as a negative, allowing for co-optation and by creating a brain drain of sorts in civil society, and as a positive by placing those with grassroots interests, connections, and ideas into the formal power structures. Further, civil society as a real locus for women's power and positive change may only exist in certain types of transitions. It proved tremendously important during the transition of socialist states,[65] but in other regimes, civil society has attracted elites, limiting the true effectiveness with which the women within these organizations can be said to speak for many or most women within the society. Finally, as with other aspects of post-conflict reconstruction, the potential strengths of civil society are substantially weakened when it "follows the money." That is, perhaps even more than in other post-conflict programs, the very existence of civil society depends upon funding.

Despite the foregoing concerns, women's groups and those concerned with gender equity may yet have much to gain by aligning with broad civil society interests. Proponents argue that civil society can be instrumental in creating a sense of security in the immediate aftermath of war and thereby instrumental to sustainable security. They point out, too, that women have been essential to building a grassroots and localized sense of security by organizing peace movements during and after war.[66] Civil society, operating from the grassroots level, has often been more adept than formal political structures at recognizing the importance of gender in post-conflict reconstruction.[67] By working within local populations, by creating a space for people to voice needs and demands, and by fostering an arena in which expression is tolerated and even appreciated, civil society can successfully create collective action and the movement more likely to change societal attitudes regarding the minimum expectations of gender equality.[68]

In general, women may be able to exercise more power from within NGOs and other alternative spheres of power (economic, cultural, or social) than within formal political structures. In Bosnia, for example, while women were virtually invisible in the initial political and governance structures created at the peace negotiations, women dominated civil society.[69] In Northern Ireland, women's organizations from across the political divide worked with a broader civil society alliance and were instrumental during the peace process in forcing such issues as equality, social and economic rights, victims' rights and remedies, as well as a range of legal devices designed to benchmark progress on all these substantive issues into the formal peace negotiations.[70] By one measure, these are very positive precedents for demonstrating venues of political influence for women.[71]

Another argument in support of promoting healthy civil society as an integral component of gender-positive post-conflict governance programs is that this may result in bringing values associated with gender issues—such as freedom to reject cultural expectations, freedom from domestic violence, and power within the family structure—out of the private sphere and into the public. In Rwanda, for example, NGOs that were focused on gender equity successfully pressured the government to pass legislation giving women equal rights to inheritance and property.[72]

Additionally, the critical set of economic and social rights is often deftly tackled by civil society operating within and around local mores rather than by formal domestic or international political or judicial structures. Real power for minority or disenfranchised groups, women among them, is being in a position of strength capable of influencing policy. A healthy and inclusive civil society should be recognized as a key component for good governance within the overall post-conflict governance; such recognition would help guarantee appropriate funding, thereby rendering it less susceptible to the wild fluctuations attendant to grasping for limited available donor funds. Because the most marginally funded and vulnerable groups are often women's organizations, ensuring adequate support for civil society generally and for women's organizations in particular is, in our view, a priority in post-conflict reconstruction. If civil society can provide a power base for women's voices to emerge and influence policy, then it is a valuable tool for engendering governance.

GOVERNANCE CONFLATED WITH ECONOMIC RECONSTRUCTION AND DEMOCRATIZATION

The international community now largely understands economic stability as necessary to post-conflict stability and often begins to address economic systems in tandem with governance stabilization.[73] For women, socioeconomic opportunity is of tremendous importance to their security and well-being throughout the reconstruction process. Post-conflict governance discourses that fail to deal with socioeconomic rights or the allocation of resources will inevitably fail women. Where socioeconomic rights are assumed to be "dealt with" by liberalizing a country's economy, women not only lose jobs, economic power, and status, but, as will be discussed below, they also fail to receive the concrete socioeconomic resources they so desperately need after a war. While governance programs have tended to emphasize the political-administrative dimension, as discussed above, the socioeconomic dimension requires considered attention, particularly for women. But not, perhaps, in the way it is currently deployed.

Market reform, now a standard component of post-conflict reconstruction, is intended to integrate the new state into the global economy by rolling back the power of the state over the economy. We argue that the socioeconomic component of governance should include the provision of social and economic rights and benefits at least, consistent with the treaty obligations of states under the International Covenant on Economic, Social, and Cultural Rights.[74] Creating post-conflict economic solutions requires grappling with the root causes of conflict and violence, which typically include elements of poverty and economic inequity. Regrettably, in some instances the opposite is done. In the name of market liberalization, benefits that might have existed for women pre-conflict are terminated; such policies can have harmful effects on women's social and economic status. No one solution fits all countries undergoing transition. Undoubtedly, it is in women's interest to ensure that markets are regulated by law, that monopolistic patterns are undone, and that corruption in the economic sphere is fully addressed. When market liberalization is undertaken, we particularly underscore the importance of political and economic transparency to counter corruption.

The Ramifications of Economic Liberalization for Women When Social Benefits Are Scaled Back or Terminated

There are serious and as yet understudied gender consequences to currently employed economic liberalization aspects of governance programs in post-conflict societies. With the emergence of a number of new and newly independent states in the last half-century,[75] many of which were ripe for both political and economic transition, the international community began to conflate post-conflict reconstruction and development with economic liberalization.

When economic stabilization includes liberalizing the economy, as has been the case in particular in transitioning countries with vestiges of socialism (e.g., Eastern European, Southeastern Europe, Central Asian and Latin American transitions), the international intervenors focus on deregulating markets, reducing taxes and government services, and privatizing business and property as part of the post-conflict governance process.[76] In some post-conflict economies, the fundamental transition may be from a highly interventionist state-supported economy to a market-driven entity with minimal regulatory oversight, though variations on this core schematic are also common. Following from this are a number of outcomes, many of which are highly gendered. First, market variation changes employment patterns, and where jobs are downsized, women and minorities are often the first to go.[77] Not only do women lose employment, but they also lose a related set of social and welfare benefits linked to their employment. In many non-open economies, women are more likely to be found in public sector jobs, with men in the private sector. In former socialist countries, when public sector jobs were largely eradicated pursuant to the international community's requirements of economic liberalization, women lost jobs while men gained them as attention and funding were channeled into the private sector where men have considerable advantages.[78] Not all men benefit, either, of course. In such sweeping market reform, many men, including those who are undereducated or who lack transferable skills, may also be affected, leading to the broader crisis of masculinity we have identified in Chapter 2. Men are more likely to see few alternatives to remaining in or joining militias and military occupations, which are often among the few paid positions after war and during economic transition, or transferring combatant skills to criminality. Evidence suggests that where women do achieve entry into a newly developing private sector, it is largely within the service industry.[79] Women of higher socioeconomic strata may retain or find employment while women of lower socioeconomic status do not.[80]

It is important to pause here and note again that we critique the "one size fits all" approach to market reform and acknowledge that in some instances, particularly in the world's poorest and least-developed countries, market reform may well serve those most in need by, for example, establishing minimum wages and providing previously nonexisting benefits to workers.[81] The point is not to extol the virtues of socialism over capitalism, but rather to point out what is lost, and particularly what is lost to women, when state spending is cut, as is now required by most international financial institutions under market reform programs.[82]

The empirical evidence affirms that when state spending is cut at the behest of states and international institutions leading governance reforms, women typically lose out. For example, in most socialist systems, childcare, maternity leave, and parental leave were subsidized. Under market reform, those programs are cut substantially or entirely. State funding for food subsidies and prenatal nutrition programs are also cut, which impact women as the caretakers of the family at a rate disproportionate to men.[83] The result is that women, due to their traditional roles in the family—and in the case of the former Soviet states these are roles that were immediately resurrected after lying dormant for two to three generations—stay home to care for children and sick family members formerly cared for by the state. Thus in terms of equality and autonomy measures, transition may result in a retrograde step for women's social and economic status.

In this way, the paradigms of economic transition that accompany post-conflict reconstruction in some countries become highly regressive movements for women, undoing benefits that may have operated to women's advantage under the previous system of governance or have been produced by conflict itself.[84] As we have consistently pointed out, this is one of the paradoxes of post-conflict transition: the presumed benefits for all are not equally shared by women.

The Gender of Liberalized Economies

In many conflicted societies, there is an extremely high overlap between the poorest communities and the sites of conflict-related violence. This cyclical and spatial connection, which ought to force deep reflection on the causes of communal violence in any society, is often overlooked or ignored when reconstruction and economic rebuilding are advanced. In Northern Ireland, for example, the poverty, employment, and social opportunity differential between Protestants and Catholics resulting from a structure of enforced discrimination and preference has been recognized as causal to the reemergence of violent conflict in the late 1960s.[85] It would seem self-evident, then, that bridging these economic and social gaps would be at the heart of the new social and economic dispensation after the signing of the Good Friday Peace Agreement, yet these differentials for historically marginalized communities persist.[86] Ongoing economic marginalization of vulnerable communities may well be a powder keg waiting to be ignited and thereby fueling ongoing cycles of violence in states that fail to fundamentally address economic disparities and inequities.

Furthermore, war itself tends to destroy economies, such that post-conflict governance programs must address both poverty and economic stabilization, both of which have gendered dimensions and gendered impacts, some positive, some negative for women. For instance, when the population at large is impoverished as a consequence of war, the continuing economies of violence in post-conflict societies can lead women into human trafficking.[87] On the other hand, war tends to change the gender divisions of labor, which can also have the effect of forcing women out of households and into the fields and the workplace, even while centering many women as new heads of household. In the economic arena as well, war and conflict create both problems and opportunities for women and men.

Feminist scholars argue that market-oriented economic liberalization policies are inherently detrimental to women in that they shift resources into male-dominated corporations and market mechanisms.[88] In post-conflict countries that privatize state assets, a small group of domestic actors benefits—male elites with international contacts.[89] As businesses and factories privatize, liberalizing the economy demands business streamlining. Not every member of the polity can be employed in a liberal economy. For both men and women, negative and gendered results emerge.[90] Where a conflict intersects with (or gives rise to or is brought on by) the dismantling of an economic system, the resultant impacts are particularly detrimental to women, as women tend to rely more heavily on public services generally which are no longer available,[91] are more likely to need social services in the aftermath of a war or conflict,[92] and are more likely to lose out in the privatization process.[93] Further, in these new private markets, the work done by women can go unrecognized and undervalued.[94]

In some former Eastern Bloc countries, which had previously prided themselves on quantitative gender equity in the workforce (whether or not it constituted genuine equity), women constituted 72 percent of the unemployed in the transitioning states.[95]

While economic liberalization has become an inherent component of post-conflict governance, it is imperative that the strict policies attaching to privatization and the elimination of public services so inequitably detrimental to women recovering from conflict be carefully examined. In this context, we endorse benchmarking with a gender impact assessment, requiring that any economic liberalization program (1) consult with women about their economic needs, (2) ensure that women are represented across all arenas including economic sites of transition, (3) assess whether programs designed to liberalize the economy will have negative gender outcomes, (4) ensure that rights discourse pervades the framework of economic transition, and finally, (5) ensure some minimal nonnegotiable provisions such as the availability of food, water, shelter, and health care through the liberalization process.

Transparency

In some conflicted and transitioning countries, the real issue of import to the governance component of post-conflict reconstruction is transparency and anticorruption. The government must be made accountable to the people in its policies, economic decisions, and allocation of resources. Transparency initiatives are designed to increase the disclosure of information to the public, thereby increasing the reliability and impartiality of those institutions. As transparency results in greater accountability by government leaders, transparent governance helps stabilize the political and economic climate of a country, which is critical for attracting long-term international development investment.

Corruption and lack of transparency are almost always present in conflicted states and interrelated with post-conflict processes. Corruption and lack of transparency can give rise to internal conflict and can also emanate from it. One strategy for reducing corruption is increasing transparency, which "works as a sealant against the corrosiveness of corruption."[96] During conflict and even in the years after conflict, black and gray market economies are rife and corruption finds easy places to hide. In other contexts, such gray zones provide for and are useful to women as the informal economy facilitates survival. Thus, there is an overlap between the dynamics of the war economy and women's limited advancement in highly fraught contexts. Particularly in resource-rich conflicted countries where those in power had an incentive to foster more conflict in order to spirit away and hide more resources, lack of transparency and corruption are rampant.[97] For example, the illegal exploitation of the Democratic Republic of the Congo (DRC)'s natural resources (gold, diamonds, cobalt, and timber) helps fuel the war in that state. Money laundering is rampant, and natural resource exploitation was so egregious that the United Nations issued a special report recommending that twenty-nine companies be subjected to financial restrictions, including a freezing of assets and a suspension of banking abilities.[98] Even in non-resource-rich states, corruption is rampant in the post-conflict scramble for political and economic power shares.[99] In order to model good governance, international actors must themselves model transparency[100] and force out corruption, with the cooperation of the new domestic elites (some of whom may also have been prewar domestic elites, and some of whom may be hiding resources and wealth).[101]

Corruption is problematic for all citizens, not just for women. When governments or domestic power holders divert funds for personal gain, the monies are not available to the people—for schooling, food, shelter, health care, or any government services. As argued above, the eradication or unavailability of government services in these particular areas tends to impact women, as care providers, greatest. Regularizing domestic government procedures decreases corruption. Increasing transparency by making government practices and economic decisions public similarly works to decrease corruption and render more funds available, which in turn can be beneficial to women if used correctly.

GENDERING GOVERNANCE

What would an engendered post-conflict governance program look like? Employing the framework we have utilized throughout, it should at a minimum be based on (1) consultation with women, (2) representation of women within governance frameworks, be they formal or informal, (3) being mindful that tipping points may need to be reached before women truly begin to feel the impact of women's representation in those systems, and (4) substantive minimums based squarely in international law, specifically, the International Covenant on Economic Cultural and Social Rights. Ideally, engendered governance would prioritize issues important to the female half of most post-conflict societies: labor training and labor equality; education access and retention; access to health care and childcare; and rights within the family structure, such as inheritance and property rights, and the rights to refuse one's family and societal dictates about marriage, divorce, and family caretaking. It would also focus less on the pro forma creation of democracy and a free market economy and more on ensuring provision of "social services justice," on which we elaborate in Chapter 11 of this book.

Good governance must come to be seen as governance that accurately assesses and then genuinely serves the needs of women as well as men. There are pragmatic reasons for domestic elites to include women in the framework of governance and reconstruction. By involving women at the core of the transformation project, outcomes can be maximized for differing interests, not least in gaining broader access for all to material resources which ultimately may work to the benefit of both men and women. In this view, creating new spaces in which masculinity can be rewarded positively is an unexpected benefit of the reconstruction process.

Retaining Wartime Gains to Bring Gender Discourse into the Public Sphere

During conflict, as has been noted elsewhere in this book, women can take on many roles, not all of which are synonymous with victimization and deprivation and some of which are, on the contrary, quite positive. However, even where women are combatants during war[102] or are able to enter the workforce as a consequence of war,[103] their status as warriors and breadwinners does not in and of itself bring gender issues and specifically women's equality and autonomy into the public domain and open to public discourse.[104] In practice, women who hold prominent and gender-bending roles during conflict tend to fade out of public view in the transition phase. As we have noted in other parts of this book, that retrenchment has multiple causes, but its effects on reconstruction policy and implementation have not generally been noted. One primary tenet of engendered governance, then, should be to bring women generally out of the private and into the public sphere, open up public discourse and negotiation through consultation with women, include women in formal political and economic institutions, and seek to ensure regular discourse between formal and informal political systems.

Focus on Women's Agency and Empowerment Rather Than "Democratization"

Governance programs centered in democracy have at least nominally contributed to political and civil rights participation for women, but their social and economic rights, all core minimal rights based on the Covenant on Economic, Social, and Cultural Rights, have not been substantively improved or acknowledged. In many instances, women's economic rights have substantially diminished as governance is conflated with democratization, which is in turn conflated with market liberalization.

While post-conflict governance programs and policies have thus far prioritized democracy and democratization, engendered governance would operate from a framework grounded in equality, the foundational tenet of democratic society, rather than democracy itself. In so doing, these governance programs would expend much less energy on instituting procedural democracy (elections and quotas for representation of women in formal, and sometimes effectively powerless, political systems), and much more energy on establishing actual, de facto social equality, in the form of economic security, political power, representation and voice, education, employment, and opportunity.[105]

We endorse certain fixtures of current reconstruction programs with respect to gender, including quotas for women in formal public office, party list requirements, and reserved seats for women. However, list inclusion must not stop with quotas and insertion of women into formal power structures, but rather has to take a sustained approach across the executive and parliamentary committee structures, and must also be applied in the civil service context, so that those who serve the state (and its elected officials) are also governed by the same principles of representation and equality of access to decision-making. Of course, many of these proposals are not new; the temporary special measures provision of the Convention on the Elimination of All Forms of Discrimination Against Women (CEDAW) has given significant juridical meaning to our understanding of the range of measures and sites that might redress historic exclusion for women.[106] The point we make is that many of these broad recommendations and the learning that has been accrued in non-conflicted societies is often not deemed relevant to the post-conflict setting by international actors with their priorities on security and other post-conflict programs. We take precisely the opposite position; post-conflict societies often provide the best setting to engage in these processes of social and political repair, which will in turn lead to longer-term security.

Democratic trappings alone will not alter long-held perceptions that men are better politicians and governors than women, but democratic and rights-based governance is better achieved when both genders are equally encouraged to engage in the political process. Furthermore, accession to regional and international legal and political structures requires adherence to and compliance with internationally acknowledged gender and equality principles. The failure to adhere and resultant nonaccession relegates the offending nation-state to that of outsider status, politically and economically. If nothing else, it is politically and economically expedient for a nation-state to adopt gender-positive governance structures and norms.

Equality itself being a term laden with potential for critique, an engendered governance scheme would specifically assert, promote, and protect legal, economic, political, and social power.[107] This would include economic opportunity, to which women and men alike need access, particularly as post-conflict governance tends to contemplate economic transition, which in the short term at least, as set out above, tends to leave women without access to income. Other economic alternatives include employing a development model initiating gender-conscious credit policies and lending programs.[108] Of parallel relevance is the need to integrate programs of reparations and remedy into the broader scheme of reconstruction, understanding that a cohesive set of initiatives, rather than a fragmented approach, is most likely to serve the vulnerable and the marginalized.

Governance programs now view economic liberalization as a necessary bedfellow to political liberalization, yet fail to fully consider the political and economic consequences of those programs to women and other vulnerable groups. This underscores our broader point about consultation processes and the extent to which programs and policies that affect women directly (and potentially negatively) ought to be subject to consultation with the groups most affected by them. While economic policies are crucial to governance programs, the focus of gender-positive governance programs should be on labor rights, economic access, and equality for all (particularly the disenfranchised, including women), rather than on the mere economic liberalization of the host nation with its flawed assumption of gender neutrality.

At a minimum, women's post-conflict equality would ensure that they are not deprived of agency to shape their own fate. In this conceptualization, we view agency and autonomy as critical values to shape the way in which policies advancing gender equality are advanced. In some cases, laws may need to be rewritten in order for women to participate fully in the electoral process. In other contexts, election procedures may need to be altered to take account of women's needs and ensure women's participation.[109] In other instances, quotas may be instituted to ensure women's inclusion in political, rule of law, or economic structures. The ability of women to attain agency, however, requires more than voting access, quotas, or the eradication of gender-discriminatory laws, although those can sometimes indicate a good place to start.[110] It also requires that women be provided opportunities for education, so that elites alone (women among them) are not the only persons in a position to function within newly developing formal power structures, and that cultural and social expectations are altered, if necessary, to make way for a place for women in the public sphere.

Public Information Campaigns to Counter Social and Cultural Gender Inequity

The persistence of asymmetrical social roles can render even the most carefully crafted election and the most well-built formal political structure moot if women's daily experience fails to provide them either with awareness of the existence of those opportunities and institutions or access to them.[111] Effecting social change requires public information campaigns, the success of which can take a generation to achieve. Therefore, every post-conflict governance effort aimed at a gender-positive outcome should expend resources on identifying social and cultural factors that would prevent women from participating in political life or accessing rights by creating a public information campaign or other broadly targeted measures aimed at overcoming those taboos. This is no easy task, as it is a more difficult and abstract task to undertake informal transformation of society's attitudes than it is to erect formal state institutions.[112]

CONCLUSION

In the post-conflict governance context, commitment to gender centrality requires inter alia identifying the masculinities that exist in the formal political and economic structures in order to reveal and yield actual opportunities for women to gain agency and traction within the political process and economic sectors. The post-conflict phase presents opportunity, but also responsibility to utilize this period in order to protect women and bring them fully into the political sphere. When a state has experienced significant gender-based atrocities, the strongest emphasis post-conflict must be placed upon protecting women's rights, centering the post-conflict work in a human rights framework, fostering equality, and preventing further discrimination. The components of effective post-conflict reconstruction include thoughtful and gender-infused understandings of democratic principles.

Both democracy and a secure economic environment are indeed critical to sustaining peace after conflict and to women's safety and women's rights. What is most important, however, is the immediate and long-term focus on securing, building, and then protecting an environment in which individual and collective rights are secure and in which men and women can be secure in the knowledge that gender-positive governance principles of equality and fairness will be applied.

CHAPTER 11

Development Infrastructure

Economics, Health, and Education

Populations and infrastructure are in disarray in the early days after formal hostilities have ended. As peace agreements are being negotiated, peacekeeping forces begin to assume their duties, and international actors begin to think about accountability mechanisms. Not only have people been displaced from their homes, but, typically, health clinics, schools, roads, businesses, and markets have deteriorated substantially or been destroyed. Many countries undergoing the post-conflict process were poverty-stricken even before the conflict started, and sustained violence generally functions to further damage economies and economic infrastructure. Of the twenty poorest countries in the world, three-quarters experienced conflict during the last twenty years of the twentieth century.[1] Not all conflicts occur in the poorest countries (Northern Ireland and the former Yugoslavia are evident exceptions), but its occurrence is more frequent in such locations.[2] Following the formal conclusion of hostilities, international actors, the national government, and aid groups turn their focus, often quickly, to development-based activities with an eye to longer-term reconstruction processes.[3] As a society begins the physical and socioeconomic reconstruction process, we suggest that the success of any development efforts depends significantly on gender integration.

The dividing lines between what constitutes development programs, as opposed to reconstruction or even rule of law reform, are not always clearly demarcated and can be murky for all actors. Rather than focus on these structural and definitional problems, however, our goal is to provide guidance on gender-centered development. Consequently, drawing on the definition advanced by the UN Development Programme (UNDP), we take development as referring not just to economic growth, but also to fostering human capabilities by improving a country's socioeconomic conditions.[4] Indeed, the general concepts bundled into development have expanded to include "measures to improve economic growth and distribution, but also measures . . . related to the social, institutional, and political factors that could impinge on economic well-being."[5]

While the terminology of development risks being used too broadly and too loosely (or may be undertaken by the wrong organizations at the wrong time), a broader view of development may in fact more accurately reflect women's needs. As such development can serve as a tool which recalibrates gender equality and gendered needs throughout the transition process. Development programs and processes provide multiple opportunities for ensuring gender centrality through post-conflict societies. Development undertaken in the immediate aftermath of war, which sometimes suffers from being viewed as inappropriate, untimely, and encroaching on the mandate of other organizations, could in practice serve as a bridge between conflict and security, running the temporal spectrum from humanitarian relief through post-conflict to longer-term development. If undertaken well, infused with a notion of what we term "social services justice" rather than market development or rehabilitation of armed groups as its core mission, then it provides critical support for a society's security and stability. Consequently, development processes must commence in tandem with the transition process with development professionals working in conjunction with local civil society groups.

The development field, more than post-conflict reconstruction, has already begun to take gender into account in structural and policy-oriented ways, and as such stands a credible chance of offering positive strategies, demonstrating how to center gender in the post-conflict process. This chapter focuses on building upon and advancing these strategies. As an initial matter, this chapter sets the stage by examining the need to integrate the fields and perspectives of development and post-conflict reconstruction, thereby creating a context in which gender centrality—ensuring equity between men and women and identifying and responding to both masculine and feminine concerns—can be made operational.

It then uses the concept of "social services justice" as the link between immediate post-conflict humanitarian aid and longer-term development measures, before examining how to make gender central throughout this time period. Social services justice should, we argue, become a critical aspect of any transitional justice and post-conflict reconstruction model, serving as a gender-central bridge between a recognition of the immediate needs of the population and long-term development. It provides a teleological justification for moving beyond the focus on formal mechanisms of accountability and of peace negotiations during the transition process. Gender is made central when post-conflict programs are grounded in the recognition of and response to the daily realities of life in a post-conflict country, where social services are often unavailable and legal accountability is often a distant dream. Social services justice is, then, a critical component of post-conflict reconstruction and has three goals: (1) to respond to the daily needs of the population post-conflict, ranging from livelihoods to health to education, (2) to expand the focus of justice and accountability mechanisms to account for the daily needs of those who have been victimized by the conflict and their visions of justice, and (3) to respond to the differing needs of women and men in order to dismantle conflict-perpetuated hypermasculinities and open space for women and men to thrive in the post-conflict environment. Finally, this chapter examines a series of strategies associated with development, assessing their gendered impact and suggesting how to promote gender centrality.

THE DIFFERING DIRECTIONS OF POST-CONFLICT AND DEVELOPMENT FIELDS

A post-conflict process will fail if it focuses only on separating the warring parties, on restoring earlier institutions, or even if only on rule of law reform along Western democratic lines allied with market liberalization. Instead, the transition process must—somehow—manage the impact of the social injustices that often helped cause the conflict and the high levels of violence that may accompany the end of the "official" war.[6] And it must do so accounting for the particular needs of the local population—women and men, girls and boys, families and communities. While conflicts are not caused by any one factor, consistent casualties across jurisdictions are social and economic disparities, including poverty, inequalities between groups, and a disintegrating economy.[7] The experience of socioeconomic inequality by outsider groups, those who are excluded based on religion, ethnicity, or other minority status, may serve as the powder keg that triggers the conflict. In turn, of course, war and conflict give rise to and exacerbate inequalities and poverty and demolish economies.

The fields of development and of post-conflict reconstruction have historically organized their scope of work and timelines somewhat differently from each other. The transition from short-term reconstruction to longer-term development is not always smooth and has been subject to critical assessment. Critiques arise due to the overlapping mandates of the organizations engaged in the work, the lack of expertise held by humanitarian organizations that engage in reconstruction and even longer-term development work, and the differing motivations of the various international actors involved.[8] For example, as discussed earlier in Chapter 5 and later in this chapter, peacekeepers will often have undertaken some development-type activities long before formal cessation of hostilities, with the goal of winning the hearts and favor of the local population.[9] The peacekeepers may have little expertise in development, nor a motivation to develop the state in transition, but rather are employing development-type activities in order to render their work (patrolling the local communities and keeping the peace) easier.[10]

Whether as a result of the lack of coherent parameters around each field or as a concerted recognition of the necessity to synthesize and harmonize their efforts, actors within each domain are beginning to build on and toward each other.[11] As discussed in Chapters 4 and 10, the disconnect and simultaneous overlap between these fields results from many factors. These include the complicated nature and messiness of the post-conflict process itself, the varying interests and motivations of donors, the desire of organizations to be on the ground first, the growing business of post-conflict reconstruction, the interests and motivations of donor states in developing their own markets and entry points into transitioning countries, regional politics, and so forth.

Differing conceptions of what the post-conflict process constitutes affects its relationship to development. If post-conflict refers only to disarmament and narrow definitions of security, then, while it may include some attention to civil and political issues, it will deem economic, social, and cultural issues to be extraneous to the core project (and may leave these issues to be taken up later by those engaged in development). The justification for electing a particular conception of post-conflict reconstruction depends upon many factors, often similar to those listed identifying why the work of the actors often overlaps. Consequently, development and post-conflict work, in all of its manifestations, have numerous common characteristics, goals, and concerns. Indeed, the connection between the two is quite clear, because, as noted earlier, the majority of armed conflicts today occur in countries with low levels of development. Poverty, inequality, and underdevelopment may not in themselves cause armed conflict and human rights abuses, but they can be contributing or enabling factors. Second, armed conflict, authoritarianism, massive corruption, and the humanitarian disasters and immense human rights abuses that often accompany them can have an immeasurably negative and long-lasting impact on a country's development. Third, and as a result, transitional justice frequently is pursued in a context of severely underdeveloped economic and social institutions, widespread scarcity of resources, and myriad competing needs. At the same time, justice initiatives come with a number of costs, so decision-makers in transitional societies face dilemmas about where to allocate available resources and how to ensure transparency in those decisions and implementation.[12]

Ensuring the interrelationship between development and post-conflict reconstruction is critical—and inevitable. For example, disarmament, demobilization, and reintegration (DDR) must be integrated with democracy promotion, gender equality, and economic and social development in order to achieve the very goals that DDR sees itself as advancing. These can also be thought of as short-, medium-, and long-term goals, with development taking over at the end of the continuum in order to maintain sustainability. Indeed, at a global level, there is general recognition that disarmament and development are linked (think "guns *and* butter" from basic economics courses),[13] and this recognition must inform ongoing post-conflict efforts.

On the other hand, a major difference between post-conflict reconstruction and development lies with the people and organizations undertaking it, and their goals and motivations in so doing. Those engaging in post-conflict reconstruction have often been present in the field following the formal cessation of hostilities and often were in the field during the armed conflict. As discussed earlier in this book, their "process" tends to be reactive—focused on addressing emergencies and putting out fires. This reactive mode may not be revised as the formal conflict phase concludes, and accordingly emergency mode extends far into the later stages of post-conflict reconstruction, when its utility becomes minimal or even counterproductive.[14] One of the consequences of working in the post-conflict "theater," employing military jargon on a daily basis, and reflexively reacting rather than planning, is that even years after the conflict, when there is less reason to treat each problem as an emergency and plenty of reason to be thoughtful in creating long-term strategies, programs, and plans, it has become habit to continue to operate in reactive mode; in this mode, women's issues rarely end up being prioritized.[15]

Nonetheless, the post-conflict reconstruction arena, which has primarily been concerned with the immediate aftermath of war on issues such as disarming the combatants and war crimes accountability, is beginning to expand its coverage. It is increasingly acknowledged that transitional justice, for instance, includes institutional reform, rule of law, constitution making and enforcement, and socioeconomic distribution within its broader competence.[16] Although conflict resolution, humanitarian aid, and development activities may have different priorities, there is growing recognition in practice and in theory of the need for each to work together[17] and of the interrelationship between each of these activities.

For example, the value of using a participatory approach—involving, consulting with, and empowering the local community and building capacity within it—is a lesson from the development field that is becoming intrinsic to post-conflict reconstruction.[18] This participatory approach, discussed throughout this book, means that in planning for societal rebuilding across its social, institutional, and economic dimensions, affected communities should be included from the outset in consultation about the form and practice of change. A participatory approach may require ingenuity, creativity, and patience in situations where funds are limited, the geography of the conflict area is vast, and ongoing security concerns may persist. Nonetheless, local ownership is critical to making long-term outcomes work. An example that shows both the ability of the development field to engage with local communities and the necessity of both development and post-conflict actors to excel at consultation with those who will be impacted by their projects involves the cook-stove project in Darfur. Engineers visited refugee camps, primarily occupied by women and children, and consulted with women and other refugee camp leaders concerning the need for an alternative to their existing stoves. The need resulted from the evidence that a preponderance of the families were missing meals because they did not have enough wood to cook their food. Moreover, women and girls were vulnerable to sexual assault when they traveled distances to collect wood to enable cooking. Engineers developed a more fuel-efficient stove which does not solve all social and vulnerability problems (it still requires wood, a valuable commodity, requiring that women find the wood), but the stoves are a much more efficient alternative and respond to an articulated need by the local female population.[19] This microexample provides us with cogent clues as to what kinds of material needs emerge from participatory forms of engagement with vulnerable communities in post-conflict societies. In this example lies a broader lesson: only by deep and practical engagement with the needs of the communities on the ground, and specifically listening to the voices of women, will advancements be made sufficient to ensure development agendas that are sustainable and transformative. Sensitivity to context also requires developing mechanisms to ensure that deference to local culture does not inscribe patriarchal attitudes toward women.

Even as we accept the broader universalist arguments for and value of accountability, as one common post-conflict reconstruction priority, we view these mechanisms as successful only if they are tied to the long-term structural changes that meet people's social, economic, and repair needs on the ground. While holding military actors accountable for their violence provides one basis for moving a society forward, the society must also deal with the concrete manifestations of that violence, providing health care for women who have been raped, providing schools for boys and girls whose educations have been disrupted, and rebuilding damaged transportation systems. Success may not be adequately determined by what the intervening international community views as progress, but its measurements ought to be deeply informed by what communities identify as their needs, rights, and capacities. If such needs assessments were undertaken more routinely, across all fields of post-conflict transitional work, then they could serve as the basis for post-conflict efforts to recalibrate its priorities.

GENDER CENTRALITY IN DEVELOPMENT

Successful transitions require development; development depends on supporting individual and communal capabilities. The forms this support might take depend on the individual's specific contexts, including gender, ethnicity, class, and other characteristics. Community capabilities may be dependent on similar variables. Many post-conflict goals cannot be implemented, or even initiated, when the population is starving, homeless, and mistrustful of government-sponsored services. Consequently, transitions must confront this dilemma in the planning process. This mandates incorporating programs and objectives traditionally viewed as within the sphere and mandate of development institutions even while firmly in the post-conflict phase. Post-conflict reconstruction programs that delve into and cross-reference development territory range from building civil society organizations, to providing education and health services, to improving the physical infrastructure and providing employment opportunities.

Development activities undertaken during the transition provide a significant opportunity to ensure that gender is central to the process because both men's and women's participation is better understood as critical to any national recovery process, socioeconomic or otherwise, and especially so in societies which have been conflicted and violent. Better understood, but not completely accepted. In many countries, the low levels of women's education, their lack of power, and cultural obstacles to women's equality hamper improvements in women's status and health even as the country as a whole seeks to recover. For women, as discussed in the Introduction to this book, the transformation of a country from "conflicted" to "peaceful" is generally partial and exclusionary. The transition process itself may frequently operate to cloak women's ongoing repression and inequality. For example, whether the country is in conflict or in recovery, men may determine whether their partners have access to or use family planning, and men are usually in charge of the family budget, determining how much is spent on nutritious foods and health items such as doctor visits.[20]

Studies undertaken with a development lens have shown that when women are in control of the finances, these needs are more highly prioritized. Indeed, if women have influence over household decision-making, they are more likely than men who are similarly situated to promote their family's interests.[21] Micropractices, at the household level, affect the macrolevels of a society's socioeconomic development, and so changes undertaken even within households offer a solid foundation for a broader social, economic, and political transformation. Although this is true regardless of whether the country is in a post-conflict phase, during the transition process, many more international donors are present. Theoretically, then, there is opportunity beyond generally available development opportunities to harness the energy, goodwill, human capacity, laws, and funding that come with post-conflict reconstruction to affect equity, in addition to the practical potential of new policies, institutions, and the presence of external actors to model gender-sensitive roles and behaviors.

A gender-central reconstruction process that unmasks existing gendered priorities would ground security and the country's forward movement in the concrete developmental needs of the population, needs that may vary for men and women. For women, these needs may range broadly from treatment centers for sexual violence victims to maternal care clinics to building roads to training police officers. In transitional societies, macroeconomic policies are often primarily focused on creating the conditions to open up markets to foreign inward investment. Free-market development is not, however, the only post-conflict economic transitional solution, and its utility is far more limited than its champions would admit. Accepting the limits of the market in the context of deeply fractured societies is also a fundamental recognition by the international community that economic advancement may be slow and that a long-term supportive presence will be necessary. This flies contrary to a concept of short-term commitments and an easy-fix approach, and recognizes that short-term market solutions do not generally work well for women.[22] Although reconstruction and development overlap substantially, a gender-sensitive reconstruction process must be integrated with development and development goals.

Throughout this book, we have emphasized that gender must be central to the ways in which the ending of violence is conceived, planned, and delivered. When it comes to reconstruction, investment in women makes a critical difference to achieving both short- and longer-term sustainable peace and development. Conflict scrambles women's roles (positively and negatively) and fosters hypermasculinity; a development focus may fundamentally assist with the difficulties of unscrambling such flux during the post-conflict process. It may also signal the possibility to post-conflict reconstruction actors that some revision of roles may benefit women and should be retained and fostered throughout the transitional process. As civilians and combatants return to their families, they must accommodate role transformation. This ranges from the shame of either having been a soldier or a sexual violence victim, to making extraordinary and routine the new identities untethered from prior gender constraints. Post-conflict and development actors working together may be able to create some space for women to retain and adjust to those new roles.

There is ample data supporting the contention that women should be central to the development process and how investing in girls and women can promote a society's economic and social growth.[23] Consider how education, a typical development priority, has implications for women. Research has shown that women with only a few years of primary education have better economic prospects, have fewer and healthier children, and are more likely in turn to ensure their own children go to school.[24] Educated mothers immunize their children 50 percent more often than mothers who are not educated, and their children have a 40 percent higher survival rate.[25] Children whose mothers are not educated are more than twice as likely not to be in primary school than are children whose mothers attended primary school, and educating women improves their children's rates of survival and nutritional status.[26] Each of these outcomes, obviously, improves both the local community and the overall development of the country as a whole.

Moreover, women's economic empowerment makes a difference; increasing women's labor force participation and earnings is linked to reducing poverty and improving growth, benefiting not just the individual women, but the larger society.[27] Finally, as discussed in Chapter 1, states that do not protect women's rights are more likely to fail, and states that cannot secure women's rights and place in the post-conflict world are not sustainable. It is imperative, therefore, that post-conflict reconstruction actors learn from lessons already internalized within the development sphere—that women matter and for transitional programs to succeed, women's concerns must not be tacked on but truly incorporated into post-conflict reconstruction projects.

SOCIAL SERVICES JUSTICE AS THE INTEGRATION OF POST-CONFLICT PROCESSES AND DEVELOPMENT

Post-conflict reconstruction processes generally contemplate criminal prosecutions and civil lawsuits to ensure the responsibility and accountability of some perpetrators, redefining governance, electoral structures, and processes and generally edging the society toward sustainable security. The needs of women, however, whether victims of violence or not, go far beyond seeing their violators punished and being able to vote.

In fact, justice for women in post-conflict contexts includes not just criminal and civil accountability (rights-based justice) but assistance of the kind traditionally associated with development. This assistance, which falls somewhere between the mandates of those engaged in humanitarian aid and development, is received more in the form of "healing" justice, because it focuses on providing critical social services to facilitate all aspects of post-conflict reconstruction.[28] Social services justice (SSJ) may be administered and funded by entities with no connection to the harms that have been experienced during conflict. While SSJ necessarily includes possible reparations programs as longer-term remedies, or as possibilities when the perpetrators are known and accept responsibility, it is also concerned with the more immediate, and often desperate, status of the victims. As such, social services justice refers to the range of potential services (social, economic, medical) that can be provided to victims both short and long term outside of the limited sphere of holding perpetrators criminally responsible and beyond attempts to measure the specific losses caused by the violence. For example, it could provide protection for women who may not have directly experienced sexual violence themselves, but who live in continuing fear of it. While social services justice draws legitimacy from the need for accountability, it also serves as an engendered bridge between conflict and security, running the temporal spectrum from humanitarian relief through post-conflict to longer-term development, any of which is inclusive of transitional justice.

Indeed, in some programs providing post-conflict reparations, this concept is being rolled into—albeit in very limited ways—the broader reparations strategy, particularly in the developing practices of communal reparations.[29] This is to be seen in the transitional justice field as it evolves to include more attention to socioeconomic rights and reparations.[30] In light of the post-conflict goals of peace, security, and healing, however, there are questions about whether mechanisms such as the International Criminal Court (ICC), reparations, or even truth commissions are critical to achieving these goals based on the needs of the local population.[31] In a study undertaken in the eastern Congo to determine needs and priorities of locals in the transitional process, more than 2,600 people (half of the respondents were women) stated that their highest individual priorities were peace, security, and livelihood concerns, such as money, education, food, and health. The highest stated priorities for the government to undertake were peace, security, education, and development. For the international community, the named priorities were development, money, peace, and food.[32] Transitional justice, which has been historically premised on achieving accountability and underpinned by the notion of "punishing those responsible," was ranked as the eighteenth priority for individuals, the twelfth for the government, and the fifteenth for the international community. The authors of this study concluded that "transitional justice must be integrated within a broader social, political, and economic transition to provide for basic needs and protection."[33] A similar survey in Uganda conducted shortly after a peace agreement was signed there found that survey participants' highest priorities were health (45 percent), peace, education, and livelihood issues, such as food and land, with justice, at 3 percent, as a much lower priority.[34] Indeed, when they were asked to consider what should be done for the victims of wartime violence, 60 percent of the respondents said that victims should be given financial compensation (51.8 percent) or cattle and goats (8.2 percent), with only 1.7 percent indicating that victims should be given "justice."[35]

While we recognize the limitations of relying on only two studies, and recognize further the methodological limitations of these kinds of studies (outlined in Chapter 1), the studies indicate the existence of a different set of priorities than has been assumed, suppositions upon which the entire basis of post-conflict reconstruction and development work has been founded. This affirms our calls throughout this book for reconceptualizing the premises upon which post-conflict work is based. The transitional process can effectively pay attention to and develop measures to modify existing structures of social and economic inequality and ensure that justice remedies, such as reparations, recognize locally articulated development-based needs.[36] This will also provide reassurance that development and post-conflict reconstruction programs, which may seem to be competing for the same funding, should not be mutually exclusive.[37]

We endorse the expansion of international justice in the post-conflict setting to include social, economic, and development-based rights.[38] "Justice" here requires responding on an individual, community, and national level to atrocities committed against the population based on sex, ethnicity, or nationality, to provide social, economic, and development-based benefits. These services should not be directly linked to legal concepts of restitution or punishment for crimes, but rather must be part of the entire post-conflict reconstruction process by providing remedies to the country from the damages inflicted by conflict.

Social services justice serves to recognize that women need resources that respond to their daily needs. In general, and in particular when seeking redress for harms inflicted on them, women may be more interested in long-term health care. The services may range, for example, from HIV/AIDS treatment (which may be traceable to crimes of sexual violence)[39] to establishing schools in communities that have been most heavily targeted by violence during a conflict. The activities for which justice is sought may not be traceable to one individual or group, but result from the conflict itself and address the conditions which created and facilitated communal violence. They may also result from the corruption and economic crimes that often accompany conflict.[40]

Justice, broadly defined, is part of an effort not just to compensate for past acts but also to deter future crimes. The basic argument we put forward here is the importance of broader conceptions of justice in post-conflict reconstruction, conceptions that require the integration of processes throughout the reconstruction period, thus creating "democratic [or engendered] space."[41]

Because women face special challenges in conflicts, as set forth in Chapter 2, they will have special needs. For example, establishing the procedures for restorative justice or civil and criminal trials is time-consuming, and by the time cases come to court, women's HIV may have become full-blown AIDS, their husbands may have married other women, they may have given birth to children born of rape, their reproductive capacities may be further compromised by lack of access to appropriate medical intervention, and/or they may be frightened to sell goods at market or work in the fields for fear of being raped en route. The list of women's needs and fears in the post-conflict context is long.

Social services justice also focuses on the consequences and effects of crime, not just accountability. Because it is unrealistic for perpetrators to provide reparations directly to the victim, victims and communities need additional resources to heal the harm and to secure the peace. Social services may be provided by the community, by the government, nongovernmental organizations, multilateral institutions, or other donors. Social services justice in this model requires a multisectoral approach that involves the community, as well as health, legal, security, and social services actors.[42] Importantly, many of the states emerging from communal violence are still bound by their international human rights treaty obligations, and we must be wary of thinking that the provision of basic needs through the social services model is above and beyond what they may be already required to do by treaty.

Ideally, the provision of social services justice would be local, but the actors providing services may be internationals working independently or with local counterparts until local capacity is sufficient to provide the services.[43] In fact, the capacity-building model applied to provision of social services and development of social services frameworks would provide a profound link between post-conflict reconstruction and longer-term development. This organic linkage belongs in every post-conflict and development context as a practical means by which gender can be made central.

Social services justice expands the meaning of post-conflict justice to provide broader—and more focused—remedies for the consequences and effects of the conflict rather than a single-minded focus on criminal accountability and legal process or the creation of government institutions. This development-based form of justice recognizes that stable and safe societies are societies in which all persons, including women, have access to basic services that enable them to restore and then live out their daily lives with some hope for the future.

Moving now to very specific conceptions of programs that gender-conscious social services justice might offer, this might, for example, take the forms of (1) supplying medical kits to test for AIDS; (2) establishing security patrols so that women can sell goods and produce at markets; or (3) developing rape clinics which provide detraumatization services, as well as legal counseling. Schooling is also critical; minimal expenditures in creating schooling opportunities for both girls and boys and encouraging attendance have an immediate payout for societal stability.[44] Gender- and culture-specific attention must be paid to factors that impact girls' attendance in different ways than boys. For instance, girls' ability to manage their menstruation cycles has a significant impact on their school attendance.[45] Boys, on the other hand, will stop attending school when they risk being picked up and conscripted by the military or rebel groups as they walk to and from school.[46] Simple yet effective ways to involve peacekeepers in a social services justice model during the early days of transition might include, for example, securing access and routes to school, as well as routes to market and for water and firewood collection. For children whose education has been interrupted because their parents fear they will be attacked if they attend school, peacekeepers can help provide the requisite physical protection and even work to develop community watch committees.[47] Having children attend school lends a tangible feel of stability and security in the post-conflict environment and is critical to addressing the legacy of intergenerational violence.

Addressing short-term developmental needs under the guise of social services justice also accords with evolving standards of international law. For example, the Declaration on the Elimination of Violence Against Women urges states to provide services for women and their children, including "rehabilitation, assistance in child care and maintenance, treatment, counseling, and health and social services facilities and programmes . . . and should take all other appropriate measures to promote their safety and physical and psychological rehabilitation."[48] A recent handbook published by the UN Division for the Advancement of Women complements the treaty requirements and is a useful tool providing a model framework for legislation in addressing violence against women based on existing treaty obligations by states "to enact, implement and monitor legislation addressing all forms of violence against women."[49]

As the conceptual basis for reparations expands, so too does the overlap with our concept of social services justice. For example, some scholars have suggested "national reparations programs" for victims of sexual violence, which could provide remedies ranging from direct monetary transfers to social services,[50] such as providing scholarships for children of sexual violence victims. Others have suggested reparations take the form of microfinance, thereby combining development goals with transitional justice goals.[51] Through microfinance, the recipients could also receive other services that are critical in a post-conflict society, ranging from health clinics to vocational training.

We acknowledge that there are potential criticisms of social services justice that may undermine its effectiveness. First, social services justice may seek to ameliorate too many wrongs, some of which were not directly caused by the conflict. Because of its breadth, like restorative justice, social services justice can be an expensive proposition in compensating the victim, her family, and her community. Second, because aspects of social services justice resemble development assistance, the social services may be emphasized at the expense of its justice and accountability aspects. Indeed, many post-conflict reconstruction programs are arguably also development programs.[52] Third, as with the other types of justice discussed earlier, its effectiveness depends on sensitive implementation, with responsiveness to and the participation of the affected communities, listening to their needs. Finally, there is a danger that we see the "goods" provided by social services justice as exceptional and as merely compensation to the community in general and perhaps by implication to specifically vulnerable victims. This may block a full appreciation of the range of existing human rights' obligations to which a state, even one emerging from conflict, is bound. Rights protection and service provision must not be viewed as exceptional or conditioned on being a "victim of a crime," but as a part of the compact involved in the ratification of treaties and as part of a broader set of obligations involved in post-conflict reconstruction for states and international institutions.

These are legitimate criticisms that must be addressed as the concept is more fully developed in theory and in practice. Because at its core it is based on the coordination and response of the different sectors concerned with prevention of and response to gender-based violence but reaches beyond that lens to address broader harms, it provides a useful model that can provide both immediate and long-term assistance. We propose applying the social services justice model not only in the context of achieving accountability and reparations goals, but as an engendered security tool, linking humanitarian relief, post-conflict reconstruction, transitional justice, and development by focusing on placing women in a position to reclaim or claim their place in society.

LONG-TERM DEVELOPMENT

Notwithstanding the need to focus on short-term development as part of the immediate post-conflict reconstruction process, the post-conflict time period is also the time to begin longer-term development projects that support broader conceptions of justice and sustained stability. As the state progresses and restores, there must also be a shift to full local ownership of economic and social development as part of its ordinary practice. Correspondingly, this points to the long-term transformative effect of post-conflict societies on the organization of government and the provision of services.

Social services justice provides the link from the immediate aftermath of conflict to longer-term development efforts. Projects begun as part of social services justice can provide the basis for these longer-term strategies, which involve, for example, making education accessible, promoting adequate livelihood support, building health care delivery, and ensuring an adequately paid, trained, and appropriately sized civil service. Indeed, as we argue above, the social services justice model can be used as the link to carry post-conflict reconstruction into longer-term development as a continuous model that may be calibrated in different ways and to different degrees in some phases over others. As the state progresses and is restored, there may be a need to move away from a specialized model to centralizing this approach through national government agencies and policymaking. The shift here is to full state ownership of development objectives as part of its ordinary practice in emerging from conflict, pointing to the long-term transformative effect of post-conflict societies on the organization of government and the provision of services. Throughout this process, gender centrality is critical.

While we focus on post-conflict reconstruction and therefore do not set out a comprehensive framework for gender-central development here, we provide an outline of various issues that should be considered, including education, health care, and economic development.

Education

Education should be a priority during all stages of the transition process. As part of our analysis of how rights hierarchies must be upended to make gender central, education is a foundational principle for helping achieve human capabilities and social stability. First, it helps to achieve the short-term post-conflict security and stability for which internationals are striving.[53] Second, it helps to establish equality of voice and rights that we argue are central to all post-conflict endeavors. For example, literacy rates for women in most post-conflict countries are abysmally low, placing them at a substantial disadvantage as actors in the public sphere. Conflict often disrupts the educational system, making it even more difficult for girls to complete their schooling. Education is crucial to post-conflict development, as education allows the country to achieve and sustain economic growth and advance meaningful democratic governance. A comprehensive developmental education policy would ensure new facilities in both urban and rural areas, with sensitivity to the language of instruction,[54] as well as to accessibility for boys and girls. Adult education is another critical component,[55] particularly given the disruptive effect of conflict on the larger education system. While improving education is not a panacea—higher literacy rates in the former Yugoslavia and Northern Ireland did not prevent violence, for example, and education can also support a patriarchal and elitist system—it nonetheless provides the basis for enhancing economic opportunities and improving health.

Studies have shown that the family of an educated mother is healthier and more economically viable. Increasing the number of girls that complete primary education can make significant improvement in advancing gender equality, as well as enhance women's social strength and autonomy. When household resources are limited, there is a tendency to spend money on boys' education rather than girls'. A family may prefer that a girl stay home to cultivate fields, collect water and firewood, cook, tend to younger siblings, or be responsible for caring for the family elders rather than attend school. Even if a girl has the opportunity to go to school, the cultural and social constraints listed above mean that she is under great pressure not only to underperform but also to drop out. Nonetheless, given the studies discussed earlier that show how educating women benefits the family and the community[56] and increases economic growth and generates more skilled workers,[57] it is critical to ensure gender equity in addressing literacy issues.

While we wish to avoid the essentialized presumption that education for women will result in peaceful societies, the link here is that the greater the levels of economic equality and opportunity within the state, the less likely the overall resort to communal violence. Beyond the basic goal of enhancing literacy, education can provide a culturally mediating role by teaching understanding and acceptance of different ethnic groups and the development of a society-wide identity: ensuring equal access for girls and women. Gender centrality might mean supporting home-based and community efforts, hiring women as teachers,[58] expanding the curriculum to include health and reproductive information,[59] and providing incentives—perhaps even financial—for girls to complete their schooling. Educational equity, then, is not just a formal human rights treaty obligation but also the right practical strategy.

Health Care

Conflicts can fundamentally affect health care and those fomenting conflict often purposely target health care infrastructure.[60] During conflict, (1) the health care infrastructure will, inevitably, be compromised, if not entirely destroyed; (2) the government may be unable to provide any funding; and (3) there may be few health care workers.[61] In East Timor, for example, more than one-third of all health care clinics were destroyed.[62] In Mozambique, 1,113 of the 1,171 primary health units were looted, forced to close, or destroyed.[63]

Building a new health care system invariably depends on international organizations working with local groups to ensure that health facilities are accessible and respond to medical needs. In East Timor, for example, UN agencies worked with local health care providers to decide where to locate new facilities and also provided salaries, ultimately resulting in a health care system that continues to function.[64]

Changing health care may start with an emergency response, and then continue to address other needs. It involves concrete steps, working with the local community. And, of course, health system transformations have incredibly gendered needs and outcomes. Consider what the International Committee of the Red Cross (ICRC) did in the Central African Republic with respect to sexual violence programs:

> Within two weeks we had trained a core, about three or four key health care staff, on providing treatment to survivors of sexual assault. . . . We had set up a very basic referral system, right, between health care, the health care, the health clinic and those providing basic counseling, psycho-social support. By June 2007, we were seeing 30 women and girls a day that were coming to us and saying that they had been raped as a result of the conflict. Eight months later we had provided services to 1200, right. . . . We have to set up these psycho-social response services, extremely basic, but still . . . addressing the issue in such a way that women feel comfortable coming forward. We start to break the silence, and we certainly reduce the health consequences.[65]

The organization astutely created a program that addressed the real needs of women and built capacity to increase that assistance, thereby providing the health benefits that responded to the community's problems.

Other more generalized gendered needs exist as well, not necessarily caused by conflict. Sierra Leone, for instance, has the highest maternal mortality rate (MMR) in the world, at 2,100 per 100,000 live births, compared to the United States, where it is 1 per 10,000 live births.[66] Beyond simple biology, women die in childbirth primarily because of inadequate health care structures, low levels of education, and low status.[67] Though maternal mortality is not linked directly to conflict, the post-conflict moment can provide the opportunity and resources to improve these gendered health outcomes through a combination of legal change together with investment in education and the health system. We assert that such transformative opportunities are few and that ensuring sustained equality and autonomy for women is highly dependent on grasping them as they arise.

Economic Development

As we think about economic development, often a priority for external states and organizations engaging with conflicted and post-conflict societies (detailed in Chapter 10 of this book), we argue that the frame of reference ought to encompass wider acceptance of the international dialogue and practice related to the right to development, which has clearly been articulated as a right premised on the grounds of no distinction on the basis of sex.[68]

Conflict disrupts the economy and, as peace takes hold, the formal employment sector may have few jobs. As an example, consider what happened in Bosnia. In 1990, two years before the siege of Sarajevo, Bosnia had a gross domestic product (GDP) of $11 billion and a per capita income of $2,400; five years later, by the time of the ceasefire, the GDP had fallen to $2 billion and the per capita income was estimated to be $500.[69] Moreover, only 20 percent of the population was employed, and they tended to work for government-related agencies (police, schools, or municipalities).[70] Among the 80 percent who were unemployed at the end of the war, some found work within international organizations. This resulted in a polarized economy and labor market, in which those who worked were employed by either the local government or the international administrative government.[71] The conflict also created an economy that was dependent on the international presence rather than sustaining itself.

Sometimes, as we have acknowledged, women make gains during conflict, such as entering the formal labor sector for the first time. Equally, women who may have assumed nontraditional jobs during the conflict frequently lose those jobs and return to their traditional roles thereafter. Even with improved legal protection, women may lack the requisite knowledge and legal literacy to take advantage of their new status.[72] Equally, the cultural and social pressures (frequently tacitly supported by external largely male intervenors) to conform to highly stratified feminine roles and responsibilities leave little space for women to contest the backsliding on status and autonomy gains in the post-conflict context.

Gender-focused economic development, which recognizes that women are often excluded, either formally or through entrenched discriminatory practices, can take many forms: for example, ensuring credit, rebuilding infrastructure, and promoting businesses. Gender centrality might lead to a focus on rural roads so that farmers (primarily women) can bring their goods to a market or can travel to a health care center, rather than rebuilding larger-scale highways.[73] It involves training women and men to develop their own livelihood, and it requires changes in attitudes toward women working. In some parts of the world, microcredit has helped women begin businesses and work their way out of poverty, although the model has been less successful in Africa than in Asia.[74]

There is a critique of economic empowerment which suggests that it can serve as a means of legitimating Western hegemonic notions of a market economy without confronting the underlying conditions of social inequality that cause women to be poor.[75] Indeed, a simple emphasis on employing women can result in cheap labor, labor exploitation, or human trafficking. Instead, we stress with others that economic development policies should operate in tandem with other aspects of the development project that result in recognizing women's civil, political, social, economic, and reproductive rights and capacities.

CONCLUSION

Development and post-conflict processes are integrally linked. In the post-conflict context, development must embrace more than mere attempts to increase the income of beneficiaries.[76] While there is a correlation between good governance (a post-conflict priority and stability indicator) and per capita income, a higher per capita income does not necessarily result in better country governance.[77] On the other hand, ensuring development for the long haul includes placing social services justice into the legislative, executive, and administrative mainstream, with the corresponding need to train and ensure competence and prevent corruption. Ultimately, development is critical to fostering sustainable peace and security. It is also critical to assisting women in developing, capturing, and securing gains they may have made during war or which they may have begun to access in the post-conflict process. Development in the post-conflict context therefore requires the coordination of activities, civil society promotion, and security safeguards based on recognition of the population's broadest socioeconomic needs. We argue that these goals are best met, both for the society as a whole and for women in particular, through the social services justice model of post-conflict development, bridging post-conflict reconstruction, transitional justice, and development programs through a mutual prioritization of social services provision.

NOTES

INTRODUCTION

1. *See* Spike Peterson, *New Wars and Gendered Economies*, 88 FEMINIST REV. 7 (2008). We draw upon Peterson's definition in which "[g]ender refers not to anatomical or biological distinctions but to the social construction, which is always culturally specific, of masculine and feminine as hierarchical and oppositional categories. Symbols, theories, practices, institutions, and, of course, individuals are gendered, meaning that their characteristics can be associated with, or construed as manifestations of, masculinity or femininity." *Id.* at 41.
2. SARA RUDDICK, MATERNAL THINKING TOWARDS A POLITICS OF PEACE 234 (1989).
3. Fionnuala Ní Aoláin has lived and worked in Belfast, Northern Ireland since 1987, as a law student, law professor, and human rights activist. From 2008 to 2010, she was a faculty member at the Hebrew University's Law Faculty and from 2007 to 2008, she was a representative of the Prosecutor of the ICTY working in the former Yugoslavia. She served as a Special Expert on Gender in Post-Conflict Settings for the United Nations Secretary-General in 2006. Dina Francesca Haynes lived and worked in Croatia, Bosnia and Herzegovina, and Serbia between 1997 and 2002, South Africa in 1995, and Chad from 1989 to 1991; Naomi Cahn lived in Kinshasa, Democratic Republic of the Congo, from 2002 to 2004.
4. FEMINIST DILEMMAS IN QUALITATIVE RESEARCH: PUBLIC KNOWLEDGE AND PRIVATE LIVES 16 (Jane Ribbons & Rosalind Edwards eds., 1998).
5. Katherine Borland, *"That's Not What I Said": Interpretive Conflict in Oral Narrative Research, in* WOMEN'S WORDS: THE FEMINIST PRACTICE OF ORAL HISTORY 71 (Sherna Berger Gluck & Daphne Patai eds., 1991).
6. Kristina Minister, *A Feminist Frame for the Oral History Interview, in* WOMEN'S WORDS, *supra* note 5, at 41.
7. As an example, a highly influential multiyear cross-jurisdictional study by the International Committee of the Red Cross (ICRC) fails entirely to acknowledge the gendered context, experience, and perpetuation of war even as it sets out to understand the causality of war and seeks methods to avoid the worst excesses of violence. *See* Daniel Muñoz-Rojas & Jean-Jacques Frésard, International Committee of the Red Cross, *The Roots of Behaviour in War: Understanding and Preventing IHL Violations*, INT'L REV. OF THE RED CROSS (2004).
8. Christine Bell & Catherine O'Rourke, *The Impact of UNSC Resolution 1325 on Peace Processes and Their Agreements*, 59 I.C.L.Q. 1 (2010).
9. VEENA DAS, CRITICAL EVENTS: AN ANTHROPOLOGICAL PERSPECTIVE ON CONTEMPORARY INDIA (1995).

10. *See generally* NADERA SHALHOUB-KEVORKIAN, MILITARIZATION AND VIOLENCE AGAINST WOMEN IN CONFLICT ZONES IN THE MIDDLE EAST: A PALESTINIAN CASE STUDY (2009) (articulating the concept of women as frontliners, women who occupy parallel and sometimes conflicting roles in violent societies).

11. *See generally* Peterson, *supra* note 1, at 13–17.

12. CHRISTINE BELL, ON THE LAW OF PEACE: PEACE AGREEMENTS AND THE LEX PACIFICATORIA (2008).

13. *Id.* at 56.

14. An example from the Palestinian/Israeli context was the Oslo, Cairo, Wye River, and the U.S.-backed "Roadmap" negotiations, which did not include women. Two Israeli women participated in the nonstate-sanctioned Geneva Accord of 2003.

15. Bell, *supra* note 12, at 60–62.

16. Bell, *supra* note 12, at 62–65.

17. Christine Bell & Kathleen Cavanaugh, *"Constructive Ambiguity" or Internal Self-Determination? Self-Determination, Group Accommodation and the Belfast Agreement*, 22 FORDHAM INT'L L.J. 1345 (1999).

18. This was the case in Bosnia and Herzegovina, with portions of the Dayton Framework Agreement for Peace, particularly those provisions devoted to property repossession and the facilitation of return. *See* Massimo Morrati, *Tackling Obstruction to Property and Return: A Critical Assessment of the Practice of Removing Housing Officials in Bosnia and Herzegovina, in* DECONSTRUCTING THE RECONSTRUCTION: HUMAN RIGHTS AND THE RULE OF LAW IN POSTWAR BOSNIA AND HERZEGOVINA (Dina Francesca Haynes ed., 2008); *see also* Charles Philpott & Rhodri C. Williams, *The Dayton Dialectic: The Significance of Property Deprivation and Repossession in the Context of Ethnic Cleansing, in* DECONSTRUCTING THE RECONSTRUCTION, *supra*, at 149.

19. *See, e.g.,* Hala Manna, *Between Dispossession and Undying Hope: The Refugees' Eternal Agony, in* WOMEN AND THE POLITICS OF MILITARY CONFRONTATION 164, 164–69 (Nahla Abdo-Zubi & Ronit Lentin eds., 2002).

20. Sheila Meintjes & Beth Goldblatt, *South African Women Demand the Truth, in* WHAT WOMEN DO IN WARTIME: GENDER AND CONFLICT IN AFRICA (Meredeth Turshen & Clotilde Twagiramariya eds., 1998).

21. *See* Maria Stratigaki, *Gender Mainstreaming vs. Positive Action: An Ongoing Conflict in EU Gender Equality Policy*, 12 EURO. J. WOMEN'S STUD. 165, 170 (2005); *see also* UNITED NATIONS, GENDER AND UN PEACEKEEPING OPERATIONS 3 (2005) (describing gender mainstreaming as the "assess[ment of] the implications for women and men of any planned action, including legislation, policies, or programmes" (quoting U.N. Econ. & Soc. Council [ECOSOC], *Agreed Conclusions 1997/2*, U.N. Doc. A/52/3 (September 18, 1997))).

22. The United Nations Office of the Special Adviser on Gender Issues and the Advancement of Women (OSAGI) defines the term *gender* as referring to the social attributes and opportunities associated with being male and female and the relationship between women and men and girls and boys, as well as relations between women and those between men. U.N. Office of the Special Adviser on Gender Issues and the Advancement of Women, GENDER MAINSTREAMING: STRATEGY FOR PROMOTING GENDER EQUALITY 1 (2001).

23. *Id.* (quoting U.N. Econ. & Soc. Council [ECOSOC], *Agreed Conclusions 1997/2*, U.N. Doc. A/52/3 (September 18, 1997)).

24. *See* S.C. Res. 1325, U.N. Doc. S/RES/1325 (October 31, 2000); UN Peacekeeping, Gender, Peacekeeping, & Peacebuilding. *See also* S.C. Res. 1880, U.N. Doc. S/

Res/1880 (2009); S.C. Res. 1888, U.N. Doc. S/Res/1888 (2009); S.C. Res. 1889, U.N. Doc. S/Res/1889 (2009).

25. *See* Stratigaki, *supra* note 21, at 170; Mark A. Pollack & Emilie Hafner-Burton, *Mainstreaming Gender in the European Union*, 7 J. EUR. PUB. POL'Y 432, 433 (2000) (citing Rees).

26. *See* Mary Daly, *Gender Mainstreaming in Theory and Practice*, 12 SOC. POL. INT'L STUD. GENDER, ST. & SOC'Y 433, 437 (2005).

27. Christine Booth & Cinnamon Bennett, *Gender Mainstreaming in the European Union: Towards a New Conception and Practice of Equal Opportunities?*, 9 EUR. J. WOMEN'S STUD. 430, 434 (2002).

28. *Id.* at 438.

29. U.N. Gender Strategy, *supra* note 22 (quoting U.N. Econ. & Soc. Council [ECO-SOC], *Agreed Conclusions 1997/2*, U.N. Doc. A/52/3 (September 18, 1997)); *see also* Booth & Bennett, *supra* note 27, at 434–38.

30. In 1998, the Council of Europe defined gender mainstreaming as: "the (re)organization, improvement, development and evaluation of policy processes, so that a gender equality perspective is incorporated in all policies at all levels and at all stages, by the actors normally involved in policy-making." COUNCIL OF EUROPE, ACTIVITIES OF THE COUNCIL OF EUROPE—1998 REPORT (1998). For an overview of gender responsive budgeting, see United Nations Development Fund for Women, Gender-Responsive Budgeting, http://www.gender-budgets.org.

31. *See* Daly, *supra* note 26, at 442–43.

32. Diane Otto, *The Exile of Inclusion: Reflections on Gender Issues in International Law over the Last Decade*, 10 MELBOURNE J. OF INT'L L. 11, 15 (2009).

33. *Id.* at 7.

34. Otto, *supra* note 32.

35. Hilary Charlesworth, *Talking to Ourselves: Should International Lawyers Take a Break from Feminism?*, in BETWEEN RESISTANCE AND COMPLIANCE? FEMINIST PERSPECTIVES ON INTERNATIONAL LAW IN AN ERA OF ANXIETY AND TERROR (Sari Kouvo & Zoe Pearson eds., 2010).

36. Sally Baden & Anne Marie Goetz, *Who Needs [Sex] When You Can Have [Gender]? Conflicting Discourses on Gender at Beijing*, in FEMINIST VISIONS OF DEVELOPMENT: GENDER ANALYSIS AND POLICY 19, 20–22 (Cecile Jackson & Ruth Pearson eds., 1998).

37. Otto, *supra* note 32, at 20 (drawing upon the work of Carol Miller & Shahra Razavi, *Gender Mainstreaming: A Study of the Efforts by the UNDP, the World Bank, and the ILO to Institutionalize Gender Issues*, 4 U.N. RES. INST. SOC. DEV. OCCASIONAL PAPER SERIES 67–69 (1995)).

38. Otto, *supra* note 32, at 21.

39. Maitrayee Mukhopadhyay, *Mainstreaming Gender or "Streaming" Gender Away: Feminists Marooned in the Development Business*, 35 INST. DEV. STUD. BULL. 95, 98 (2004).

40. *Id.*

41. *Id.*

42. *See* Daly, *supra* note 26, at 448.

43. U.N. Gender Strategy, *supra* note 22 (quoting U.N. Econ. & Soc. Council [ECO-SOC], *Agreed Conclusions 1997/2*, U.N. Doc. A/52/3 (September 18, 1997)).

44. *Id.*

45. *See* Committee on Economic, Social, and Cultural Rights Optional Protocol, G.A. Res. 63/117, U.N. Doc. A/RES/63/117 (December 10, 2008) (addressing the

justiciability of economic, social, and cultural rights); *see also* World Conference on Human Rights, June 14–25, 1993, *Vienna Declaration and Program of Action*, U.N. Doc. A/CONF.157/23 (July 12, 1993).

46. Other works have examined the aspects of gender and post-conflict reconstruction. *See, e.g.*, THE AFTERMATH: WOMEN IN POST-CONFLICT TRANSFORMATION (Sheila Meintjes, Anu Pillay, & Meredith Turshen eds., 2001); GENDERED PEACE: WOMEN'S STRUGGLES FOR POST-WAR JUSTICE AND RECONCILIATION (Donna Pankhurst ed., 2007).

47. Aisling Swaine, *Assessing the Potential of National Action Plans to Advance Implementation of United Nations Security Council Resolution 1325*, 12 YEARBOOK OF INTERNATIONAL HUMANITARIAN LAW 403 (2009).

48. *See* United Nations Millennium Declaration G.A. Res. 55/2, U.N. Doc. A/RES/55/2 (September 18, 2000); WORLD BANK, GLOBAL MONITORING REPORT 2007 (2007). 2_20070411162802/Rendered/PDF/394730GMR02007.pdf. A broader critique is the extent to which the goals are linked to the neoliberal economic policies that trace to the "Washington Consensus" and have contributed considerably to the limitation of the capacities of states in the Global South and hence to the decline in their legitimacy.

49. H.R.C. Res. 5/1, ¶ k, U.N. Doc HR/RES/5/1 (June 18, 2007).

50. *See* S.C. Res 1820, U.N. Doc. S/RES/1820 (June 19, 2008); *see generally UN Classifies Rape a "War Tactic,"* BBC NEWS, June 20, 2008.

51. G.A. Res. 62/277, U.N. Doc. A/RES/62/277 (October 7, 2008).

52. Bell & O'Rourke, *supra* note 8, at 9–19 (2011).

53. Leti Volpp, *Feminism v. Multiculturalism*, 101 COLUM. L. REV. 1181, 1294 (2001); *see also* Catherine Powell, *Lifting Our Veil of Ignorance: Culture, Constitutionalism, and Women's Human Rights in Post–September 11 America*, 57 HASTINGS L.J. 331 (2005).

54. They are also survivors, and there has been much discussion over whether to label them victims or survivors. Some humanitarian organizations use the term "survivor" because "victim" "connotes powerlessness and stigma" rather than the "strength and resilience" associated with "survivor." *See* Kelly D. Askin, *The Quest for Post-Conflict Gender Justice*, 41 COLUM. J. TRANSNAT'L L. 509, 515 (2003).

55. *See* Marcia Greenberg & Elaine Zuckerman, *The Gender Dimensions of Post-Conflict Reconstruction, in* MAKING PEACE WORK: THE CHALLENGES OF SOCIAL AND ECONOMIC RECONSTRUCTION (Tony Addison & Tilman Bruck eds., 2009).

CHAPTER 1

1. *See, e.g.*, Catherine Powell, *Lifting our Veil of Ignorance: Culture, Constitutionalism, and Women's Human Rights in Post–September 11 America*, 57 Hastings L.J. 331, 331–34 (2005).

2. HUMAN RIGHTS WATCH, BETWEEN HOPE AND FEAR: INTIMIDATION AND ATTACKS AGAINST WOMEN IN PUBLIC LIFE IN AFGHANISTAN 1 (2005) (briefing paper). *See also* Chapter 3, *infra* at 71–72.

3. *See, e.g.*, Mayra Buvinic, Monica Das Gupta, & Ursula Casabonne, *Gender, Poverty and Demography: An Overview*, 23 THE WORLD BANK ECONOMIC REVIEW 347 (2009).

4. WORLD HEALTH ORGANIZATION, WOMEN AND HEALTH: TODAY'S EVIDENCE TOMORROW'S AGENDA xvi (2009).

5. *See, e.g.*, 2008–2009 UNITED NATIONS SYSTEM WIDE ACTION PLAN ON UNITED NATIONS SECURITY COUNCIL 1325 (2000) ON WOMEN, PEACE AND SECURITY.

6. Note thanks to Dr. Jeremy Sarkin, Report Integration of Gender into the Human Rights Council's Universal Periodic Review Process.
7. *See* Sarah White, *Men, Masculinities, and the Politics of Development*, 5(2) GENDER AND DEVELOPMENT 14, 16 (1997) (noting that "In the gender and development literature, men appear very little, often as hazy background figures.").
8. Both the Optional Protocol to the International Covenant on Economic, Social and Cultural Rights and Article 11 of the International Covenant for Civil and Political Rights provides some means to garner concrete and focused information. *See generally* Committee on Economic, Social and Cultural Rights Optional Protocol, G.A. Res. 63/117, U.N. Doc. A/RES/63/117 (December 10, 2008); International Covenant on Civil and Political Rights art. 11, December 16, 1966, 999 U.N.T.S. 14668.
9. *See generally* Organisation for Economic Co-operation and Development, Social Institutions and Gender Index 2009, http://genderindex.org [hereinafter Gender Index]. The data produces SIGI rankings. The data indicates that there is a moderate, though by no means clear, correlation between conflict countries and SIGI outcomes. *See infra* at 31–34.
10. *See infra* at 34–36.
11. World Health Organization, *supra* note 4, at 4.
12. Explained generally as a combination of inherent biological advantage and reflecting behavioral differences between men and women.
13. World Health Organization, *supra* note 4, at 6. *See also* WORLD HEALTH ORGANIZATION, WORLD HEALTH STATISTICS 2009 (2009).
14. World Health Organization, *supra* note 4, at 6. Lower mortality rates among children under five and overall declining fertility rates result in an aging population and characterize demographic transition. The declines are largely due to the increasing use of contraception. Epidemiological transition reflects a shift in the main causes of death and disease away from infectious diseases toward noncommunicable diseases (e.g., stroke and cancer). Finally, risk transition is characterized by a reduction in risk factors for infectious diseases (under nutrition, unsafe water, and poor sanitation). *Id.*
15. Buvinic et al., *supra* note 3, at 348–49.
16. World Health Organization, *supra* note 4, at 8.
17. Michelle Mendez & Linda Adair, *Severity and Timing of Stunting in the First Two Years of Life Affect Performance on Cognitive Tests in Late Childhood*, 129 J. NUTRITION 1555 (1999).
18. Buviniv et al., *supra* note 3, at 362.
19. *See* THE WORLD BANK GENDER DEVELOPMENT GROUP, ENGENDERING DEVELOPMENT: THROUGH GENDER EQUALITY IN RIGHTS, RESOURCES AND VOICE 15–17 (2001).
20. *See, e.g.,* AMANDA HESLOP & MARK GORMAN, CHRONIC POVERTY AND OLDER PEOPLE IN THE DEVELOPING WORLD 12 (Chronic Poverty Resource Center, Working Paper No. 10, 2002).
21. *See, e.g.,* AUSTRALIAN INSTITUTE OF HEALTH AND WELFARE, AUSTRALIA'S HEALTH 2008 at 267 (2008).
22. *See generally* THE WORLD BANK, WORLD DEVELOPMENT INDICATORS: LABOR AND SOCIAL PROTECTION, http://data.worldbank.org/indicator.
23. Even in the European Union, women continue to earn on average 17.6 percent less than men for every hour worked. EUROPEAN COMMISSION, REPORT ON EQUALITY BETWEEN WOMEN AND MEN 2010 at 17–18 (2010).

24. World Health Organization, *supra* note 4, at 10.
25. *Id.* Furthermore, data shows that on average, a woman heads one in five households and that these households are particularly susceptible to poverty. *Id.*
26. *Id.* at 11 (citing WORLD HEALTH ORGANIZATION, GENDER AND HEALTH IN DISASTERS (2002)).
27. *See, e.g.*, Katharina Pistor, Antara Haldar, & Amrit Amirapu, *Social Norms, Rule of Law and Gender Reality* (World Justice Forum Vienna, Working Draft, 2008).
28. *Id.* at 1.
29. *Id.*
30. *Id.* at 2.
31. *See generally* RICHARD L. ABEL, POLITICS BY OTHER MEANS: LAW IN THE STRUGGLE AGAINST APARTHEID (1995).
32. UNICEF, GENDER EQUALITY—THE BIG PICTURE (2007) (reporting that women perform 66 percent of the world's work, produce 50 percent of the food, but only earn 10 percent of the income and own 1 percent of the property).
33. World Health Organization, *supra* note 4, at 9–10.
34. THE UNITED NATIONS, THE MILLENNIUM DEVELOPMENT GOALS REPORT (2007).
35. There is an ample literature on the capacity of social groups to govern themselves in the absence of formal law. *See, e.g.*, ROBERT C. ELLICKSON, ORDER WITHIN LAW: HOW NEIGHBORS SETTLE DISPUTES (1991); FRANK K. UPHAM, LAW AND SOCIAL CHANGE IN POSTWAR JAPAN (1987).
36. Pistor et al., *supra* note 27, at 13.
37. *See, e.g.*, Spike Peterson, *New Wars and Gendered Economies*, 88 FEMINIST REV. 7 (2008).
38. *See generally* Mark Duffield, *Reprising Durable Disorder: Network War and the Securitisation of Aid*, *in* GLOBAL GOVERNANCE IN THE 21ST CENTURY: ALTERNATIVE PERSPECTIVES ON WORLD ORDER (Bjorn Hettne & Bertil Oden eds., 2002).
39. *See generally* William Reno, *Shadow States and the Political Economy of Civil Wars*, *in* GREED AND GRIEVANCE: ECONOMIC AGENDAS IN CIVIL WARS 47–54 (Mats Berdal & David M. Malone eds., 2000) (describing economic characteristics of shadow states and various reasons why they remain shadow states).
40. Colleen Duggan, Claudia Paz y Bailey, & Julie Guillerot, *Reparations for Sexual and Reproductive Violence: Prospects for Achieving Gender Justice in Guatemala and Peru*, 2 INTL J. TRANS JUST. 192, 209 (2008).
41. Statistics reveal that one in three women around the world has been beaten, coerced into sex, or otherwise abused in her lifetime. U.N. Secretary General, In-Depth Study on All Forms of Violence Against Women: Report of the Secretary General, U.N. Doc A/61/122/Add.1 (July 6, 2006).
42. Caroline Moser & Cathy McIlwaine, *Gender and Rebuilding Social Capital in the Context of Political Violence: A Case Study of Colombia and Guatemala* 21 (background paper presented at the World Bank conference, Gender, Armed Conflict and Political Violence, Washington, D.C., June 10–11, 1999).
43. *Id.*
44. UNITED NATIONS DEVELOPMENT PROGRAMME, HUMAN DEVELOPMENT REPORT FOR EUROPE AND THE COMMONWEALTH OF INDEPENDENT STATES (1998).
45. Gender Index, *supra* note 9.
46. Organisation for Economic Co-operation and Development, Social Institutions and Gender Ranking 2009, http://genderindex.org/ranking. Compare SIGI values for El Salvador .0082581, Cambodia .0220188, Myanmar .0462871, Colombia .012727, Afghanistan .582304, Iraq .2755243, Congo .204482; with Norway, Switzerland,

the United Kingdom. We think it important to note that the correlation is moderate and the degree of its significance may leave some room for contestation.

47. The World Bank, Gender Stats, http://go.worldbank.org/YMPEGXASH0.

48. *See infra*, Appendix A.

49. We do note some caveats to this conclusion. The usefulness of the data is limited by a number of factors. In particular, the small size for certain regions (i.e., South Asia) and the lack of data for certain measures (i.e., for women in nonagricultural work). In addition, the designation of "conflict countries" is problematic because there are many countries in which localized or regional conflict areas cannot be easily labeled as conflict or non-conflict nations. There are also countries such as the United States with foreign military operations that cannot be easily identified as conflict or non-conflict nations. In many contexts, there is a lack of clear guidelines and state practice on what combination of factors, or what extent of human suffering and economic damage, are sufficient to make a nation "in conflict" or not.

50. As of June 2010, Rwanda had 55,062 refugees; Somalia had 1,842 refugees and 1,277,200 internally displaced persons; Burundi had 21,093 refugees and 100,000 internally displaced persons; and Colombia had 170 refugees and 3,000,000 internally displaced persons. Naomi Cahn & Fionnuala Ní Aoláin, *Gender, Masculinities, and Transition in Conflicted Societies*, 44 New England L.R. 101 (2010).

51. The most recent version of the report highlights a number of initiatives developed based on the findings in 2007. *See* The World Bank, Global Monitoring Report 2010 143 (2010).

52. World Bank, *Promoting Gender Equality and Women's Empowerment, in* Global Monitoring Report 2007 107–08 (2007). These statements are based on data provided by the U.N. Millennium Project Task Force on Gender Equality 2005. *See id.* at 145.

53. Caren Grown, Geeta Rao Gupta, & Aslihan Kes, Millennium Project, Taking Action: Achieving Gender Equality and Empowering Women 110 (2005).

54. *See* CIA, The World Factbook, https://www.cia.gov/library/publications/the-world-factbook/(choose country from drop-down menu).

55. *See* Terry M. Dworkin & Cindy A. Schipani, *Gender Voice and Correlations with Peace*, 36 Vand. J. Transnat'l L. 527, 531–33 (2003); Terry M. Dworkin & Cindy A. Schipani, *Linking Gender Equity to Peaceful Societies*, 44 Am. Bus. L.J. 391 (2007) [hereinafter Dworkin & Schipani, *Linking Gender*].

56. Heidelberg Institute for International Conflict Research, http://www.hiik.de/en/index.html.

57. *See* UNDP, Human Development Report 2007–2008 326 (2007). The GDI supplements the Human Development Index, and it assesses the inequalities between men and women in four different areas. *Id.*, 356, 358.

58. Dworkin & Schipani, *Linking Gender, supra* note 55, 391–92.

59. *Id.* at 398–99, 414.

60. *See* Mary Caprioli & Michael A. Boyer, *Gender, Violence and International Crisis*, 45 J. Conflict Resol. 503 (2001). For one potential explanation, *see* Jedediah Purdy, *The New Biopolitics: Autonomy, Demography, and Nationhood*, 2006 BYU L. Rev. 889, 949–52.

61. *See* Mary Caprioli, *Gendered Conflict*, 37 J. Peace Res. 51, 55 (2000).

62. *See* Purdy, *supra* note 60, at 893.

63. *See, e.g.*, Mary Caprioli, Valerie M. Hudson et al., *Walking a Fine Line: Addressing Issues of Gender with Women Stats* 5 (2007) (presented at International Studies Association Conference, Chi., Ill.). *See also* Valerie Hudson & Andrea Den Boer, *A Surplus of Men, A Deficit of Peace*, 26 INT'L SECURITY 5 (2002).

64. Valerie H. Hudson & Carl H. Brinton, *Women's Tears and International Fears: Is Discrepant Enforcement of National Laws Protecting Women and Girls Related to Discrepant Enactment of International Law by Nation-States?*, 8–12 (2007) (presented at the annual meeting of the American Political Science Association, Chi., Ill.).

65. For two examples of analysis of the state socialization and norm acculturation process, see Ryan Goodman & Derek Jinks, *Colloquy—How to Influence States: International Law and State Socialization: Conceptual, Empirical, and Normative Challenges*, 54 DUKE L.J. 983 (2005); Ryan Goodman & Derek Jinks, *Incomplete Internalization and Compliance with Human Rights Law*, 19 EUR. J. INT'L L. 725 (2008).

66. CLARA MORGAN, AFGHANISTAN: THE STATUS OF WOMEN 2 (Parliamentary Information and Research Services Publication PRB 07-34E, January 10, 2008).

67. HUMAN RIGHTS WATCH, "WE HAVE THE PROMISES OF THE WORLD": WOMEN'S RIGHTS IN AFGHANISTAN 55 (December 6, 2009).

68. AFGHAN MINISTRY OF PUBLIC HEALTH, MATERNAL MORTALITY IN AFGHANISTAN: MAGNITUDE, CAUSES, RISK FACTORS, AND PREVENTABILITY 4–5 (November 6, 2002).

69. HEALTH AND DEVELOPMENT SERVICE, AFGHANISTAN: REPRODUCTIVE HEALTH RESOURCES ASSESSMENT 8–9 (2003).

70. MORGAN, *supra* note 66, at 2.

71. We are mindful of the "cultural relativism" arguments and postcolonial critiques. *See* discussion *infra* Introduction 4–7.

72. Fionnuala Ní Aoláin, *Political Violence and Gender during Times of Transition*, 15 COLUM. J. GENDER & L. 829, 830–31 (2006). *See also* Fionnuala Ní Aoláin & Catherine Turner, *Gender, Truth & Transition*, 16 UCLA WOMEN'S L.J. 229, 279 (2007).

73. See, e.g., Dianne Otto, *The Exile of Inclusion: Reflections on Gender Issues in International Law over the Last Decade*, 10 MELBOURNE J. INTL. L. 11, 21–24 (2009).

CHAPTER 2

1. *See, e.g.*, FIONNUALA NÍ AOLÁIN, THE POLITICS OF FORCE: CONFLICT MANAGEMENT AND STATE VIOLENCE IN NORTHERN IRELAND 218–47 (2000).

2. For an account of the complexity and essentialism that follows from the depiction of women in war, see Aubrey Graham, *Re-Contextualizing the Visual Victim: Talk and Photographic Exhibit* (on file with authors).

3. As Rosemary Ridd has noted, "when a community is involved in open conflict and all resources are directed towards an external threat . . . there is likely to be some fluidity in social ordering." Simona Sharoni, *Rethinking Women's Struggles in Israel— Palestine and in the North of Ireland*, *in* VICTIMS, PERPETRATORS OR ACTORS? GENDER, ARMED CONFLICT, AND POLITICAL VIOLENCE 87 (Caroline N. O. Moser & Fiona C. Clark eds., 2001) (citing WOMEN AND POLITICAL CONFLICT: PORTRAITS OF STRUGGLE IN TIMES OF CRISIS 3 (Rosemary Ridd & Helen Callaway eds., 1987)).

4. As Rick Wilford has noted, "Women . . . are commonly constructed as the symbolic form of the nation whereas men are invariably represented as its chief agents and, with statehood achieved, emerge as its major beneficiaries." Rick Wilford, *Women, Ethnicity and Nationalism: Surveying the Ground* in Women, ETHNICITY AND NATIONALISM: THE POLITICS OF TRANSITION (ed. Rick Wilford & Robert Miller

1998), at 1; *see also* KUMARI JAYAWARDENA, FEMINISM AND NATIONALISM IN THE THIRD WORLD IN THE 19TH AND EARLY 20TH CENTURIES 259 (1986) (confirming that "[o]nce independence had been achieved, male politicians, who had consciously mobilized women in the struggle, pushed them back to their 'accustomed place.'").

5. *See, e.g.*, Ruth Seifert, *The Second Front: The Logic of Sexual Violence in War*, WOMEN'S STUD. INT'L. FORUM, January–April 1996, at 35; Fionnuala Ní Aoláin, *Sex-Based Violence and the Holocaust—A Reevaluation of Harms and Rights in International Law*, 12 YALE J.L. & FEMINISM 43 (2000).

6. *See* NIRA YUVAL-DAVIS, GENDER AND NATION (Bryan S. Turner ed., 1997).

7. Karen Engle, *Judging Sex in War*, 106 MICH. L. REV. 941, 942 (2008). *See also* Karen Engle, *Feminism and Its (Dis)contents: Criminalizing Wartime Rape in Bosnia and Herzegovina*, 99 AM. J. INT'L. L. 778 (2005).

8. Engle, *Judging Sex in War*, *supra* note 7, at 951. *See also* Clare McGlynn, *Rape as "Torture"? Catherine Mackinnon and Questions of Feminist Strategy*, 16 FEMINIST LEGAL STUD. 71 (2008).

9. Ronit Lentin, *Introduction: (En)gendering Genocides*, *in* GENDER AND CATASTROPHE 12 (Ronit Lentin ed., 1997).

10. *See* MIRANDA ALISON, WOMEN AND POLITICAL VIOLENCE: FEMALE COMBATANTS IN ETHNO-NATIONAL CONFLICT 1 (2008).

11. For an exception to this lack of research, see CYNTHIA ENLOE, DOES KHAKI BECOME YOU? THE MILITARIZATION OF WOMEN'S LIVES (1983).

12. Simona Sharoni, *Rethinking Women's Struggles in Israel—Palestine and in the North of Ireland*, *in* VICTIMS, PERPETRATORS OR ACTORS? GENDER, ARMED CONFLICT, AND POLITICAL VIOLENCE 85, 86 (Caroline N. O. Moser & Fiona C. Clark eds., 2001).

13. *See, e.g.*, YUVAL-DAVIS, *supra* note 6; *see also* J. McKinley, *Eritrea's Women Fighters Long for Equality of War*, THE GUARDIAN, May 6, 1995.

14. Miranda Alison, *Women as Agents of Political Violence: Gendering Security*, 35 SECURITY DIALOGUE 447 (2004); Megan MacKenzie, *Securitization and Desecuritization: Female Soldiers and the Reconstruction of Women in Post-Conflict Sierra Leone*, 18 SECURITY STUD. 241 (2009). In her study of fifty female former combatants in Sierra Leone, Megan MacKenzie found that:

Every woman responded positively to the question: "Would you define yourself as a former soldier?" Women were quick to point out which armed group they were a part of, what rank they held, and what roles they carried out: one woman identified herself as a commander with the RUF; another woman specified that she was a soldier "because [she] was given one week training on how to fire a gun and subsequently became active"; another woman identified as a soldier because she "took part in most of the horrible activities of the evil conflict in SL."

MacKenzie, *supra*, at 247.

15. *See* Alison, *supra* note 14, at 450.

16. *See* http://humanrights.change.org/blog/view/women_as_perpetrators_of_war.

17. *See, e.g.*, MARIA MCGUIRE, TO TAKE ARMS: A YEAR IN THE PROVISIONAL IRA (1973); NELL MCCAFFERTY, THE ARMAGH WOMEN (1981).

18. *See* Alison, *supra* note 14, at 456 (referencing specifically the use of behavior and dress as a means to gain access to targets, premised on the reluctance of mainly male agents of the state to defy conventions around searching women).

19. *See* Carol S. Lilly & Jill A. Irvine, *Negotiating Interest: Women and Nationalism in Serbia and Croatia 1990–1997*, 16 E. EUR. POL. & SOC'Y 109 (2002).

20. Barbara Ehrenreich, *Prison Abuse; Feminism's Assumptions Upended: A Uterus Is Not a Substitute for a Conscience. Giving Women Positions of Power Won't Change Society by Itself*, L.A. TIMES, May 16, 2004, at M1.

21. Beth Goldblatt & Sheila Meintjes, *South African Women Demand the Truth*, in WHAT WOMEN DO IN WARTIME: GENDER AND CONFLICT IN AFRICA 27, 45 (Meredeth Turshen & Clotilde Twagiramariya eds., 1998).

22. *See* FIONA C. ROSS, BEARING WITNESS: WOMEN AND THE TRUTH AND RECONCILIATION COMMISSION IN SOUTH AFRICA 17–20 (2003) ("[W]omen who had been active in opposing the Apartheid State seldom gave public testimony."). *See also* WHAT WOMEN DO IN WARTIME, *supra* note 21, at 37–45.

23. *See* YUVAL-DAVIS, *supra* note 6, at 103–05.

24. As Wilford has noted, "[F]ighting alongside men to achieve independence does not provide a guarantee of women's inclusion as equal citizens," and "even where women have been active as warriors . . . they invariably are left holding the wrong end of the citizenship stick." Wilford *supra* note 4.

25. Full egalitarian involvement is variable. For seemingly full integration of non-state forces in the context of Namibian independence, see Teckla Shikola, *We Left Our Shoes Behind*, in WHAT WOMEN DO IN WARTIME, *supra* note 21, at 138–49.

26. *See, e.g.*, SUSAN BROWMILLER, AGAINST OUR WILL: MEN, WOMEN, AND RAPE (1975).

27. *See, e.g.*, THE PUBLIC NATURE OF PRIVATE VIOLENCE (Martha Albertson Fineman & Roxanne Mykitiuk eds., 1994); Symposium, *Domestic Violence and the Law: Theory, Policy and Practice*, 23 SAINT LOUIS U. PUB. L. REV. 7 (2004).

28. Violence against women in most societies comes in a variety of forms, including: sex-selective abortion, female infanticide, genital mutilation, incest and sexual abuse, kidnapping and sale, sex trafficking, sexual harassment, rape by strangers and acquaintances, spousal or partner battering, immolation of wives and widows, and murder. *See* Jane L. Dolkart, *Hostile Environment Harassment: Equality, Objectivity, and the Shaping of Legal Standards*, 43 EMORY L. J. 151, 178–79 (1994).

29. By sex-based violence, we mean a wide variety of violence and victimizing acts directed at women because of their gender. *See* Ní Aoláin, *supra* note 5, at 65–73.

30. *See, e.g.*, GARY SOLIS, THE LAW OF ARMED CONFLICT (2010).

31. Geneva Convention Relative to the Protection of Civilian Persons in Times of War (Fourth Geneva Convention) art. 27, Aug. 12, 1949, 75 U.N.T.S. 287; Geneva Conventions of 1949, Common Art. 3(1)(c), 6 U.S.T. 3114; Protocol Additional to the Geneva Conventions of 12 August 1949 and Relating to the Protection of Victims of International Armed Conflicts (Protocol I), Dec. 7, 1978, 1125 U.N.T.S. 3; Protocol Additional to the Geneva Conventions of 12 August 1949 and Relating to the Protection of Victims of Non-International Armed Conflicts (Protocol II), art. 4(2)(e), Dec. 7, 1978, 1125 U.N.T.S. *See generally* FRITZ KALSHOVEN & LIESBETH ZEGVELD, CONSTRAINTS ON THE WAGING OF WAR (2001).

32. *See* CYNTHIA COCKBURN, THE SPACE BETWEEN US: NEGOTIATING GENDER AND NATIONAL IDENTITIES IN CONFLICT (1998).

33. Margaret Urban Walker, *Gender and Violence in Focus: A Background for Gender Justice in Reparation*, in THE GENDER OF REPARATIONS: UNSETTLING SEXUAL HIERARCHIES WHILE REDRESSING HUMAN RIGHTS VIOLATIONS 29–30 (Ruth Rubio-Marín ed., 2009).

34. *See, e.g.,* Sheila Meintjes, Anu Pillay, & Meredeth Turshen, *There Is No Aftermath for Women, in* THE AFTERMATH: WOMEN IN POST-CONFLICT TRANSFORMATION, *supra* note 17, at 4.

35. *See* Prosecutor v. Kunarac et al., Case No. IT-96-33, 23/1; Prosecutor v. Delalic et al., Case No. IT-96-21; Prosecutor v. Furundzija, Case No. IT-95-17/1; Prosecutor v. Jean-Paul Akayesu, Judgment, Case No. ICTR 96-4-T (September 2, 1998).

36. *See, e.g.,* Katherine Lusby, *Hearing the Invisible Women of Political Rape: Using Oppositional Narrative to Tell a New War Story,* 25 U. TOL. L. REV. 911 (1994).

37. Empirical work on gender-based violence and the Holocaust by one of this book's authors has clearly demonstrated this link in the context of violence experienced by women during the Holocaust. *See* Ní Aoláin, *supra* note 5.

38. *Id.* at 56–65.

39. *See, e.g.,* Doris E. Buss, *The Curious Visibility of Wartime Rape: Gender and Ethnicity in International Criminal Law,* 25 WINDSOR Y.B. ACCESS JUST. 3 (2007).

40. *See* Statute of the International Criminal Tribunal for the Former Yugoslavia, S.C. Res. 827, art. 5(g), U.N. Doc. S/RES/827 (May 25, 1993) (naming rape as a crime against humanity within the jurisdiction of the Tribunal). *See also* Statute of the International Criminal Tribunal for Rwanda, S.C. Res. 955, arts. 3(g), 4(e), U.N. Doc. S/RES/955 (May 25, 1993) (1994) (naming rape as a crime against humanity, and "outrages upon personal dignity, in particular humiliating and degrading treatment, rape, enforced prostitution and any form of indecent assault" as a violation of common article 3 of the Geneva Conventions and Additional Protocols thereto, thus coming within the jurisdiction of the Tribunal).

41. Indictments for rape have been issued by the ICTR against Karema Ngirumpatse, Case No. ICTR-98-44; Nzirorera, Case No. ICTR-98-44-I; Muvunyi, Case No. ICTR-2000-55; Bizimungu, Nzuwonemeye, and Sagahutu, Case No. ICTR-2000-56; Bikindi, Case No. ICTR-01-72-I; Nzabirindam Case No. ICTR-01-77-I. *See also* Kunarac, Delalic, Furundzija, *supra* 35, for cases dealing with rape before the ICTY.

42. *See* Prosecutor v. Kunarac, *supra* note 35; Prosecutor v. Jean Paul Akayesu, *supra* note 35.

43. BEST PRACTICES MANUAL FOR THE INVESTIGATION AND PROSECUTION OF SEXUAL VIOLENCE CRIMES IN SITUATIONS OF ARMED CONFLICT LESSONS FROM THE INTERNATIONAL CRIMINAL TRIBUNAL FOR RWANDA (2008) (on file with authors).

44. *See* Meintjes, Pillay, & Turshen, *supra* note 34, at 4. We eschew a narrow choice between a needs-based or rights-based approach to post-conflict rebuilding. A needs-based approach is often focused exclusively on physical and immediate material needs in devastated societies. A rights-based approach is primarily aimed at implementing fundamental human rights, justice, and equality with a strong emphasis on avoiding impunity in similar contexts. Neither framework "recognizes the real need women feel for social transformation rather than reconstruction of the past." *Id.*

45. *See* Brandon Hamber, Paddy Hillyard, Amy Maguire, Monica McWilliams, Gillian Robinson, David Russell, & Margaret Ward, *Discourses in Transition: Re-Imagining Women's Security,* 20 INT'L REL. 487 (2006).

46. We recall the importance of Sarat's insights that:

   [L]aw depends on violence and uses it as a counterpunch to the allegedly more lethal and destructive violence situated just beyond law's boundaries. But the violence on which law depends always threatens the values for which law stands. . . . Moreover the pain that these acts produce is everywhere, in the drama of law's sporadic vengeance as well as in the ordinary lives of those made subject to legal regulation.

As cited in Maguire, *"Security Starts with the Law": The Role of International Law in the Protection of Women's Security Post Conflict, in* THE ROLE OF INTERNATIONAL LAW IN REBUILDING SOCIETIES AFTER CONFLICT: GREAT EXPECTATIONS 218, 231–32 (Brett Bowden, Hilary Charlesworth, & Jeremy Farrall eds., 2009).

47. *See* Rita Manchanda, *Ambivalent Gains in South Asian Conflicts, in* THE AFTERMATH: WOMEN IN POST-CONFLICT TRANSFORMATION, *supra* note 34, at 99.

48. For detailed discussions of such compromises across a number of negotiations sites see, Chapter 9 focused in part on the crossover between peace agreements and constitutional pacts at 205–207.

49. *Id* at Manchandra *supra* note 47, at 100.

50. *See* GARY BARKER & CHRISTINE RICARDO, THE WORLD BANK, YOUNG MEN AND THE CONSTRUCTION OF MASCULINITY IN SUB-SAHARAN AFRICA: IMPLICATIONS FOR HIV/AIDS, CONFLICT, AND VIOLENCE 24 (Social Development Papers: Conflict Prevention and Reconstruction, No. 26, 2005).

51. *See* CYNTHIA COCKBURN, THE SPACE BETWEEN US: NEGOTIATING GENDER AND NATIONAL IDENTITIES IN CONFLICT (1998).

52. *Id.* at 433.

53. *See* LESLEY ABDELA, KOSOVO: MISSED OPPORTUNITIES, LESSONS FOR THE FUTURE (2000) (report from the former Deputy-Director, NGO, Civil Society Building for the OSCE Mission—Kosovo) (on file with author) (detailing the consistent lack of integration of women and gender-related issues into the planning of the Interim Arrangements for Kosovo). *See also* Human Rights Watch, Not on the Agenda: The Continuing Failure to Address Accountability in Kosovo Post–March 2004.

54. As Cockburn and Sarkov's edited collection explores, the loosening of rigid gender roles from the social flux that conflict inevitably creates is not necessarily sealed off at conflict's end or transition by national male leadership, but rather this role is taken up by the male international development community, "whose own sense of patriarchy-as-normal is quite intact." Zarkov & Cockburn, *supra* note 22. *See also* ARMS TO FIGHT, ARMS TO PROTECT: WOMEN SPEAK OUT ABOUT CONFLICT (Olivia Bennett, Jo Bexley, & Kitty Warnock eds., 1995).

55. *See, e.g.*, JOSHUA S. GOLDSTEIN, WAR AND GENDER: HOW GENDER SHAPES THE WAR SYSTEM AND VICE VERSA (2001); YUVAL-DAVIS, *supra* note 6.

56. *See, e.g.*, NANCY J. CHODOROW, FEMININITIES, MASCULINITIES, SEXUALITIES: FREUD AND BEYOND (1994); R. W. CONNELL, GENDER AND POWER: SOCIETY, THE PERSON AND SEXUAL POLITICS (1987).

57. *See, e.g.*, MICHAEL KIMMEL, MANHOOD IN AMERICA: A CULTURAL HISTORY (1996).

58. THE POSTWAR MOMENT: MILITARIES, MASCULINITIES AND INTERNATIONAL PEACEKEEPING (eds. Dubravka Zarkov and Cynthia Cockburn, 2008).

59. Here we draw on the foundational questions posed by Bartlett in identifying feminist legal method: (1) asking "the woman question," (2) feminist practical reasoning (a focus on the specific factual context of a complex dilemma), and (3) consciousness-raising (testing the validity of accepted legal principles through the lens of personal experiences). *See* Katharine T. Bartlett, *Feminist Legal Methods*, 103 HARV. L. REV. 829 (1990).

60. *See* Angela P. Harris, *Gender, Violence, Race, and Criminal Justice*, 52 STAN. L. REV. 777, 793 (2000).

61. *See, e.g.*, Kimberly Theidon, *Reconstructing Masculinities: The Disarmament, Demobilization, and Reintegration of Former Combatants in Colombia*, 31 HUM. RTS. Q. 1 (2009).

62. *Id.* at 23–30.

63. Kimberly Theidon, *Transitional Subjects: The Disarmament, Demobilization, and Reintegration of Former Combatants in Colombia*, 1 INT'L. J. TRANSITIONAL JUST. 66, 76 (2007).

64. *See* Kirsten Anderson, *Violence Against Women: State Responsibilities in International Human Rights Law to Address Harmful Masculinities*, 26 NETH. Q. HUM. RTS. 173, 175 (2008).

65. For a review of the effects of such integration in a variety of post-conflict and health-related programs, see BARKER & RICARDO, *supra* note 50.

66. *See* Marko Zivkovic, *Ex-Yugoslav Masculinities Under Female Gaze, or Why Men Skin Cats, Beat Up Gays, and Go to War*, 34 NATIONALITIES PAPERS 257 (2006).

67. *See* discussion *supra* Chapter 1 31–34 in endnote 50, 54.

68. *Id.*

69. BARKER & RICARDO, *supra* note 50, at 24–36.

70. *Id.* (analyzing the limits on access to land in Sub-Saharan Africa, which is pivotal for the transmission of social status, marriage opportunity, and independence for young men).

71. U.N. DEVELOPMENT FUND FOR WOMEN, GETTING IT RIGHT, DOING IT RIGHT: GENDER AND DISARMAMENT, DEMOBILIZATION, AND REINTEGRATION 19 (2004).

72. Brandon Hamber, "We Must Be Careful How We Emancipate Our Women": Shifting Masculinities in Post-Apartheid South Africa, Paper Presented at the Re-Imaging Women's Security: A Comparative Study of South Africa, Northern Ireland, and Lebanon Round Table, United Nations University (October 12–13, 2006) (on file with authors).

73. Maguire, *supra* note 46, at 226.

74. *See* Aleksandra Sasha Milićević, *Joining the War: Masculinities, Nationalism and War Participation in the Balkans War of Secession, 1991–1995*, 34 NATIONALITIES PAPERS 265 (2006) (arguing that one of the underlying rationales to male hostilities in the conflict in the former Yugoslavia was a desire to restore traditional societal gender roles and to undo some of the structural effects of equality-driven socialism).

75. *See, e.g.*, Mary Caprioli, *Gendered Conflict*, 37 J. OF PEACE RES. 53 (2000).

76. *See* Mackenzie, *supra* note 14, at 247.

77. This capacity is acknowledged in the case of *Prosecutor v. Kunarac*, *supra* note 35, at 6273–74.

CHAPTER 3

1. SUSAN E. RICE & STEWART PATRICK, BROOKINGS INSTITUTION, INDEX OF STATE WEAKNESS IN THE DEVELOPING WORLD 22 (2008).

2. Stef Jensen, *"Home" and Return in the Foreign Intervention in Bosnia and Herzegovina: An Anthropological Critique*, in DECONSTRUCTING THE RECONSTRUCTION (Dina Francesca Haynes ed., 2008).

3. *See generally* SECURITY: A MULTIDISCIPLINARY NORMATIVE APPROACH (Cecilia Bailliet ed., 2009). For a discussion and critique of "human security," see GARETH EVANS, THE RESPONSIBILITY TO PROTECT: ENDING MASS ATROCITY CRIMES ONCE AND FOR ALL 34–35 (2008); V. M. HUDSON & A. M. DEN BOER, BARE BRANCHES: THE SECURITY IMPLICATIONS OF ASIA'S SURPLUS MALE POPULATION 1–3 (2004).

4. *See* Johan Galtung, *Violence, Peace, and Peace Research*, 6 J. PEACE RES. 167 (1969); KENNETH BOULDING, STABLE PEACE (1978).

5. *See* Johan Galtung, PEACE BY PEACEFUL MEANS: PEACE AND CONFLICT, DEVELOPMENT AND CIVILIZATION 197 (1996) (emphasis in the original).

6. *Id.* at 32.

7. Christine Bell, *Women and the Problems of Peace Agreements*, in WOMEN, PEACEMAKING, AND CONSTITUTIONS (Radhika Coomaraswamy ed., 2005); Fionnuala Ní

Aoláin, *Political Violence and Gender in Times of Transition*, 15 COLUM. J. GENDER & L. 829 (2006).

8. For example, there is an extensive literature on the experiences of Indian Sikhs following the assassination of Indira Ghandi (October 31, 1984), specifically in New Delhi. *See* Amrit Srinivasan, *The Survivor in the Study of Violence*, in MIRRORS OF VIOLENCE: COMMUNITIES, RIOTS, AND SURVIVORS IN SOUTH ASIA 305, 311 (Veena Das ed., 1990). *See generally* Andrea Bartoli, *Learning from the Mozambique Peace Process: The Role of the Community of Sant'Egidio*, in PAVING THE WAY: CONTRIBUTIONS OF INTERACTIVE CONFLICT RESOLUTION TO PEACEKEEPING 79 (Ronald J. Fisher ed., 2005).

9. *See* Jensen, *supra* note 2, at 41, 48.

10. *See* NATALIE FLOREA HUDSON, GENDER, HUMAN SECURITY, AND THE UNITED NATIONS: SECURITY LANGUAGE AS A POLITICAL FRAMEWORK FOR WOMEN (2009).

11. *See* Kristin Valasek, *Security Sector Reform and Gender* 6–11, in GENDER AND SECURITY SECTOR REFORM TOOLKIT (Megan Bastick & Kristin Valasek eds., 2008).

12. VASUKI NESIAH ET AL., INT'L. CTR. FOR TRANSITIONAL JUSTICE, TRUTH COMMISSIONS AND GENDER: PRINCIPLES, POLICIES, AND PROCEDURES 43–44 (2006).

13. VANESSA A. FARR, VOICES FROM THE MARGINS (2004).

14. EVANS, *supra* note 3, at 171.

15. MEASURING PROGRESS IN CONFLICT ENVIRONMENTS 21 (Michael Dziedzic, Barbara Sotirin, & John Agoglia eds., 2008).

16. *See* ORGANISATION FOR ECONOMIC CO-OPERATION & DEVELOPMENT ("OECD"), OECD DAC HANDBOOK ON SECURITY SYSTEM REFORM 22 (2007).

17. THEODOR H. WINKLER, GENEVA CENTRE FOR THE DEMOCRATIC CONTROL OF ARMED FORCES, MANAGING CHANGE: THE REFORM AND DEMOCRATIC CONTROL OF THE SECURITY SECTOR AND INTERNATIONAL ORDER 5 (2002). *Cf.*, Fionnuala NíAoláin, *Women, Security and the Patriarchy of Internationalized Transitional Justice*, 31 HUMAN RTS. Q. 1055 (2009).

18. NICOLE BALL, TSJEARD BOUTA, & LUC VAN DE GOOR, ENHANCING DEMOCRATIC GOVERNANCE OF THE SECURITY SECTOR: AN INSTITUTIONAL ASSESSMENT FRAMEWORK 12 (2003).

19. A good example is provided by the Netherlands. "Peace and stability are preconditions for development and poverty reduction, which makes security a sustainable development issue." *Id.* at Preface.

20. However, one clear issue in this context is to ensure recognition of a holistic vision of SSR that the "development community" is not homogenous. *See* FARR, *supra* note 13, at 3.

21. *See generally* SAMUEL HUNTINGTON, THE SOLDIER AND THE STATE: THE THEORY AND POLITICS OF CIVIL-MILITARY RELATIONS (1957).

22. Valasek, *supra* note 11, at 2.

23. OECD, SECURITY SYSTEM REFORM AND GOVERNANCE 137 (2005).

24. *See* WINKLER, *supra* note 17, at 3.

25. There are also grassroots challenges to the dominance of the state from such community-based initiatives as restorative justice programs. For further discussion of restorative justice, *see* Chapter 7.

26. For analysis of the relationship between security and poverty, *see* NICOLE BELL & MICHAEL BRZOSKA, VOICE AND ACCOUNTABILITY IN THE SECURITY SECTOR, BICC Paper 21 (2002) (charting the positive and progressive relationship between improved security and poverty reduction).

27. *See, e.g.*, Deborah Harrison, *Violence in the Military Community*, in MILITARY MASCULINITIES: IDENTITY AND THE STATE 71–90 (Paul R. Higate ed., 2003).

28. *See* Cynthia Cockburn, The Space Between Us: Negotiating Gender and National Identities in Conflict 8 (1999).

29. Commission on Human Security, Human Security Now 2–6 (2003).

30. United Nations, Millennium Development Goals, http://www.un.org/millennium goals/ (last visited January 8, 2010).

31. Report of the Secretary-General, United Nations Security Council, The Rule of Law and Transitional Justice in Conflict and Post-Conflict Societies, Report No. S/2004/616, at 2–4 (August 2004).

32. *See, e.g.,* Alix J. Boucher & Madeline L. England, Security Sector Reform: Current Challenges and US Policy 6 (2009).

33. *See* Ní Aoláin, *Political Violence and Gender in Times of Transition, supra* note 7.

34. *See* Michael Brzoska, Development Donors and the Concept of Security Sector Reform 5 (2003).

35. *See* Fionnuala Ní Aoláin, *Women, Security, and the Patriarchy of Internationalized Transitional Justice*, 31 Human Rts. Q. 1055, 1079 (2009); *see generally* Heiner Hanggi & Vincenza Scherrer, *Towards an Integrated Security Sector Reform Approach in UN Peace Operations*, 15 Int'l Peacekeeping 486 (2008).

36. For a thorough articulation of the priorities for security sector reform, *see* Bell *supra* note 26.

37. The ICTJ Briefing Paper, *supra* note 12, articulates the notion of a "comprehensive and coherent transitional justice policy."

38. *See* Fionnuala Ní Aoláin & Catherine Turner, *Gender, Truth, & Transition*, 16 UCLA Women's L.J. 229, 279 (2007).

39. Farr, *supra* note 13, at 2.

40. *Id.* at 2.

41. *See generally* Brenda Cossman et al., *Gender, Sexuality, and Power: Is Feminist Theory Enough?*, 12 Colum. J. Gender & L. 601 (2003).

42. *See* Eilish Rooney, *Engendering Transitional Justice: Questions of Absence and Silence*, 3 Int'l J.L. in Context 173 (2007).

43. *See* Mary Caprioli, *Democracy and Human Rights versus Women's Security: A Contradiction?*, 35 Security Dialogue 411 (2004).

44. *See, e.g.,* Thokozani Xaba, *Masculinity and Its Malcontents: The Confrontation Between Struggle Masculinity and Post-Struggle Masculinity, in* Changing Men in Southern Africa (Robert Morrell ed., 2001); Charles Ukeje, *Youths, Violence, and the Collapse of Public Order in the Niger Delta of Nigeria*, 26 African Dev. 337 (2001).

45. *See* Hudson, *supra* note 10 at Chapter 3.

46. *See generally* J. Ann Tickner, Gender in International Relations: Feminist Perspectives on Achieving Global Security (1992).

47. Donna Pankhurst, *Post-War Backlash Violence Against Women: What Can "Masculinity" Explain?, in* Gendered Peace: Women's Struggles for Post-War Justice and Reconciliation (Donna Pankhurst ed., 2007).

48. Empirical findings may be more complex than they initially appear. *See* Ní Aoláin, *Political Violence and Gender in Times of Transition, supra* note 7, at 847–48.

49. *See* Monica McWilliams & Lynda Spence, Taking Domestic Violence Seriously: Issues for the Civil and Criminal Justice System 103 (1996); Monica McWilliams & Joan McKiernan, Bringing It Out in the Open: Domestic Violence in Northern Ireland (1993).

50. Harvard Humanitarian Initiative, "Now, the World Is Without Me": An Investigation of Sexual Violence in Eastern Democratic Republic of Congo 2 (2010).

51. *Id.* at 3.

52. Some commentators have made further distinctions between different kinds of countries that have high priority in security sector reform. *See* Damian Lilly et al., The Privatization of Security and Security Sector Reform (2000), who identify five types of country groups: (1) consolidating democracies, (2) lapsing or stalled democracies, (3) transitional democracies, (4) conflict-torn societies, and (5) states under reconstruction.

53. Bell, *Women Address the Problems of Peace Agreements, supra* note 7, at 100–16.

54. Diane Otto notes the shift from the images of women in Resolution 1325, in which they are imagined as independent actors, to Resolution 1820, in which women are imagined as needing protection. *See* Dianne Otto, *The Exile of Inclusion: Reflections on Gender Issues in International Law over the Last Decade*, 10 Melbourne J. Intl. L. 11 (2009).

55. *See, e.g.*, Kristin Valasek & Kaitlin Nelson, Securing Equality, Engendering Peace: A Guide to Policy and Planning on Women, Peace, and Security (U.N. SCR 1325) 1 (2006).

56. *See, e.g.*, Sasha Gear, Wishing Us Away: Challenges Facing Ex-Combatants in the "New" South Africa (Ctr. for the Study of Violence & Reconciliation, Violence & Transition Series, vol. 8, 2002).

57. *See* Brandon Hamber, *"We Must Be Very Careful How We Emancipate Our Women": Shifting Masculinities in Post-Apartheid South Africa*, Paper Presented at Re-Imagining Women's Security: A Comparative Study of South Africa, Northern Ireland and Lebanon Round Table, United Nations University (October 10, 2006).

58. One exception is the work of LaShawn Jefferson. *See, e.g.*, LaShawn R. Jefferson, *In War as in Peace: Sexual Violence and Women's Status, in* World Report 2004: Human Rights and Armed Conflict 325 (Human Rights Watch 2004).

59. Nesiah et al., *supra* note 12, at 25.

60. *See* Farr, *supra* note 13, at 4.

61. *See* The Aftermath: Women in Post-Conflict Transformation (Sheila Meintjes, Anu Pillay, & Meredith Turshen eds., 2001).

62. *See* Human Rights Watch, "Killing You Is a Very Easy Thing for Us": Human Rights Abuses in Southeast Afghanistan 73 (2003). Examples also abound in "post-conflict" Zimbabwe, Namibia, Eritrea, Mozambique, and Algeria. *See* Donna Pankhurst, Women, Gender, and Peacebuilding 6 (Centre for Conflict Resolution, Department of Peace Studies, Working Paper No. 5, 2000).

63. Global Rights, Living with Violence: A National Report on Domestic Abuse in Afghanistan (2008).

64. UNIFEM, Facts and Figures on Peace and Security (2010).

65. *See Engendering Transitional Justice, supra* note 42.

66. This requires consideration of the need for applying quotas to ensure women's representation.

67. *See, e.g.*, Emily Wax, *Park Offers Women Heady Taste of Freedom; "This Is the One Place That's Ours,"* Wash. Post, April 11, 2010, at A14.

68. *See* Valasek, *supra* note 11, at 16–17.

69. Brzoska, *supra* note 34, at 16.

70. Some governments have developed National Action Plans to implement Resolution 1325 to ensure gender mainstreaming in military trainings (especially for peacekeeping missions) and development programs for post-conflict countries. NGO Working Group on Women, Peace, and Security, From Local to Global: Making Peace Work for Women at Chapter 2 (2005); Andrew Sherriff

& Karen Barnes, Enhancing the EU Response to Women and Armed Conflict with Particular Reference to Development Policy 61, Annex 4 (2008); UNIFEM, INTRODUCTORY BRIEF & SUGGESTIONS: FORMULATING NATIONAL ACTION PLANS (NAPS) TO END VIOLENCE AGAINST WOMEN AND GIRLS (2010).

71. UNIFEM, GENDER SENSITIVE POLICE REFORM IN POST CONFLICT SOCIETIES 4 (2007).

72. OECD, OECD DAC HANDBOOK ON SECURITY SYSTEM REFORM: SECTION 9: INTEGRATING GENDER AWARENESS AND EQUALITY 11 (2009).

73. OECD Handbook (2007), *supra* note 16, at 55–56.

74. *E.g.*, OECD Handbook, Integrating Gender Awareness, *supra* note 16, at 2.

75. THE LIBERIA NATIONAL ACTION PLAN FOR THE IMPLEMENTATION OF UNITED NATIONS RESOLUTION 1325 (2009).

76. *See* Aisling Swaine, *Assessing the Potential of Action Plans to Advance Implementation of United Nations Security Council Resolution 1325 by Member States*, YEARBOOK OF INTERNATIONAL HUMANITARIAN LAW (forthcoming 2011).

77. Annie Jones-Demen, *Dynamics of Gender Relations in War-Time and Post-War Liberia: Implications for Public Policy, in* WAR TO PEACE TRANSITION: CONFLICT INTERVENTION AND PEACEBUILDING IN LIBERIA 99, 109 (Kenneth Omeje ed., 2009).

78. UNIFEM, *supra* note 71, at 7.

79. OECD, Section 9: Integrating Gender Awareness and Equality, *supra* note 16, at 11.

80. *See, e.g.*, Living with Violence, *supra* note 63, at 51.

81. Commission on Human Security *supra* note 29.

82. BETH VANN, GENDER-BASED VIOLENCE: EMERGING ISSUES IN PROGRAMS SERVING DISPLACED POPULATIONS 10 (2003).

83. For further analysis of differences in views of the meaning of women's security, see Fionnuala Ní Aoláin, *Women, Security and the Patriarchy of Internationalized Transitional Justice*, 31 HUM. RTS. Q. 1055 (2009).

84. Elaine Zuckerman & Marcia Greenberg, *The Gender Dimensions of Post-Conflict Reconstruction: An Analytical Framework for Policymakers*, 12:3 GENDER & DEV. 9–10 (2004).

85. *See* Stephen Lewis, Remarks Delivered at the 10th Annual V-Day Celebrations (April 12, 2008).

CHAPTER 4

1. U.N. Charter art. 2, para. 4; U.N. Charter art. 51.

2. *See, e.g.*, S.C. Res. 1264, U.N. Doc. S/RES/1264 (September 15, 1999) (East Timor); S.C. Res. 814, U.N. Doc. S/RES/814 (March 26, 1993) (Somalia). *See also* General Framework Agreement for Peace in Bosnia and Herzegovina, December 14, 1995, Bosn. & Herz.-Croat.-Yugo., 35 I.L.M. 75 (placing Bosnia and Herzegovina (BiH) under the administration of the High Representative, appointed by the interested states constituting the Peace Implementation Council for post-conflict BiH); S.C. Res. 1244, U.N. Doc. S/RES/1244 (June 10, 1999) (placing Kosovo under U.N. administration); S.C. Res. 1483, U.N. Doc. S/RES/1483 (May 22, 2003) (endorsing the international administration of Iraq subsequent to the invasion); S.C. Res. 1383, U.N. Doc. S/RES/1383 (December 6, 2001) (endorsing the establishment of provisional "arrangements . . . pending the reestablishment of permanent government institutions" in Afghanistan).

3. We deal separately with peacekeeping in Chapter 5 of this book. Because peacekeeping is not addressed in the U.N. Charter, the authority for such missions is sometimes referred to as "Chapter VI and a half" authority, meaning that it falls

somewhere between. *See* UNITED NATIONS, *United Nations Peacekeeping*, http://www.un.org/en/peacekeeping/ (last visited May 17, 2010).

4. The Security Council has authorized "coalitions of the willing" to use all means necessary in Kuwait and Iraq in 1990–1991; Somalia in 1992; Rwanda in 1994; Haiti in 1994; Bosnia in 1995; Kosovo in 1999; and East Timor in 1999. It has sometimes characterized this as permitting member states to "cooperate" with an aggressed state. *See* UNITED NATIONS, *50 Years of United Nations Peacekeeping Operations*, http://www.un.org/en/peacekeeping/sites/50years/2.htm (last visited February 12, 2010). *See also* Gary Wilson, *The Legal, Military and Political Consequences of the "Coalition of the Willing" Approach to UN Military Enforcement Action*, 12 J. CONFLICT SECURITY LAW 295 (2007).

5. *See, e.g.*, U.N. Charter art. 33 (dealing with dispute resolution); U.N. Charter art. 41 (dealing with sanctions).

6. U.N. Charter art. 42.

7. Additional Chapter VII mandated interventions include intervention in the Dem. Rep. Congo (MONUC), the establishment of the International Criminal Tribunal for Rwanda, the second intervention in Angola (UNAVEM II 1991), and the second intervention in Somalia (UNOSOM II 1993), S.C. Res. 814, U.N. Doc. S/RES/814 (March 26, 1993).

8. *See, e.g.*, Max du Plessis, *Chinese Arms Destined for Zimbabwe over South African Territory: The R2P Norm and the Role of Civil Society*, 17 AFR. SECURITY REV., 17, 18 (2008).

9. In the year 2009 alone, active peacekeeping missions contain more than 81,000 military personnel, 10,000 police, and 8,000 civilians, while peacebuilding operations contain 318 military, 15 police, and 880 civilians within U.N.-led operations. In non–U.N.-led operations, such as those led by the European Union (e.g., Somalia, Israel), the United States (Iraq, Afghanistan), or the OSCE (Bosnia, Serbia, Montenegro, Albania), there are more than 224,000 military, 500 police, and 300 civilians. For an overview of the operations, see United Nations Peace Operations, Year in Review (2010).

10. UNITED NATIONS INTERVENTIONISM, 1991–2004 at ix–x (Mats Berdal & Spyros Economides eds., rev. and updated ed. 2007).

11. International organizations and NGOs have been more willing to recognize the need to consider gender issues when characterizing the intervention as "an emergency" or "humanitarian assistance." BRIDGET BYRNE & SALLY BADEN, GENDER, EMERGENCIES, AND HUMANITARIAN ASSISTANCE (listing the "gender approach" taken by organizations ranging from the ICRC and GTZ to WFP and UNICEF as early as 1995 in the context of humanitarian assistance under the rubric of "women in development").

12. For example, one author of this book directed the OSCE's Human Rights Department in post-conflict Bosnia. Human rights officers working in that department who had come from different organizations and different nations with different legal backgrounds (e.g., an Englishman formerly with ICRC, a Spaniard formerly with Amnesty International, a Frenchwoman formerly with Médecins Sans Frontières, and an American formerly with the Department of State) had very different ideas regarding how to interpret the OSCE's broad mandate to "ensure democratic principles."

13. CHRISTINE BELL, PEACE AGREEMENTS AND HUMAN RIGHTS 33–35 (2000). *See also* Nozizwe Madlala-Routledge & Sybert Liebenberg, *Developmental Peacekeeping What Are the Advantages for Africa?*, 13 AFR. SECURITY REV. 125, 125–26 (2004)

(proposing something called "developmental peacekeeping" to bridge what they view as the too-long gap between peacekeeping and post-conflict reconstruction); U.N. Special Committee on Peacekeeping Operations, 64th sess., 212th & 213th mtgs., U.N. Doc. GA/PK/203 (February 22, 2010).

14. It is also sometimes undertaken as a purely internal dynamic (e.g., Northern Ireland and Spain), without overt international involvement.

15. See U.N. DEP'T OF PEACEKEEPING OPERATIONS [DPKO], GENDER RESOURCE PACKAGE FOR PEACEKEEPING OPERATIONS, ix, U.N. Sales No. E.04.IV.6 (2004); Dianne Otto, *The Exile of Inclusion: Reflections on Gender Issues in International Law over the Last Decade*, 10 MELB. J. INT'L L. 11, 15–19 (2009).

16. Daniel J. Whelan & Jack Donnelly, *The West, Economic and Social Rights, and the Global Human Rights Regime: Setting the Record Straight*, 29 HUM. RTS. Q. 908, 915 (2007) (citing Ruth Gavison, *On the Relationship Between Civil and Political Rights, and Social and Economic Rights*, in THE GLOBALIZATION OF HUMAN RIGHTS at 54 n.46 (Jean-Marc Coicaud, Michael W. Doyle, & Anne-Marie Gardner eds., 2003); Louise Arbour, *Economic and Social Justice for Societies in Transition*, N.Y.U. J. INT'L L. & POL. 1, 3 n. 4 (2007), ("[T]he vindication of economic, social, and cultural rights in transitional justice is not only a matter of principle, but also one of effectiveness . . ."). *See also* Shedrack C. Agbakwa, *A Path Least Taken: Economic and Social Rights and the Prospects of Conflict Prevention and Peacebuilding in Africa*, 47 J. AFR. L. 38, 40 (2003).

17. As argued by Dina Francesca Haynes in *The Deus ex Machina Descends: The Laws, Priorities and Players Central to the International Administration of Post-Conflict Bosnia and Herzegovina*, in DECONSTRUCTING THE RECONSTRUCTION 3, 8–9 (Haynes ed., 2008); Dina Francesca Haynes, *Lessons from Bosnia's Arizona Market: Harm to Women in a Neoliberalized Postconflict Reconstruction Process*, 158 U. PA. L. REV. 6 at 1779 (2010). Liberal scholars question the deeply paternalistic, imperialist, and undemocratic nature of imposing rules, obligations, and political and economic ideology in the name of "democracy." *See* DAVID CHANDLER, BOSNIA: FAKING DEMOCRACY AFTER DAYTON 197 (2d ed. Pluto Press 2000).

18. Some international interventions approved by the Security Council, explicitly for the purpose of securing or restoring democracy, typically where a coup has occurred, include Haiti (1991–1994) and Sierra Leone (1997–1998). *See generally* ROLAND I. PERUSSE, HAITIAN DEMOCRACY RESTORED 1991–1995 (1995); JOHN L. HIRSCH, SIERRA LEONE: DIAMONDS AND THE STRUGGLE FOR DEMOCRACY (2001).

19. The practice of "democratization" in state building feigns neutrality, allowing those who engage in "democratization" to pretend that they merely have taken the role of facilitator in an inevitable political transition. For more on this, in the context of Bosnia, see Haynes, *The Deus ex Machina Descends, supra* note 17 at 3, 14.

20. *See* Thomas Carothers, *The End of the Transition Paradigm*, 13 J. DEMOCRACY 5, 6 (2002).

21. Fionnuala Ní Aoláin & Michael Hamilton, *Gender and the Rule of Law in Transitional Societies, Rule of Law Symposium*, 18 MINN. J. INT'L L. 380, 387 (2009).

22. The Secretary-General and the Chairman of the Panel on United Nations Peace Operations, Report of the Panel on United Nations Peace Operations, delivered to the President of the General Assembly and the President of the Security Council, U.N. Doc. A/55/305–S/2000/809 (August 21, 2000).

23. *See generally* BOB BREEN, MISSION ACCOMPLISHED, EAST TIMOR: THE AUSTRALIAN DEFENCE FORCE PARTICIPATION IN THE INTERNATIONAL FORCES EAST TIMOR (INTERFET) (2001). *See also* SIMON CHESTERMAN, JUST WAR OR JUST PEACE?: HUMANITARIAN INTERVENTION AND INTERNATIONAL LAW 135 (2001).

24. Violence erupted again over the following eight years, and in 2006, tens of thousands were again displaced when rioting broke out over alleged rampant discrimination. Prior to this, the economy had all but collapsed with the departure of the international community. *See, e.g.*, Michael Bhatia, *The Political Economy of Intervention*, 11 GLOB. GOV. (2005).

25. *See* Cynthia Alkon, *The* Cookie Cutter *Syndrome: Legal Reform Assistance Under Post-Communist Democratization Programs*, J. DISP. RESOL. 327, 335–38 (2002).

26. In September of 2009, the General Assembly of the United Nations voted in favor of a draft resolution consolidating all U.N. agencies and divisions addressing women's issues into a single entity, U.N. Women. As Secretary-General Ban Ki-moon stated: "U.N. gender architecture lacks a recognized driver. It is fragmented. It is inadequately funded, and insufficiently focused on country-driven demands." As of this writing, the newly operating agency, whose longer name is the UN Entity for Gender Equality and the Empowerment of Women, is headed by Michele Bachelet, former president of Chile. Press Release, *Press Conference by Under-Secretary-General for Gender Equality, Women's Empowerment*, U.N. Dept. of Info. (September 22, 2010).

27. UNIFEM is one of the agencies slated to be consumed by U.N. Women in January 2011.

28. "Security touches on many aspects of the way we live and are governed. The OSCE's comprehensive view of security covers three 'dimensions': the politico-military; the economic and environmental; and the human. The OSCE's activities cover all three of these areas, from 'hard' security issues such as conflict prevention to fostering economic development, ensuring the sustainable use of natural resources, and promoting the full respect of human rights and fundamental freedoms."
OSCE, About the OSCE, http://www.osce.org/what.

29. *See generally* INTERNATIONAL LAW: MODERN FEMINIST APPROACHES (Doris Buss & Ambreena Manji eds., 2005); HILARY CHARLESWORTH & C. M. CHINKIN, THE BOUNDARIES OF INTERNATIONAL LAW: A FEMINIST ANALYSIS (2000); DORINDA G. DALLMEYER, RECONCEIVING REALITY: WOMEN AND INTERNATIONAL LAW (1993).

30. By way of example, the country contributions to the 2007 budget for the Office of the High Representative, the de facto governor of post-conflict Bosnia and Herzegovina, broke down as follows: EU: 53 percent; USA: 22 percent; Japan: 10 percent; Russia: 4 percent; Canada: 3.03 percent; OIC: 2.5 percent; and others: 5.47 percent. *See* Office of the High Representative and EU Special Representative (OHR), *Status, Staff, and Funding of the OHR* (May 11, 2006).

31. *See* Stef Jansen, *"Home" and Return in the Foreign Intervention in Bosnia and Herzegovina: An Anthropological Critique, in* DECONSTRUCTING THE RECONSTRUCTION 29, 31–32 (Dina Francesca Haynes ed., 2008).

32. *Id.* at 29, 40.

33. *Id.* at 29.

34. DAVID CHANDLER, BOSNIA: FAKING DEMOCRACY AFTER DAYTON 197 (2d ed. Pluto Press 2000); SIMON CHESTERMAN, YOU, THE PEOPLE: THE UNITED NATIONS, TRANSITIONAL ADMINISTRATION, AND STATE-BUILDING (2004).

35. Chandler, *supra* note 34. *See also* Massimo Morrati, *Tackling Obstruction to Property Rights and Return: A Critical Assessment of the Practice of Removing Housing Officials in Bosnia and Herzegovina, in* DECONSTRUCTING THE RECONSTRUCTION 177, 189–90 (Dina Francesca Haynes ed., 2008).

36. Meredeth Turshen, *Engendering Relations of State to Society in the Aftermath, in* THE AFTERMATH: WOMEN IN POST CONFLICT TRANSFORMATION 78 (Sheila Meintjes, Anu Pillay, & Meredeth Turshen eds., 2002).

37. Fionnuala Ní Aoláin, *Political Violence and Gender During Times of Transition*, 15 COLUM. J. GENDER & L. 829, 836–37 (2006).

38. *See* Letter dated October 25, 2004, from the Permanent Representatives of Jordan, South Africa, Sweden, and the United Kingdom of Great Britain and Northern Ireland to the United Nations, Addressed to the Secretary-General, ¶53, U.N. Doc. S/2004/862 (October 26, 2004). *But see*, for example, positive examples such as the Danish Refugee Council which has holistically reformulated its work to take women's issues into account, establishing "minimum requirements" that all programs must "Benefit men and women, Recognise and utilize their respective capacities; Recognise and take into consideration their special needs; Support positive changes in gender relations, i.e. changes in terms of greater gender equality; and Avoid undermining women's decision making capacities, and increasing their work load." Danish Refugee Council, *Gender*, http://www.drc.dk/dk/relief-work/how-we-work/operational-principles/gender (last visited November 3, 2010).

39. Gayle Tzemach Lemmon, *Extending the Horizon for Woman's Aid Projects in Afghanistan*, N.Y. TIMES, August 14, 2009.

40. *See, e.g.*, Haynes, *Lessons from Bosnia's Arizona Market*, *supra* note 17 (containing the following vignette: "a development organization passed through [Chad] spoke with the local leaders and ultimately presented every household with a new, efficient wood burning stove. The goal was to reduce the amount of wood burned, as people (women and girls) walked further and further each day to find firewood with which to cook. . . . When the development agency returned in a year's time to evaluate the success of the project, they discovered the stoves being used as stools. . . . Had the organization ever asked a woman whether she would use a stove created for outdoor use, they would have learned that their project was worthless.").

41. *See, e.g.*, THE WOMEN'S INITIATIVES FOR GENDER JUSTICE, 2009 GENDER REPORT CARD ON THE INTERNATIONAL CRIMINAL COURT (ICC), 10 (2009) (establishing that the ICC has reached gender parity with both professional staff and with 53 percent of judges now being women).

42. As of 1989, women in upper-level positions, after concerted efforts were made to attract, retain, and promote more women, were still: P-2 administrative (43.2 percent), P-3 low level but not always administrative (39 percent), P-4 senior level (23 percent), P-5 more senior (12.4 percent), D-1 very senior (8.6 percent), D-2 (5.7 percent), Assistant Secretary-General (5.3 percent), Under-Secretary-General (7.7 percent), Secretary-General (0 percent). RUMKI BASU, PERSONNEL ADMINISTRATION IN UNITED NATIONS 69 (1989).

43. *Id.* at 68.

44. One author recalls that "[a]s a junior UN officer (P-3), I was asked to participate in a task force to assess the problem the UN was having in retaining women. . . .[T] he problem lay in the fact that very few postings were available for couples, or for women with children." Dina Francesca Haynes, *Ethics of International Civil Service: A Reflection on How the Care of United Nations' Staff Impacts the Ability to Fulfill Their Role in "Harmonizing" the World*, 30 HAMLINE J. PUB. L. & POL'Y. 175, 196 n.62 (2008).

45. Of men and women who were P-1 and P-2s in 1954, and were still on staff in 1974, 64 percent of the women had remained in low positions of P-4 or lower, while only 39 percent of the men had remained in these low grades. *Id.* at 197 n.63.

46. *See generally* Adali v. Turkey, App. No. 38187/97 Eur. Ct. H.R. (2005) (challenging the measure and weakening the requirement somewhat via a recent European Court of Human Rights judgment on Cyprus).

47. *See* Hilary Charlesworth, Christine Chinkin, & Shelley Wright, *Feminist Approaches to International Law*, 85 AM. J. INT'L L. 613, 621–23 (1991). *See also* Haynes, *Ethics of International Civil Service, supra* note 44 at 195.

48. *See also* Haynes, *Ethics of International Civil Service, supra* note 44 at 209–12.

49. *Id.* at 209–11.

50. *Id.*

51. *Id.*

52. Simon Harris, *Gender, Participation, and Post-Conflict Planning in Northern Sri Lanka, in* GENDER, PEACEBUILDING, AND RECONSTRUCTION 61 (Caroline Sweetman ed., 2005).

53. Madeline Morris, *By Force of Arms: Rape, War, and Military Culture*, 45 DUKE L.J. 651, 733 (1996) (quoting a female U.S. military officer as saying that "the units that work with females every day seem to be able to relate [to women and gender issues] better."); ANU PILLAY, GENDER, PEACE, AND PEACEKEEPING: LESSONS FROM SOUTHERN AFRICA, 3 (2006) (citing WOMEN IN AN INSECURE WORLD: VIOLENCE AGAINST WOMEN, FACTS, FIGURES, AND ANALYSIS 247–53 (Marie Vlachová & Lea Biason eds., Geneva Centre for Democratic Control of Armed Forces (DCAF) 2005).

54. *See, e.g.*, Sheila Meintjes, *War and Post-War Shifts in Gender Relations, in* AFTERMATH: WOMEN IN POST-CONFLICT TRANSFORMATION 63, 64 (Sheila Meintjes, Anu Pillay, & Meredeth Turshen eds., 2002) (relating the fact that women fought in the Zimbabwe, Eritrean, and South African "liberation wars").

55. In fact, some scholars argue that gender shifts are fragile and the reversal of those wartime shifts are inevitable because it is always men who broker the peace and conceive of plans to "right" the imbalance as part of the work of placing the country "back on track." *Id.* at 73.

56. Fionnuala Ní Aoláin, *Political Violence and Gender During Times of Transition*, 15 COLUM. J. GENDER & L. 829, 829 (2006).

57. *See, e.g.*, Jackie Kirk, *Promoting a Gender Just Peace, in* GENDER, PEACEBUILDING, AND RECONSTRUCTION 50, 52 (Caroline Sweetman ed., 2005) (stating that in some countries and regions, war and migration combine to make the ratio of women to men even higher. In Southern Sudan it is almost 2:1.).

CHAPTER 5

1. Some limited exceptions to UN-led peacekeeping include the African Union-deployed troops through the Economic Community of West African States Monitoring Group (ECOMOG) in Sierra Leone and Liberia; NATO deployment of International Forces (IFOR) and then Special Forces (SFOR) troops in Croatia and Bosnia; and a deployment by the EU under its Foreign and Security Pillar of a Rapid Reaction Force to Montenegro. *See* David Quayat, The United Nations and Regional Organizations: A New Paradigm for Peace? Presentation at the Conference of Defence Associations Institute Second Annual Graduate Symposium, Univ. of Calgary, Can. 12 (November 13, 1999).

2. U.N. DEP'T OF PEACEKEEPING OPERATIONS (DPKO) BEST PRACTICES UNIT, GENDER RESOURCE PACKAGE FOR PEACEKEEPING OPERATIONS, at ix, U.N. Sales No. E.04.IV.6 (2004) [hereinafter DPKO, GENDER RESOURCE PACKAGE].

3. *See* Pamela Scully, *Expanding the Concept of Gender-Based Violence in Peacebuilding and Development*, J. OF PEACEBUILDING & DEV. (SPECIAL ISSUE ON GENDER VIOLENCE AND GENDER JUSTICE) (2011).

4. *See, e.g.,* PAUL HIGATE, INST. FOR SECURITY STUD., GENDER, AND PEACEKEEPING CASE STUDIES: THE DEMOCRATIC REPUBLIC OF THE CONGO AND SIERRA LEONE at 15 (ISS Monograph Ser. No. 91, 2004).

5. Note that abuse of the local population, including gendered abuse, is not limited to peacekeepers, but has been perpetrated by U.N. staff, humanitarian workers, and other internationals in the field. *See* Dina Francesca Haynes, *Used, Abused, Arrested, and Deported: Extending Immigration Benefits to Protect the Victims of Trafficking and to Secure the Prosecution of Traffickers*, 26 HUM. RTS. Q. 221, 236 (2004). *See also* HIGATE, *supra* note 4, at 15, 43–44. This chapter, however, is limited to discussing peacekeeping missions, and its focus is therefore on abuses by peacekeepers.

6. U.N. Charter, Preamble (1945).

7. *See* United Nations Peacekeeping home page, http://www.un.org/en/peacekeeping/ (last visited November 4, 2010).

8. Because peacekeeping is not specifically mentioned in either chapter, it is sometimes referred to as justified by "Chapter VI and a half," meaning that the authority of Chapters VI and VII, taken together, justify the missions. See *id.*

9. Involvement requires that such activities are consistent with the purposes and principles outlined in Chapter I of the Charter. U.N. DEP'T OF PEACEKEEPING OPERATIONS, UNITED NATIONS PEACEKEEPING OPERATIONS: PRINCIPLES AND GUIDELINES, at 13 (2008) [hereinafter DPKO, BEST PRACTICES GUIDELINES].

10. *Id.* at 13–14 (noting that the Security Council need not refer to a specific Chapter of the Charter when passing a resolution authorizing the deployment of a U.N. peacekeeping operation).

11. *See, e.g., id.* at 13 ("In fulfilling [its] responsibility, the Security Council may adopt a range of measures, including the establishment of a United Nations peacekeeping operation. The legal basis for such action is found in Chapters VI, VII, and VIII of the Charter.").

12. *Id.* at 8.

13. *See* U.N. Secretary-General & Chairman of the Panel on U.N. Peace Operations, *Rep. of the Panel on U.N. Peace Operations, delivered to the President of the General Assembly and the President of the Security Council*, U.N. Doc. A/55/305–S/2000/809 (August 21, 2000); DPKO, BEST PRACTICES GUIDELINES, *supra* note 9, at 8–10.

14. *See* DPKO, BEST PRACTICES GUIDELINES, *supra* note 9, at 20.

15. *Id.* at 23 fig. 2.

16. *See* Dianne Otto, *The Exile of Inclusion: Reflections on Gender Issues in International Law over the Last Decade*, 10 MELB. J. INT'L L. 11, 15–19 (2009).

17. *See, e.g.,* DPKO, BEST PRACTICES GUIDELINES, *supra* note 9 (rarely mentioning gender, though written long after Resolution 1325 went into effect).

18. U.N. Dep't of Pub. Info., *Background Notes: November 30, 2009*, at 1, U.N. Doc. DPI/1634/Rev.103 (October 2010). *See also* U.N. SCOR, 64th sess., 6075th mtg. at 7, U.N. Doc. S/PV.6075 (January 23, 2009) (relating the Department Field Support's involvement in 16 peacekeeping missions, 18 special political missions, and in the administration of 22,000 international and local civilian staff, as well as the operation and maintenance of more than 250 medical facilities, 300 aircraft, 18,000 vehicles, and 40,000 computers).

19. *See* Pekka Hirvonen, *Stingy Samaritans: Why Recent Increases in Development Aid Fail to Help the Poor*, GLOBAL POLICY FORUM (August 2005), http://www.global policy.org/home/240/45056.html (providing examples of relief efforts funded and supported by the United States (Israel), France (Cote d'Ivoire), and Australia (East Timor)).

20. *See* HIGATE, *supra* note 4, at 11–12.

21. For example, three peacekeepers were killed in the Democratic Republic of the Congo in 2003, and their peacekeeper colleagues believe that two had been cannibalized. HIGATE, *supra* note 4, at 13.

22. *See* THE POSTWAR MOMENT: MILITARIES, MASCULINITIES, AND INTERNATIONAL PEACEKEEPING 13 (Dubravka Zarkov & Cynthia Cockburn eds., 2002).

23. *See* HIGATE, *supra* note 4, at 14–15. *See also* Dina Francesca Haynes, *Lessons from Bosnia's Arizona Market: Harm to Women in a Neoliberalized Postconflict Reconstruction Process*, 158 U. PA. L. REV. 1779 (2010) (remarking on the increased supply and demand for human trafficking in the wake of peacekeeping operations).

24. *See, e.g.*, Andrew Bickford, *See the World, Meet Interesting People, Have Sex with Them: Tourism, Sex, and Recruitment in the U.S. Military*, NAT'L SEXUALITY RES. CTR. (July 1, 2003).

25. HIGATE, *supra* note 4, at 13. *See also* Dina Francesca Haynes, *Ethics of International Civil Service: A Reflection on How the Care of United Nations' Staff Impacts the Ability to Fulfill Their Role in "Harmonizing" the World*, 30 HAMLINE J. PUB. L & POL'Y 175 (2008).

26. *See* R. W. Connell, *Masculinities, the Reduction of Violence, and the Pursuit of Peace*, *in* THE POSTWAR MOMENT, *supra* note 22, at 33, 34.

27. *See id.*

28. For instance, MONUC, the U.N. Mission to the Democratic Republic of the Congo, has fewer than 5 percent women among its ranks, and the Gender Adviser, appointed to handle the gender mainstreaming of the MONUC mission, operates without a budget. *See* Emily Schroeder, *A Window of Opportunity in the Democratic Republic of the Congo: Incorporating a Gender Perspective in the Disarmament, Demobilization, and Reintegration Process*, PEACE, CONFLICT, & DEV., July 2004, at 11–12.

29. *See* Haynes, *infra* note 37 and accompanying text, for discussion of the victim/ savages/savior paradigm.

30. *See* HIGATE, *supra* note 4, at 18–20.

31. *See id.*

32. *Id.* at 19 (stating that peacekeepers tended to forget the gender components of training, which constituted forty minutes of their total training, but remembered radio operation, military protocols, vehicle maintenance, care of electrical equipment, and medical trainings. Some expressed the belief that gender should fall under HIV/AIDS training).

33. *See* RAY MURPHY, UN PEACEKEEPING IN LEBANON, SOMALIA, AND KOSOVO: OPERATIONAL AND LEGAL ISSUES IN PRACTICE 216 (2007).

34. The annual income of a local in the DRC in 2003, for instance, was $100, while the Mission Subsistence Allowance (which is *daily* U.N. pay in addition to whatever, if anything, one's own country pays its own troops when deployed as peacekeepers) was $138. HIGATE, *supra* note 4, at 11, 13.

35. *Id.* at 11 (establishing that the average life expectancy in the DRC in 2003, for example, is forty-seven for men and fifty-one for women).

36. Women and children make up 80 percent of refugees and displaced persons during war. BRIDGET BYRNE & SALLY BADEN, BRIDGE, REPORT NO. 33, GENDER, EMERGENCIES AND HUMANITARIAN ASSISTANCE 9 (1995).

37. Dina Francesca Haynes, *Client-Centered Human Rights Advocacy*, 13 CLINICAL L. REV. 379, 388–90 (2006).

38. HIGATE, *supra* note 4, at 7.

39. Agence France-Presse, *Ex–UN Worker on Trial for Rape*, September 10, 2008, http://news.asiaone.com/News/AsiaOne%2BNews/World/Story/A1Story20080910-86865.html.

40. *See* Dina Francesca Haynes, *The* Deus ex Machina *Descends: The Laws, Priorities, and Players Central to the International Administration of Post-Conflict Bosnia and Herzegovina, in* DECONSTRUCTING THE RECONSTRUCTION: HUMAN RIGHTS AND RULE OF LAW IN POSTWAR BOSNIA AND HERZEGOVINA 3, 16 (Dina Francesca Haynes ed., 2008). *See also* HIGATE, *supra* note 4, at 12 (noting that peacekeepers in the DRC expressed fatalistic views of the country, describing it as "dysfunctional" and lacking a future due to "lazy" locals).

41. *See generally* Refugee Studies Centre & U.N. Population Fund, *Sexual Violence: Weapon of War, Impediment to Peace*, FORCED MIGRATION REV. (January 2007).

42. *See* Fionnuala Ní Aoláin & Colm Campbell, *The Paradox of Transition in Conflicted Democracies*, 27 HUM. RTS. Q. 172 (2005).

43. HIGATE, *supra* note 4, at 46–47 (noting that when some women in the Sierra Leone did not have available clothes with which to cover up, the predominantly Muslim peacekeepers supplied them).

44. *Id.*

45. *Id.*

46. *See* HIGATE, *supra* note 4, at 15, 43–44 (citing the MONUC personnel who felt that local women relied economically on their regular payment for sexual services and UNAMSIL peacekeepers who purchased cell phones for women and "put them up" in apartments in Freetown to have regular access to sex, ignoring the exploitative nature of the relationship wherein the women were in it to survive).

47. *See, e.g.,* HIGATE, *supra* note 4, at 44–45.

48. *See, e.g.,* BOB BREEN, A LITTLE BIT OF HOPE: AUSTRALIAN FORCE—SOMALIA (1998) (stating that the Australian role in Somalia has been hailed as one to emulate). *See also* Letter dated August 17, 2000, from the Chairman of the Panel on United Nations Peace Operations to the Secretary-General, *Report of the Panel on United Nations Peace Operations*, ¶¶ 48–64, U.N. Doc. A/55/305–S/2000/809 (August 21, 2000) (tasked with ensuring that peacekeeping missions have a "robust doctrine and realistic mandates" to avoid repeating scenarios like those in Rwanda and Srebrenica).

49. Meaning that they shot and killed several Somalis whom locals identified as murderers and criminals, described as "effectively channeling their warrior ethos." BREEN, A LITTLE BIT OF HOPE, *supra* note 48, at 85–87.

50. *See* U.N. MINE ACTION SERV., GENDER GUIDELINES FOR MINE ACTION PROGRAMMES 24 (March 2010) [hereinafter U.N., GENDER GUIDELINES].

51. *Id.* at 25.

52. Even the "Rosie the Riveters" gave the steel plant jobs back to the men when they returned from war, and although it is quite likely that such gender role shifts will not be permanent, some space may open up for women to move somewhat more freely. *See* Rosie the Riveter, http://www.rosietheriveter.org/shipyards.htm (last visited November 14, 2010).

53. DPKO, GENDER RESOURCE PACKAGE, *supra* note 2, at 8.

54. *See, e.g.*, U.N., GENDER GUIDELINES, *supra* note 50.

55. In Bosnia, women constituted the majority of locals hired by international missions, as women were more likely to speak English and have the desired administrative skills. *See* Haynes, *supra* note 23, at 1783 n.12 (2010).

56. Haynes, *supra* note 25, at 209–12 (listing the sexual harassment problems rife in the field where such large gender and power disparities exist between internationals and locals).

57. *See International Association of Women Judges: Stopping the Abuse of Power for Purposes of Sexual Exploitation: Naming, Shaming, and Ending Sextortion*, COUNTER BALANCE INT'L, Vol. 16, No. 1 (IAWJ, Summer 2010).

58. *See* Haynes, *supra* note 23, at 1780–81.

59. *See id.*

60. DPKO, GENDER RESOURCE PACKAGE, *supra* note 2, at 63.

61. *See* HIGATE, *supra* note 4, at 6–7, 16–17.

62. *See* Lyn S. Graybill, *Peacekeepers in Africa and Gender Violence*, GLOBAL SECURITY AND COOPERATION Q. (2002) (referencing photographs of peacekeepers inserting explosives into a woman's vagina after raping her that led to twelve peacekeepers being disciplined, but no charges were brought against them).

63. *See id. See also* Max du Plessis & Stephen Pete, *Who Guards the Guards? The ICC and Serious Crimes Committed by United Nations Peacekeepers in Africa*, 13 AFRICAN SECURITY REV., no. 3, 2004 at 5 (describing Italian troops in Somalia alleged to have raped a woman with a flare gun and Canadian troops alleged to have beaten a sixteen-year-old boy to death after raping him with a baton).

64. *See* Haynes, *supra* note 5, at 236.

65. HIGATE, *supra* note 4, at 41.

66. Lindsay Murdoch, *UN's Legacy of Shame in Timor*, THE AGE, July 22, 2006.

67. Haynes, *supra* note 23, at 1795–96.

68. *See* Haynes, *supra* note 5, at 221, 236; Haynes, *supra* note 23, at 1780–81; 1794–96.

69. *See* HIGATE, *supra* note 4, at 44.

70. U.N. Secretary-General on the activities of the Office of Internal Oversight Services, *Investigation by the Office of Internal Oversight Services into Allegations of Sexual Exploitation and Abuse in the United Nations Organization Mission in the Democratic Republic of Congo*, ¶ 11, U.N. Doc. A/59/661 (January 5, 2005) [hereinafter U.N., *Investigation into Allegations of Sexual Exploitation and Abuse*].

71. *See* Protocol to Prevent, Suppress, and Punish Trafficking in Persons, Especially Women and Children, Supplementing the United Nations Convention against Transnational Organized Crime, G.A. Res. 55/25, Annex II, U.N. Doc. A/RES/55/25 (January 8, 2001).

72. As was the case, for instance, in Cambodia (UNAMIC and subsequently UNTAC) and, arguably, is the case in the former Yugoslavia and Bosnia (UNPROFOR and subsequently UNMiB).

73. *See* Madeline Morris, *By Force of Arms: Rape, War, and Military Culture*, 45 DUKE L.J. 651, 676 (1996).

74. *See id.* at 701. *See also* CHARLOTTE LINDSEY, INTERNATIONAL COMMITTEE OF THE RED CROSS (ICRC), WOMEN FACING WAR 24–25, 51–61 (2001).

75. *See* Morris, *supra* note 73, at 698–700.

76. *See* Susan A. Notar, Note, *Peacekeepers as Perpetrators: Sexual Exploitation and Abuse of Women and Children in the Democratic Republic of the Congo*, 14 J. GENDER, SOCIAL POL'Y & THE L. 413, 417 (2006).

77. *See, e.g.*, ANU PILLAY, GENDER, PEACE, AND PEACEKEEPING: LESSONS FROM SOUTHERN AFRICA, at 7 (Inst. for Security Stud., ISS Paper Ser. 128, October 2006).

78. U.N. DEP'T OF PEACEKEEPING OPERATIONS, DPKO POLICY DIRECTIVE: GENDER EQUALITY IN UN PEACEKEEPING OPERATIONS (November 3, 2006). *See also* Press release, Security Council, Security Council Recalling Resolution 1325 (2000), Seeks Measures to Strengthen Role of Women in Peacekeeping, Post-Conflict Situations, U.N. Doc SC/8858 (October 26, 2006).

79. The recommendations included more research into cultural interactions between peacekeepers and the local populace; increasing gender-awareness training; more robust response of supervisors to allegations of sexual misconduct; education of key senior personnel about the issue; sharpening of Codes of Conduct; and, importantly, the need for more women in peacekeeping missions. *See, e.g.*, HIGATE, *supra* note 4, at 8; DPKO, GENDER RESOURCE, *supra* note 2, at x (announcing the appointment of full-time gender advisors to missions in Afghanistan, Liberia, the DRC, East Timor, Kosovo, and Sierra Leone).

80. *See, e.g.*, Murdoch, *supra* note 66 (noting that no one in the Timor case was ever charged).

81. Sam Vaknin, *The Sergeant and the Girl: Anatomy of a Double Standard*, CENTRAL EUROPE REVIEW, September 17, 2000.

82. *See* Agence France-Presse, *French Give UN Pedophile Didier Bourguet a Slap on the Wrist*, TERRITORY, September 11, 2008.

83. Agence France-Presse, *Ex–UN Worker on Trial for Rape*, *supra* note 39.

84. U.N., *Investigation into Allegations of Sexual Exploitation and Abuse*, *supra* note 70, ¶¶ 8, 12. In the DRC, sixty-eight military personnel and four civilians were investigated for sexually exploiting young girls, some who had already suffered rape during the war, and offering them food or small sums of money in exchange for sex. Allegations against three of the civilians were found not to be substantiated. None of the peacekeepers investigated admitted to the acts, but the report stated that "the evidence against them is strong and has been corroborated." *Id.* ¶¶ 8, 11.

85. U.N. Secretary-General, *Implementation of the Recommendations of the Special Committee on Peacekeeping Operations*, Annex ¶ 2, U.N. Doc. A/60/640 (December 29, 2005). It should be noted that the Department of Peacekeeping Operations highlights the fact that humanitarian workers, not just peacekeepers, were accused of sexually abusing refugee women and girls in West Africa. *See* DPKO, GENDER RESOURCE PACKAGE, *supra* note 2, at 51.

86. *See* U.N., *Investigation into Allegations of Sexual Exploitation and Abuse*, *supra* note 70, ¶ 29.

87. *See* CONGRESSIONAL RESEARCH SERVICE, STATUS OF FORCES AGREEMENT (SOFA): WHAT IS IT AND HOW HAS IT BEEN UTILIZED? (2011).

88. *See, e.g.*, Special Representative of the Secretary-General, *On the Status, Privileges, and Immunities of KFOR and UNMIK and Their Personnel in Kosovo*, U.N. Doc. UNMIK/REG/2000/47 (August 18, 2000) (establishing immunity for personnel under local jurisdiction and exclusive jurisdiction to individual sending countries). In Bosnia, the terms of the General Framework on the Agreement for Peace (GFAP aka the Dayton Peace Accord) specified that exclusive jurisdiction rests with the sending country. *See* General Framework on the Agreement for Peace in

Bosnia and Herzegovina, Annex 1A, Appendix B, December 14, 1995, Bosn. & Herz.-Croat.-Yugo., 35 I.L.M. 75.

89. The situation improved only slightly with a compromise by the Security Council that adopted a resolution that, in effect, granted peacekeepers a one-year immunity from investigations by the International Criminal Court. *See* Jim Wurst, *ICC: UN Council Resolves Immunity Debate*, UN WIRE, July 15, 2002. Resolution 1422 permitted a single twelve-month deferral if the ICC wants to investigate or prosecute a peacekeeper from a state that is not a party to the ICC, a category that includes the United States. *Id.* The one-year deferral has been repeatedly renewed since its initial passage in 2002, effectively rendering the ICC without jurisdiction over peacekeepers from nonsignatory countries.

90. *See World Signatures and Ratifications*, COALITION FOR THE INTERNATIONAL CRIMINAL COURT (2008). Currently, the Rome Statute has 139 signatories and 111 ratifications. *Id.*

91. *See* U.N. Dep't of Pub. Info., Special Comm. on Peacekeeping, *Special Committee on Peacekeeping Concludes 2007 Session, Finalizes Draft Memorandum of Understanding Between United Nations, Troop Contributors*, U.N. Doc. GA/PK/195 (June 11, 2007).

92. *See* Katherine Andrews, *Signs of Progress in Improving Peacekeeper Accountability*, THE HENRY L. STIMSON CENTER (October 15, 2007).

93. Behrami v. France; Saramati v. France, Germany, and Norway, Joint App. Nos. 71412/01 & 78166/01, Eur. Ct. H.R. (2007).

94. *See id.*

95. *See* Mark Leon Goldberg, *The Trouble with Peacekeeper Accountability*, UN DISPATCH (May 23, 2008), http://www.undispatch.com/the-trouble-with-peacekeeper-accountability.

96. *See, e.g.,* Andrews, *supra* note 92. In July of 2007, an entire Moroccan contingent was sent home from Cote d'Ivoire for unspecified "misconduct," and it has been contended that the United Nations is getting better at preventing those accused of misconduct from being reassigned to future missions or assigned to different U.N. agencies. *Id.*

97. *See* U.N., *Investigation into Allegations of Sexual Exploitation and Abuse*, *supra* note 70, ¶ 38 (expressing vexation that although commanders met with and expressed willingness to assist, over time all save one unit failed to respond to requests for assistance).

98. HIGATE, *supra* note 4, at 45.

99. *See id.* at 18 (describing training to Bangladeshi police arriving in the Democratic Republic of the Congo).

100. *See* Haynes, *supra* note 5, at 236–37; HIGATE, *supra* note 4, at 58–62.

101. *See* Minna Lyytikäinen, *Gender Training for Peacekeepers: Preliminary Overview of United Nations Peace Support Operations* 9 (United Nations Int'l Research & Training Inst. for the Advancement of Women (U.N.-INSTRAW): Gender, Peace, and Security, Working Paper No. 4, 2007).

102. DPKO, GENDER RESOURCE PACKAGE, *supra* note 2, at 46. *See* Lyytikäinen, *supra* note 101, at 7–12.

103. DPKO, GENDER RESOURCE PACKAGE, *supra* note 2, at 45.

104. HIGATE, *supra* note 4, at 26 (quoting a male MONUC peacekeeper on his perception of the value of the MONUC Code of Conduct).

105. There is some concern, however, that Codes of Conduct merely push the inevitable activity underground. HIGATE, *supra* note 4, at 40 (including arguments by UNAMSIL staff that this was the case).

106. U.N. Dep't of Peacekeeping Operations, Ten Rules: Code of Personal Conduct for Blue Helmets (1998).

107. *Id.*

108. Sending countries are, however, bound by the Geneva Conventions; accordingly, failure to address grave breaches of rights is not (formally at least) a matter of discretion. Geneva Convention Relative to the Protection of Civilian Persons in Time of War, art. 146, August 12, 1949, 6 U.S.T. 3516, 75 U.N.T.S. 287.

109. Higate, *supra* note 4, at 15.

110. Higate, *supra* note 4, at 25.

111. *See, e.g.,* Sulaiman Momodu, SEA Incidents Decrease, UNMIL Today, Vol. 5, Issue 3, at 1 (August 2008).

112. Some international organizations working in post-conflict settings have signed onto the Statement of Commitment on Eliminating Sexual Exploitation and Abuse by U.N. and Non-U.N. Personnel (December 4, 2006); *see, e.g.,* International Rescue Committee, Inc., IRC Code of Conduct on Sexual Exploitation and Abuse in Humanitarian Crises (2002).

Others, such as the Danish Refugee Council, subscribe to *The Code of Conduct: Principles of Conduct for the International Red Cross and Red Crescent Movement and NGOs in Disaster Response Programmes*, which contains provisions relating to sexual exploitation.

113. *See* Higate, *supra* note 4, at 26 (noting that one peacekeeper believed that superiors were not implementing the Code because they were also regularly breaching the Code).

114. *See* U.N., Gender Guidelines, *supra* note 50, at 18, 20, 27.

115. Higate, *supra* note 4, at 42.

116. *See* DPKO/OMA Statistical Report on Female Military and Police Personnel in UN Peacekeeping Operations Prepared for the 10th Anniversary of the SCR 1325 (2010).

117. *Id.*

118. In 2006, women constituted 4 percent of police personnel in U.N. peacekeeping missions. *See* U.N. Peacekeeping, Gender, Peacekeeping, & Peacebuilding: Background on Gender and U.N. Peace Operations, http://www.unac.org/peacekeeping/en/un-peacekeeping/fact-sheets/gender-peacekeeping-peacebuilding/ (last visited November 20, 2010). The Department of Peacekeeping Operations asserts that in 2003, women constituted 33 percent of the civilian forces. DPKO, Gender Resource Package, *supra* note 2, at 4.

119. Women currently represent 30 percent. U.N., Background on Gender, *supra* note 118.

120. Currently 28 percent. *Id.*

121. U.N. Peace & Security Section, Dep't of Pub. Info., U.N. Peace Operations 2009 Year in Review, at 18 (2009); IRIN Humanitarian News & Analysis, Gender: Women U.N. Peacekeepers—More Needed (May 20, 2010).

122. *See* U.N., Background on Gender, *supra* note 118; U.N., Office of the Special Adviser on Gender Issues & Advancement of Women, The Status of Women in the United Nations System & in the Secretariat (February 2010), http://www.un.org/womenwatch/osagi/ianwge/Factsheet%20as%20of%20FEB%202010.pdf. *See also* Haynes, *supra* note 25, at 191–92 (noting the historically low percentages of women in all U.N. agencies).

123. Some feminists argue that like women serving in the military, it would be "buying into the androcentric war culture" for women to serve. *See* Pillay, *supra* note 77, at 5.

124. *See* Morris, *supra* note 73, at 733 (quoting a female U.S. military officer as saying, "The units that work with females every day seem to be able to relate [to women and gender issues] better.").

125. *See* PILLAY, *supra* note 77, at 3, 6 (commenting on the mission dynamics of UNOMSA when led by Angela King as consultative, hands-on, unhierarchical, and providing space for personal growth and markedly void of locker room talk, as compared to the dynamics of the final phase of the UNOMSA mission led by Ladhdar Brahimi, described as inaccessible, surrounded by a male entourage, tense, and distant).

126. *See* IRIN, GENDER, *supra* note 121.

127. *See, e.g.*, U.N. Peacekeeping, Gender Statistics by Mission for the Month of November 2009 (December 8, 2009). In 2009, of the 83,000 peacekeeping troops in U.N. missions, approximately 2,000 were women. *Id.* In the year 2003, only 4 percent of civilian police positions and 1.5 percent of military personnel positions supplied by countries contributing personnel (e.g., contractors and nonprofessional U.N. staff) were women. DPKO, GENDER RESOURCE, *supra* note 2, at 4.

128. Resolution on the Improvement of the Status of Women in the United Nations System, G.A. Res. 57/180, ¶ 3, U.N. Doc. A/RES/57/180 (January 30, 2003).

129. *See* Department of Peacekeeping Operations Under-Secretary-General, *Statement on Gender Mainstreaming* (March 29, 2005).

130. *See* U.N. SECRETARY-GENERAL, WOMEN, PEACE, AND SECURITY: STUDY SUBMITTED BY THE SECRETARY-GENERAL PURSUANT TO SECURITY COUNCIL RESOLUTION 1325 (2000), ¶ 263, U.N. Sales No. E.03.IV.1 (2002).

131. *See* PILLAY, *supra* note 77, at 6–7 (noting that the mission, led in its initial phases by Angela King, comprising 46 percent and 53 percent women throughout its duration and acknowledging that it was able to obtain gender balance due to its status as a civilian mission, not a traditional peacekeeping mission; its mandate was not just to observe the elections, but also to quell the potential for violence).

132. *Id.* (citing evidence that U.N. peacekeeping missions with better gender-balanced staff have been highly effective).

133. While it is not clear whether the liaisons are men or women, if the role is not performed adeptly and discreetly, such a role can do further harm to the goal of encouraging local women to come forward and report problems they have had with peacekeepers. *See* HIGATE, *supra* note 4, at 7 (reporting that "less discrete" liaisons were serving to actually drive underground some of the exploitation).

134. Nicholas D. Kristof & Sheryl WuDunn, *The Women's Crusade*, N.Y. TIMES MAG., August 23, 2009, at MM28.

135. *See* U.N., GENDER GUIDELINES, *supra* note 50, at 23–24.

136. For instance, one author of this book was offered a position with UNHCR to "promote the education of women and girls" in Kandahar, Afghanistan, in 1998, under the Taliban. Although local customs and Taliban law dictated that no women could be present unaccompanied by a male relative, let alone meet with local male officials, the United Nations was nevertheless willing to send this author to do work that could not be carried out, in conditions that would inevitably lead to violence. This fear was borne out when a female U.N. official visited the region and was slapped in the face by the mayor of Kandahar for the offense of traveling unaccompanied by a male relative.

137. "The added value of ensuring that women, girls, boys and men enjoy equal access to and participate in . . . programmes as beneficiaries, employees and decision-makers is tangible and has ensured better programmes that benefit communities as a whole." U.N., GENDER GUIDELINES, *supra* note 50, at 58.

138. *See* U.N., Gender Guidelines, *supra* note 50, at 14–27.

139. *See id.* at 20.

CHAPTER 6

1. Tsjeard Bouta, Assessment of the Ituri Disarmament and Community Reinsertion Program (DCR) 21 (2005). For case studies of DDR programs, *see, e.g.*, Jessica Schafer, *A Baby Who Does Not Cry Will Not Be Suckled: AMO-DEG and the Reintegration of Demobilised Soldiers*, 24 J. S. Afr. Stud. 207 (1998).

2. *See, e.g.*, Lomé Accord art. VI(2)(vi), Sierra Leone-RUF, July 7, 1999.

3. *See, e.g.*, Kess Kingma, Bonn Int'l Ctr. for Conversion, Demobilisation and Reintegration of Ex-Combatants in Post-War and Transition Countries (Deutsche Gesellschaft für Technische Zusammenarbeit 2001); UN Dep't for Disarmament Affairs (DDA), Gender Perspectives on Disarmament, Demobilization, and Reintegration (DDR) 1 (2001) [hereinafter Gender Perspectives on DDR]; Maya Oza Ollek, Forgotten Females: Women and Girls in Post-Conflict Disarmament, Demobilisation, and Reintegration Programs (2007).

4. *See* United Nations, *Integrated Disarmament, Demobilization, and Reintegration Standards* (IDDRS) 5.10. The standards acknowledge that women are rarely included even in the planning.

5. In doing so, DDR can help positively disturb "not only the traditional narrative of women's weakness and vulnerability . . . but is also disruptive of the gendered ways of thinking that have served to legitimate armed conflict." Dianne Otto, *The Exile of Inclusion: Reflections on Gender Issues in International Law over the Last Decade*, 10 Melb. J. Int'l L. 11, 17 (2009).

6. Examples of DDR planning during the peace process may be found in Koth, *supra* note 1, at 1, 5 (Colombia); Mark Knight & Alpaslan Ozerdem, *Guns, Camps, and Cash: Disarmament, Demobilization, and Reinsertion of Former Combatants in Transitions from War to Peace*, 41 J. Peace Res. 4 (2004) (Congo); Kris Brown & Corinna Hauswedell, Bonn Int'l Ctr. for Conversion, Burying the Hatchet: The Decommissioning of Paramilitary Arms in Northern Ireland 4 (2002) (Northern Ireland).

7. These programs, worldwide, cost more than $1.5 billion per year, and generally occur in some of the poorest countries. *See, e.g.*, United Nations, Peace and Security Through Disarmament (2007).

8. *See* Nicole Ball & Luc van de Goor, Neth. Inst. of Int'l Relations, Disarmament, Demobilization, and Reintegration 5–6 (2006).

9. *See, e.g.*, Ball & van de Goor, *id.* at 11.

10. *Id.*

11. *See, e.g.*, Susan McKay & Dyan Mazurana, Where Are the Girls? Girls in Fighting Forces in Northern Uganda, Sierra Leone, and Mozambique: Their Lives During and After War 98 (2004) (traditional pattern observation in Sierra Leone DDR program); United Nations, Conference Report on DDR and Stability in Africa 19, 24 (June 23, 2005) (Mozambique and Zimbabwe DDR programs following the traditional pattern).

12. Lisa J. LaPlante & Kimberly Theidon, *Transitional Justice in Times of Conflict: Colombia's Ley de Justicia y Paz*, 28 Mich. J. Int'l L. 49, 58–59 (2006).

13. *See* Bart Klem & Pyt Douma, The Struggle After Combat: The Role of NGOs in DDR Processes: Synthesis Study 10–14 (2008).

14. *See* Vanessa Farr, Gender-Aware Disarmament, Demobilization, and Reintegration (DDR): A Checklist 6 (2008).

15. *See* Ollek, *supra* note 3.

16. Naomi Cahn & Fionnuala Ní Aoláin, *Gender, Masculinities, and Transition in Conflicted Societies*, 44 New Eng. L. Rev. 101 (2010).

17. Chapter 2 provides further discussion of these issues.

18. Section 8 of the Belfast, or "Good Friday" Agreement in Northern Ireland deals with security, referring to the "normalisation" of security arrangements and practices. *See* Belfast Agreement Sec. 8, Gr. Brit.-Ir. (April 10, 1998).

19. United Nations, Integrated Disarmament, Demobilization, and Reintegration Standards, Sec. 5.10 7–10 (2006) [hereinafter IDDRS].

20. *See* U.N. DDR Resource Center, Afghanistan, *available at* http://unddr.org/countryprogrammes.php?c=121&search=afghanistan_reintegration#activity.

21. Those forcibly taken for sex or any other forced labor should also, of course, be included.

22. *See* Prosecutor v. Germain Katanga, ICC-01/04-01/07, Warrant of Arrest, at 5 (July 2, 2007); Prosecutor v. Mathieu Ngudjolo Chui, ICC-01/04-01/07, Warrant of Arrest, at 5 (July 6, 2006). Both warrants charged both defendants with sexual slavery under Article 7(1)(g) of the Rome Statute.

23. The international community is moving toward recognition of the need to include those in noncombat roles. *See, e.g.*, U.N. Children's Fund, Cape Town Principles and Best Practices (1997) (providing a comprehensive definition of child soldier that recognizes not all soldiers have carried weapons).

24. *See* Sally Baden & Anne Marie Goetz, *Who Needs [Sex] When You Can Have [Gender]? Conflicting Discourses on Gender at Beijing, in* Feminist Visions of Development: Gender Analysis and Policy 19, 22 (Cecile Jackson & Ruth Pearson eds., 1998).

25. Theidon, *supra* note 12, at 19 (emphasis in original).

26. *See* Farr, *supra* note 14, at 6.

27. *See* Joshua S. Goldstein, War and Gender: How Gender Shapes the War System and Vice Versa 9 (2001); La Plante & Theidon, *supra* note 12.

28. U.N. Dev. Fund for Women, Getting It Right, Doing It Right: Gender Disarmament, Demobilization, and Reintegration 19 (2004).

29. United Nations, Operational Guide to the Integrated Disarmament, Demobilization, and Reintegration Standards 195 (2006) [hereinafter DDRS]; Megan Bastick, Karin Grimm & Rahel Kunz, Sexual Violence in Armed Conflict: Global Overview and Implications for the Security Sector 182, 187 (2007).

30. Human Rights Watch, Between Hope and Fear: Intimidation and Attacks Against Women in Public Life in Afghanistan 9, 18 (October 2003).

31. Consider the Sierra Leone process, often hailed as a success. Nonetheless, as Women Waging Peace concluded, "Sierra Leone's DDR process failed women and girls." Women Waging Peace, From Combat to Community: Women and Girls of Sierra Leone (2004).

32. Addressing masculinities requires paying attention to the ways in which women often actively facilitate and support men's militarized masculinity. *See, e.g.*, Kimberly Theidon, *Reconstructing Masculinities: The Disarmament, Demobilization, and Reintegration of Former Combatants in Colombia*, 31 Hum. Rts. Q. 1, 29 (2009). *See also* Joshua S. Goldstein, War and Gender: How Gender Shapes the War System and Vice Versa 306 (2001).

33. *See, e.g.*, Amnesty Int'l, The Impact of Guns on Women's Lives (2003).
34. *Id.* at 2.
35. *See* Gender Perspectives on DDR, *supra* note 3.
36. *See* Matt Hobson, Save the Children, Forgotten Casualties of War: Girls in Armed Conflict 19–20 (2005).
37. McKay, *supra* note 11, at 98–99.
38. Ollek, *supra* note 3, at 2.
39. McKay, *supra* note 11, at 101–02.
40. In such programs, participants receive some form of personal benefit for turning over weapons. For example, "In El Salvador, successful personal incentives included in-kind vouchers for consumer goods, while in Mozambique farm implements or other tools to assist with productive opportunities worked well." Forum on the Policies and Practices of Small Arms and Light Weapons Disarmament in Post-Conflict Transitions, Swords for Ploughshares Micro-disarmament in Transitions from Conflict 16 (2000). For descriptions of the Sierra Leone compensation for weapons program, *see* Dyan Mazurana & Khristopher Carlson, From Combat to Community: Women and Girls of Sierra Leone 8 (Sanam Anderlini ed., 2004); Andrew Sherriff with Karen Barnes, European Centre for Development Policy Management, Enhancing the EU Response to Women and Armed Conflict with Particular Reference to Development Policy 17 (2008).
41. The World Bank, Technical Annex for a Proposed Grand of SDR 68.1 Million (US$100 Million Equivalent) to the Democratic Republic of Congo for an Emergency Demobilization and Reintegration Project 2 (2004). *See also* Women's Comm'n for Refugee Women & Children, Precious Resources: Adolescents in the Reconstruction of Sierra Leone April–July 2002 at 7 (2002) [hereinafter Precious Resources].
42. Tsjeard Bouta, Neth. Inst. of Int'l Relations, Gender and Disarmament, Demobilization, and Reintegration: Building Blocs for Dutch Policy 10–11 (2005).
43. Sherriff, *supra* note 40, at 17.
44. Both reasons are from Bouta, *supra* note 42, at 11.
45. *See, e.g.*, Bouta, *supra* note 1.
46. *See* Jeffrey Isima, *Cash Payments in Disarmament, Demobilisation, and Reintegration Programmes in Africa*, 2 J. Sec. Sector Mgmt. (2004). *See also* U.S. Dep't of State, Bureau of African Affairs, Background Note: Sierra Leone (2011).
47. Isima, *supra* note 46.
48. World Bank Technical Annex, *supra* note 41, at 16.
49. *See* U.N. DDR Resource Center, Afghanistan, *supra* note 20.
50. *See, e.g.*, Nicholas D. Kristof & Sheryl WuDunn, Half the Sky: Turning Oppression into Opportunity for Women Worldwide (2009).
51. Gender Perspectives on DDR, *supra* note 3, at 2.
52. *See* Theidon, *supra* note 32, at 10 (quoting U.N. Disarmament, Demobilization, and Reintegration Resource Ctr., Integrated Disarmament, Demobilization, and Reintegration Standards II.2.4 (2006)).
53. *Id.* at 9.
54. *Id.* at 33–34.
55. *See* Stephanie Hanson, *Disarmament, Demobilization, and Reintegration (DDR) in Africa*, Council on Foreign Relations, February 16, 2007.
56. *See* IDDRS, *supra* note 19, at 10.

57. *Id.* at 4.
58. *See* Christine Bell & Catherine O'Rourke, *The Impact of UNSC Resolution 1325 on Peace Processes and Their Agreements*, 59 I.C.L.Q. 1 (2010).
59. *See* KINGMA, *supra* note 4, at 35–38 (the special attention runs to nine lines of a 51-page report); Emily Schroeder, *A Window of Opportunity in the Democratic Republic of Congo: Incorporating a Gender Perspective on the Disarmament, Demobilization, and Reintegration Process*, 5 J. PEACE, CONFLICT, & DEV. 1, 3 (2003).
60. *See* Otto, *supra* note 5, at nn. 62–64.
61. *See, e.g.*, MCKAY *supra* note 11; HOBSON, *supra* note 36; Beth Verhey, Save the Children and the NGO Group: CARE, IFESH and IRC, *Reaching the Girls: Study on Girls Associated with Armed Forces and Groups in the Democratic Republic of Congo* (2005).
62. *See, e.g.*, BOUTA, *supra* note 42, at 15–16.
63. Ollek, *supra* note at 3, 89. *See* TSJEARD BOUTA, GEORG FRERKS, & IAN BANNON, GENDER, CONFLICT AND DEVELOPMENT 49–51 (2005).
64. BOUTA, *supra* note 42, at 52.
65. *See, e.g.*, Christine Chinkin, *Gender, Human Rights, and Peace Agreements*, 18 OHIO ST. J. ON DISP. RESOL. 867, 877 (2003) (arguing that peace agreements "may have to address a three-way relationship between the designated leaders, the local population, and international agencies").
66. *See* FARR, *supra* note 14.
67. ORG. FOR ECON. CO-OPERATION & DEV., *Section 9: Integrating Gender Awareness and Equality, in* OECD DAC HANDBOOK ON SECURITY SYSTEM REFORM 17 (2009 ed. 2008); MEGAN BASTICK, INTEGRATING GENDER IN POST-CONFLICT SECURITY SECTOR REFORM 17–18 (2008).
68. *See, e.g.*, PRECIOUS RESOURCES, *supra* note 41. Although the recommendations are tailored to Sierra Leone, they provide useful insights for other DDR programs.
69. *Id.*
70. WORLD BANK, MDRP, *supra* note 41.
71. *Id.*
72. *See* Schroeder, *supra* note 59, at 24.
73. *Id.*
74. *Id.*
75. *See* NICOLE BALL & LUC VAN DE GOOR, NETH. INST. OF INT'L RELATIONS, DISARMAMENT, DEMOBILIZATION, AND REINTEGRATION 5–6, 17 (2006).
76. FARR, *supra* note 14, at 10–11.
77. As the World Bank notes:

Specific prejudices include the assumption that the women have been sexually abused and hence have lost their "purity." Host communities are also fearful of the aggressive behavior they believe the women may have acquired while away and that members of their military group may follow them to their communities. The women's own assumptions reinforce these perceptions and they sometimes choose [sic] to marginalize themselves from the community.

The World Bank, *In DRC, MDRP Helps Female Ex-Combatants Regain a Livelihood*, N&N No. 10 (October 24, 2008).
78. VANESSA FARR, GENDERING DEMILITARIZATION AS A PEACEBUILDING TOOL 41–47 (2002). Farr has developed an extensive checklist of issues, which seeks "to draw attention to the particular challenges that face women combatants, the wives of

male soldiers and war widows during the demobilization phase and the process of reintegration. . . ." *Id.* at 40.

79. Some post-conflict programs in other contexts have tried to work effectively around these gender roles by providing childcare to women so that they might attend informational meetings, ensuring that men and women eat at different times so that women are not expected to cook for men, etc. *See* UNITED NATIONS, GENDER GUIDELINES FOR MINE ACTION PROGRAMMES 22, 24, 31 (2010).

80. *See* FARR, *supra* note 78, at 4.

81. *See* KRISTIN VALASEK, GENEVA CENTRE FOR THE DEMOCRATIC CONTROL OF ARMED FORCES, GENDER, AND SSR TOOLKIT: SECURITY SECTOR REFORM AND GENDER 19 (2008).

82. *See* IDDRS, *supra* note 19, at 202.

83. *See* Anna Cutter Patel, *Transitional Justice and DDR*, *in* SECURITY AND POST-CONFLICT RECONSTRUCTION: DEALING WITH FIGHTERS IN THE AFTERMATH OF WAR 248, 262 (Robert Muggah ed., 2009).

84. *See* IDDRS, *supra* note 19, at Table 5.10.6.

85. *See generally* BRANDON HAMBER, "We Must Be Careful How We Emancipate Our Women": Shifting Masculinities in Post-Apartheid South Africa 22–24, 26 (2006) (detailing the post-conflict conditions of women by considering the three case studies of South Africa, Northern Ireland, and Lebanon).

86. *See, e.g.,* Anu Pillay, *Violence Against Women in the Aftermath*, *in* THE AFTERMATH: WOMEN IN POST-CONFLICT TRANSFORMATION 35, 43 (Sheila Meintjes, Anu Pillay, & Meredith Turshen eds., 2001).

87. *See* Fionnuala Ní Aoláin & Catherine Turner, *Gender Truth and Transition*, 16 UCLA WOMEN'S L. J. 229 (2007).

88. *See* Ruth Rubio-Marín, *The Gender of Reparations in Transitional Societies*, *in* THE GENDER OF REPARATIONS: UNSETTLING SEXUAL HIERARCHIES WHILE REDRESSING HUMAN RIGHTS VIOLATIONS 63 (Ruth Rubio-Marín ed., 2009).

89. *Theidon*, *supra* note 32, at 32.

90. *See, e.g., MDRP Launches Learning for Equality, Access, and Peace Program*, NEW & NOTEWORTHY, December 4, 2007.

91. *See* PEACEBUILD: THE CANADIAN PEACEBUILDING NETWORK, EMERGING ISSUES: YOUTH, GENDER, AND THE CHANGING NATURE OF ARMED CONFLICT 13, 15 (2008).

92. *See generally* MIRANDA ALISON, WOMEN AND POLITICAL VIOLENCE: FEMALE COMBATANTS IN ETHNO-NATIONAL CONFLICT (2009).

93. UN OFFICE FOR THE COORDINATION OF HUMAN AFFAIRS, DISCUSSION PAPER 2: THE NATURE, SCOPE, AND MOTIVATION FOR SEXUAL VIOLENCE AGAINST MEN AND BOYS IN ARMED CONFLICT 1, 3, 4 (2008).

94. *See* Colleen Duggan et al., *Reparations for Sexual and Reproductive Violence*, 2 INT'L J. TRANS. JUST. 192, 202 (2008).

95. *See, e.g.,* Prosecutor v. Thomas Lubanga Dvilo, ICC-01-02-01/06, Warrant of Arrest (February 10, 2006).

96. *See* DDRS, *supra* note 29, at 195–96; Megan Bastick, *Integrating Gender in Post-Conflict Security Sector Reform*, *in* GENEVA CENTRE FOR THE DEMOCRATIC CONTROL OF ARMED FORCES: POLICY PAPER NO. 29, at 18 (2008).

97. *See* Jeffrey Gettleman, *Symbol of Unhealed Congo: Male Rape Victims*, N.Y. TIMES, August 5, 2009, at A1.

98. *See generally* UNDPKO, A New Partnership Agenda: Charting a New Horizon for UN Peacekeeping 23 (2009).

99. *See generally* ROGER DUTHIE, TRANSITIONAL JUSTICE AND SOCIAL REINTEGRA-
TION (n.d.).

100. *See* INT'L PEACE ACAD., A FRAMEWORK FOR LASTING DISARMAMENT, DEMOBILIZA-
TION, AND REINTEGRATION OF FORMER COMBATANTS IN CRISIS SITUATIONS 5 (2002).

101. *Id.* at 4.

102. *Id.*

103. *Id.*at 5.

104. *See, e.g.*, DUTHIE, *supra* note 99, at 22.

105. DUTHIE, *supra* note 99, at 18.

106. *See, e.g.*, HUMAN RIGHTS WATCH, SEEKING JUSTICE: THE PROSECUTION OF SEXUAL
VIOLENCE IN THE CONGO WAR 8 (2005).

107. *See* Kees Kingma, *The Role of Demobilisation in the Peace and Development Process in
Sub-Saharan Africa: Conditions for Success*, 5 AFRICAN SEC. REV. 1 (1996).

108. For example, the thousands of trials that would need to be conducted would certainly overwhelm the justice system in many post-conflict countries.

109. *See* Stephanie K. Wood, *A Woman Scorned for the "Least Condemned" War Crime:
Precedent and Problems with Prosecuting Rape as a Serious War Crime in the International Criminal Tribunal for Rwanda*, 13 COLUM. J. GENDER & L. 274, 318
(2004).

110. *See generally* PETER SHIRLOW & KIERAN McEVOY, BEYOND THE WIRE FORMER
PRISONERS AND CONFLICT TRANSFORMATION IN NORTHERN IRELAND (2008).

111. *See, e.g.*, Joel R. Reidenberg, *Resolving Conflicting International Data Privacy
Data Rules in Cyberspace*, 52 STAN. L. REV. 1315, 1326–27 (2000) (identifying
ten principles to which an organization must adhere with respect to personal
information).

112. *See, e.g.*, Antonia Sherman, Note, *Sympathy for the Devil: Examining a Defendant's
Right to Confront Before the International Crimes Tribunal*, 10 EMORY INT'L L. REV. 833
(1996).

113. *See generally* Roman David, *Lustration Laws in Action: The Motives and Evaluation of
Lustration Policy in the Czech Republic and Poland (1989–2001)*, 28 LAW & SOC. IN-
QUIRY 387, 388 (2003); Eric A. Posner & Adrian Vermeule, *Transitional Justice as
Ordinary Justice*, 117 HARV. L. REV. 762, 805 (2004) ("lustration law forces one to
reveal those parts of one's past that are of great relevance to the present."); CTR.
FOR DEMOCRACY & RECONCILIATION IN SOUTHEAST EUROPE, DISCLOSING
HIDDEN HISTORY: LUSTRATION IN THE WESTERN BALKANS (2005) (discussing
implementation of lustration in the Balkans).

114. *See, e.g.*, AMNESTY INT'L, DEMOCRATIC REPUBLIC OF CONGO: MASS RAPE: TIME
FOR REMEDIES 29–30 (2004).

115. DUTHIE, *supra* note 99, at 22.

116. Beth Dougherty considers a study conducted by a Sierra Leonean NGO on the
views of ex-combatants toward the Sierra Leone Truth and Reconciliation Commission (SLTRC):

A majority of ex-combatants had heard about the SLTRC, supported it, and expressed
a willingness to testify before it . . . in any case only 15% of those surveyed believed
they had done anything wrong. . . .
　　Concern about the SCSL [Special Court for Sierra Leone] and fears for their security (witness protection was rudimentary at best) initially kept ex-combatant participation low. But as the hearings went on, and the SCSL did not pursue those who
testified, more and more ex-combatants came forward. Many ex-combatants wanted
to return to their communities but were afraid of their reception; participating in the
SLTRC was a means of easing the path of reintegration.

Beth K. Dougherty, *Searching for Answers: Sierra Leone's Truth and Reconciliation Commission*, 8 AFR. STUD. Q. 39, 48 (2004).

117. DUTHIE, *supra* note 99.

CHAPTER 7

1. Fionnuala Ní Aoláin, *Towards a Feminist Theory of Harm in Post-Conflict Societies*, 35 QUEENS L.J. 219 (2009).

2. *See, e.g.*, SUSAN BROWNMILLER, AGAINST OUR WILL: MEN, WOMEN, AND RAPE (1975).

3. *See generally* BEVERLY BALOS & MARY LOUISE FELLOWS, LAW AND VIOLENCE AGAINST WOMEN: CASES AND MATERIALS ON SYSTEMS OF OPPRESSION (1994); SUSAN ESTRICH, REAL RAPE (1987).

4. Violence against women in most societies comes in a variety of forms including sex-selective abortion, female infanticide, genital mutilation, incest and sexual abuse, kidnapping and sale, sex trafficking, sexual harassment, rape by strangers and acquaintances, spousal or partner battering, immolation of wives and widows, and murder. *See* Jane L. Dolkart, *Hostile Environment Harassment: Equality, Objectivity, and the Shaping of Legal Standards*, 43 EMORY L. J. 151, 178–79 (1994).

5. By sex-based violence we mean "a wide variety of violence and victimizing acts directed at women because of their gender." *See* Fionnuala Ní Aoláin, *Sex-Based Violence and the Holocaust—A Reevaluation of Harms and Rights in International Law*, 12 YALE J.L. & FEMINISM 43, 44 (2000). *But see* Elisabeth Jean Wood, *Armed Groups and Sexual Violence: When Is Wartime Rape Rare?*, 37 POL. & SOC'Y 131 (2009) (exploring how and why certain conflicts do not manifest persistent resort to sexual violence as a method and means of warfare).

6. *See, e.g.*, Prosecutor v. Miroslav Kvocka et al., Case No. IT-98-30/1-T, Judgment, (November 2, 2001); Prosecutor v. Jean-Paul Akayesu, Judgment, Case No. ICTR 96-4-T (September 2, 1998). *See generally* PATRICIA VISEUR SELLERS, THE PROSECUTION OF SEXUAL VIOLENCE IN CONFLICT: THE IMPORTANCE OF HUMAN RIGHTS AS MEANS OF INTERPRETATION (2006) (noting varying definitions of rape in different international tribunals and arguing that "gender-competent interpretation of the elements of rape is pivotal" for women's equal access to justice under international human rights norms).

7. *See, e.g.*, Katherine Lusby, *Hearing the Invisible Women of Political Rape: Using Oppositional Narrative to Tell a New War Story*, 25 U. TOL. L. REV. 911 (1994).

8. Empirical work on gender-based violence has clearly demonstrated this link in the context of violence experienced by women during the Holocaust. *See* Ní Aoláin, *supra* note 5, at 50–56.

9. Ní Aoláin, *supra* note 1.

10. *See, e.g.*, ROBIN WEST, CARING FOR JUSTICE (1997).

11. *See* Ní Aoláin, *supra* note 5; Ní Aoláin, *supra* note 1.

12. *See* Frances Stewart, *Crisis Prevention: Tackling Horizontal Inequalities*, 28 OXFORD DEV. STUD. 245 (2000). *See also* Ismael Muvingi, *Sitting on Powder Kegs: Socioeconomic Rights in Transitional Societies*, 3 INT'L J. TRANSITIONAL JUST. 163 (2009).

13. The law on the matter has developed piecemeal. Sexual assault in war could have come under some of the following sanctions but lacked primary recognition in its own right. Draft Code of Crimes Against the Peace and Security of Mankind, Art. 21, *in* Rep. of the Int'l Law Comm'n, 46th sess., U.N. Doc A/46/10 (1991). For gendered crime as torture, see Universal Declaration of Human Rights, art. 5, G.A. Res. 217(III) A, U.N. Doc. A/RES/217(III) (December 10,

1948); International Covenant on Civil and Political Rights, art. 7, 999 U.N.T.S. 171 (December 16, 1966); Convention Against Torture and Other Cruel, Inhuman, and Degrading Treatment or Punishment, G.A. Res. 39/46, U.N. Doc A/39/51 (December 10, 1984).

14. *See, e.g.*, Declaration on the Elimination of Violence Against Women, G.A. Res. 48/104, U.N. Doc. A/Res/48/104 (December 20, 1993).

15. U.N. WAR CRIMES COMM'N, 13 LAW REPORTS OF TRIALS OF WAR CRIMINALS 122, 123 (1949).

16. *See, e.g.*, KELLY DAWN ASKIN, WAR CRIMES AGAINST WOMEN: PROSECUTION IN INTERNATIONAL WAR CRIMES TRIBUNALS 44 (1997).

17. *See* United States v. Karl Brandt et al. (*The Medical Case*), 1 NMT 694–738 (1947); 6 TRIAL OF THE MAJOR WAR CRIMINALS BEFORE THE INTERNATIONAL MILITARY TRIBUNAL 211–13 (1947) [hereinafter INTERNATIONAL MILITARY TRIBUNAL].

18. *See* 7 INTERNATIONAL MILITARY TRIBUNAL, *supra* note 17, at 456–57.

19. *See id.* at 406, 455, 467. Notably the link between the criminalization of sex between Germans and non-Aryans made the link between rape and murder an inevitable one in many contexts. *See* INGO MÜLLER, HITLER'S JUSTICE: THE COURTS OF THE THIRD REICH 97 (Deborah Lucas Schneider trans., 1991).

20. Council Control Law No. 10, Punishment of Persons Guilty of War Crimes, Crimes Against Peace and Against Humanity, December 20, 1945, 3 OFFICIAL GAZETTE CONTROL COUNCIL FOR GERMANY 50–55 (1946).

21. "[P]risoners of war were murdered, beaten, tortured and otherwise ill-treated, and female prisoners were raped by members of the Japanese forces." IMT for the Far East, Indictment, app. D § I, *reprinted in* NEIL BOSITER & ROBERT CRYER, THE TOKYO INTERNATIONAL MILITARY TRIBUNAL: A REAPPRAISAL 59 (2008).

22. ASKIN, *supra* note 16, at 167 n.556.

23. *See generally* THE TOKYO WAR CRIMES TRIAL: THE COMPLETE TRANSCRIPTS OF THE PROCEEDINGS OF THE INTERNATIONAL MILITARY TRIBUNAL FOR THE FAR EAST (John R. Pritchard & Sonia M. Zaide eds., 1981) [hereinafter TOKYO WAR CRIMES TRIAL].

24. 2 TOKYO WAR CRIMES TRIAL, *supra* note 23, at 2572–73 (testimony of Hsu Chuan-Ying).

25. *Id.* at 4470 (affidavit of Mr. James McCallum).

26. 6 TOKYO WAR CRIMES TRIAL, *supra* note 23, at 13, 641–42 (statement of Major de Weerd).

27. For example, the President of the IMFTE, Justice Webb, interrupted defense counsel during a line of questioning by saying "[y]ou are assuming that, if the Japanese [raped], they were just reprisals. Rape and murder of women . . . could never be reprisals, and it is useless to continue your cross examination along these lines." 2 TOKYO WAR CRIMES TRIAL, *supra* note 23, at 2585. This was not true of all justices. *See, e.g.*, *id.* at 1063–68 (Justice Pal, dissenting).

28. Dianne Luping, *Investigation and Prosecution of Sexual and Gender-Based Crimes Before the International Criminal Court*, 17 AM. U. J. GENDER SOC. POL'Y & L. 431, 439 (2009).

29. Geneva Convention Relative to the Protection of Civilian Persons in Time of War, art. 27, ¶ 2, August 12, 1949, 6 U.S.T. 3516, 75 U.N.T.S. 287 [hereinafter Fourth Geneva Convention].

30. Protocol Additional to the Geneva Conventions of August 12, 1949, and Relating to the Protection of Victims in International Armed Conflicts, Annex I, June 8, 1977, U.N. Doc. A/32/144, 16 I.L.M. 1391 [hereinafter Protocol I].

31. *See generally* Danise Aydelott, *Mass Rape During War: Prosecuting Bosnian Rapists Under International Law*, 7 EMORY INT'L. L. REV. 585 (1993); Laurel Fletcher, Allyn Taylor, & Joan Fitzpatrick, *Human Rights Violations Against Women*, 15 WHITTIER L. REV. 319 (1994); Kathleen M. Pratt & Laurel E. Fletcher, *Time for Justice: The Case for International Prosecutions of Rape and Gender-Based Violence in the Former Yugoslavia*, 9 BERKELEY WOMEN'S L.J. 77 (1994).

32. The four Conventions are: Geneva Convention for the Amelioration of the Condition of Wounded and Sick in Armed Forces in the Field, August 12, 1949, 6 U.S.T. 3114, 75 U.N.T.S. 31 [hereinafter First Geneva Convention]; Geneva Convention for the Amelioration of the Condition of Wounded, Sick, and Shipwrecked Members of Armed Forces at Sea, August 12, 1949, 6 U.S.T. 3217, 75 U.N.T.S. 85 [hereinafter Second Geneva Convention]; Geneva Convention Relative to the Treatment of Prisoners of War, August 12, 1949, 6 U.S.T. 3316, 75 U.N.T.S. 135 [hereinafter Third Geneva Convention]; Fourth Geneva Convention, *supra* note 29.

33. Thus, commentators such as Theodor Meron argued that "[u]nder a broad construction, Article 46 of the Hague Regulations can be considered to cover rape. . . ." Theodor Meron, *Rape as a Crime Under International Humanitarian Law*, 87 AM. J. INT'L. L. 424, 425 (1993).

34. International Tribunal for the Prosecution of Persons Responsible for Serious Violations of International Humanitarian Law Committed in the Territory of the Former Yugoslavia Since 1991, Updated Statute of the International Criminal Tribunal for the Former Yugoslavia, U.N. Doc. S/25704 at 36, annex (1993) and S/25704/Add.1 (1993), adopted by Security Council on May 25, 1993, U.N. Doc. S/RES/827 (1993) [hereinafter ICTY Statute].

35. "The International Tribunal shall have the power to prosecute persons committing or ordering to be committed grave breaches of the Geneva Conventions of August 12, 1949, namely the following acts against persons or property protected under the provisions of the relevant Geneva Convention . . . (b) torture or inhuman treatment, including biological experiments . . ." *Id.* art. 2.

36. In parallel, developments in post-conflict accountability for sexual violence have been accompanied by concurrent jurisprudence from the European Human Rights Convention system acknowledging rape to constitute torture and inhuman treatment. *See* Cyprus v. Turkey, App. no. 6780/74 and 6950/75, 4 Eur. H.R. Rep. 482, 537 (1982) (recognizing acts of rape by Turkish soldiers in Cyprus to be "inhuman treatment," although not recognizing them as torture). *See also* Aydin v. Turkey, App. No. 25660/94, Eur. Ct. H.R. (2005) (defining rape as torture). Specifically, rape unequivocally violates prohibitions against torture under certain circumstances, particularly where the violence is carried out by a public official acting in a public capacity. *See, e.g.*, U.N. Commission of Experts, *Report of the Commission of Experts Established Pursuant to Security Council 780*, ¶ 135, U.N. Doc. S/1994/674 (May 27, 1994).

37. *See* Catharine A. MacKinnon, *Turning Rape into Pornography: Postmodern Genocide*, *in* MASS RAPE: THE WAR AGAINST WOMEN IN BOSNIA-HERZEGOVINA 73, 75 (Alexandra Stiglmayer ed., 1994).

38. ICTY Statute, *supra* note 34, art. 4(2)(b).

39. *Id.* art. 4 (2)(d).

40. *Id.* art. 5(g).

41. *See* Rome Statute of the International Criminal Court, adopted by the U.N. Diplomatic Conference of Plenipotentiatics on the Establishment of an International Criminal Court on July 17, 1998, arts. 1, 15, 126, U.N. Doc. A/CONF. 183/9 (1998), 37 I.L.M. 999 [hereinafter Rome Statute].

42. *Id.* art. 3.
43. *Id.* art. 7(1)(g).
44. *Id.* at art. 7 (defining a crime against humanity as prohibited conduct that is part of an "attack," against "any civilian population," which involves the multiple commission of specified acts "pursuant to or in furtherance of a State or organizational policy to commit such an act," and clarifying that the violations must be systematic or widespread).
45. *See, e.g., id.* at art. 68(2) (creating a provision for the presentation of sensitive evidence, such as sex-based crimes). On this basis, the trial can move to an in camera hearing to protect confidential or sensitive evidence.
46. The language of Article 43(6) of the Rome Statute creating a permanent international criminal court is drawn from the ad hoc tribunals, and one would expect its practices to follow. *See generally* International Criminal Court, Victims and Witnesses Unit, http://www.icc-cpi.int/Menus/ICC/Structure+of+the+Court/Protection/Victims+and+Witness+Unit.htm (last visited November 30, 2010) (describing the work of the ICC Victims and Witnesses Unit); INTERNATIONAL CRIMINAL COURT, SUMMARY REPORT ON THE ROUND TABLE ON THE PROTECTION OF VICTIMS AND WITNESSES APPEARING BEFORE THE INTERNATIONAL CRIMINAL COURT (2009).
47. International Tribunal for the Prosecution of Persons Responsible for Serious Violations of International Humanitarian Law Committed in the Territory of the Former Yugoslavia since 1991, Rules of Procedure and Evidence 34, U.N. Doc. IT/32/Rev. 43 (July 24, 2009) [hereinafter ICTY R. EVID.].
48. *See* ESTRICH, *supra* note 3, at 10–11.
49. *See* Nicola Henry, *Witness to Rape: The Limits and Potential of International War Crimes Trials for Victims of Wartime Sexual Violence*, 3 INT'L J. TRANSITIONAL JUST. 114 (2009).
50. *See generally* Gaëlle Breton-Le Goff, *Analysis of Trends in Sexual Violence Prosecutions in Indictments by the International Criminal Tribunal for Rwanda, Coalition for (ICTR) From November 1995 to November 2002*, COALITION FOR WOMEN'S HUMAN RIGHTS IN CONFLICT SITUATIONS (November 28, 2002), http://www.womensrightscoalition.org/site/advocacyDossiers/rwanda/rapeVictimssDeniedJustice/analysisoftrends_en.php (documenting that more than half of the ICTR prosecutions initiated between 1995 and 2002 involved crimes of sexual violence).
51. *See* Emily Haslam, *Law, Civil Society, and Contested Justice at the International Criminal Tribunal for Rwanda, in* PATHS TO INTERNATIONAL JUSTICE: SOCIAL AND LEGAL PERSPECTIVES 57, 61–62 (Marie-Bénédicte Dembour & Tobias Kelly eds., 2007).
52. Despite a reputation for greater inclusivity of gender crimes, similar concerns have been raised in the context of the Special Court for Sierra Leone. *See* SARA KENDALL & MICHELLE STAGGS, U. C. BERKELEY WAR CRIMES STUD. CTR., SILENCING SEXUAL VIOLENCE: RECENT DEVELOPMENTS IN THE CDF CASE AT THE SPECIAL COURT FOR SIERRA LEONE 7–9 (2005).
53. *See* Doris Buss, *Re-thinking "Rape as a Weapon of War,"* FEM. LEG. STUD. (2009), at 145.
54. *See, e.g.,* Prosecutor v. Dragoljub Kunarac, Radomir Kovac, Zoran Vukovic, Case No. IT-96-23-T & IT-96-23/1-T, Judgment (Int'l Crim. Trib. for the Former Yugoslavia February 22, 2001).
55. The Security Council established the International Tribunal pursuant to Resolution 808. *See* S.C. Res. 808, U.N. Doc. S/RES/808 (February 22, 1993).

56. *See* Marlise Simons, *U.N. Court, for First Time, Defines Rape as War Crime*, N.Y. TIMES, June 28, 1996, at A1, A10.

57. *See* AMNESTY INTERNATIONAL, BOSNIA-HERZEGOVINA: RAPE AND SEXUAL ABUSE BY ARMED FORCES (1993); HELSINKI WATCH, WAR CRIMES IN BOSNIA-HERZEGOVINA (1992); THE INTERNATIONAL'S WOMEN'S HUMAN RIGHTS CLINIC OF THE CITY UNIVERSITY OF NEW YORK, GENDER JUSTICE AND THE CONSTITUTION OF THE WAR CRIMES TRIBUNAL PURSUANT TO SECURITY COUNCIL RESOLUTION 808 (1993).

58. *See, e.g.*, Submission of the National Alliance of Women's Organizations to the Secretary General and Others, March 31, 1993, *in* 2 VIRGINIA MORRIS & MICHAEL P. SCHARF, AN INSIDER'S GUIDE TO THE INTERNATIONAL CRIMINAL TRIBUNAL FOR THE FORMER YUGOSLAVIA: A DOCUMENTARY HISTORY AND ANALYSIS 399 (1995) [hereinafter National Alliance of Women's Organizations].

59. *See, e.g.*, Akayesu, Case No. ICTR-96-4-T, ¶596 (defining rape as "a physical invasion of a sexual nature, committed on a person under circumstances which are coercive").

60. *See* Prosecutor v. Delalic et al. ("Celebici Camp"), Case No. IT-96-21-T, Judgment (Int'l Crim. Trib. for the Former Yugoslavia November 16, 1998). Joint Trial of Delalic, Mucic, Delic, and Landzo for various offenses in relation to charges including killing, torture, sexual assault, inhumane conditions, and unlawful confinement of civilians.

61. *See* Akayesu, Case No. ICTR-96-4-T.

62. *See* Int'l Crim. Ct., Review Conference of the Rome Statute, *Stocktaking of International Criminal Justice Impact of the Rome Statute System on Victims and Affected Communities*, Doc. No. RC/ST/V/1 (June 10, 2010) [hereinafter Review Conference, Stocktaking].

63. See *id.* at ¶ 16 (contribution of Ms. Rehn).

64. *See* Patricia M. Wald, *Guest Blogger*, INTLAWGRRLS (October 5, 2009, 6:06 AM), http://intlawgrrls.blogspot.com/2009/10/guest-blogger-patricia-m-wald.html. Judge Wald served as a judge on the ICTY.

65. Note that at time of writing, thirty-four programs were currently in place in the eastern Democratic Republic of Congo, in northern Uganda, and, in the near future, in the Central African Republic, reaching approximately 42,000 individuals. The Fund, however, continues to require state contributions (which are voluntary), making it susceptible to cuts and lack of priority for member states. Review Conference, Stocktaking, *supra* note 62, ¶ 31.

66. The Statute of the Yugoslav Tribunal was originally published as Annex to the Report of the Secretary-General pursuant to paragraph 2 of Security Council resolution 808. Article 15 states, "The judges of the International Tribunal shall adopt rules of procedure and evidence for the conduct of the pre-trial phase of the proceedings, trials and appeals, the admission of evidence, the protection of victims and witnesses and other appropriate matters." ICTY Statute, *supra* note 34, art. 15.

67. ICTY R. EVID., *supra* note 47, 89(a).

68. *See, e.g.*, BROWNMILLER, *supra* note 2; ANDREA DWORKIN, INTERCOURSE (1987); SUSAN S. M. EDWARDS, FEMALE SEXUALITY AND THE LAW (C. M. Campbell & Paul Wiles eds., 1981); Susan Estrich, *Rape*, 95 YALE L. REV. 1087 (1986).

69. EDWARDS, *supra* note 68, at 49.

70. The Rules of Procedure and Evidence find their basis in the Secretary-General's report that recommended the preparation and adoption of rules by the judicial

bench as a whole. *See* U.N. Secretary-General, *Report of the Secretary-General Pursuant to Paragraph 2 of Security Council Resolution 808*, U.N. Doc. S/25704 (1993); Kate Fitzgerald, *Problems of Prosecution and Adjudication of Rape and Other Sexual Assaults Under International Law*, 8 EUR. J. INT'L. L. 638 (1997). Jennifer Green, Rhonda Copelon, Patrick Cotter, & Beth Stephens, *Affecting the Rules for the Prosecution of Rape and Other Gender-Based Violence Before the International Criminal Tribunal for the Former Yugoslavia: A Feminist Proposal and Critique*, 5 HASTINGS WOMEN'S L.J. 171 (1994).

71. ICTY R. EVID., *supra* note 47, 34(b) (stating, "Due consideration shall be given, in the appointment of staff, to the employment of qualified women.").

72. *See* INTLAWGRRLS, *supra* note 64.

73. National Alliance of Women's Organizations, *supra* note 58, at 401. NGO submission to the judicial chamber stressed the significance of equal gender representation, specifically the need to have those who dealt with victims of sex crimes to be primarily women.

74. *See* ICTY R. EVID., *supra* note 47, 69(A), 75(B). The Rule also allows that proceedings may be held in camera.

75. General Framework Agreement for Peace in Bosnia and Herzegovina, 35 I.L.M. 75 (1995) [hereinafter Dayton Agreement]. *See generally* John R. W. D. Jones, *The Implications of the Peace Agreement for the International Criminal Tribunal for the Former Yugoslavia*, 7 E.J. INT'L. L. 226 (1996).

76. Repatriation and reintegration were ostensible cornerstones of the Dayton Agreement, guaranteed by the Constitution of Bosnia and Herzegovina. *See* Dayton Agreement, *supra* note 75, at Annex 4; James A. Goldstone, *Crime Still Pays in Bosnia*, WALL ST. J., November 26, 1996.

77. *See* AMNESTY INTERNATIONAL, *supra* note 57, at 1–2.

78. The Report of the UN Special Rapporteur on the Former Yugoslavia to the 49th Session of the U.N. Commission on Human Rights has recorded that:

> Fear of reprisals against themselves and their families, some of whom may still be in the areas affected by the conflict, also makes victims unwilling to speak. . . . Some of the women met by the team of experts felt exploited by the media and the many missions "studying" rape in the former Yugoslavia. Furthermore, health care providers were concerned about the effects on women of repeatedly recounting their experiences without adequate psychological and social systems in place.

> U.N. Special Rapporteur on the Former Yugoslavia to the 49th Session of the U.N. Commission on Human Rights, ¶¶ 51–52, U.N. Doc. E/CN.4/1993/50 (1993).

79. The general principles on the admissibility of evidence are contained in Rules 89 of the ICTY and ICTR Rules. The provisions allow the judicial chamber to admit any relevant evidence that it deems to have probative value. ICTY R. EVID., *supra* note 47, 89(c).

80. ICTY R. EVID., *supra* note 47, 101(b)(i).

81. *See* Alexandra Stiglmayer, *The Rapes in Bosnia-Herzegovina*, in MASS RAPE, *supra* note 37, at 82 (recounting the stories of women raped during the war).

82. *See, e.g., id.* at 119 (relating another woman's story who said, "My daughter was raped along with me. First he raped me, and then I had to watch while he raped my little girl.").

83. For example, Rule 96 of both the ICTY and ICTR statutes specifically relates to the presentation of evidence in cases of sexual assault.

84. *See also* C. P. M. Cleiren & M. E. M. Tijssen, *Substantive and Procedural Issues: Rape and Other Forms of Sexual Assault in the Armed Conflict in the Former Yugoslavia: Legal, Procedural, and Evidentiary Issues*, 5 Crim. L.F. 471, 505 (1994).

85. Susan Estrich points out that while the formal requirement has been abandoned by American jurisdictions, in practice it remains a critical factor in determining the disposition of rape charges today. Estrich, *supra* note 3, at 43.

86. The ICTR and ICTY rules of evidence specifically prohibit the prior sexual conduct of the victim from being admitted into evidence. ICTY R. Evid., *supra* note 47, 96(iv).

87. Note the so-called Rape Shield provisions of the United States. *See* Fed. R Evid. 412(b).

88. Universal Declaration of Human Rights, G.A. Res. 217 (III) A, arts. 1–2, U.N. Doc. A/810 (December 10, 1948); International Covenant on Civil and Political Rights (ICCPR), G.A. Res. 2200A(XXI), arts. 2–3, U.N. Doc. A/6316 (December 16, 1966); Declaration on the Elimination of Discrimination Against Women, G.A. Res. 2263, at 35, U.N. Doc. A/6716 (November 7, 1967); Convention on the Elimination of All Forms of Discrimination Against Women, G.A. Res. 34/180, at 193, U.N. Doc. A/34/36 (December 18, 1979).

89. ICTY R. Evid., *supra* note 47, 96(ii)(a)–(b).

90. *See, e.g.*, Lotta Teale, *Addressing Gender-Based Violence in the Sierra Leone Conflict: Notes from the Field*, 9 Afr. J. Conflict Resolution 69, 76 (November 2009) (describing the reports on the costs of the Sierra Leone Tribunal and explaining that by mid-2008 the Court had already cost more than US$150 million, in a country where 75 percent of the population live on less than US$2 a day).

91. *See, e.g.*, Criminology, Conflict Resolution, and Restorative Justice (Kieran McEvoy & Tim Newburn eds., 2003).

92. *See* Deepak Mehta & Roma Chatterji, *Boundaries, Names, Alterities: A Case Study of a "Communal Riot" in Dharavi, Bombay*, in Remaking a World: Violence, Social Suffering, and Recovery 200, 221 (Veena Das et al. eds., 2001). *See also* Renos K. Papadopoulos, *Destructiveness, Atrocities, and Healing: Epistemological and Clinical Reflections*, 43 J. Analytical Psych. 455, 466 (1998).

93. *See* Mehta & Chatterji, *supra* note 92, at 207.

94. *See* Henry, *supra* note 49, at 121.

95. *See generally* Allison Morris, *Critiquing the Critics*, 42 Brit. J. Criminology 596, 609 (2002) (arguing that while critics of restorative justice may say it incites vigilantism, its core principles are fundamentally at odds with abusive self-help remedies).

96. *See* Allison Corey & Sandra F. Joireman, *Retributive Justice: The Gacaca Courts in Rwanda*, 103 Afr. Aff. 73 (2004).

97. The *Gacaca* courts were established by Rwandan organic law number 40/2000 on January 26, 2001. The law applies to persons who, between October 1990 and December 31, 1994, committed crimes of genocide or crimes against humanity and war crimes as defined by the Genocide Convention of 1948 and the Geneva Conventions of 1949 with the Additional Protocols of 1979. *See Organic Law No. 40/2000 of 26/01/2001 Setting Up "Gacaca Jurisdictions" and Organizing Prosecutions for Offenses Constituting the Crime of Genocide or Crimes Against Humanity Committed Between October 1, 1990 and December 31, 1994 (Rwanda)*.

98. *But see* Human Rights Watch, Struggling to Survive: Barriers to Justice for Rape Victims in Rwanda (2004) [hereinafter HRW, Struggling to Survive].

99. Clotilde Twagiramariya & Meredeth Turshen, *"Favours" to Give and "Consenting" Victims: The Sexual Politics of Survival in Rwanda, in* What Women Do in Wartime: Gender and Conflict in Africa 101, 113–14 (Meredeth Turshen & Clotilde Twagiramariya eds., 1998).

100. *See* Corey & Joireman, *supra* note 96, at 84.

101. *See* HRW, Struggling to Survive, *supra* note 98, at 30.

102. *Id.*

103. *See id.* at 2 (documenting various obstacles facing the *Gacaca* system even with the advent of the new safeguards).

104. *Id.* at 33.

105. *Id.* at 3.

106. The lack of significance attributed to sexual violence, and rape in particular, is illustrated by the fact that the Restatement (Third) on Foreign Relations Law of the United States largely ignores the issue.

107. *See, e.g.,* Françoise Nduwimana, The Right to Survive: Sexual Violence, Women and HIV/AIDS 34–35 (2004).

108. It is worth noting that domestic law of the now defunct Socialist Federal Republic of Yugoslavia (SFRY) was distinctly deficient in relation to gender-specific violence. *See* National Alliance of Women's Organizations, *supra* note 58, at 402.

CHAPTER 8

1. *See* Brandon Hamber & Steve Kibble, From Truth to Transformation: The Truth and Reconciliation Commission in South Africa 1–3 (1999).

2. *See generally* Priscilla Hayner, Unspeakable Truths: Confronting State Terror and Atrocity (2001).

3. *See, e.g.,* Nahla Abdo, *Nationalism and Feminism: Palestinian Women and the Intifada—No Going Back, in* Gender and National Identity Women and Politics in Muslim Societies 152–57 (Valentine Moghadem ed., 1994).

4. For general examples of the broad and deep literature on criminal accountability for harms against women, *see* Beverly Allen, Rape Warfare: The Hidden Genocide in Bosnia-Herzegovina and Croatia (1996); Rhonda Copelon, *Gendered War Crimes: Reconceptualizing Rape in Times of War, in* Women's Rights, Human Rights: International Feminist Perspectives 197–214 (Julie Peters & Andrea Wolper eds., 1995); Christine Chinkin, *Rape and Sexual Abuse of Women in International Law,* 5 Eur. J. Int'l L. 326 (1994).

5. An issue that arises at the outset is whether truth or truths are the appropriate terminology to utilize in this context. We prefer "truths," as the term captures a wider array of complexities and captures the incompatibilities that arise when dealing with complicated pasts.

6. *See, e.g.,* Hayner, *supra* note 2.

7. Rama Mani, *Dilemmas of Expanding Transitional Justice, or Forging the Nexus Between Transitional Justice and Development,* 2 Intl J. Transitional Just. 253 (2008).

8. *See, e.g.,* Impunity and Human Rights in International Law and Practice (Naomi Roht-Arriaza ed., 1995); Diane F. Orentlicher, *Settling Accounts: The Duty to Prosecute Human Rights Violations of a Prior Regime,* 100 Yale L.J. 2537 (1991); Anonymous, *Human Rights in Peace Negotiations,* 18 Hum. Rts. Q. 249 (1996).

9. *See, e.g.,* Andrea Bartoli, *Learning from the Mozambique Peace Process: The Role of the Community of Sant'Egidio, in* Paving the Way: Contributions of Interactive Conflict Resolution to Peacemaking 79 (Ronald J. Fisher ed., 2005); Sara B.

Miller, *Spain Begins to Confront Its Past*, CHRISTIAN SCI. MONITOR, February 6, 2003.

10. *See, e.g.*, Tom Hadden, *Punishment, Amnesty, and Truth: Legal and Political Approaches, in* DEMOCRACY AND ETHNIC CONFLICT 196 (Adrian Guelke ed., 2004).

11. Sheila Meintjes, *"Gendered Truth"? Legacies of the South African Truth and Reconciliation Commission*, 9 AFR. J. OF CONFLICT RESOL. 101, 109 (2009).

12. As Angela Hegarty critically notes, truth processes should not be assumed to have positive political motives. Rather, they can be established as mechanisms to hide, distort, and manipulate the truth. Angela Hegarty, *Truth, Law, and Official Denial: The Case of Bloody Sunday*, 15 CRIM. L.F. 199, 200, 212 (2004). *See also* LOUISE MALLINDER, AMNESTY HUMAN RIGHTS AND POLITICAL TRANSITIONS: BRIDGING THE PEACE AND JUSTICE DIVIDE (2008).

13. Former ICTY Prosecutor Richard Goldstone has argued (in the context of Bosnia) that "[w]hile [the international] judicial process is essential for reconciliation to begin, it is insufficient alone to satisfy the human need for knowing the truth of a tragic series of events. In addition to criminal prosecutions, it is necessary for a damaged society to arrive at a wider understanding of the causes of its suffering. For no matter how well the tribunal does its job, the scope of history is far broader than proving the guilt of a few specific individuals." Richard J. Goldstone, *Ethnic Reconciliation Needs the Help of a Truth Commission*, INT'L HERALD TRIB., October 24, 1998, Opinion, at 6.

14. HAYNER, *supra* note 2, at 24–31.

15. Although some truth processes premise the absence of criminal accountability on full and frank disclosure, there is increasing agreement that certain categories of crime cannot be excluded from the scope of criminal accountability, notably Genocide and Crimes Against Humanity. *See, e.g.*, HAYNOR *id.* at 43 (discussing South Africa's amnesty provisions). For consideration of the status of amnesties for international crimes, note the decision of the Special Court for Sierra Leone in Prosecutor v. Kallon (Case no. SCSL-2004-15-AR72(E)) and Prosecutor v. Kamara (Case No. SCSL-2004-16-AR72(E)). These decisions considered, inter alia, the effect of Security Council Resolution 1315, which states that the "United Nations hold the understanding that the amnesty provisions of the Agreement shall not apply to international crimes of genocide, crimes against humanity, war crimes, and other serious violations of international humanitarian law." *See* S.C. Res. 1315, Preamble, U.N. Doc. S/RES/1315 (August 14, 2000).

16. *See, e.g.*, REPORT OF THE CHILEAN NATIONAL COMMISSION ON TRUTH AND RECONCILIATION 792 (Philip E. Berryman trans., 1993) [hereinafter CHILEAN REPORT]. The first chapter of the Report is dedicated to the political context in which the violations under consideration occurred. The Report states, "[I]t is absolutely essential that we understand the crisis of 1973, both in order to understand how subsequent human rights violations we were charged to investigate came about and to prevent their recurrence." *Id.* at 47.

17. *See* Kader Asmal, *Truth, Reconciliation, and Justice: The South African Experience in Perspective*, 63 MOD. L. REV. 1, 12–13 (2000).

18. *See, e.g.*, HAYNER, *supra* note 2, at 27–28.

19. Kirk Simpson, *Victims of Political Violence: A Habermasian Model of Truth Recovery*, 6 J. HUM. RTS. 325, 329 (2007).

20. HAYNER, *supra* note 2, at 28.

21. *Id.*

22. *Id.*

23. *Id.* at 24–31.

24. The Chilean Report acknowledges these characteristics when it states, "Our study of the crisis will deal basically with its immediate causes, especially with those of a political and ideological nature. The Commission is well aware that the crisis had deeper social and economic roots, but to explore them any further than simply mentioning them would have meant going beyond its task and beyond the direct object of the present chapter." CHILEAN REPORT, *supra* note 16, at 47.

25. *See, e.g.*, Vasuki Nesiah, *Truth Commissions and Gender: Principals, Policies, and Procedures* 43–44 (International Center for Transitional Justice, July 2006).

26. As an example, Sierra Leone's TRC extensively analyzed the causes of conflict and the patterns of social injustice and recommended a series of measures to provide redress and prevent recurrence. *See, e.g.*, Lotta Teale, *Addressing Gender-Based Violations in the Sierra Leone Conflict: Notes from the Field*, 9 AFR. J. CONFLICT RESOL. 69 (2009) (noting that beyond its analysis of the causes of the conflict, the Sierra Leone TRC made substantial efforts to support witnesses and victims).

27. *See* Anne Orford, *Commissioning the Truth*, 15 COLUM. J. GENDER & L. 813, 856–64 (2006); Fionnuala Ní Aoláin & Catherine Turner, *Gender, Truth, and Transition*, 16 UCLA L. REV. 229 (2008).

28. In many conflicts, such groups tend to disproportionately experience the human rights violations because of their vulnerability as the minority group. There are exceptions to this, such as in South Africa, where the majority population experienced the human rights violations.

29. *See, e.g.*, Christine Bell, *Dealing with the Past in Northern Ireland*, 26 FORDHAM INT'L L.J. 1095 (2003); FIONNUALA NÍ AOLÁIN, THE POLITICS OF FORCE—CONFLICT MANAGEMENT AND STATE VIOLENCE IN NORTHERN IRELAND (2000).

30. *See, e.g.*, FIONA ROSS, BEARING WITNESS: WOMEN AND THE TRUTH AND RECONCILIATION COMMISSION IN SOUTH AFRICA 50 (2003).

31. HAMBER & KIMBLE, *supra* note 1.

32. For example, Veena Das has conducted a highly relevant study of widows among urban Punjabi families, some of whom had been displaced after the Partition of India, and examines the subjectivity of women in the context of violence and subject formation. She notes that "to be vulnerable is not the same as to be a victim, and those who are inclined to assume that social norms or expectations of widowhood are automatically translated into oppression need to pay attention to the gap between a norm and its actualization." Veena Das, *The Act of Witnessing: Violence, Poisonous Knowledge, and Subjectivity, in* VIOLENCE AND SUBJECTIVITY 205, 209 (Veena Das et al. eds., 2000).

33. *See, e.g.*, Article 15 of the European Convention on Human Rights (ECHR), which specifics the right to life, the right to be free from torture, freedom from slavery, and freedom from ex post facto laws as the sole nonderogable rights under the ECHR.

34. Vasuki Nesiah, Paper presented to a conference on Women and Human Rights in Belfast, May 20, 2005 (on file with authors).

35. Fionnuala Ní Aoláin, *Towards a Feminist Theory of Harm in Conflicted and Post-Conflict Societies*, 35 QUEENS L. REV. 219 (2009).

36. Nesiah, *supra* note 34, at 909.

37. *See* Amrit Srinivasan, *The Survivor in the Study of Violence, in* MIRRORS OF VIOLENCE: COMMUNITIES, RIOTS, AND SURVIVORS IN SOUTH ASIA 305, 311 (Veena Das ed., 1990).

38. Even in more recent truth commission formats, where attempts have been made to involve women more centrally, success has been limited. In 2002 Ghana's National Reconciliation Committee elected to "mainstream" gender throughout its operation and therefore did not hold separate public hearings for women. With good intentions, gender-based violations were subsumed into the broader catalogue of violations. Women submitted less than 20 percent of all testimonies. *See* Helen Scanlon & Kelli Muddell, *Gender and Transitional Justice in Africa: Progress and Prospects*, 9 AFR. J. OF CONFLICT RESOL. 9, 12 (2009).

39. Some limited evidence of this exists through the testimony of women to the El Salvador Truth Commission. *See generally* U.N Commission on Human Rights, *Final Report on the Situation of Human Rights in El Salvador Submitted to the Commission on Human Rights by Professor José Antonio Pastor Ridruejo in Fulfillment of the Mandate Conferred Under Commission Resolution 1985/53.* U.N. Doc. E/CN.4/1986/22 (February 3, 1986).

40. *See* Simona Sharoni, *Rethinking Women's Struggles in Israel-Palestine and in the North of Ireland, in* VICTIMS, PERPETRATORS, OR ACTORS? GENDER, ARMED CONFLICT, AND POLITICAL VIOLENCE 87 (Moser & Clark eds., 2001). Sharoni also notes that "[i]n both Palestine and the North of Ireland . . . women's political involvement began with their attempts to protect their homes, families and communities rather than with a conscious attempt to move beyond the confines of the private sphere into the broader political arena." *Id.* at 93.

41. For an exploration of how this maps onto Northern Ireland, see ALLEN FELDMAN, FORMATIONS OF VIOLENCE: THE NARRATIVES OF BODY AND POLITICAL TERROR IN NORTHERN IRELAND 85–97 (1991). Feldman notes that it was in the collective experiences of daily violation of local traditions, of "moral right" community and familial and domestic integrity by the army and police rather than a fully worked-out resistance ideology that contributed to ordinary women's politicization. *Id.*

42. The range of truth processes in Africa alone include: Uganda (1974), Zimbabwe (1985), Uganda (1986), Chad (1991), Rwanda (1992), Burundi (1995), South Africa (1995), Nigeria (1999), Sierra Leone (2002), Ghana (2002), and Liberia (2007). Recent peace processes in Burundi, Togo, and Kenya also have had commitments to truth commissions.

43. An extensive amount of literature documents the experiences of Indian Sikhs following the assassination of Indira Ghandi, specifically in New Dehli. As Amrit Srinivasan notes: "The violation of the home, whether religiously or domestically defined, formed a common thread in the Sikhs' own perception of Operation Bluestar (a military operation) as an outrage of essentially the same order as the November killings (a populist action)." Srinivasan, *supra* note 37.

44. Thus, a study of riots in a shanty town called Dharavi in Bombay (December 7, 1992), following the destruction of a significant mosque (Babri Masjid) in Ayodhya, Uttar Pradesh, describes the violation of the home in the words of one victim (Faridabi) as follows:

On the twenty-fourth the police came to my house. . . . The "scene-shot" was like this: when I opened the door they asked me to show them where the men were hidden. I told them there was no one in this house. They wouldn't listen. They took my two alarm clocks and a Citizen wall clock. When I protested they rifle-butted me in the stomach. Ever since my stomach has become hard. . . . One of them kicked the cupboard. Now it doesn't close. . . .

See Deepak Mehta & Roma Chatterji, *Boundaries, Names, Alterities: A Case Study of a Communal Riot, in* REMAKING A WORLD: VIOLENCE SOCIAL SUFFERING AND RECOVERY 200, 221 (Veena Das ed., 2001).

45. Colm Campbell & Ita Connolly, *A Model for the "War Against Terrorism"? Military Intervention in Northern Ireland and the 1970 Falls Curfew*, 30 J.L. AND SOC'Y. 341, 372–73 (2003).

46. Nthabiseng Motsemme, *The Mute Always Speak: On Women's Silences at the Truth and Reconciliation Commission*, 52 CURRENT SOC. 905, 924 (2004). *See also* Veena Das, *Our Work to Cry, Your Work to Listen, in* MIRRORS OF VIOLENCE: COMMUNITIES, RIOTS, AND SURVIVORS IN SOUTH ASIA 345 (Veena Das ed., 1990); Metha & Chatterji, *supra* note 81.

47. Fionnuala Ní Aoláin, *Sex-Based Violence and the Holocaust—A Reevaluation of Harms and Rights in International Law*, 12 YALE J.L. & FEMINISM 43, 57 (2000) (describing how in the context of sex-based violence experienced by women during the Holocaust, perpetrators understood exactly the harms that they were inflicting as did the victim, only the law failed to name appropriately).

48. ROSS, *supra* note 30, at 42–43.

49. Carole Pateman, *Feminist Critiques of the Private/Public Dichotomy, in* PUBLIC AND PRIVATE IN SOCIAL LIFE 281 (S. I. Benn & G. F. Gaus eds., 1983) (noting that "[t]he dichotomy between the private and the public is central to almost two centuries of feminist writing and political struggle, it is, ultimately, what the feminist movement is about."). *See also* Tracy E. Higgins, *Reviving the Public/Private Distinction in Feminist Theorizing*, 75 CHI.-KENT L. REV. 841 (2001).

50. Thanks to Martha Fineman for opening up these ideas.

51. Motsemme, *The Mute Always Speak, supra* note 46, at 910.

52. *Id. See also* Carol M. Kaplan, *Gender and Justice in Africa: Voices Rising: An Essay on Gender, Justice, and Theater in South Africa*, 3 SEATTLE J. SOC. JUST. 711 (2005).

53. *See generally* IRIS MARION YOUNG, THROWING LIKE A GIRL AND OTHER ESSAYS IN FEMINIST PHILOSOPHY (1990); IRIS MARION YOUNG, INCLUSION AND DEMOCRACY (2000) (describing Western notions of agency in respect of elevated forms of speech in political life).

54. *See* ELAINE SCARRY, THE BODY IN PAIN (1985).

55. Das, *Our Work to Cry, supra* note 46. *See also* SCARRY, THE BODY IN PAIN, *supra* note 54.

56. Das, *Our Work to Cry, supra* note 46.

57. ROSS, *supra* note 30, at 50.

58. *Id.* at 17 (noting that "although approximately equal proportions of men and women made statements, for the most part women described the suffering of men whereas men testified about their own experiences of violation.").

59. INTERNATIONAL CENTER FOR TRANSITIONAL JUSTICE, TRUTH COMMISSIONS AND GENDER: PRINCIPLES, POLICIES, AND PROCEDURES (2002).

60. TRUTH AND RECONCILIATION COMMISSION OF PERU, FINAL REPORT OF THE TRUTH AND RECONCILIATION COMMISSION OF PERU, VI § 1.5, VIII § 2.1 (International Center for Transitional Justice trans., 2003).

61. TRUTH AND RECONCILIATION COMMISSION OF PERU, SUMMARY OF THE COMPREHENSIVE REPARATIONS PLAN § 2.2.2.1 (International Center for Transitional Justice trans., 2003) (quoting an earlier summary prepared by the Commission's technical staff on reparations).

62. Our conceptualization and approach to reparations in this section is drawn from THE GENDER OF REPARATIONS, UNSETTLING GENDER HIERARCHIES WHILE REDRESSING HUMAN RIGHTS' VIOLATIONS (Ruth Rubio-Marín ed., 2009).

63. Pablo de Greiff, *Introduction, in* THE HANDBOOK OF REPARATIONS 1, 1–18 (Pablo de Greiff ed., 2006).

64. *See id.* at 4.

65. Ruth Rubio-Marín, *Introduction: A Gender and Reparations Taxonomy, in* THE GENDER OF REPARATIONS, UNSETTLING GENDER HIERARCHIES WHILE REDRESSING HUMAN RIGHTS' VIOLATIONS 1, 17 (Ruth Rubio-Marín ed., 2009).

66. As Ruth Rubio-Marín so cogently reminds us, reparations promise a means to link "individual rights to a broader political project, namely, one that may require the transformation of a pre-existing order when it systematically subordinated certain groups." Ruth Rubio-Marín, *The Gender of Reparations in Transitional Societies, in* THE GENDER OF REPARATIONS, UNSETTLING GENDER HIERARCHIES WHILE REDRESSING HUMAN RIGHTS' VIOLATIONS 63, 70 (Ruth Rubio-Marín ed., 2009) (drawing on Brandon Hamber, *Narrowing the Micro and Macro—A Psychological Perspective on Reparations in Societies in Transition, in* THE HANDBOOK OF REPARATIONS (Pablo de Greiff ed., 2006)).

67. G.A. Res. 60/147 U.N. Doc. A/RES/60/147 (March 21, 2006).

68. For the most comprehensive overview of the theory and practice of this failure, see generally THE GENDER OF REPARATIONS, *supra* note 62, at 1–17.

69. Rubio-Marín, *The Gender of Reparations in Transitional Societies, supra* note 66, at 66.

70. González et al. v. Mexico (*Cotton Field*), 2009 Inter-Am. Ct. H. R. at 148 (November 16, 2009). The court specifically ordered that:

The investigation shall include a gender perspective; undertake specific lines of inquiry concerning sexual violence, which must involve lines of inquiry into the respective patterns in the zone; be conducted in accordance with protocols and manuals that comply with the guidelines set out in this Judgment; provide the victims' next of kin with information on progress in the investigation regularly and give them full access to the case files; and be conducted by officials who are highly trained in similar cases and in dealing with victims of discrimination and gender-based violence.

71. COALITION FOR WOMEN'S HUMAN RIGHTS IN CONFLICT SITUATIONS, NAIROBI DECLARATION ON WOMEN'S AND GIRLS' RIGHT TO A REMEDY AND REPARATION (2007) [hereinafter NAIROBI DECLARATION].

72. In this context, "[g]endered violence is a part of a socio-political economy based on the patriarchal motivation to control women's sexuality and their productive and reproductive capacity." Colleen Duggan, Claudia Paz y Bailey, & Julie Guillerot, *Reparations for Sexual and Reproductive Violence: Prospects for Achieving Gender Justice in Guatemala and Peru,* 2 INT'L J. TRANSITIONAL JUST. 192, 208 (2008).

73. Colleen Duggan & Adila Abusharaf, *Reparation of Sexual Violence and Democratic Transition: In Search of Gender Justice, in* THE HANDBOOK OF REPARATIONS (Pablo de Grief ed. 2006).

74. Rubio-Marín, *The Gender of Reparations in Transitional Societies, supra* note 66, at 78–79.

75. *See generally* Ní Aoláin, *Sex-Based Violence During the Holocaust, supra* note 47.

76. For an example in the South African context, see Beth Goldblatt, *Evaluating the Gender Content of Reparations, in* WHAT HAPPENED TO THE WOMEN? GENDER AND REPARATIONS FOR HUMAN RIGHTS VIOLATIONS 48 (Ruth Rubio-Marín ed., 2006).

77. Rubio-Marín, *The Gender of Reparations in Transitional Societies*, supra note 66, at 73–79.

78. Galuh Wandita, Karen Campbell-Nelson, & Manuela Leong Pereira, *Learning to Engender Reparations in Timor-Leste: Reaching Out to Female Victims, in* WHAT HAP-PENED TO THE WOMEN? GENDER AND REPARATIONS FOR HUMAN RIGHTS VIOLA-TIONS 284, 309 (Ruth Rubio-Marín ed., 2007).

79. We are reminded that "in societies organized around a family structure . . . reflect[ing] a patriarchal culture," women can experience unique "material harm linked to the absence or loss of a . . . breadwinner." *Id.* at 91, 93.

80. NAIROBI DECLARATION, *supra* note 71, at § 3H.

81. Rubio-Marín, *The Gender of Reparations in Transitional Societies*, supra note 66, at 101–08.

82. Clause XI in the U.N. Principles on Reparation, whereby, "the application and in-terpretation of these Principles and Guidelines must be consistent with interna-tional human rights law and international humanitarian law and be without any discrimination of any kind or ground, without exception."

83. *See* Rubio-Marín, *The Gender of Reparations in Transitional Societies*, supra note 66, at 84–85.

84. Jamesina King, *Gender and Reparations in Sierra Leone: The Wounds of War Remain Open, in* WHAT HAPPENED TO THE WOMEN? GENDER AND REPARATIONS FOR HUMAN RIGHTS VIOLATIONS 246, 267–68 (Ruth Rubio-Marín ed., 2007).

85. IER Report (in Arabic) at http://www.ier.ma.

86. Colleen Duggan, Claudia Paz y Bailey, & Julie Guillerot, *Reparations for Sexual and Reproductive Violence: Prospects for Achieving Gender Justice in Guatemala and Peru*, 2 INT'L J. TRANSITIONAL JUST. 192 (2008).

87. *Id.* at 193.

88. *See* Sunila Abeysekera, *Maximizing the Achievement of Women's Rights in Conflict Transformation: The Case of Sri Lanka*, 41 COLUM. J. TRANSNAT'L L. 523, 538–39 (2003). Here it would recognize the effects that sexual harm has on the short-, medium-, and long-term capacity of women to feed, to care, and to support those dependent upon them, including elderly family members and abandoned or orphaned children.

89. JUSTICE AS PREVENTION: VETTING PUBLIC EMPLOYEES IN TRANSITIONAL SOCI-ETIES 17 (Alexander Mayer-Rieckh & Pablo de Greiff eds., 2007).

90. *See generally id.* at 17–20.

91. Ruben Zamora & David Holiday, *The Struggle for Lasting Reform: Vetting Process in El Salvador, in* JUSTICE AS PREVENTION: VETTING PUBLIC EMPLOYEES IN TRANSITIONAL SOCIETIES 80, 87 (Alexander Mayer-Rieckh & Pablo de Greiff eds., 2007).

92. *See generally* Dimitri Sotiropoulos, *Swift Gradualism and Variable Outcomes: Vetting in Post-Authoritarian Greece, in* JUSTICE AS PREVENTION: VETTING PUBLIC EM-PLOYEES IN TRANSITIONAL SOCIETIES 120 (Alexander Mayer-Rieckh & Pablo de Greiff eds., 2007).

93. *See generally* Valeria Barbuto, *Strengthening Democracy: Impugnación Procedures in Argentina, in* JUSTICE AS PREVENTION: VETTING PUBLIC EMPLOYEES IN TRANSI-TIONAL SOCIETIES 40 (Alexander Mayer-Rieckh & Pablo de Greiff eds., 2007).

94. *See generally* Zamora & Holiday, *The Struggle for Lasting Reform*, supra note 91.

95. Jonathan Klaaren, *Institutional Transformation and the Choice Against Vetting, in* JUSTICE AS PREVENTION: VETTING PUBLIC EMPLOYEES IN TRANSITIONAL SOCI-ETIES 146 (Alexander Mayer-Rieckh & Pablo de Greiff eds., 2007).

96. Those with least fanfare, and least formal legal sanction, are often surprisingly the most effective. In Argentina, the operation of the Junta de Calificaciones (qualifying commission) empowered to evaluate promotions decisions within the military was effective in unexpected ways. *See* Barbuto, *Strengthening Democracy, supra* note 95, at 49. While clearly a forward-looking mechanism, it has had interesting past accountability effect by focusing attention on past behavior within a seemingly neutral assessment process that "bites" at the records of military officers seeking advancement, effectively catching prior abuses. In parallel, the operation of the little known work of the Ad Hoc Commission in the El Salvador context (formed after the Peace Agreements to vet the military officer corps) demonstrates that the most effective institutional operators for vetting can be those for whom the least expectations are created. *See* Zamora & Holiday, *The Struggle for Lasting Reform, supra* note 91, at 89.
97. *See, e.g.*, Women, Crime, and Criminal Justice Original Feminist Readings (Claire M. Renzetti & Lynne Goodstein eds., 2000).
98. We note our thanks to Professor Colm Campbell for the origin of this concept and its application to this context.

CHAPTER 9

1. *See generally* Helen Irving, Gender and the Constitution Equity and Agency in Comparative Constitutional Design 1 (2008) (noting that "constitutions frame women's membership of, or absence from, the constitutional community" and "can promote, or alternatively, present obstacles to gender equity and agency").
2. This draws on Helen Irving's important collation of both these concepts as necessary to understanding the full gendered impact of constitutions. *Id.* at 2–3.
3. In this we concur with Irving, who observed that to emphasize provisions on rights alone and statement of equality is to "focus primarily on future judicial review; it is to anticipate a struggle between the legislative and the judicial branches, between the legislative usurper and the constitutional fortress." *Id.* at 29.
4. This section draws heavily on Fionnuala Ní Aoláin & Michael Hamilton, *Gender and the Rule of Law in Transitional Societies*, 18 Minn. J. Int'l. L. 380 (2008).
5. Katherine Pistor, *Launching a Global Rule of Law Movement: Next Steps November 10, 2005*, 25 Berkeley J. Int'l Law 100, 103 (2007) (arguing that indicators need to be developed capable of measuring processes, not merely technocratic outcomes). *See also* Katharine Pistor, Antara Haldar, & Amrit Amirapu, *Social Norms, Rule of Law, and Gender Reality* (July 2–5, 2008) (preliminary draft of paper for World Justice Forum).
6. As Margaret Jane Radin has noted, "when the ideal [of the rule of law] developed, and during most of its long history, it was inconceivable that any individuals who were not 'men' could be a part of political life." Margaret Jane Radin, *Reconsidering the Rule of Law*, 69 B.U. L. Rev. 781, 781 n.1 (1989).
7. Pistor, Halder, & Amirapu, *supra* note 5, at 24.
8. Balakrishnan Rajagopal, *Invoking the Rule of Law in Post-Conflict Rebuilding: A Critical Examination*, 49 Wm. & Mary L. Rev. 1347, 1349 (2007).
9. *See, e.g.*, Frank Upham, *Mythmaking in the Rule of Law Orthodoxy, Carnegie Endowment for International Peace* 7, 14–20 (Carnegie Endowment for International Peace, Rule of Law Paper Series, Working Paper No. 30, 2002).
10. Lynne Henderson, *Authoritarianism and the Rule of Law*, 66 Ind. L.J. 379, 383 (1991). An example of the dangers of a jurisprudential preoccupation with the

duty to obey law is seen in the United States' "long history of governmental tolerance of private oppression of women and children through violence." *Id.*

11. *See* JOSEPH RAZ, THE AUTHORITY OF LAW: ESSAYS ON LAW AND MORALITY 214–18, 221 (Oxford Univ. Press 1979). *But see* Patricia Williams, THE ALCHEMY OF RACE AND RIGHTS (1992).

12. *See generally* Heinz Klug, *Transnational Human Rights: Exploring the Persistence and Globalization of Human Rights*, 1 ANN. REV. L. SOC. SCI. 85, 96–97 (2005) (noting the rise of world constitutionalism, but arguing that "the jury is still out when it comes to judging either the meaningful implementation or effectiveness of these new institutions.").

13. *See, e.g.*, Thomas Carothers, *Rule of Law Temptations* 7 (July 2–5, 2008) (preliminary draft of paper for World Justice Forum). Carothers warns that the concept is "so capacious that it is open to significantly different interpretations and operational emphasis," and that therefore "international attention to the rule of law is arguably as much about the fraying of an international consensus on political values as convergence." *Id. See also* Thomas Carothers, *The Rule of Law Revival*, 77 FOREIGN AFF. 95, 99 (1998).

14. Upham, *supra* note 9, at 14.

15. *See, e.g.*, Jeremy Waldron, *The Rule of Law in Contemporary Liberal Theory*, 2 RATIO JURIS 79, 84–85 (1989).

16. Hilary Charlesworth, *Alienating Oscar? Feminist Analysis of International Law*, in RECONCEIVING REALITY: WOMEN AND INTERNATIONAL LAW 1, 9–10 (Dorinda G. Dallmeyer ed., 1993).

17. Feminist theorists have long articulated that the most pervasive harms to women tend to occur within the inner sanctum of the private realm, within the family. For a fascinating recent contribution, *see* SALLY ENGLE MERRY, HUMAN RIGHTS & GENDER VIOLENCE: TRANSLATING INTERNATIONAL LAW INTO LOCAL JUSTICE (2006).

18. *See* Celestine Nyamu-Musembi, *Ruling Out Gender Equality? The Post-Cold War Rule of Law Agenda in Sub-Saharan Africa*, 27 THIRD WORLD Q. 1193 (2006) (asserting that post–Cold War rule of law efforts in Sub-Saharan Africa have focused on improving the market rather than gender equality).

19. *See also* Fionnuala Ní Aoláin & Catherine Turner, *Gender, Truth, and Transition*, 16 UCLA WOMEN'S L.J. 16 (2007).

20. *See generally* ENGLE MERRY, *supra* note 17.

21. The concept of "legal opportunity structures" borrows from that of "political opportunity structures" in social movement theory and describes the constraints and incentives that operate on particular (here, gendered) actors at a given time vis-à-vis their interaction with legal institutions. *See* Chris Hilson, *New Social Movements: The Role of Legal Opportunity*, 9 J. EUR. PUB. POL'Y 238 (2002); Bruce M. Wilson & Juan Carlos Rodríguez Cordero, *Legal Opportunity Structures and Social Movements: The Effects of Institutional Change on Costa Rican Politics*, 39 COMP. POL. STUD. 325 (2006). For a discussion of how this has played out in India, *see* Pistor, Halder, & Amirapu, *supra* note 5, at 21–22.

22. Office of the High Commissioner for Human Rights, RULE-OF-LAW TOOLS FOR POST-CONFLICT STATES: REPARATIONS PROGRAMMES (2008).

23. Office of the High Commissioner for Human Rights, *supra* note 22, at 37.

24. Fionnuala Ní Aoláin & Eilish Rooney, *Underenforcement and Intersectionality: Gendered Aspects of Transition for Women*, 1 INT'L J. TRANSITIONAL JUST. 338, 346, 348, 351 (2007).

25. *See* Fundación para las Relaciones Internacionales y el Diálogo Exterior (FRIDE), Justice for Women: Seeking Accountability for Sexual Crimes in Post-Conflict Situations 3 (Seminar Report, Brussels, May 13–14, 2008).

26. For example, there are some significant transitional constitutions that follow the model of a constitutional compact like the Philadelphia Convention of 1787, or the 1891 Convention, to start drafting the Constitution of the Commonwealth of Australia. The South African post-apartheid constitution in its drafting and structures has overlap with these traditional models, but this type of holistic post-conflict constitution making tends to be the exception and not the norm.

27. For example, Art. II of the General Framework Agreement for Peace (BiH) brings the European Convention on Human Rights into the domestic legal framework of the Bosnian state.

28. *See* Susan Alberts, Chris Warshaw, & Barry R. Weingast, *Democratization and Countermajoritarian Institutions: The Role of Power and Constitutional Design in Self-Enforcing Democracy,* Paper presented at the University of Chicago Law School (October 16 and 17, 2009). *See also* Timothy William Waters, *Assuming Bosnia: Taking Polities Seriously in Ethnically Divided States, in* Deconstructing the Reconstruction (Dina Francesca Haynes ed., 2008) (arguing that the constitution created by the international community for post-conflict Bosnia will fail, along with the state).

29. Constitutional Design Group, Option Reports: Transitional Justice (2009). The Constitutional Design Group is composed of scholars dedicated to distributing data and analysis useful to those engaged in constitutional design. The primary intent of the reports is to provide current and historical information about design options in written constitutions, as well as representative and illustrative text for important constitutional provisions.

30. Christine Bell, On the Law of Peace: Peace Agreements and the Lex Pacificatoria 56, 60–65 (2008).

31. Joint Declaration on Peace: The Downing Street Declaration, UK-Ireland, December 15, 1993.

32. Many of these principles are then imported fully into the final peace agreement: The Good Friday/Belfast Agreement Reached in the Multi-party Negotiations, UK-Northern Ireland, April 10, 1998, U.K. Cm. Paper 3883.

33. Joint Declaration on Peace: The Downing Street Declaration, *supra* note 31. Important constitutional principles first advanced by this document included the notion of "parity of esteem" between the two communities in Northern Ireland.

34. *See* Hilary Charlesworth, *The Constitution of East Timor,* 2 Int'l J. Const. L. 328 (2002).

35. Martha I. Morgan & Monica Maria Alzate Buitrago, *Constitution Making in a Time of Cholera: Women and the 1991 Colombian Constitution,* 4 Yale J.L. & Feminism 373 (1991–1992).

36. Inter-Parliamentary Union, *Seminar on the Process of Engendering a New Constitution for Rwanda* (2001) (noting the degree of external support to facilitate the internal process).

37. These are, in some sense, the classic peace agreements. Examples of these classic framework agreements include, for example, the Burundi Peace Agreements, the Belfast Agreement, the Lomé Accords in Sierra Leone, and the South African Interim Constitution. *See* Bell, *supra* note 30, at 60–62.

38. An example is Rwanda, where the transitional Government of National Unity (GNU) created the Legal and Constitutional Commission (LCC) to prepare a draft

constitution in consultation with public opinion. REPUBLIC OF RWANDA LEGAL & CONSTITUTIONAL COMMISSION, TOWARDS A CONSTITUTION FOR RWANDA: ACTION PLAN 2002–2003 (April 2002).

39. *See* Christine Bell & Catherine O'Rourke, *Peace Agreements or Pieces of Paper? The Impact of UNSC Resolution 1325 on Peace Processes and their Agreement*, 59 INT. & COMP. L. Q 941 (2010). This study assessing the effects of Resolution 1325 on the inclusion of women in peace agreements also tracks whether the involvement of the United Nations or other international party had a significant effect on the substance of women's inclusion and the substance of the agreement. Their data concludes that out of the agreements in which the United Nations was mentioned as a third party, forty agreements (6.7 percent) made references to women. Of these, sixteen (4 percent of pre–Resolution 1325 agreements) date from before Resolution 1325, and twenty-four (12 percent of post–Resolution 1325 agreements) date from after Resolution 1325. In their view "[t]his shows a significant rise in peace agreement references in which the UN was involved as a third party." *Id.*

40. For critical discussions on the impact of this resolution, *see* Jessica Neuwirth, *Women and Peace and Security: The Implementation of U.N. Security Council Resolution 1325*, 9 DUKE J. OF GENDER, L., & POL'Y 253, 253–60 (2002); Dianne Otto, *A Sign of "Weakness"? Disrupting Gender Certainties in the Implementation of Security Council Resolution 1325*, 13 MICH. J. OF GENDER & L. 113, 113–76 (2006).

41. S.C. Res. 1272 on *The Situation in East Timor*, U.N. Doc. S/RES/1272 (1999).

42. Hilary Charlesworth & Mary Wood, *Women and Human Rights in the Rebuilding of East Timor*, 71 NORDIC J. INT'L L. 325 (2002).

43. *See* Jeanne Izabiliza, *The Role of Women in Reconstruction: Experience of Rwanda* (2003).

44. *See* Angela M. Banks, *Participatory Constitution-Making in Post-Conflict Societies*, 101 AM. SOC'Y INT'L L. PROC. 138, 140–42 (2007).

45. By way of another example, in East Timor, the First Women's Congress of 2000 produced a Platform for Action of the Advancement of East Timorese Women, which emphasized the need for increased women's participation in the transitional administration and the constitution-drafting process. Sherrill Whittington, *Gender and Peacekeeping: The United Nations Transitional Administration in East Timor*, 28 SIGNS: J. OF WOMEN IN CULTURE AND SOC. 1283, 1285 (2003). It demanded that 30 percent of elected decision-making positions be reserved for women and recommended a "consultative process for constitution-building." *See* UNTAET Press Office, Fact Sheet 11: Gender Equality Promotion (2002). At the same time, a working group on Women and the Constitution, which received support from the UNTAET Gender Affairs Unit (GAU), organized meetings and consultations with women nationwide, resulting in a *Women's Charter of Rights in East Timor*, which thousands of East Timorese women signed.

46. *See generally* SUSAN H. WILLIAMS, CONSTITUTING EQUALITY: GENDER EQUALITY AND COMPARATIVE CONSTITUTIONAL LAW (2009).

47. Bell & O'Rourke, *supra* note 39. Their empirical work indicates that while references to women are typically found under five headings: (1) Respect for human rights of women and girls; (2) Special measures for women and girls in post-conflict processes e.g., repatriation; (3) Measures supporting local women's peace initiatives; (4) Measures dealing with the issue of sexual violence; (5) Measures providing for women's needs in DDR contexts—that many of the references are tangential to the core of the agreement, and many are limited in their implementation capacity. *Id. See also*

INTERNATIONAL PEACEKEEPING, WOMEN, PEACE, AND CONFLICT: A DECADE AFTER RESOLUTION 1325 (Susan Willett ed., 2010).

48. Fionnuala Ní Aoláin, *Women, Security, and the Patriarchy of Internationalized Transitional Justice*, 31 HUM. RTS. Q. 1055 (2009).

49. KATE FEARON, WOMEN'S WORK: THE STORY OF THE NORTHERN IRELAND WOMEN'S COALITION (1999).

50. Public authorities must also prepare an Equality Impact Assessment, along the lines suggested by Christopher McCrudden. *See* CHRISTOPHER MCCRUDDEN, BENCHMARKS FOR CHANGE: MAINSTREAMING FAIRNESS IN THE GOVERNANCE OF NORTHERN IRELAND 13–16 (Belfast: Committee on the Administration of Justice, 1998).

51. *Id.*

52. *See, e.g.*, GENDER ACTION FOR PEACE AND SECURITY, GLOBAL MONITORING CHECKLIST ON WOMEN, PEACE, AND SECURITY (2009). *See also* United Nations Secretary-General, *Women Peace and Security*, U.N. Doc/S/2010/173 (2010).

53. *See* United Nations Secretary-General, *Women, Peace, and Security*, U.N. Doc. S/2004/814 (2004); United Nations Secretary-General, *Women, Peace, and Security*, U.N. Doc. S/2008/622 (2008).

54. *See* discussion *supra* Chapter 1, at 34–36.

55. ISSER, LUBKEMANN, & N'TOW, LOOKING FOR JUSTICE: LIBERIAN EXPERIENCES AND PERCEPTIONS OF LOCAL JUSTICE OPTIONS 26 (2009).

56. *See, e.g.*, ISSER, LUBKEMANN, & N'TOW, *supra* note 55.

57. This point was cogently recognized, for example, by the Kenyan Constitutional Review Commission's report, which included the requirement that customary rules "must conform to constitutional principles" and was significantly shaped by a 2002 Report entitled *Gender and Constitution Making in Kenya*. KENYAN CONSTITUTIONAL REVIEW COMMISSION, THE PEOPLE'S CHOICE: REPORT OF THE CONSTITUTION OF KENYA REVIEW COMMISSION 13 (September 2002). The new Kenyan Constitution was defeated by a referendum in 2005, and its future remains uncertain.

58. Rita Manchanda, *Ambivalent Gains in South Asian Conflicts*, *in* THE AFTERMATH WOMEN IN POST-CONFLICT TRANSFORMATION 99, 108 (Meintjes, Pillay, & Turshen eds., 2001).

59. Fadwa Allabadi, *Secular and Islamist Women in Palestinian Society*, 15 EUR. J. OF WOMEN'S STUD. 181, 182 (2008).

60. Adrien Katherine Wing & Hisam Kassim, *Hamas, Constitutionalism, and Palestinian Women*, 50 HOW. L.J. 479 (2006).

61. For example, Article 9 of the Basic Law, Equality Clause declares "All Palestinians are equal under the law and judiciary, without discrimination because of race, sex, color, religion, political views or disability." However, these lofty provisions are tempered by the parallel confirmation in the draft Constitution that Shari'a will be a "major source" for legislation. Complexity is compounded by the religious platform advanced by Hamas, which has made the very notion of "women's rights" a point of controversy. In its election platform, Hamas has stated that Shari'a should be the principle source of legislation in Palestine, in contrast with the Third Draft of the Constitution, which currently identifies Shari'a as a major source but not the major source of law.

62. Wing & Kassim, *supra* note 60, at 491.

63. This is potently illustrated by the fact that the 2006 Fatah legislation to establish a constitutional court with nine judges was invalidated after Hamas' decisive 2006 electoral victory.

64. *See* Nadera Shalhoub-Kevorkian, Militarization and Violence Against Women in Conflict Zones in the Middle East: A Palestinian Case Study (2009).

65. Hallie Ludsin, *Putting the Cart Before the Horse: The Palestinian Drafting Process*, 10 UCLA J. Int'l L. & For. Aff. 443, 494 (2005).

66. Ludsin, *supra* note 65, at 452 n.35. Women in Palestinian society continue to experience discrimination in almost every facet of public and private life. Many women's primary access to justice is through the customary and religious systems that do not recognize equal justice between women and men. The customary tradition, known as *urf*, handles matters related to family law, education, honor killings, and domestic violence. Discriminatory practices under customary law include, for example, women being encouraged to marry at a very young age and not allowing women to live independently, and customary law tolerates the practice of "honor" killings. Women are generally excluded from acting as mediators or negotiators in the customary system, offering them little opportunity to change the practices. Civil land criminal law codes are based on the Ottoman, Jordanian, and Egyptian systems, some of which have not been revised since the nineteenth century.

67. Irving, *supra* note 1, at 3.

68. Bell, *supra* note 30, at 62–65.

69. Christine Bell & Kathleen Cavanaugh, *"Constructive Ambiguity" or Internal Self-Determination? Self-Determination, Group Accommodation, and the Belfast Agreement*, 22 Fordham Int'l L.J. 1345 (1998–1999).

70. Cogent examples of implementation agreements include the Israeli/Palestinian Interim Agreement (Oslo II) intended to take forward and implement parts of the Oslo I Agreement, as well as the more successful South African Final Constitution.

71. Anne Smith, The Drafting Process of a Bill of Rights for Northern Ireland Public Law 526 (2004). We note that a separate Constitutional Convention might be called to advance the specific work of agreement on legal principles and values. The success of such bespoke approaches for advancing women's interests and needs remains open. Nonetheless, results and success for women have been mixed.

72. Northern Ireland Act 1998, §§ 68–69.

73. The NIHRC has been tasked with advising on the scope of rights supplementary to the rights contained in the European Convention on Human Rights, and the inclusion of social and economic rights is obviously additional to the ECHR. The NIHRC must also bear in mind the need to recognize the principles of mutual respect for both communities in Northern Ireland. The NIHRC has given its advice to the UK government on the scope and content of a bill of rights. The government response was disappointing in its response to both the civil society and NIHRC proposals, indicating that a seriously amputated version of the proposals would emerge, and that developments for the jurisdiction would be taken in tandem with wider constitutional developments in the United Kingdom as a whole.

74. Christine Bell & Johanna Keenan, *Human Rights, Non-governmental Organizations, and the Problems of Transition*, 26 Hum. Rts. Q. 330 (2004) (noting inter alia that the conflict context can, despite the evident pressures of violence and threat, provide greater incentive to support NGOs, as well as greater opportunities to interface with key international and local actors. At conflict's end the assumption that the "war is over" and fears that criticism might unhinge the deals may paradoxically limit the maneuvering space for NGOs).

75. Vijaya Joshi, Creating and Limiting Opportunities: Women's Organizing and the UN in East Timor 5 (2005).

76. Kathleen Sullivan's hypothetical question which asks, "What choices would a hypothetical set of feminist drafters face if they were to constitutionalize women's equality from scratch?" Sullivan then offers a typology largely based on equality provisions. See Kathleen Sullivan, Constitutionalizing Women's Equality, 90 Cal. L. Rev. 735, 763 (2002).

77. Helen Irving stresses the dangers of a focus on a "rights centered paradigm . . . [that] overlooks structurally prior questions surrounding constitutional design of the institutions in which the judges who interpret and enforce the rights are appointed and work . . ." Irving, supra note 1, at 29.

78. Paula Monopoli suggests that the singular executive with plenary power based on a model of masculine authority is "the least likely to result in women's ascending to executive office." Paula A. Monopoli, Gender and Constitutional Design, 115 Yale L.J. 2643, 2644–45 (2006).

79. Arend Lijphart notes that among the wide array of constitutional models available to newly independent countries, consociational models may offer a better model for deeply fractured societies. See Arend Lijpart, Constitutional Design for Divided Societies, 15 J. of Democracy 96 (2004).

80. Susan H. Williams, supra note 46.

81. In this way, they provide a route for the "temporary special measures" provision of the Convention on the Elimination of All Forms of Discrimination Against Women (CEDAW) to be operationalized. Article 4; "Adoption by States Parties of temporary special measures aimed at accelerating de facto equality between men and women shall not be considered discrimination as defined in the present Convention. . . ."

82. Irving, supra note 1, at 117. Irving quotes a 2007 survey by the Inter-Parliamentary Union of 180 countries in which not one enjoyed "parity," namely genuine numerical equality between men and women in representation. Rwanda had the highest score with 48.8 percent. Id.

83. See Meredeth Turshen, Engendering Relations of State to Society, in The Aftermath: Women in Post-Conflict Transformation 78, 86 (Sheila Meintjes, Anu Pillay, & Meredith Turshen eds., 2001).

84. Charlesworth, supra note 34, at 332.

85. See Milena Pires, East Timor and the Debate on Quotas 38 (2002).

86. Saras Jagwanth & Christine Murray, "No Nation Can Be Free When One Half of It Is Enslaved": Constitutional Equality for Women in South Africa, in The Gender of Constitutional Jurisprudence 237 (Beverley Baines & Ruth Rubio-Marín eds., 2005).

87. Charlesworth, supra note 34, at 333.

88. See Susan Harris Rimmer, Surfacing Gender and the Constitution of Timor Leste, in The Constitution of Timor Leste 6 (William Binchy ed., 2009).

89. Id. at 9 (citing U.N. Development Programme, Annual Report 15–16 (2006)).

90. Commission for Reception, Truth, and Reconciliation in East Timor (CAVR), Women and the Conflict, National Public Hearing (April 28–29, 2003).

91. Hilary Charlesworth, Mainstreaming Gender in International Peace and Security: The Case of East Timor, 26 Yale J. Int'l. L. 313, 315 (2001).

92. Christine Chinkin, The Protection of Economic, Social, and Cultural Rights Post Conflict (Office of the High Commissioner for Human Rights, 2008).

93. *Id.* at 4.

94. *See* Lisa J. Laplante, *Transitional Justice and Peacebuilding: Diagnosing and Addressing the Socioeconomic Roots of Violence through a Human Rights Framework*, 2 INT'L J. OF TRANSITIONAL JUST. 331 (2008) (observing such riots in countries like Chile, South Africa, and Guatemala).

95. PAUL FARMER, PATHOLOGIES OF POWER: HEALTH, HUMAN RIGHTS, AND THE NEW WAR ON THE POOR (2003).

96. Ismael Muvingi, *Sitting on Powder Kegs: Socioeconomic Rights in Transitional Societies*, 3 INT'L J. OF TRANSITIONAL JUST. 163 (2009).

97. This kind of thinking is also clearly evident in the development sector. For example, the World Bank's *Empowerment and Poverty Reduction: A Sourcebook* now calls for "the expansion of assets and capabilities of poor people to participate in, negotiate with, influence, control and hold accountable institutions that affect their lives." *See* DEEPA NARAYAN, EMPOWERMENT AND POVERTY REDUCTION: A SOURCEBOOK 14 (2002).

98. Irving decisively notes that the "attempts at gender-inclusive language are not merely a matter of legal precision and formal inclusion. This involves the recognition of language as a form of representation." IRVING, *supra* note 1, at 42.

99. *See generally* Sandra Petersson, *Locating Inequality—The Evolving Discourse on Sexist Language*, 32 U. OF BRIT. COLUM. L. REV. 55 (1998).

100. *See* Christina Murray, *A Constitutional Beginning: Making South Africa's Final Constitution*, 23 U. ARK. LITTLE ROCK L. REV. 809 (2001).

101. Words matter and in the case before the South African Constitutional Court, *Bhe and Others v. Magistrate* concerned a 1993 constitutional challenge to the customary rule of male primogeniture in inheritance as codified in the South African Black Administration Act. The presiding judge found that the removal of gender discrimination in inheritance was consistent with the preamble that set out to "improve the quality of all citizens and free the potential of each person." *Bhe and Others v. Magistrate* 2005 (1) BCLR 1 (CC) (S. Afr.).

102. Without conceding to biological essentialism, we accept that "even full achievement of formal equality and comprehensive demonstrations of equal capacity would still leave women different from men. . . . Women bear and give birth to children, where men do not." IRVING, *supra* note 1, at 189.

103. *See* WORLD HEALTH ORGANIZATION, WOMEN AND HEALTH TODAY'S EVIDENCE TOMORROW'S AGENDA (2009).

104. *See* Beverley Baines & Ruth Rubio-Marín, *Towards a Feminist Constitutional Agenda*, *in* THE GENDER OF CONSTITUTIONAL JURISPRUDENCE 83 (Beverley Baines & Ruth Rubio-Marín eds., 2005) (discussing a comparative reproductive analysis).

105. The provision also sets out that the state take "reasonable legislative and other measures, within its available resources, to achieve the progressive realization of . . . [such] rights." S. AFR. CONST., 1996.

106. *See* Rachel Rebouche, An Anti-Model for Reproductive Rights Reform: The South African Example (unpublished manuscript) (on file with author).

107. *South African Rape Survey Shock*, BBC NEWS, June 18, 2009.

108. At least on its face, this liberation was carried out in the Bonn Process of December 2001, under which the Emergency Loya Jirga (Grand Council) met in June 2002 to form a two-year transitional government. In 2003, the Constitutional Loya Jirga approved an interim constitution. The accord was signed by representatives of the militia forces who fought with the U.S.-led coalition, representatives of the former king of Afghanistan, and representatives of various other exiled Afghani groups.

109. "The citizens of Afghanistan—whether man or woman—have equal rights and duties before the law." AFGHAN CONST. OF 2004, art. 22.

110. AFGHANISTAN ONLINE (2007), http://www.afghan-web.com/woman/equality_fades.html.

111. The World Bank, *Afghanistan Girls' Schools: Achieving Results in a Difficult Environment* (2007).

112. THE WORLD BANK, AFGHANISTAN: THE ROLE OF WOMEN IN AFGHANISTAN'S FUTURE (2005). Among Afghan women, 87 percent are illiterate, while 30 percent of girls have access to education. Forty-four years is the life expectancy for women.

113. Article 12:1 states: "Parties shall take all appropriate measures to eliminate discrimination against women in the field of health care in order to ensure, on the basis of equality to men and women, access to health care services, including those related to family planning."

   Article 12:2 states: "Parties shall ensure to women appropriate services in connection with pregnancy, confinement and the post-natal period, granting free services where necessary, as well as adequate nutrition during pregnancy and lactation."

   Article 14:2 states: "Parties shall take all appropriate measures to eliminate discrimination against women in rural areas . . . and, in particular, shall ensure to such women the right: . . . (b) to have access to adequate health care facilities, including information, counseling and services in family planning."

114. WORLD HEALTH ORGANIZATION, MATERNAL MORTALITY IN 2000: ESTIMATED DEVELOPED BY WHO, UNICEF, AND UNFPRA (2004).

115. Charles Ngwena, *An Appraisal of Abortion Laws in Southern Africa from a Reproductive Health Rights Perspective*, 32 J. OF L., MED. & ETHICS 708 (2004).

116. International World Conference on Population and Development, Program of Action (Cairo 1994).

117. *See* DAVID CHANDLER, BOSNIA: FAKING DEMOCRACY AFTER DAYTON 12–13 (2d ed. Pluto Press 1999) (citing Richard Rose, *Where Are Post Communist Countries Going?*, 8 J. DEMOCRACY 92, 97 (1997)).

118. Pistor, Halder, & Amirapu, *supra* note 5, at 24.

119. Launching a worldwide campaign to promote the rule of law in September 2005, then-President of the International Bar Association (IBA), Francis Neate, declared: "We lawyers have a duty, as well as an interest, to respond. Business can only flourish when there is adherence to the Rule of Law. Without it, freedom and democracy cannot exist. Nor can lawyers. We lawyers understand what the Rule of Law means—why it is important—how it works." HANS CORELL, CREATING A GLOBAL RULE OF LAW MEETING POINT 4 (2007).

120. *See generally* U.N. Secretary General, *The Rule of Law and Transitional Justice in Conflict and Post-Conflict Societies: Report of the Secretary General*, U.N. Doc. S/2004/616 (August 3, 2004).

121. Duncan Ivison, *Pluralism and the Hobbesian Logic of Negative Constitutionalism*, 47 POL. STUD. 83, 83–89 (1999).

122. *See* JOSEPH RAZ, THE AUTHORITY OF LAW: ESSAYS ON LAW AND MORALITY 214–18 (Oxford Univ. Press 1979). Premised on the notion that "the law must be capable of guiding the behaviour of its subjects," Raz argues that the law must be prospective, open, clear, and relatively stable. *Id.* at 214. In addition, the independence of the judiciary, adherence to the principles of natural justice (particularly in guaranteeing open and fair hearings), the power of the courts to review the implementation of these principles, and the accessibility of the courts

must all be ensured, and "[t]he discretion of crime-preventing agencies should not be allowed to pervert the law." *Id.* at 218.

123. *See* Kenneth L. Karst, *Woman's Constitution*, DUKE L. REV. 447–49 (1984). However, the authors note the dangers of essentializing the "morality and world view characteristic" of women as outlined by Karst.

124. A deeper analysis of the fundamental relationship between intersectionality, inequality, and underenforcement is undertaken by Ní Aoláin and Rooney, *supra* note 24. Seeing these relationships is the start of probing the benefits of intersectional analysis as a tool for analyzing the problematics of underenforcement, particularly as they negatively impact upon those women and children who constitute the group most seriously affected by armed conflict and repression. In this view, underenforcement and equality are structurally linked.

CHAPTER 10

1. F. R. G. MINISTRY FOR ECON. COOPERATION & DEV., PROMOTING GOOD GOVERNANCE IN POST-CONFLICT SOCIETIES 3 (2005) [hereinafter GTZ Report].

2. *Id.* at 5 ("[T]here is no comprehensive set of political guidelines for the promotion of good governance in fragile environments to date").

3. *See generally* U.N. Special Adviser on Gender Issues and Advancement of Women, Dep't of Pol. Aff., *Enhancing Women's Participation in Electoral Processes in Post-Conflict Countries*, U.N. Doc. EGM/ELEC/2004/REPORT (February 20, 2004) (explaining the link between gender and post-conflict governance programming).

4. Constitutions and administrative legal structures can also be considered formal political structures, but we deal with constitutions and rule of law separately in this book.

5. *See* JÜRGEN HABERMAS, BETWEEN FACT AND NORMS: CONTRIBUTING TO A DISCOURSE THEORY OF LAW AND DEMOCRACY 329 (1998).

6. *See* Janet Halley, Prabha Kotiswaran, Hila Shamir, & Chantal Thomas, *From the International to the Local in Feminist Legal Responses to Rape, Prostitution/Sex Work, and Sex Trafficking: Four Studies in Contemporary Governance Feminism*, 29 HARV. J. L. & GENDER 335 (2006).

7. As we will argue in Chapter 11, a better bridge for women would be the provision of "social services justice."

8. GTZ Report, *supra* note 1, at 1 ("The task is thus to build transparent, efficient and participative governance structures that can help to stabilise the volatile transformation of post-conflict societies. A political and administrative system that satisfies the principles of good governance can prevent outbreaks of new violence by providing more peaceful procedures of conflict resolution").

9. *See, e.g.*, U.N. Special Adviser on Gender Issues and Advancement of Women, Dep't of Political Affairs, *supra* note 3, at 12.

10. PAUL COLLIER, WARS, GUNS, AND VOTES: DEMOCRACY IN DANGEROUS PLACES 21 (2009); Dina Francesca Haynes, *The Deus ex Machina Descends: The Laws, Priorities, and Players Central to the International Administration of Post-Conflict Bosnia and Herzegovina*, in DECONSTRUCTING THE RECONSTRUCTION 3, 27–28 (Dina Francesca Haynes ed., 2008).

11. GEORGINA WAYLEN, ENGENDERING TRANSITIONS: WOMEN'S MOBILIZATION, INSTITUTIONS, AND GENDER OUTCOMES 11, 34 (2007) [hereinafter WAYLEN, ENGENDERING TRANSITIONS].

12. Security Council Resolution 1325 calls on member states "to ensure increased representation of women at all decision-making levels in national, regional and international institutions and mechanisms for the prevention, management, and

resolution of conflict," S.C. Res. 1325, ¶ 1, U.N. Doc. S/RES/1325 (October 31, 2000). It also calls upon actors to "ensure the protection of and respect for human rights of women and girls, particularly as they relate to the constitution, the electoral system, the police and the judiciary." *Id.* at ¶ 8 (c).

13. GTZ Report, *supra* note 1, at 3–5. It is important to note that because there is so little doctrine and so few norms in post-conflict reconstruction, each profession tends to see its issue as the umbrella under which all other post-conflict reconstruction elements are organized. Here, GTZ sees governance as the overarching goal of post-conflict reconstruction, and so organizes security and economics as elements under that umbrella. Military actors might see security as the primary goal and organize governance as a component of security. Human rights actors might see human rights as the umbrella and organize governance and security under it, and so forth. For more on the difficulties caused by lack of doctrine combined with professional and institutional bias, *see generally* Haynes, *supra* note 10, at 3.

14. Georgina Waylen, *Women and Democratization: Conceptualizing Gender Relations in Transition Politics*, 46 WORLD POL. 327, 330 (1994) [hereinafter Waylen, *Women and Democratization*] (citing Guillermo A. O'Donnell, *Introduction to the Latin American Cases, in* TRANSITIONS FROM AUTHORITARIAN RULE: LATIN AMERICA 3 (Guillermo O'Donnell, Philippe C. Schmitter, & Laurence Whitehead eds., 1986)). *See also* ANU PILLAY, GENDER, PEACE, AND PEACEKEEPING: LESSONS FROM SOUTHERN AFRICA 4 (2006) (calling democratization one of the "four main inter-related components" of peacebuilding, along with demilitarization, social reconstruction and development).

15. Jean d'Aspremont, *Post-Conflict Administrations as Democracy-Building Instruments*, 9 CHI. J. INT'L L. 1, 7 (2008) (citing generally Marc Cogen & Eric De Brabandere, *Democratic Governance and Post-Conflict Reconstruction*, 20 LEIDEN J. INT'L L. 669 (2007)). *See also* Waylen, *Women and Democratization, supra* note 14, at 330 (calling democratization "unashamedly normative" and considered "desirable per se").

16. Fionnuala Ní Aoláin, *Women, Security, and the Patriarchy of Internationalized Transitional Justice*, 31 HUM. RTS. Q. 1055, 1058–63 (2009).

17. *See generally* CHANTAL MOUFFE, THE DEMOCRATIC PARADOX (2000); IRIS MARION YOUNG, INCLUSION AND DEMOCRACY (2000); BONNIE HONIG, POLITICAL THEORY AND DISPLACEMENT OF POLITICS (1993) (relating feminist perspectives of democratic political theory).

18. COLLIER, *supra* note 10, at 21.

19. *See* Jean d'Aspremont, *supra* note 15, at 7–8.

20. *Id.* at 3–4 (cautioning "this customary legal obligation to adopt a democratic regime must not be exaggerated," as it is not *jus cogens*).

21. *Id.* at 3 (citing the examples of Pakistan and Myanmar). *See also* Thomas M. Franck, *The Emerging Right to Democratic Governance*, 86 AM. J. INT'L L. 46 (1992).

22. *See* Haynes, *supra* note 10, at 8–9 (addressing "governance by fiat").

23. *See also* Rebecca Everly, *Assessing the Accountability of the High Representative, in* DECONSTRUCTING THE RECONSTRUCTION (Dina Francesca Haynes ed., 2008).

24. Also sometimes referred to by the similarly paternalistic moniker of "nation-building." *See, e.g.,* DAVID CHANDLER, BOSNIA: FAKING DEMOCRACY AFTER DAYTON 169 (2000).

25. Ralph Wilde, *Understanding the International Territorial Administration Accountability Deficit: Trusteeship and the Legitimacy of International Organizations, in*

INTERNATIONAL PEACEKEEPING: THE YEARBOOK OF INTERNATIONAL PEACE
OPERATIONS 93 (Harvey Langholtz, Boris Kondoch, & Alan Wells eds., 2008).

26. Nancy Bermeo, *Democratization After War: What the Democratization Literature Says—And Fails to Say—About Democracy in Post-Conflict Settings*, 9 GLOBAL GOVERNANCE 159, 165 (2003).

27. *See* Haynes, *supra* note 10, at 14 (citing the General Framework Agreement for Peace in Bosnia and Herzegovina and alleging that it was a mistake to hold elections so early, as it legitimated nationalists who rose to power in the wake of ethnic cleansing and because the elections were poorly undertaken; for example, there were more votes cast than voters). *See also* Waylen, *Women and Democratization, supra* note 14, at 332 (noting that classical democracy scholars concentrated narrowly on "democracy as simply an institutional arrangement [such that] wider definitions of democracy couched in terms of the real distribution of power in society are considered illegitimate.").

28. *See, e.g.*, WAYLEN, ENGENDERING TRANSITIONS, *supra* note 11, at 335.

29. *See generally* CHANTAL MOUFFE, THE DEMOCRATIC PARADOX (2000); IRIS MARION YOUNG, INCLUSION AND DEMOCRACY (2000); BONNIE HONIG, POLITICAL THEORY AND DISPLACEMENT OF POLITICS (1993).

30. *See* Kenneth Roth, *Ballots and Bullets*, N.Y. TIMES, March 20, 2009, at BR16.

31. *See* International Covenant on Civil and Political Rights arts. 3, 25, 26, December 19, 1966, 6 I.L.M. 368, 999 U.N.T.S. 171; Convention on the Elimination of All Forms of Discrimination Against Women arts. 2, 7, 18, December 18, 1979, 19 I.L.M. 33, 1249 U.N.T.S. 13. *See also* Universal Declaration of Human Rights, G.A. Res. 214A (III), U.N. Doc. A/810 (December 10, 1948).

32. U.N. Special Adviser on Gender Issues and Advancement of Women, *supra* note 3, at 7–8.

33. *See* S.C. Res. 1325, *supra* note 12, at ¶ 8(c) (calling on actors to adopt "measures that ensure the protection of and respect for human rights of women and girls, particularly as they relate to the constitution, the electoral system, the police and the judiciary"). In 2003, the Secretary-General highlighted the important role of national election commissions in promoting women's participation in elections in post-conflict countries, including "the need to ensure that agreements contain provisions for the conduct of elections," establishment of "an independent and neutral national electoral commission that includes an equal number of women and men and whose membership and mandate is the result of consultations with civil society groups, including women's organizations." U.N. Secretary-General, *Rep. of the Secretary-General to the Commission on the Status of Women*, U.N. Doc. E/CN.6/2004/10 (December 22, 2003), at 15.

34. Women are more likely than men to be illiterate. U.N. Econ. & Soc. Comm'n for W. Asia (ESCWA), *Where Do Arab Women Stand in the Development Process? A Gender-Based Statistical Analysis*, U.N. Doc. E/ESCWA/SDD/2004/Booklet.1 (January 12, 2004), at 21. Furthermore, "according to UNESCO data and the World Development Indicators (WDI), less than a quarter of Iraqi women are literate, whereas literacy for men is 55%. This is the second largest gender gap in literacy in the Middle East (after Yemen), and one of the largest in the world." *Post-Conflict Reconstruction: The Importance of Women's Participation in Afghanistan and Iraq: Hearing Before the Congressional Human Rights Caucus*, 108th Cong. (2004) (testimony of Isobel Coleman, Senior Fellow, Director of U.S. Foreign Policy and Women Initiative Council on Foreign Relations).

35. In Afghanistan, for instance, not only had popular elections never been held, "but the political role of women had been greatly circumscribed by a socio-political tradition that had changed little over the centuries. In addition, women in Afghanistan had more recently been subjected to extreme repression under the Taliban regime. It was clear from the beginning that a number of special measures would need to be undertaken." U.N. Dep't of Pub. Info., Women and Elections: Guide to Promoting the Participation of Women in Elections 51 (2005).

36. One author, supervising elections in post-conflict Bosnia and Herzegovina, regularly saw illiterate (or allegedly illiterate) women accompanied to the polls by male relatives acting as "helpers." While the electoral procedures permitted an illiterate person to be read the ballot by a helper, verbally state his or her preference, be directed to the appropriate place to mark his or her preference, and so mark it, what actually took place in almost every instance was that the male "helper" simply voted for her, with her standing idly by. In some instances it appeared that the women were bused in by party members who then acted as helpers.

37. Collier, *supra* note 10, at 31–36, 155 (citing countries, such as Côte d'Ivoire and Kenya, where the integrity of the electoral process arguably was not protected).

38. Elections are also hugely susceptible to corruption and fraud. *See, e.g.*, Richard Oppel Jr. & Archie Tse, *One in 4 Afghan Ballots Face Check for Possible Fraud*, N.Y. Times, September 21, 2009, at A6.

39. Collier, *supra* note 10, at 49.

40. Prompting the Commission on the Status of Women to adopt specific benchmarks for implementing women's increased electoral participation "not only . . . as voters, but also as candidates." Press Release, Commission on the Status of Women, 48th Session, Delegates to Women's Commission Stress Need to Engage Males in Eliminating Stereotypes, Discrimination, U.N. Doc. WOM/1439 (March 4, 2004). *See also* Collier, *supra* note 10, at 31–36, 155.

41. Waylen, Engendering Transitions, *supra* note 11, at 128–32 (2007) (relating the use of quotas in post-transition periods in Argentina and Brazil). *See also* Women, Quotas, and Politics 250 (Drude Dahlerup ed., 2006) (discussing how quotas have taken varying forms ranging from voluntary party quotas adopted by the ruling (liberation) parties in Mozambique and South Africa to constitutionally guaranteed quotas in Rwanda, Afghanistan, and Iraq, where the international community has been influential in their adoption); Marcia E. Greenberg & Elaine Zuckerman, *The Gender Dimensions of Post-Conflict Reconstruction: The Challenges in Development Aid*, *in* Making Peace Work: The Challenges of Social and Economic Reconstruction 101 (Tony Addison & Tilman Brück eds., 2009) (noting that post-conflict quotas were instituted in East Timor).

42. Greenberg & Zuckerman, *supra* note 41, at 101 (identifying post-conflict Rwanda and East Timor as states in which women constituted 30 percent of candidates for election after institution of quotas).

43. E-mail from Susan H. Williams, Professor of Law and Director, Center for Constitutional Democracy, Indiana University Maurer School of Law, to Fionnuala Ní Aoláin, Dorsey & Whitney Chair in Law, University of Minnesota Law School and Professor of Law and Director, Transitional Justice Institute, University of Ulster, Northern Ireland (March 11, 2010, 13:53 CST) (on file with author). *See also* Susan H. Williams, *Equality, Representation, and Challenge to Hierarchy: Justifying Electoral Quotas for Women*, *in* Constituting Equality: Gender Equality and

COMPARATIVE CONSTITUTIONAL LAW 53 (Susan H. Williams ed., 2009). *See generally* ANNE PHILLIPS, THE POLITICS OF PRESENCE 57–84 (1995).

44. ANU PILLAY, GENDER, PEACE, AND PEACEKEEPING: LESSONS FROM SOUTHERN AFRICA 2 (Inst. for Security Studies, ISS Paper Ser. 128, 2006).

45. Greenberg & Zuckerman, *supra* note 41.

46. Susan Williams responds to this concern with the following useful observation: "In this democratic model, the representatives elected under a quota don't represent women, rather they *are* women and their various views have all been shaped by that life experience, and that is what makes it important to have them in the legislature." Susan H. Williams, *supra* note 43.

47. Maja Tjernström & Linda Ederberg, *Common Arguments for and Against Quotas*, ACE: THE ELECTORAL KNOWLEDGE NETWORK, http://aceproject.org/ero-en/topics/parties-and-candidates/Quotas.doc/view.

48. This particular argument was made in critiquing the most recent elections in India, for example, even while the attitude toward quotas was largely favorable. *See* Lydia Polgreen, *Uproar in India Over Female Lawmaker Quota*, N.Y. TIMES, March 10, 2010, at A4.

49. This last set of pros and cons was added by the authors of this book and was not included in the ACE table.

50. Be it voluntary, legally mandated in party lists, or through reserved seats. *See* International Institute for Democracy and Electoral Assistance (International IDEA), *Quota Project: Global Database of Quotas for Women*, http://www.quotaproject.org (last visited June 3, 2010).

51. Quotas for appointing female judges and prosecutors, for instance, have been discussed in chapters 8 and 9.

52. U.N. DEP'T OF PUB. INFO., *supra* note 35, at 24.

53. U.N. DEP'T OF PUB. INFO., *supra* note 35, at 24. Countries adopting this system include Argentina, where party lists must have a minimum of 30 percent women, placed in positions likely to result in election; Costa Rica, where party lists must include at least 40 percent women; and Bosnia and Herzegovina, where party lists must include at least 30 percent women. U.N. DEP'T OF PUB. INFO., *supra* note 35, at 28. *See also* OFFICE OF DEMOCRATIC INSTS. & HUMAN RIGHTS (ODIHR), BOSNIA AND HERZEGOVINA: GENERAL ELECTIONS OCTOBER 5, 2002 FINAL REPORT 17–18 (2003).

54. WAYLEN, ENGENDERING TRANSITIONS, *supra* note 11, at 112–13 (citing VALERIE SPERLING, ORGANIZING WOMEN IN CONTEMPORARY RUSSIA: ENGENDERING TRANSITIONS 117 (1999)).

55. Eva-Marie Svensson, *Contemporary Challenges in Nordic Equality Policies and Law* (Equality and Diversity in Europe, International Interdisciplinary Conference in Helsinki January 12–13, 2006, Working Paper); Heje Skjeie & Mari Teigen, *Political Construction of Gender Equality: Traveling Towards . . . A Gender Balanced Society?*, 13 NORDIC J. OF WOMEN'S STUD. 187 (2005).

56. Even the United Nations, which supports quotas, acknowledges that quota reservations risks tokenism and may even be counterproductive. U.N. DEP'T OF PUB. INFO., *supra* note 35, at 27 (citing U.N. Special Adviser on Gender Issues and Advancement of Women, Dep't of Political Affairs, *Enhancing Women's Participation in Electoral Processes in Post-conflict Countries*, U.N. Doc. EGM/ELEC/2004/REPORT (2004).

57. Subsequent to the Beijing Women's Conference Platform for Action, where women's underrepresentation in formal political institutions was widely criticized, quotas were adopted for elections to national parliament in about forty countries,

and political parties in more than fifty other countries voluntarily established quotas for women. WAYLEN, ENGENDERING TRANSITIONS, *supra* note 11, at 11 (citing WOMEN, QUOTAS, AND POLITICS 3 (Drude Dahlerup ed., 2006)). In Djibouti, 10 percent of seats are reserved; in India, 33 percent of seats in all local bodies (panchayats and municipalities) are reserved; in Jordan, 6 of the 110 seats in the House of Deputies are reserved; in Pakistan, 60 of 342 National Assembly seats (17.5 percent) are to be allocated to women; in Tanzania, 20 percent of the seats in parliament are reserved; in Uganda, at least one woman from each of the 54 districts is guaranteed a seat (out of 304 seats). U.N. DEP'T OF PUB. INFO., *supra* note 35, at 28 (citing U.N. Special Adviser on Gender Issues and Advancement of Women, Dep't of Political Affairs, *Enhancing Women's Participation in Electoral Processes in Post-conflict Countries*, U.N. Doc. EGM/ELEC/2004/ REPORT (2004).

58. In Argentina, for example, quotas resulted in the percentage of women occupying parliamentary seats to rise from 6.7 percent in 1990 to 36.2 percent in 2005. *See* WAYLEN, ENGENDERING TRANSITIONS, *supra* note 11, at 94, 129. In South Africa, however, the ANC instituted quotas for women within its party, which increased the profile of women and women candidates across all political parties.

59. UNITED NATIONS DEVELOPMENT FUND FOR WOMEN (UNIFEM), PROGRESS OF THE WORLD'S WOMEN 2008/2009: WHO ANSWERS TO THE WOMEN? GENDER AND ACCOUNTABILITY 30 (2009).

60. For example, Bosnia's ombudsmen's office and Serbia's Ministry of Human Rights and Minorities.

61. *See* United Nations Enable: Rights and Dignity of Persons with Disabilities, *Chapter Seven: Creating National Institutions to Implement and Monitor the Convention*, http://www.un.org/disabilities/default.asp?id=245 (last visited May 30, 2010) (explaining the "Paris Principles" and corresponding citations).

62. Whether political liberalization is actually associated with real long-term security will be discussed below.

63. *See* GOVERNING WOMEN: WOMEN'S POLITICAL EFFECTIVENESS IN CONTEXTS OF DEMOCRATIZATION AND GOVERNANCE REFORM 175 (Anne Marie Goetz ed., 2009) (citing the positive example of South Africa); *but see* GTZ Report, *supra* note 1, at 22 (cautioning that "[r]elying too heavily on NGOs, however, creates a danger of substituting and delegitimizing state organizations and thus potentially undermines long-term efforts to strengthen them.").

64. Catherine O'Rourke, *The Shifting Signifier of Community in Transitional Justice: A Feminist Analysis*, 23 WIS. J.L. GENDER & SOC'Y 269, 272–73 (2008). *See also* ANNE PHILLIPS, MULTICULTURALISM WITHOUT CULTURE (2007).

65. *See* WAYLEN, ENGENDERING TRANSITIONS, *supra* note 11, at 50.

66. *See, e.g.*, GTZ Report, *supra* note 1, at 19 (2005).

67. As noted by Madeline Rees, former Head of OHCHR in Bosnia, NGOs and even the Bosnian government were far more adept at recognizing the importance of gender in postwar reconstruction than was the international community. Madeleine Rees, *International Intervention in Bosnia-Herzegovina: The Cost of Ignoring Gender*, *in* THE POSTWAR MOMENT: MILITARIES, MASCULINITIES, AND INTERNATIONAL PEACEKEEPING IN BOSNIA AND THE NETHERLANDS 51 (Cynthia Cockburn & Dubravka Zarkov eds., 2002). *See also* Georgina Waylen, *Women and Democratization*, *supra* note 14, at 336 (describing the impact of human rights groups in Chile and Argentina in the 1970s, comprising primarily mothers of the disappeared, who carried that organizational momentum into rallying for women's role in society and governance in the '80s and '90s). The focus of those later movements

was economic rights, natural given the greater impact on women during times of economic stress, as discussed above.

68. In recognizing the importance of attaining substantive gender equality, proponents of gender mainstreaming note that "the ability of social movements to organize and to influence policy . . . is dependent . . . upon *mobilizing structures*," not on "political opportunities." Mark A. Pollack & Emilie Hafner-Burton, *Mainstreaming Gender in the European Union*, 7 J. EUR. PUB. POL'Y 432 (2000) (emphasis in original).

69. Madeleine Rees, *supra* note 67, at 56 (citing M. Walsh, *Rising to the Challenge: Gendered Impacts of Conflict and the Role of Women's Organizations in Post-Conflict Bosnia and Herzegovina*, Report to the United States Agency for International Development (1999)).

70. KATE FEARON, WOMEN'S WORK: THE STORY OF THE NORTHERN IRELAND WOMEN'S COALITION 5 (1999).

71. Regrettably, in Northern Ireland, initial electoral success for the Women's Coalition was followed by capture and domination of the legislature and executive by traditional parties, mostly identified by their ethno-national politics, indicating the long-term challenges of maintaining these gendered opportunities. Christine Bell & Fionnuala Ní Aoláin, *Forward to Women's Rights in Transitioning and Conflicted Societies*, *in* WOMEN AND THE IMPLEMENTATION OF THE GOOD FRIDAY/BELFAST AGREEMENT (Catherine O'Rourke ed., Transitional Justice Inst. 2005).

72. Greenberg & Zuckerman, *supra* note 41 at 6–9.

73. *See, e.g.,* GTZ Report, *supra* note 1, at 6.

74. International Covenant on Economic, Social, and Cultural Rights, G.A. Res. 2200A (XXI), U.N. Doc. A/6316 (1966); 993 UNTS 3 (1967).

75. Examples include Bosnia, Croatia, Slovenia, Serbia, Montenegro, Macedonia, Czech Republic, Slovakia, Lithuania, Latvia, Chad, Congo, the DRC, and Rwanda.

76. Privatization is ostensibly seen by international donors to "play a part in improved socio-economic governance in post-conflict nations [because] [p]ublic sector corporations are frequently unable to finance themselves, and have to be permanently subsidized." GTZ Report, *supra* note 1, at 17.

77. *See* WAYLEN, ENGENDERING TRANSITIONS, *supra* note 11, at 181–82.

78. *See id.* at 83–84 (identifying the loss of female positions to men post transition). *See also* R. W. CONNELL, GENDER 149–50 (2002) (asserting that "[m]en control almost all market-based institutions, such as corporations, and acquire most of the income distributed through markets, such as salaries and wages. Neo-liberalism, in exalting the power of markets, has thus tended to restore the power and privilege of men".).

79. *See* WAYLEN, ENGENDERING TRANSITIONS, *supra* note 11, at 183.

80. *Id.* at 184.

81. *See, e.g.,* Naomi Cahn & Anthony Gambino, *Towards a Typology of Corporate Responsibility in Different Governance Contexts: What to Do in the Absence of Responsible Country Governance?*, 39 GEO. J. INT'L L. 655, 675 (2008) (arguing that multinational companies (MNCs) can and should provide needed investments and, through their presence, improve the foundations of civil society and governance systems).

82. BENJAMIN KEEN, A HISTORY OF LATIN AMERICA xi (5th ed. 1996) (describing neo-liberalism as "the policies of privatization, austerity, and trade liberalization dictated to dependent countries by the International Monetary Fund and the World Bank as a condition for approval of investment, loans, and debt relief."). *See also*

Joseph E. Stiglitz, *The End of Neoliberalism*, NEW EUR., August 2008 (calling neoliberalism, "that grab-bag of ideas based on the fundamentalist notion that markets are self-correcting, allocate resources efficiently, and serve the public interest well.").

83. *See* WAYLEN, ENGENDERING TRANSITIONS, *supra* note 11, at 185–88. *See also* Julie Cupples, *Counter Revolutionary Women: Gender and Reconciliation in Post-War Nicaragua, in* GENDER, PEACEBUILDING, AND RECONSTRUCTION 8, 9 (Caroline Sweetman ed., 2004) (arguing that the structural adjustment programs (SAPs) regularly required by the World Bank have a distinctly gendered impact in that the attendant reduction of social services that accompanies a liberalizing economy drastically increases the burdens on women who become the caretakers for those formerly cared for in part by the government).

84. *But see* WAYLEN, ENGENDERING TRANSITIONS, *supra* note 11, at 62–65 (acknowledging that state socialist regimes had both benefits and drawbacks for women and noting that in many contexts, women's emancipation was limited based on selective canonization of the works of Marx and Lenin and the control that Communist parties exercised over civil society meant that women's organizations were contained).

85. *See* MICHAEL FARRELL, NORTHERN IRELAND: THE ORANGE STATE (2d ed. 1976).

86. COMM. ON THE ADMIN. OF JUSTICE (CAJ), EXAMINATION OF THE UNITED KINGDOM'S 5TH PERIODIC REPORT TO THE UN COMMITTEE ON ECONOMIC, SOCIAL, AND CULTURAL RIGHTS 5–6 (2008).

87. Dina Francesca Haynes, *Lessons from Bosnia's Arizona Market: Harm to Women in a Neoliberalized Post Conflict Reconstruction Process*, 6 U. PENN. L. REV. 158 (2010).

88. CONNELL, *supra* note 78, at 149–50 ("Men control almost all of the market based institutions, such as corporations, and acquire most of the income distributed through markets, such as salaries and wages. Neoliberalism, in exalting the power of markets, has thus tended to restore the power and privilege of men."). *See also* Ambreena Manji, *"The Beautyful Ones" of Law and Development, in* INTERNATIONAL LAW: MODERN FEMINIST APPROACHES 169–71 (Doris Buss & Ambreena Maji eds., 2005) (critiquing market-oriented development models and asking for analysis as to why a "global and capitalist order is always a contingent social construct," and suggesting that the continuity of this order be scrutinized).

89. Greenberg & Zuckerman, *supra* note 41, at 5.

90. Tatjana Djuric Kuzmanovic, *Introduction to Feminist Economics: Household, Market, and State*, GLOBALIZACIJA: J. FOR POL. THEORY AND RESEARCH ON GLOBALIZATION, DEV. AND GENDER ISSUES (2008). *See also* TAMAR SABEDASHVILI, GENDER AND DEMOCRATIZATION: THE CASE OF GEORGIA 1991–2006 at 12 (2007) (citing that women were most likely to be made redundant or have their pay cut during privatization in Georgia, and that subsequent wages were so low that they would not cover the transportation costs of getting to and from the job).

91. *See, e.g.,* THE POSTWAR MOMENT: MILITARIES, MASCULINITIES, AND INTERNATIONAL PEACEKEEPING BOSNIA AND THE NETHERLANDS 55–56 (Cynthia Cockburn & Dubravka Zarkov eds., 2002) (citing UNITED NATIONS CHILDREN'S FUND (UNICEF); SITUATION ANALYSIS FEDERATION OF BiH 1999 (1999) (noting that at the end of the war in BiH, when the economy was decimated, around two-thirds of the population was female and the health and welfare services needed to support them had collapsed)). According to the Women's Commission for Refugee Women and Children, four out of five of the world's nearly 35 million displaced people are women, children, and young people. WOMEN'S COMMISSION FOR REFUGEE WOMEN AND CHILDREN, WOMEN'S COMMISSION FACT SHEET 1 (2008).

92. *See, e.g.*, Tamar Sabedashvili, Gender and Democratization: The Case of Georgia 1991–2006 at 11 (2007) (stating that women constituted 55 percent of all internally displaced persons (IDPs)).

93. In Bosnia and Mozambique, for instance, women had the most difficulty acquiring and holding on to land during the privatization process. Greenberg & Zuckerman, *supra* note 41, at 5.

94. For example, women generally earn "77 percent of what men earn (compared with 59 cents on the male dollar 40 years ago). . . ." Stephen J. Rose & Heidi I. Hartmann, Inst. for Women's Policy Research, Still A Man's Labor Market: The Long-Term Earnings Gap iii (2004). *See also* Sabedashvili, *supra* note 90, at 12 (stating that Georgian women were concentrated, post-privatization, into the lowest positions within the least profitable sectors of the economy, despite the so-called "Soviet legacy," which considered women as integral to any reform process).

95. Sergei Blagov, *Equal Opportunities Remain a Pipedream*, Asia Times Online, March 10, 2000 (stating that "some 70% of Russian unemployed with college degrees are women and in some regions, women make up almost 90% of the unemployed."). The Soviet legacy was not all it was touted to be. By 1980, although women constituted 50 percent of the workforce in Central and Eastern Europe, "they were concentrated in low-paid, low-status, and gender-segregated jobs." Waylen, *Women and Democratization*, *supra* note 14, at 345.

96. Naomi Cahn & Anthony Gambino, *Towards a Typology of Corporate Responsibility in Different Governance Contexts: What to Do in the Absence of Responsible Country Governance?*, 39 Geo. J. Int'l L. 655, 675 (2008).

97. For example, approximately US$4 billion of oil money went missing in Angola between 1997 and 2002. Matthew Genasci & Sarah Pray, *Extracting Accountability: The Implications of the Resource Curse for CSR Theory and Practice*, 11 Yale Hum. Rts. & Dev. L.J. 37, 49 (2008). In Nigeria, the former governor of an oil-producing region has been charged with 128 counts of money laundering and related crimes and reportedly provided substantial sums of money for the presidential campaign of the current Nigerian president. Not surprisingly, little of the 13 percent provided by the state to the oil-producing regions made it to the people within the state. In the DRC, "instability, coupled with widespread corruption . . . is currently a major deterrent to foreign investment." Cahn & Gambino, *supra* note 96, at 657–59.

98. Cahn & Gambino, *supra* note 96, at 655, 669 (2008) (citing U.N. SCOR, *Report of Panel of Experts on the Illegal Exploitation of Natural Resources and Other Forms of Wealth of the Democratic Republic of the Congo*, U.N. Doc. S/2003/1027 (October 23, 2003)).

99. In Bosnia, for instance, the former Prime Minister Bicakcic was accused of diverting international funds designated to create jobs and pay government employees to families of soldiers killed in the war and his own political party, as a way of rewarding his own ethnic group. Sebastian van de Vliet, *Addressing Corruption and Organized Crime in the Context of Re-establishing the Rule of Law*, in Deconstructing the Reconstruction 205, 212 (Dina Francesca Haynes ed., 2008).

100. Everly, *supra* note 23, arguing that the Office of the High Representative administering governance in postwar Bosnia was not sufficiently transparent and had insufficient accountability for its own decision-making.

101. Matthew Genasci & Sarah Pray, *Extracting Accountability: The Implications of the Resource Curse for CSR Theory and Practice*, 11 Yale Hum. Rts. & Dev. L.J. 37, 49

(2008) (citing Steve Levine & John Tagliabue, *Swiss Freeze Bank Account Linked to Kazakh President*, N.Y. TIMES, October 16, 1999, at A6). *See also* GLOBAL WITNESS, TIME FOR TRANSPARENCY: COMING CLEAN ON OIL, MINING, AND GAS REVENUES 7–17 (2004).

102. For example, young women in Nepal were given a level of authority within the Maoist insurgency that traditional culture simply did not allow for. U.S. AGENCY FOR INT'L DEV., CONDUCTING A CONFLICT ASSESSMENT: A FRAMEWORK FOR STRATEGY AND PROGRAM DEVELOPMENT 24 (2005).

103. *See, e.g.*, Naomi Cahn, *Women in Post-Conflict Reconstruction: Dilemmas and Directions*, 12 WM. & MARY J. WOMEN & L. 355, 337–38 (2006).

104. *See, e.g.*, SABEDASHVILI, *supra* note 90, at 13.

105. For example, under Communist rule, where women's political representation was obligatory, the women who held office to satisfy party quotas were referred to as "milkmaid politicians." Waylen, *Women and Democratization, supra* note 14, at 345.

106. Convention on the Elimination of All Forms of Discrimination Against Women, *supra* note 31.

107. *See* Cahn & Gambino, *supra* note 96, at 656.

108. Critiques of microcredit have argued that in the post-conflict it is not a suitable model to address economic needs, particularly when tied into the need to compensate and provide reparations to multiple victims. In this context, it has been argued that microfinance may provide a better model. Anita Bernstein, *Tort Theory, Microfinance, and Gender Equality Convergent in Pecuniary Reparations, in* THE GENDER OF REPARATIONS: UNSETTLING SEXUAL HIERARCHIES WHILE REDRESSING HUMAN RIGHTS VIOLATIONS 291 (Ruth Rubio-Marín ed., 2009).

109. In Afghanistan, for example, the United Nations recommended instituting women-only registration, offering a choice between a fingerprint and a photograph for identification, and explaining to male religious leaders why it was important for women to vote. U.N. DEP'T OF PUB. INFO., *supra* note 35, AT 51; U.N. ESCOR, Comm. on the Status of Women, *Report of the 48th Session of the Commission on the Status of Women*, at 15, U.N. Doc. E/2004/27-E/CN.6/2004/14 (March 1–12, 2004).

110. *See, e.g.*, SABEDASHVILI, *supra* note 90, at 19–20 (stating that the second "gender analysis" submitted by the government of Georgia to CEDAW stated that evidence of Georgia's compliance was that "there are no provisions stipulating discrimination against women" in the country's legislation). *See also* Unity Dow v. Attorney General (1992) 103 I.L.R. 128 (Bots. Ct. App.)) (case in which female lawyer, Unity Dow, challenged gender discriminatory citizenship laws, won, was invited to become Attorney General and make the requisite gender positive changes to the law, and ultimately was appointed as the first woman on the High Court of Botswana).

111. The drafters of CEDAW understood this problem, and therefore CEDAW encourages states to regulate discriminatory customs and social taboos that would deter women from accessing their rights. *But see* the multitudinous reservations to CEDAW.

112. *See, e.g.*, Charles T. Call, *Democratization, War, and State-Building: Constructing the Rule of Law in El Salvador*, 35 J. OF LATIN AM. STUD. 827, 857 (2003) (noting that the post-peace inclusion of women in the police in El Salvador improved the formal place of women, but "informally [El Salvador] exhibited considerable continuity with the past, as cultural patterns were slow to change. . . ." Peace exposed women to increased domestic violence as combatants returned home.).

CHAPTER 11

1. *See* Hugh Waters, Brinnon Garrett, & Gilbert Burnham, *Rehabilitating Health Systems in Post-Conflict Situations, in* MAKING PEACE WORK: THE CHALLENGES OF SOCIAL AND ECONOMIC RECONSTRUCTION 200 (Tony Addison & Tilman Bruck eds., 2009).

2. *See* Frances Stewart, *Horizontal Inequalities and Conflict: An Introduction and Some Hypotheses, in* HORIZONTAL INEQUALITIES AND CONFLICT: UNDERSTANDING GROUP VIOLENCE IN MULTIETHNIC SOCIETIES 3, 4 (Frances Stewart ed., 2008).

3. *See generally* TSJEARD BOUTA, GEORG FRERKS, & IAN BANNON, GENDER, CONFLICT, AND DEVELOPMENT 117–19 (2005).

4. *See, e.g.*, UNITED NATIONS DEVELOPMENT PROGRAMME, HUMAN DEVELOPMENT REPORT 2009 (2009); AMARTYA SEN, DEVELOPMENT AS FREEDOM (2000); Roger Duthie, Introduction to TRANSITIONAL JUSTICE AND DEVELOPMENT: MAKING CONNECTIONS (Pablo de Greiff & Roger Duthie eds., 2009).

5. *Id.* at 18.

6. *See* Rama Mani, *Dilemmas of Expanding Transitional Justice, or Forging the Nexus Between Transitional Justice and Development*, 2 INT'L J. TRANS. J. 253 (2008).

7. *See, e.g.*, Frances Stewart, *Root Causes of Violence Conflict in Developing Countries*, 324 BRIT. MED. J. 342 (2002); Frances Stewart, *Policies Toward Horizontal Equities in Post-Conflict Reconstruction* 6 (2005).

8. *See* Ron Waldman, *Rebuilding Health Services After Conflict: Lessons from East Timor and Afghanistan* (Overseas Development Institute 2003). For more on the differing motivations of international actors, *see* Chapter 4 of this book.

9. For the translation of this practice into policy in the U.S. context, see DEPARTMENT OF THE ARMY, COUNTERINSURGENCY (2006).

10. The United Nations has recognized the need to contextualize peacekeeping efforts. *See* United Nations Dept. of Peacekeeping Operations and Department of Field Support, *A New Partnership Agenda: Charting a New Horizon for UN Peacekeeping* (2009).

11. *See* Pablo de Greiff, *Articulating the Links Between Transitional Justice and Development: Justice and Social Integration, in* TRANSITIONAL JUSTICE AND DEVELOPMENT, *supra* note 4, at 29, 31–32; Duthie, *supra* note 4, at 17–19 (observing that development is the "processes whose most general aim is to improve the socioeconomic conditions of people"); Marcia E. Greenberg & Elaine Zuckerman, *The Gender Dimensions of Post-Conflict Reconstruction: The Challenges in Development Aid, in* MAKING PEACE WORK, *supra* note 1, at 101.

12. Roger Duthie, *Toward a Development-Sensitive Approach to Transitional Justice*, 2 INT'L J. TRANS. J. 292, 295 (2008).

13. *See, e.g.*, David Koplow & Philip Schrag, *Carrying a Big Carrot: Linking Multilateral Disarmament and Development Assistance*, 91 COLUM. L. REV. 993 (1991); Lawrence R. Klein, *World Peace and Economic Prosperity, in* UNITED NATIONS DEPARTMENT OF DISARMAMENT AFFAIRS, SYMPOSIUM ON THE RELATIONSHIP BETWEEN DEVELOPMENT AND DISARMAMENT 1–2 (2004).

14. *See* Dina Haynes, *The Deus ex Machina Descends: The Laws, Priorities, and Players Central to the International Administration of Post-Conflict Bosnia and Herzegovina, in* DECONSTRUCTING THE RECONSTRUCTION (2008).

15. Dina Haynes, *Lessons from Bosnia's Arizona Market: Harm to Women in a Neoliberalized Post-Conflict Reconstruction Process*, 158 U. PA. L. REV. 1779 (2010).

16. *See, e.g.*, Louise Arbour, *Economic and Social Justice for Societies in Transition*, 40 N.Y.U. J. INT'L. L. & POL. 1, 26–27 (2007); UNITED NATIONS HUMAN RIGHTS

Council, Annual Report of the United Nations High Comm. of Human Rights and Reports of the Office of the High Commissioner and the Secretary-General: Analytical Study on Human Rights and Transitional Justice (2009); Mani, *supra* note 6, at 253–54.

17. *See* Gerd Junne & Willemijn Verkoren, *The Challenges of Postconflict Development*, *in* Post Conflict Development: Meeting New Challenges 1, 3–5 (Gerd Junne & Willemijn Verkoren eds., 2005).

18. *See* Patricia Lundy & Mark McGovern, *The Role of Community in Participatory Transitional Justice*, *in* Transitional Justice from Below: Grassroots Activism and the Struggle for Change 108 (Kieran McEvoy & Lorna McGregor eds. 2008); Duthie, *supra* note 12, at 20–21.

19. *See, e.g.,* Darfur Cookstoves, http://darfurstoves.lbl.gov (last visited January 13, 2010); James F. Smith, *Efficient Wood Stoves Help Women of Darfur*, Boston.com, June 3, 2009.

20. *See* The United Nations Children's Fund, *Equality in the Household*, *in* The State of the World's Children 2007: Women and Children: The Double Dividend of Gender Equality 16 (Patricia Moccia et al. eds., 2006).

21. *See* Sonalde Desai & Kiersten Johnson, *Women's Decisionmaking and Child Health: Familial and Social Hierarchies*, *in* A Focus on Gender: Collected Papers on Gender Using DHS Data 55, 56 (Sunitor Kishor ed., 2005); Lisa C. Smith et al., The Importance of Women's Status for Child Nutrition in Developing Countries 22 (2003); Nicholas D. Kristof & Sheryl WuDunn, Half the Sky: Turning Oppression into Opportunity for Women Worldwide (2009).

22. See discussion on harms of market liberalization on women set forth in Chapter 10, and in Dina Haynes, *Lessons from Bosnia's Arizona Market: Neoliberalism, Democracy, and Harms Towards Women*, 6 U. Pa. L. Rev. 158 (2010).

23. *See, e.g.,* Kristof & WuDunn, *supra* note 21, at xx.

24. *See* OECD, Investing in Women and Girls (n.d.).

25. *See* Goal: Promote Gender Equality and Empower Women, Unicef (2005).

26. The United Nations Children's Fund, *supra* note 20, at 24.

27. World Bank Group, *Gender Equality as Smart Economics: A World Bank Group Gender Action Plan* 2 (2006).

28. *See* Naomi Cahn, *Beyond Retribution and Impunity: Responding to War Crimes of Sexual Violence*, 1 Stan. J. Civ. Rts. & Civ. Lib. 217 (2005); Duthie, *supra* note 12, (referring to "social justice").

29. *See* The Gender of Reparations: Unsettling Sexual Hierarchies While Redressing Human Rights Violations 29–30 (Ruth Rubio-Marín ed., 2009).

30. *See id.*

31. *See* Patrick Vinck & Phuong Pham, *Ownership and Participation in Transitional Justice Mechanisms: A Sustainable Human Development Perspective from Eastern DRC*, 2 Int'l J. Trans. J. 398, 399 (2008).

32. *Id.* at 403.

33. *Id.* at 409.

34. Phuong Pham, Patrick Vinck, Eric Stover, Andrew Moss, Marieke Wierda, & Richard Bailey, When the War Ends: A Population-Based Survey on Attitudes about Peace, Justice, and Social Reconstruction in Northern Uganda 3, 22 (2007).

35. *Id.* at 32–33.

36. *See* Mani, *supra* note 6, at 256.

37. *See id.* at 256–57; Vinck & Pham, *supra* note 31, at 409–10.
38. For example, the International Covenant on Economic, Social, and Cultural Rights, Arts. 6, 11, January 3, 1976, 993 U.N.T.S. 3, recognizes the "right to work," to "an adequate standard of living," etc. *See, e.g.,* Fionnuala Ní Aoláin & Eilish Rooney, *Underenforcement and Intersectionality: Gendered Aspects of Transition for Women*, 1 INT'L J. TRANS. J. 338 (2007).
39. *See* Chapter 7 (the Rwanda Tribunal ultimately made antiretroviral drugs available to witnesses (usually rape victims) who had been infected as a result of their rape during the genocide).
40. *See* Ruben Carranza, *Plunder and Pain: Should Transitional Justice Engage with Corruption and Economic Crimes?*, 2 INT'L J. TRANS. J. 310, 329 (2008); Duthie, *supra* note 12, at 17, 19–20.
41. As Wangari Maathai defines it, this is not necessarily democracy, but the space for people to exercise their rights, including the right to expression. Wangari Maathai on Voice of America, The Green Belt Movement (2005).
42. *See* JEANNE WARD, IF NOT NOW, WHEN? ADDRESSING GENDER-BASED VIOLENCE IN REFUGEE, INTERNALLY DISPLACED, AND POST-CONFLICT SETTINGS 11 (April 2002) ("best practices" for gender-based violence is now recognized as a "multi-sectoral model," which includes a variety of individuals, including teachers, traditional birth attendants, nurses, microcredit banks, judges, police, and other military). On the need to address justice issues beyond the formal legal sector, see Naomi R. Cahn, *Women in Post-Conflict Reconstruction: Dilemmas and Directions*, WM. & MARY J. WOMEN & L., 335 (2005–2006); Rubio-Marin, THE GENDER OF REPARATIONS, *supra* note 29.
43. We are not suggesting letting states off the hook from providing what they must pursuant to treaty obligations, but are, instead, being realistic in providing to the state what it needs to meet those obligations if, for example, the "state" is not yet stable (or is too corrupt) to provide these services itself so that people do not further suffer.
44. Providing money ($6) to girls for school uniforms every one and a half years significantly reduced both drop out and pregnancy rates for girls in Kenya. Nicholas D. Kristof & Sheryl WuDunn, *The Women's Crusade*, N.Y. TIMES MAG., August 23, 2009, at MM28. Providing school fees significantly reduces human trafficking. Dina Francesca Haynes, *Exploitation Nation: The Thin and Grey Legal Lines Between Trafficked Persons and Abused Migrant Laborers*, 23 NOTRE DAME J.L. ETHICS & PUB. POL'Y 1, 16 (2009).
45. Aid workers in Africa are providing toilets and sanitary pads to discourage absenteeism, which leads to decreased drop-out rates. *See* Jackie Kirk & Marni Sommer, *Menstruation and Body Awareness: Linking Girls' Health with Girls' Education*, WASH IN SCHOOLS, 2006; Nicholas D. Kristof & Sheryl WuDunn, The Women's Crusade, *supra* note 44, at MM28.
46. One author's personal experience in Chad: her students (95 percent male) would virtually disappear just before each coup d'etat.
47. *See* Marion Pratt & Leah Werchick et al., U.S. Agency for Int'l Dev., Dev. Fund for Women, *Sexual Terrorism: Rape as a Weapon of War in Eastern Democratic Republic of Congo: An Assessment of Programmatic Responses to Sexual Violence in North Kivu, South Kivu, Maniema, and Orientale Provinces* 13 (2004).
48. Declaration on the Elimination of Violence Against Women, U.N. Doc. A/RES/48/104 Art. 4(g) (December 20, 1993).
49. UNITED NATIONS, HANDBOOK FOR LEGISLATION ON VIOLENCE AGAINST WOMEN (2009).

50. *See* Naomi Cahn, *Beyond Retribution and Impunity: Responding to War Crimes of Sexual Violence*, 1 STAN. J. C.R. & C.L. 217, 244–45 (2005).

51. *See* Anita Bernstein, *Tort Theory, Micro-Finance, and Gender Equality Convergent in Pecuniary Reparations*, *in* Rubio-Marin, THE GENDER OF REPARATIONS, *supra* note 29.

52. Greenberg & Zuckerman, *supra* note 11, at 14.

53. *See, e.g.*, Stef Jansen, *"Home" and Return in the Foreign Intervention in Bosnia and Herzegovina: An Anthropological Critique*, *in* HAYNES, DECONSTRUCTING THE RECONSTRUCTION, *supra* note 14.

54. *See* Wondem Asres Degu, *Reforming Education*, *in* POST CONFLICT DEVELOPMENT, *supra* note 17, at 129.

55. *See, e.g.*, Bouta, *supra* note 3, at xxvi, 112.

56. *See, e.g.*, Kristof, *supra* note 13 (citing a study that for each year of primary education, a girl is likely to have .26 fewer children).

57. Dina Abu-Ghaida & Stephan Klausen, *The Economic and Human Development Costs of Missing the Millennium Development Goal on Gender Equity* 9–10 (World Bank 2004).

58. *See* Bouta, *supra* note 3, at 119–21.

59. One of the authors was involved in a post-conflict survey of youths' understanding of reproduction and their use of various birth control methods, which found low levels of knowledge around these issues. Personal Experience of Naomi Cahn, Kinshasa, Congo, 2003–2004.

60. One of the authors worked in Chad in 1989 when a UTA flight was bombed by Libyans (who had recently been warring with Chad over contested territory and natural resources). All on board were killed, and although the wife of the U.S. ambassador was on board, many speculate that the real target was all of the doctors in the country of Chad who were traveling to a conference in Paris. Needless to say, their deaths significantly set back the already minimal health care infrastructure by years.

61. *See, e.g.*, APRIL HARDING ET AL., CHILD HEALTH AND THE MISSING LINK: WORKING WITH THE PRIVATE SECTOR FOR BETTER RESULTS (2010).

62. Vanessa Van Schoor, *Reviving Health Care*, *in* POST CONFLICT DEVELOPMENT, *supra* note 17, at 147, 149.

63. Harding et al., *supra* note 61, at 11.

64. Van Schoor, *supra* note 62, at 150–51, 160.

65. HEIDI LEHMANN, FROM RELIEF TO DEVELOPMENT: GENDER-BASED VIOLENCE INTERVENTIONS IN CONFLICT AND POST-CONFLICT CONTEXTS (Lehmann ed., 2008).

66. *See* Kristof, *supra* note 21, at 98.

67. *Id.* at 113–16.

68. As the U.N. Office of the High Commissioner for Human Rights explains:

    The right to development can be rooted in the provisions of the Charter of the United Nations, the Universal Declaration on Human Rights and the two International Human Rights Covenants. Through the United Nations Charter, Member States undertook to "promote social progress and better standards of life in larger freedom."

    Office of the High Commissioner for Human Rights, Development—Right to Development, http://www.ohchr.org/EN/Issues/Development/Pages/DevelopmentIndex.aspx (last visited April 7, 2011).

69. Haynes, *Lessons from Bosnia's Arizona Market*, *supra* note 22 (citing the World Bank Group, "Reconstruction of Bosnia and Herzegovina: Priorities for Recovery

and Growth," formerly at http://www.worldbank.org/html/extdr/extme/bhgen.html (on file with author)).

70. *Id.*

71. *Id.* In an odd gender twist, many have noted that the majority of locals hired by international organizations (IOs) in some countries tended to be women. The roles taken by women tend to be lower level secretarial/ administrative posts creating an inflated potential for sexual harassment. For more on the gender disparity in hiring among IOs, *see* Dina Haynes, *Ethics of International Civil Service: A Reflection on How the Care of UN Staff Impacts the Ability to Fulfill Their Role in "Harmonizing" the World*, Hamline J. Int'l L. (2011).

72. *See, e.g.*, Greenberg & Zuckerman, *supra* note 11, at 108.

73. *See id.* at 101, 122–23.

74. *See, e.g.*, Kristof, *supra* note 21, at 191.

75. *See, e.g.*, Deborah M. Weissman, *Gender and Human Rights: Between Morals and Politics, in* Gender Equality: Dimensions of Women's Citizenship 409, 426 (Linda McClain & Joanna Grossman eds., 2009).

76. Research shows that good governance results in improved development, but that increasing incomes does not, by itself, result in good governance. *See* Daniel Kaufmann & Aart Kraay, *Growth Without Governance*, 3 Economia 169, 210–11 (Fall 2002).

77. *Id.*

INDEX

goals and conditions, 131–133,
135–136
including women and families in,
134, 136–137, 140, 141, 142, 146
linked to development programs,
257–258
masculinities in, 22–23, 51–52, 132,
133, 134, 135–136, 138, 140,
144–147
transformative potential in, 23, 137,
138, 142, 143, 144, 146, 147
women combatants in, 44–45, 133,
137, 141, 142, 143–144, 146
Declaration on the Elimination of
Violence Against Women, 266
demobilization. *See* DDR programs
Democratic Republic of Congo
DDR programs, 137, 145, 150
exploitation of natural resources in,
249
interventions in, 85
peacekeeper misconduct, 111, 115,
117, 119, 121, 125–126
post-conflict needs surveys, 263
sexual violence, 70
development infrastructure
economic development, 270–272
education, 261, 265, 268–269
gender centrality in, 254–255,
259–262
importance of participatory
approach, 258–259
long-term development, 267–271
and post-conflict disarray, 254
social services justice, 255–256,
262–267, 271
See also post-conflict reconstruction
disarmament, demobilization and
reintegration. *See* DDR programs
Division for the Advancement of
Women (DAW), 17
domestic violence
spikes post-conflict, 60, 70, 71,
144–146
by Western military personnel, 64
DPKO. *See* UN Department of
Peacekeeping Operations
(UNDPKO)
"durable disorder," 35
Dyilo, Thomas Lubanga, 161

Eastern Slavonia, 83
East Timor
civil society funding, 214
constitutional negotiations, 206,
207–208, 216, 217
governance quotas, 238
health care, 269
international administration, 89
interventions, 83, 84, 85
post-conflict operations, 86
reparations program, 190, 191–192
sexual violence by peacekeepers, 115
socioeconomic hardships for women,
217–218
women in reconstruction process, 100
economics
of conflict settings, 35–36, 247, 249,
256
economic reconstruction, 244–248
false economies built around
peacekeepers, 6, 89, 114, 116
International Covenant on Economic,
Social and Cultural Rights, 245,
250, 251
in post-conflict reconstruction, 6,
35–36, 80, 89, 114, 244–248, 249,
251–253, 254, 261, 270–271
socioeconomic rights for women, 29,
33–34, 65, 68, 198, 244–245, 246,
262, 270–271
El Salvador, 193, 194
Eritrea, 115
European Court for Human Rights
(ECHR), 100, 121
European Union, gender mainstreaming
critique, 14

Feminist Conversations (Fineman), xi
feminist theory
bringing private violence into open,
45, 153
difficulty acknowledging female
violence, 43
and essentialization of women, 10,
39, 41, 42–44
as framework, 4
intersections with masculinities, 50
and Martha Fineman, xi
and subordination of women, 110
Fineman, Martha, xi

implementation phase of peace process
  impact on constitution making,
    212–215
  involvement of women in, 9, 212,
    213–215
  scope of, 9, 212
Inter-American Court, 188
international actors
  charges of colonialism, 18, 94–95
  false economies built around, 6, 89,
    114, 116
  gender-central focus needed by,
    93–94, 103
  imposition of biases on post-conflict
    states, 50, 92–93, 94–95
  international organizations and
    NGOs, 89–92
  masculinities accompanying, 50, 91,
    94–95
  motives and interests of, 92–94
  nation-states, 92–93
  women poorly represented among,
    91, 92, 99–101
  See also governance; interventions;
    peace agreements; post-conflict
    reconstruction; security sector
    reform; United Nations
international administration, 89, 234
International Center for Transitional
  Justice, 185
International Committee of the Red
  Cross (ICRC), 90–91, 269–270
International Covenant on Economic,
  Social and Cultural Rights, 245,
  250, 251
International Criminal Court (ICC)
  attempted prosecution of
    peacekeepers, 120–121
  sexual violence and, 48, 134, 147,
    155, 159, 161, 163, 167, 172
  Trust Fund for Victims, 160, 163–164
  and war crimes/crimes against
    humanity, 48, 134, 155, 159
International Institute for Research and
  Training for the Advancement of
  Women (INSTRAW), 17
International Labour Organization
  (ILO), 13
International Military Tribunal at
  Nuremberg, 156

International Military Tribunal for the
  Far East (IMFTE), 156–157
International Monetary Fund (IMF),
  37, 91
international organizations (IOs). See
  IOs (international organizations)
International Peace Academy (IPA), 148
interventions
  charges of colonialism in, 18, 94–95
  core commonalities in, 81–82, 85–87,
    95
  gender centrality urged in, 82, 84–85,
    88, 89, 90, 91–92, 93–97, 102–104
  imposition of cultural biases by
    interveners, 18, 86, 92–93,
    94–95, 99
  international actors in, 82, 86–87,
    89–94
  legal parameters for, 81–82, 83–85
  masculinities in, 82, 86, 99, 103
  motives of international actors, 92–94
  multiple types of, 81, 82, 83–84,
    87–88
  needs assessments of citizens in, 82,
    88, 93–94, 97–98, 99, 103–104
  post-conflict models of, 85–89, 92
  social science scholarship sidelined
    in, 98–99
  See also peacekeeping operations;
    post-conflict reconstruction
intrafamilial violence. See domestic
  violence
IOs (international organizations)
  involvement in interventions, 89–90
  women poorly represented in, 91, 92,
    99–101
Iraq, 83, 85, 206
Ireland, 77
  See also Northern Ireland

Japan, war crimes prosecutions,
  156–157

Kosovo, 83, 115, 121

Lebanon, post-conflict distrust of law
  in, 49
legal reform
  as central to peace and security,
    77–79, 197, 204, 222

legal reform (*continued*)
transformative potential of, 78–79
See also constitution making; criminal accountability; Rule of Law
Liberia
all-female peacekeeping unit, 127
DDR programs in, 137, 141
implementation of Resolution 1325, 16, 77
security action plan, 77
sexual abuse by peacekeepers, 115, 119
sexual violence, 116
literacy rates
in Afghanistan, 39, 134
in post-conflict settings, 80, 268
lustration and vetting. *See* remedy processes

Macedonia, 115, 119
mainstreaming of gender. *See* gender mainstreaming
masculinities
as field of study, 50
See also conflict settings; DDR programs; domestic violence; hypermasculinity; international actors; interventions; military; peacekeeping operations; post-conflict reconstruction
maternal mortality. *See* women
military
masculine culture of, 69, 109–110, 116, 126, 130, 135
in peacekeeping operations, 107, 108, 109–110, 116, 123, 127
in security sector reform, 73
Western, 64
women in, 127
Millennium Development Goals (UN), 16, 34–35, 65
Mine Action (United Nations), 61, 113, 128, 139
MONUC (UN Mission in the Democratic Republic of Congo), 117, 125–126
Morocco, 192
Mozambique, 115, 269
Multi-Country Demobilization and Reintegration Program (MDRP), 141–142

Nairobi Declaration on Women's and Girls' Rights to a Remedy and Reparation, 188–189
Namibia, 128
National Action plans, 16, 77, 185
nation-states, 92–93
NATO, 16, 83, 92
NGOs (nongovernmental organizations), 89–90, 91, 149
Northern Ireland
bill of rights, 213
Civil Rights Protests, 182
economic issues, 247
equality provisions, 203, 209–210, 213, 244
peace negotiations, 8, 206, 209, 244
post-conflict implementation phase, 214
reparations in, 188
violation of homes, 182
women as combatants in, 43
Women's Coalition, 209, 210, 213
Nuremberg Tribunals, 156

Office of the Special Advisor on Gender Issues and the Advancement of Women (OSAGI), 17
Organization for Economic Co-operation and Development (OECD), Social Institutions and Gender Index of 2009, 36–37
Organization for Security and Cooperation in Europe (OSCE), 91, 92–93
OSCE (Organization for Security and Cooperation in Europe), 91, 92–93
Otto, Diane, 13

Palestine, 43, 211–212
Palestine Liberation Organization (PLO), 211
peace
as goal of interventions, 82
negative vs. positive, 59
See also peace agreements; peacekeeping operations; security
peace agreements
commitments to DDR in, 131, 132, 148

as constitutional documents, 198,
205–210
exclusions of women from, 5, 8, 41,
69, 71, 72, 205
formal agreement phase of, 69
framework agreements, 8–9,
207–210
gender equality language in, 203
implementation agreement, 212–213
inclusion of women in, 140–141
post-conflict implementation phase,
69
prenegotiation agreements, 8, 69,
205–207
role of international actors in,
207–208, 213–214
See also accountability processes;
criminal accountability
peacekeeping operations
authorizations required for,
83–84, 106
core business of, 107
development projects in, 256–257
employment of locals by, 113–114
false economies built around, 113,
114, 116
gender-positive reform urged in,
105–106, 110, 112, 117–118, 120,
122–125, 129–130
gender representation in, 108, 111,
118, 124, 127–129, 130
gender-sensitivity training for,
122–125
goals of, 86, 105
international reevaluation of
approach to, 106–108
legal accountability in, 106, 118–122,
126–127
masculinities in, 105, 107–108,
109–110, 111, 116, 122, 123,
128, 130
modeling appropriate gender
interactions in, 113, 114–115, 124,
128–129
power differentials, 110–112, 115
professionals employed in, 107,
108–109, 123
sexual exploitation and violence by
peacekeepers, 111–112, 114,
115–117, 119, 126

stabilizing influence of, 112–113,
117
UN Codes of Conduct for, 109, 121,
125–127
See also security; United Nations
Peru, 36
reparations program, 188, 189–190
Truth and Reconciliation Commission
(TRC), 147, 186
Poland, 193
politics
participation by gender, 34–35
participation without capacity to
affect change, 219
See also governance
"positive action" programs, 11–12
post-conflict interventions
core commonalities in, 86–87
imposition of cultural biases in, 86
interfaces with women and gender,
87, 88
masculinities in, 86
types and phases of, 85–89
See also post-conflict reconstruction
post-conflict reconstruction
core ideals for, 95–96
criminality in, 35, 53, 68, 114, 147
economic issues, 6, 35–36, 80, 89,
114, 244–248, 249, 251–253, 254,
261, 270–271
failure to grasp extent of harms to
women in, 45–49, 55, 70, 152–156,
163, 172, 173, 181–182
gender centrality in, 12–15, 18–19,
21–22, 235
gendered assessment of, 4–5, 88,
95–98, 99, 102–104, 128, 261
gender equality in, 5, 22, 54, 61, 102,
230, 252–253
importance of consulting with
community members, 7, 60–61,
97–98, 250, 252, 258–259
international actors in, 41, 49–50,
60–61, 88, 89–95, 254, 258
masculinities and patriarchal
structures in, 49–50, 51–54,
69–70, 99, 102, 105, 144–145,
260, 261
models, theories and critiques of,
87–89

post-conflict reconstruction (*continued*)
    reassertion of traditional gender roles
        in, 41, 44, 54–55, 65, 102, 137,
        143, 270–271
    regression of female gains in, 49, 229,
        246–247, 250, 251, 270–271
    return to violence possible in, 59–60,
        63, 114
    social science scholarship sidelined
        in, 98–99
    transformative opportunities
        available in, 3, 21, 22, 62, 95–96,
        102, 137, 143
    UN authorizations for, 84
    violence against women, 47, 49, 52,
        68, 70, 71
    women as key actors in, 6–7, 36,
        261–262
    See also accountability processes;
        DDR programs; development
        infrastructure; governance; legal
        reform; peacekeeping operations;
        security sector reform; social status
        of women; violence against women
poverty
    addressed in UN Millennium Goals,
        65
    in durable disorder, 35
    intergenerational transmission of, 32
    and sexual exploitation, 117
    of women, 33, 197
prenegotiation phase of peace process
    DDR programs discussed in,
        132, 140
    exclusion of women from, 8, 205–207
    impact on constitution making,
        205–207
    scope of, 8, 205
Prosecutor vs. Akayesu, 163
prostitution, forced, 116, 157
Protocols Additional to the Geneva
    Conventions, 40
Pupavac, Vanessa, 159–160

Ramphosa, Cyril, 219
rape
    children born of, 264
    by civilians post-conflict, 70
    criminal accountability for, 16,
        77–79, 157, 166–168

international legal prohibitions, 16,
    156–157, 158, 159, 162–163
by peacekeeping forces, 115, 116–117
sexually-transmitted diseases from,
    5, 33, 153, 171–172, 189
as weapon of war, 116, 147, 157,
    167–168
See also criminal accountability;
    sexual violence
Rape of Nanking, 157
reconstruction. *See* post-conflict
    reconstruction
Red Cross. *See* International Committee
    of the Red Cross (ICRC)
refugees
    and gender roles, 101–102
    IOs focusing on, 90
reintegration. *See* DDR programs
remedy processes
    attention to victims in, 171–172,
        178–179, 185–186
    failure to capture extent of harms in,
        178–179, 180, 181–182, 183–185,
        189–190, 194
    lustration and vetting, 149, 150, 175,
        192–195, 203
    overview, 175–176
    reparations, 175, 176, 186–192, 203,
        252
    restorative justice programs, 153,
        168–172
    shortcomings of, 195–196
    transformative potential of, 185, 187,
        188, 190–191, 196, 252
    truth processes, 175–185, 203
reparations. *See* remedy processes
reproductive rights, 219–222
Resolution 1325
    in DDR programs, 139
    and governance, 232
    and National Action plans, 16, 77, 185
    in peace agreements, 10, 203,
        208–209
    in peacekeeping operations, 91,
        107–108, 113
    in security sector reform, 68, 71, 77
    in truth recovery processes, 185
    vision and impact, 11, 208, 210
Resolution 1820, 16, 203
Resolution 1888, 16, 203

Printed in Great Britain
by Amazon.co.uk, Ltd.,
Marston Gate.